God's Bestseller

Also by Brian Moynahan

Airport International
Fool's Paradise
Claws of the Bear
Comrades
The Russian Century
Rasputin
The British Century
The Faith

The gospell of S. Mathew.

The fyrst Chapter.

Hys ys the boke of the generaciō of Jesus Christ the sonne of David/The sonne also of Abra (ham: *Abraham and David are fyrst rehearsid/ because that christe was chefly promysed vnto them.*

C Abraham begatt Isaac:

Isaac begatt Jacob:

Jacob begatt Judas and hys brethren:

Judas begat Phares:

and Zaram ofthamar:

Phares begatt Esrom:

Esrom begatt Aram:

Aram begatt Aminadab:

Aminadab begatt naassan:

Naasson begatt Salmon:

Salmon begatt boos of rahab:

Boos begatt obed of ruth :

Obed begatt Jesse:

Jesse begatt david the kynge:

C David the kynge begatt Solomon/of her that was the wyfe of vry:

Solomon begat roboam:

Roboam begatt Abia:

Abia begatt asa:

Asa begatt iosaphat:

Josaphat begatt Joram:

Joram begatt Osias:

Osias begatt Joatham:

Joatham begatt Achas:

Achas begatt Ezechias :

Ezechias begatt Manasses:

Manasses begatt Amon:

Amon begatt Josias:

Josias begatt Jechonias and his brethren about the tyme of the captivite of babilon

C After they were led captive to babilon / Jechonias begatt

Saynct mathew leveth out certeyne generacions/ z describeth Christes linage from solomō/after the lawe of Moses / but Lucas describeth it accordyng to nature/frō nathan solomōs brother. For the lawe calleth them a mannes childrē which his brover begatt of his wyse lefte behynde hym after his deathe. deu.xxv.c.

God's Bestseller

William Tyndale, Thomas More, and
the Writing of the English Bible –
A Story of Martyrdom and Betrayal

BRIAN MOYNAHAN

St. Martin's Press New York

Endpapers: The first pages of Tyndale's New Testament 1525. Only a fragment of the book is known to exist.

www.stmartins.com

Library of Congress Cataloging-in-Publication Data

Moynahan, Brian, 1941–.
   God's bestseller : William Tyndale, Thomas More, and the writing of the English Bible—a story of martyrdom and betrayal / Moynahan.— 1st U.S. ed.
         p. cm.
      ISBN 0-312-31486-8
   1. Tyndale, William, d. 1536. 2. More, Thomas, Sir, Saint, 1478–1535. 3. Bible—English—Versions—Tyndale. 4. Reformation—England—Biography. I. Title.

BR350.T8M578 2003
270.6'092—dc21
[B]   2003043124

First published in Great Britain by Little, Brown
An imprint of Time Warner Books UK

First U.S. Edition: August 2003

10 9 8 7 6 5 4 3 2 1

For Alison Taylor,
my god-daughter

CONTENTS

Contents

PREFACE

On the Burning of Heretics

arly in the year of Our Lord 1428, the mortal remains of a former rector of the parish were exhumed from beneath the flagstones in the chancel of St Mary's Church in Lutterworth, a market town in the English Midlands. An array of powerful men stood out from the plain crowd of local people in the church. Richard Fleming, the bishop of Lincoln, in whose see Lutterworth then lay, was present with his chancellor, his suffragan bishops and the priors and abbots of the diocese. The high sheriff of Leicestershire was attended by his officers. A coterie of canons and lawyers huddled round the gravediggers as they worked. An executioner looked on with professional interest.

The coffin was raised, and opened, and its contents were exposed to the onlookers. The body was then taken out through a small door in the south side of the chancel, as the dying rector had been carried by his parishioners forty-four years before, after he suffered a stroke while celebrating mass in December 1384. His remains were borne in solemn procession, under the dripping yews in the churchyard, along the streets of the town and down the wooded hillside to a field next to the hump back bridge that crossed the River Swift.

This was a field of execution. Public hangings continued here into coaching days, when Lutterworth was an important staging post on the route north from London past Leicester. The dead rector, however, was thought too evil to hang. A stake had been set up in the ground and piled with timber and kindling. Iron chains were attached to it at shoulder height. He was to be burnt.

A brief ceremony was held. Bishop Fleming confirmed that he was carrying out the command sent to him from Rome by Pope Martin V on 16 December last. This ordered him to carry out the sentence that had been passed on the body in 1415 by the great Council of the Church meeting at Constance on the German–Swiss border. The council had condemned two hundred propositions put forward by the dead man, John Wycliffe, the former master of Balliol College at Oxford and rector of Lutterworth, that touched on core doctrines of the Catholic faith. The council found that 'since the birth of Christ no more dangerous heretic has arisen, save Wycliffe'. It instructed that his body be removed from the consecrated ground in the chancel at Lutterworth and destroyed.

Tradition allowed for the body to be dressed in the vestments that the rector had worn to celebrate mass, so that these could be stripped from him, chasuble and stole, one by one, to signify that he was 'unfrocked' and deposed from the priesthood. We do not know if this ritual was observed, or whether Wycliffe's skull and fingers were scraped, to represent the removal of the oil with which he had been anointed at his ordination. Certainly, the bishops solemnly cursed him and commended his soul to the devil.

Heresy had been declared to be 'treason against God' by Pope Innocent III in 1199, and was thus regarded as the worst of all crimes. Its 'vileness' was said to 'render pure even Sodom and Gomorrah', while the great medieval theologian St Thomas Aquinas declared that it separated man from God more than any other sin. The Church imposed a double jeopardy on heretics. The earthly *poena sensus*, the punishment of the senses, was achieved by the stake and the fire. If, like Wycliffe, the person was convicted after he was dead, the penalty was imposed on his remains. The *poena damni* proclaimed by the bishops on Wycliffe pursued his soul into the life everlasting. It damned him to absolute separation from God and to an eternity in hell.

The Church could not itself carry out a burning. To do so would defy the principle that *Ecclesia non novit sanguinem*, the Church does not shed blood. Pope Lucius III had bypassed this inconvenience in 1184 by decreeing that unrepentant heretics should be handed over to the secular authorities for sentence and execution. After cursing the remains, Bishop Fleming therefore delivered them up to the high sheriff of the county, as the representative of the civil power. The sheriff declared that they should be burnt by the executioner.

The executioner attached the dead man to the stake with the iron chains before setting fire to the kindling. He made sure that the bones and skull were burnt to ash in the fire, breaking them into small pieces with a mattock to help the process, until they merged into an indistinguishable grey pile of ash and embers. These were carefully scraped into a barrow. When the last particles of dust were swept clean from the patch of scorched earth, the barrow was tipped into the waters of the Swift.

Only then was the bishop sure that he had fulfilled the papal instructions, to rid the world of all physical trace of the heretic. Any relic might otherwise be gathered up by the dead man's supporters and placed in a shrine to perpetuate his accursed memory.

Fleming did his work well enough; he earned his altar-tomb in Lincoln Cathedral, where his bones lie undisturbed, and his renown as the founder of Lincoln College at Oxford. Only a few physical scraps remain that connect directly with Wycliffe: a fragment of his cope, an ancient pulpit and a font that he may have used.[1] Disposing of Wycliffe's ideas was another matter. The ashen waters of the Swift, his followers noted, flowed into the Avon, the Avon into the Severn, and the Severn into the sea, so that 'the whole world and all Christendom became his sepulchre'.

Wycliffe was the first of the 'Bible-men', a term of fear and abuse coined by a bishop of Chichester to describe the poor preachers, dressed in modest russet cloth, who spread Wycliffe's Bible-based theology at impromptu gatherings in churchyards and at markets, and who translated the Bible into English at his behest. More than a century later, the ferocity aroused by this translation was to colour the life of William Tyndale, the subject of our book, in the most violent hues.

'This wicked kindred,' Wycliffe said of the clergy, 'wulde that ye gospel slepte.' He was correct. The medieval Church had no desire to share the secrets of its trade. Its monopoly of faith was bolstered by its near monopoly of Latin. It opposed the translation of the authorised Vulgate Bible into any native, or vernacular, language. The Vulgate was written in the Latin of the fourth century. It was incomprehensible to the great majority of laymen and women, who also had little understanding of the Latin rites and ceremonies used in everyday worship. They were dependent on the clergy to interpret the mysteries of the faith for them. The Church feared that translations would open its dogmas to question and challenge its spiritual dominion.

It was through the rector of Lutterworth and his followers that this general dread acquired a distinct and bloody edge in England.

A fierce and blunt-spoken Yorkshireman, and a fine scholar, Wycliffe had become master of Balliol in 1360 at the age of about thirty. Generations of scholars had paid lip service to the Bible, of course. They mined it for individual texts to use in debates and sermons, and they wrote copious notes and glosses on passages within it. But their approach was logical and scholastic; they did not think of it as a work that was alive and breathing, like the God who had created it. It was a priestly text, dusty, locked up in Latin, safely beyond the reach of the English at large. Religion had come to mean the Church itself, and its traditions.

Wycliffe stood this on its head. He looked back to the scriptures and the early Fathers, before the Church had established its rituals and its wealth. He gave a series of lectures on the whole of the Bible, a sweeping commentary that – remarkably – had never been attempted before. He gathered round him, the Church noted with alarm, 'many disciples in his depravity, living together in Oxford, clad in long russet gowns of one pattern, going on foot, ventilating his errors among the people and publicly preaching them in sermons'.

The Bible, Wycliffe declared, was the 'highest authority for every Christian, and the standard of faith and all human perfection'. All that was within it must be obeyed. All that was not – the deep patina of lore, ritual, law, hierarchy and dogma that had built up for more than a thousand years – was mere human invention and superstition. No institution that God had not sanctioned, foremost among them the papacy, was to be trusted or obeyed. Wycliffe noted that the Bible did not mention the pope. 'What good doeth hys gabblyng that ye pope wolde be caled moost holy father?' he demanded. The dignities and privileges that Rome bestowed were 'not worthe a fly's foote', and men should 'shake awey al ye lawe that ye pope hath maad', and return to the laws of God.

He stressed the importance of personal faith in Christ, rather than the merits of obedience to the Church. 'As belief is the first virtue and the ground of all others,' he wrote, 'so unbelief is the first sin of all others.' This belief was not gained through the intercession of the Church, he said; it flowed from the individual and the reading of the scripture, and the decadence of churchmen was an obstacle to it. Christ had been the 'porest man of alle'. True priests should be 'moost pore men and moost meke in spirit', for they were created 'by power that Crist gyveth' and not by bishops. No cleric had the right to be wealthy, yet they were rich and sleek and self-contented, for they drank the 'podel water of ye canal' and not the pure wisdom of the gospels.

This was, of course, heresy, and Wycliffe's Bible reading led him into further clashes with fundamental Catholic dogma. A list of fifty charges against him was prepared for Simon Sudbury, the archbishop of Canterbury. Most were theological, touching on such things as the nature of the sacraments and the efficacy of auricular confession. His attacks on the powers of the pope, and the wealth of the Church, however, were highly attractive to powerful laymen, who cast a jealous eye on clerical privileges and landed estates and buildings.

Wycliffe was summoned to London to explain himself in 1377 in front of the archbishop and William Courtenay, the bishop of London. He had powerful protectors, however. Lord Percy, the earl marshal of England, escorted him with a number of barons in a large retinue. What followed between the lords spiritual and temporal was farce; a century and a half later, it would be replayed in earnest. Percy and the barons sat with the archbishop and bishops in the Lady Chapel of St Paul's.

Percy told Wycliffe 'to sytt down, for because, sayed he, he haythe much to answeare, he hath neade of a better seate'. The fiery Courtenay claimed it 'to be agaynst reason that he sholde sytt there, and also contrary to the lawe for hym to sytt'. Hereupon, 'very contumelyous wordes did ryse betwene Syr Henrye Percy and the bishopp, and the whoole multytude begane to be troubled.' Percy advanced on the bishop, 'swearynge that he wolde pulle down both the pryde of hym and of all the bishopps in Englande . . . [and] whysperynge in his eare sayed he had rather draw hym forthe of the churche by the eare . . .'. When they heard this, Londoners 'angerlye with a loud voice cryed out, swearynge they wolde not suffer theyr Bishopp to be injured . . .'. The court broke up in confusion. The following day a mob attacked Percy's palace in the Savoy, plundering it and forcing him to escape by river to Kennington.

Pope Gregory XI sent bulls to the king and the Oxford author-itics, chiding the university for its 'idleness and sloth' in allowing Wycliffe to 'vomit' heresies 'from the poisonous confines of his breast', and demanding that he be thrown into prison. Wycliffe's supporters said darkly that the university proctors should not arrest an Englishman 'at the command of the pope lest they sholde seeme to gyve the pope dominyon and royale powere in Englande'. The vice-chancellor merely forbade Wycliffe to leave his rooms.

Within a year, Gregory was dead and the papacy sank into a moral squalor that greatly aided Wycliffe's cause. Successive popes had undergone a 'Babylonian captivity' since 1309, when they had been torn from Rome and relocated at Avignon under pres-sure from the French crown. Gregory had returned to Rome shortly before his death. A Roman mob terrorised the conclave that met to choose his successor, fearful that the cardinals would elect a Frenchman, who would return with his high-spending court to Avignon. To back their demands for a Roman pope, they piled firewood in the rooms above the conclave and banged on the floor with pikes and halberds. A fake pope, an elderly Roman car-dinal, was got up in papal robes and paraded for the benefit of the crowd. In fact, the conclave elected Bartolomeo Priganano, the absentee archbishop of Bari, who took the name of Urban VI.

Urban had been sober, even austere, but his elevation unhinged him. He became violent and drank heavily, declaring that 'I can do anything, absolutely anything I like.' A group of cardinals fled from Rome, and declared Urban's election invalid since it was held under the threat of mob violence. They elected Robert, the cardinal bishop of Geneva, in his place. He took the name of Clement VII. The existing curia, the papal court, followed

Clement back to Avignon. Urban created twenty-nine new cardinals to make up a new curia of his own, and stayed in Rome.

There had been two popes and two courts before, but never had
there been two popes elected by the same cardinals. A Great
Schism was born, tearing at the loyalties of nations and religious
orders. The two popes excommunicated one another, and placed
supporters of their rival under interdict. France, Burgundy, Savoy,
Naples, the Spanish kingdoms and Scotland declared for Clement.
England, Germany, Poland, Hungary and the Scandinavian kingdoms were faithful to Urban, a thankless task, for his mania
continued unchecked; when he found that five cardinals had consulted a jurist to see whether insanity was just grounds for
dethroning him, he had them tortured within earshot of the
garden where he strolled, reading his breviary oblivious to their
screams. Four of them were not seen again.

Wycliffe revelled in this proof of papal depravity. 'I always knew
that the pope had cloven feet,' he mocked. 'Now he has a cloven
head.' The pope – both popes – were the 'most cursed of dippers
and purse-heavers' who 'vilified, nullified and utterly defaced' the
commandments of God. Wycliffe justified the power and wealth
enjoyed by secular princes and lords, a concession that many of
them would later find tempting, on the grounds that it was necessary for them to 'teach the fear of God by harshness and worldly
fear'.

He held that auricular confession, heard by a priest, was superfluous; the only effective confession was that made silently by the
sinner to God. He ridiculed pilgrimages, prayers to saints, the sale
of pardons and indulgences, and the veneration of relics – all parts
of the fabric of medieval faith, and cash cows for the Church – as
non-scriptural and inefficacious. He challenged the Catholic doctrine of the real presence, denying that the consecration of the
bread and wine during the Eucharist changed their substance into
the body and blood of Christ. Worshippers had treated the Host

with special reverence for generations. Bells were rung and candles lit as it was elevated during the mass, the faithful gazing up at it as evidence of Christ's Passion and of their own salvation. It was 'Goddys' flesh', 'Cristes own bodi . . . as hale as he toke it of that blessed maiden'; it bound the faithful to the Church, for only an ordained priest could celebrate its mysteries. Yet Wycliffe insisted that it was no more than a symbol – 'neither Christ nor any part of him, but the efficacious sign of him' – and this denial struck at the heart of Catholic grandeur.

A peasants' revolt broke out in May 1381, sparked off by the imposition of a poll tax, but blamed in part on Wycliffe's radical preaching and his championship of the poor. The mob, led by Wat Tyler and Jack Straw, was inflamed by a sermon preached on Blackheath – '[T]here shall be neither vassal nor lord . . . Are we not all descended from the same parents, Adam and Eve?' – and broke into London, sacking palaces and dragging Archbishop Sudbury from the Tower, where he had fled for shelter, and killing him.

William Courtenay, a tougher man, a hounder of heretics, replaced him as archbishop. He convoked a council that met at Blackfriars in London on 17 May 1382. It condemned twenty-four of Wycliffe's propositions as 'heretical and erroneous'. A powerful earthquake shook the city as it sat. Courtenay described the tremors as a portent of the purging of noxious heresies from the bowels of the earth. To Wycliffe, they were proof of God's anger at the Church.

He was forbidden to teach at Oxford and forced to retire to his rectory at Lutterworth. From here he continued to rail against the clergy, who paraded with 'costly saddles, bridles with dangling bells, rich garments and soft furs', happy to 'see the wives and children of their neighbours dying with hunger'. He whittled his sharp and early sense of English nationalism. 'Already a third and more of England is in the hands of the Pope,' he thundered.

'There cannot be two temporal sovereigns in one country; either Edward is King or Urban is king. We make our choice. We accept Edward of England and refute Urban of Rome.'

Spurning Latin as the language of Church oppression, he wrote almost entirely in English now. Since 'the truth of God standeth not in one language more than in another', he said, the Bible should be translated into English so that 'it may edify the lewd people as it doth clerks in Latin . . . No man is so rude a scholar but he may learn the gospel according to its simplicity.' He posed an apparently unanswerable question: 'Why may we not write in English the gospel and other things dedicating the gospel to the edification of men's souls?'

Why not, indeed? The Vulgate then in use across Catholic Christendom was itself a translation, of course. It had been painstakingly rendered from the original Greek and Hebrew at the end of the fourth century by St Jerome, in order to resolve the many differences in earlier Latin manuscripts, and became the standard *editio vulgata*. The Bible had also existed in Syriac, Coptic, Gothic, Ethiopic, Armenian, Georgian and Aramaic for a millennium or more before Wycliffe. By the ninth century, it had been translated into Persian and Arabic, and the brothers Cyril and Methodius had created the outline of the Cyrillic alphabet to render it into Slavonic.

The earliest Old English translations to survive were made by Caedmon, a seventh-century monk at Whitby and a former cowherd who had felt a divine urge to learn to read and write. 'He sang of the world's creation, the origins of the human race, and all the story of Genesis,' the scholar and theologian the Venerable Bede wrote of Caedmon; 'he sang of Israel's exodus from Egypt and entry into the Promised Land . . .' An Anglo-Saxon translation of the gospels made from the Vetus Italica, the pre-Vulgate Latin Bible, was said to be the work of Bede himself. His student Cuthbert described how the great scholar completed his work on

St John's gospel on his deathbed in the monastery at Jarrow in May 735. 'In the evening, his pupil said, Dear Master, one sentence is still wanting,' Cuthbert recalled. 'Write it quickly, exclaimed Bede. When it was finished . . . he repeated the Gloria Patria, and expired in the effort.' Passages from Exodus and the first fifty psalms were translated into Anglo-Saxon in the ninth century, perhaps by the pious King Alfred. A section of Genesis was worked on by the grammarian abbot Aelfric in the late tenth century. An anonymous scholar translated the four gospels into West Saxon. Metrical versions of Genesis and Exodus existed in Middle English from the mid-thirteenth century; before his death in 1349, the Yorkshire mystic-poet Richard Rolle had translated and glossed, or made comments and explanations, on the Psalter in English.

Nothing resembling a complete version of the Bible had been attempted before Wycliffe. The earliest work was done under his follower Nicholas Hereford, a fellow of Queen's College at Oxford. He had translated the Old Testament from Genesis to Baruch when he was condemned with Wycliffe by the 1382 Blackfriars council, and fled abroad for fear that Archbishop Courtenay would have him burnt. The task was continued by John Purvey, who worked at Lutterworth until Wycliffe's death at the end of 1384. The new English Bibles were eagerly sought after – it was said that a man would give a cartload of hay for a few sheets of St Paul – but bulky and time-consuming to produce. Each was an individual labour of magnitude, painstakingly hand-copied on to parchment and bound between boards. The English language was in headlong development – Latin was resented as alien and ecclesiastical; French, falling from fashion during the long French wars, was banned from use in the law courts in 1362, the year before parliament was opened with speeches in English for the first time – and the language in the Wycliffe Bibles would soon seem almost as outdated as Anglo-Saxon.

'Nellen ge deman,' a verse in the Anglo-Saxon gospel runs,

'daet ge ne syn fordemede.' In Wycliffe, that is rendered: 'Nyle ze deme, that se be nat demyd.' But the sentence in Tyndale – 'iudge not, lest ye be iudged' – needs only the substitution of '*you*' for '*ye*', to pass muster in our own English.

Nicholas and Purvey worked from the Vulgate, rather than the Greek and Hebrew originals. If much of their translation was a plodding word-for-word affair, they sometimes captured a graceful lilt – 'If I speke with tungis of men and aungels, sothli I haue not charite' – and above all they gave the English their first direct contact with the word of God in their own language.

The Church was angered and frightened. The Bible, the ecclesiastical chronicler Knighton observed, was now 'more open to the laity, and even to women who were able to read, than formerly it had been even to the scholarly and most learned of the clergy'. Knighton did not find this admirable. To him, it meant that 'the gospel pearl is thrown before swine and trodden underfoot . . . and become a joke, and this precious gem of the clergy has been turned into the sport of the laity . . .'.

Hostility to Wycliffe's followers escalated. The term 'Lollard' was applied to them, a derivation from the Dutch *lollen*, to mumble, and used in English to describe religious eccentrics and vagabonds. A violent opponent, Thomas Netter, railed at 'so many of this sect of Wycliffe, standing in the line of battle, provoking the Church to war; fearlessly they preach, they publish their doctrines, they boast of their strength . . .' Unlicensed preachers roamed the dioceses, ignoring summons to be silent. Lollards kept schools and held disputations and Bible readings; they made some progress among gentry and merchants, though most were artisans, weavers, millers, thatchers, butchers, and many were women.

The 'Bible-men' denied all rituals that were non-biblical. They ate meat on fast days. They did not keep Sunday as a special day. They did not confess. They failed to gaze up when the Host was elevated at mass. Some held that the sacramental bread had not even a symbolic significance. Eleanor Higges of Burford was arraigned for putting the sacrament in her oven and eating it.

A list of the teachings in secret Lollard conventicles was prepared for Thomas Arundel, who succeeded Courtenay as archbishop of Canterbury. They were said to mock confession, indulgences, pilgrimage and the use of images; two Lollard chaplains at Leicester used a wooden statue of St Katherine as fuel to cook a meal. The pope, the Church hierarchy and the 'private religions' of monks and friars were described as conspiracies against the scriptures. Lollards maintained that only God could beatify; the pope was powerless to make a saint. The sacraments were described as 'dead signs of no value . . . a mouthful of bread with no life'.

Virginity and the celibacy of the priesthood were 'not states approved by God', and were inferior to wedlock. The Church was 'nothing but a synagogue of Satan'; none should be baptised by priests, and purgatory was an invention. Forgiveness of sins flowed from belief, 'because, as they say, whatever is stands in faith, as Christ said to Mary Magdalene, "Thy faith hath made thee whole."' Lollards held many Church rituals to be magic and the craft of the devil. 'Exorcisms and hallowings, made in the Church, of wine, bread and wax, water, salt and oil and incense, the stone of the altar, upon vestments, mitre, cross and pilgrims' staves, be the very practice of necromancy, not of holy theology . . .'

As yet only England was affected by these ideas. Here, they aroused such fear of civil unrest that Arundel was able to press the king and parliament for powers to pursue and execute heretics. In 1401, at the archbishop's urging, parliament passed an act whose Latin title displayed its lethal intent, *De Haeretico Comburendo*, On the Burning of Heretics. The English bishops were empowered to arrest Lollards and try them by the canon law of the Church. Prisoners convicted of heresy by the Church courts were to be handed to a secular court, which would 'cause [them] to be burnt that such punishment may strike fear to the minds of others'.

No heretic had been burnt in England since a deacon was convicted of converting to Judaism almost two centuries before. This laxness was swiftly remedied. Even before the legislation had been enacted, a special parliamentary sanction was granted in March 1401 for the execution of the Lollard William Sawtrey, a priest from Lynn in Norfolk. Sawtrey was defiant. 'I, sent by God, tell thee that thou and thy whole clergy, and the King also,' he told Archbishop Arundel during his trial, 'will shortly die an evil death . . .' He was burnt, alive and in public, at Smithfield in London.

Arundel now turned on the Lollard Bible. He created the Constitutions of Oxford in 1408 to deal with translations of the scriptures. 'It is a dangerous thing, as witnesseth blessed St Jerome,' the Constitution said of the translator of the Vulgate, 'to translate the text of the holy Scripture out of one tongue into another, for in the translation the same sense is not always easily kept . . . We therefore decree and ordain, that no man, hereafter, by his own authority translate any text of the Scripture into English or any other tongue, by way of a book, libel or treatise; and that no man can read any such book, libel or treatise, now lately set forth in the time of John Wycliffe, or since, or hereafter to be set forth, in part or in whole, privily or apertly, *sub pena maioris excommunicationis*, upon pain of greater excommunication . . .' The penalty was comprehensive; it condemned its victims 'to be accursed eating and drinking, walking and sitting, rowing and riding, laughing and weeping, in house and in field, on water and on land . . . Cursed be their head and their thoughts, their eyes and their ears, their tongues and their lips, their teeth and their throats . . .' If they relapsed, they were to be burnt.

Arundel ordered that all Wycliffe's works be burnt, and sent the pope a list of 267 heresies and errors 'worthy of the fire' that had been found in them. He described Wycliffe in the covering letter as the 'son of the Serpent, herald and child of Antichrist'; his worst sin, so the archbishop said, which 'filled up the measure of his malice', was to devise 'the expedient of a new translation of Scripture into the mother tongue'.

The Council of the Church that met at Constance in 1414 had good reason to take good note of these comments. Wycliffe's heresies had passed from the Lollard villages of England to Prague and Bohemia. From here, the brilliant preacher John Huss spread them through the central European heartlands. He was summoned to Constance on an imperial safe conduct to explain himself. There were now three popes. John XXIII, who had summoned the council, was Antipope to two rivals. Gregory XII, although nearing ninety, clung to office, pawning his papal tiara to pay off his gambling debts; Benedict XIII endured imprisonment in the papal castle at Avignon rather than abdicate. John himself was an impoverished Neapolitan aristocrat who had restored the family fortunes through piracy before adopting an equally remunerative and less stressful career in religion. He was not ordained until the day before his papal coronation; he was said never to have confessed or to have taken the sacraments. Cynics chanted a new version of the creed: 'I believe in three holy Catholic churches.'

The need for reform, stressed by Wycliffe and by Huss, was obvious. The council was in no mood to grant it. Despite his safe conduct, 'John Huss, the Wycliffite, . . . was taken into custody to prevent his further teaching of that doctrine.' Wycliffe himself was condemned to the exhumation later carried out at Lutterworth by Bishop Fleming. Huss was convicted of a catalogue of heresies: the 'accused not does believe in the transubstantiation . . . despises the belief in the infallibility of the Pope . . . disputes the power of absolution by a vicious priest and confession to him . . . rejects the absolute obedience to worldly superiors . . . rejects the prohibition of marriage for priests . . . calls the indulgence a simony, sinning against the Holy Spirit'. He was led from the cathedral of Constance, past a bonfire of his writings that had been set alight in the cemetery, to a stake that had been prepared for him on the banks of the Rhine.

A remarkable Herefordshire knight gave a final twist to the Bible men. Sir John Oldcastle was rich, a soldier, and so close to the future Henry V that Shakespeare dubbed him Prince Hal's 'boon companion' and based the character of Falstaff on him. Oldcastle abandoned a brilliant career for rebellion and heresy, using his wife's fortune to support Lollard preachers and to have Lollard Bibles copied and distributed. He was arrested and brought before a Church court in 1413, which declared him a 'most pernicious and detestable heretic . . . against the faith and religion of the holy and universal Church of Rome'. He was committed to the secular power for execution.

He escaped from the Tower of London before the sentence was carried out. From hiding, using secret emissaries, Oldcastle planned an uprising. Informers disclosed a plot to stage a mumming, a play to entertain the court, and 'under colour of this mumming to destroy the king and the Holy Church'. Foiled in this, Oldcastle then arranged for a great muster of Lollards to take place in St Giles' Fields in London on a January night in 1414. A number of conspirators, seized at an inn at Bishopsgate, revealed the plans for the rebellion. Henry V led armed men to the Fields and fell upon the rebels, thirty-eight of whom were hanged or burnt.

Oldcastle escaped to become the most wanted fugitive in the country. Freedom from taxation and a reward of 1000 marks was offered to the city or borough that discovered him. Judges, justices of the peace and sheriffs were required to take an oath to put down 'heresies and errors commonly called Lollardies'. The possession of any biblical manuscript in English was taken as evidence of Lollardy. Oldcastle survived in hiding for more than three years. He was captured in Wales at the end of 1417 and taken to London. He was convicted of heresy and treasonable conspiracy to kill the king and the bishops. He was laid on a hurdle and dragged to St Giles' Fields, and suspended in a stout chair from a gallows while a fire was lit beneath him.

As he was hanged for his treason, he was simultaneously burnt for his heresy. A particular quality of horror was thus attached to the translation of the scripture into English. Here, in England, it was a heresy punishable by the fire under the terms of *De Haeretico Comburendo*, and it was also a harbinger of sedition and rebellion.

'Lollards' towers' were prepared for the imprisonment of the Bible men, in the palaces of the English bishops and in the archbishop of Cantebury's great palace at Lambeth; and 'Lollard pits' were assigned as the places where they were to be burnt.

'This picture represents, as far as art could, William Tyndale': so runs the Latin inscription beneath this portrait in the dining-hall of Hertford College, Oxford. No likeness dates from Tyndale's lifetime. As a fugitive, even the roughest sketch would have helped his pursuers identify him, and he made sure none was made. By the time this portrait was made, after his death, it was safe to embellish it with the two Latin lines of Protestant propaganda that appear under his hand, which have been translated as:

> To scatter Roman darkness by this light
> The loss of land and life I'll reckon slight

(Mary Evans Picture Library)

1

Youth

Tidy up his spelling, and in particular transpose 'u' and 'v', so that 'euer' becomes 'ever', and use 'j' for 'i', and the 1520s prose of William Tyndale is instantly familiar.

Those great rolling phrases that boom through the English-speaking mind – 'the laste enemy that shalbe destroyd is deeth', 'blessid are they that mourne for they shalbe comforted', 'though I speke with the tonges of men and angels' – are his. The English Paternoster is his: 'O oure father which arte in heuen, halowed be thy name . . .' So is the sadness and rejoicing of the Eucharist: 'this ys my bloude of the newe testamente, which shalbe shedde for many for the forgeuenes of synnes'.

In defying the Constitutions of Oxford, and translating the Bible, Tyndale fathered what is probably the best known and certainly the most quoted work in the English language. A complete analysis of the Authorised Version, known down the generations as 'the AV' or 'the King James', was made in 1998. It shows that Tyndale's words account for 84 per cent of the New Testament, and for 75.8 per cent of the Old Testament books that he translated. The fifty-four divines appointed by James I to produce the final work provided marginal notes and scholarly revisions to

Tyndale's existing translation, but the King James itself is, so *The Oxford Companion to Literature* states, 'practically the version of Tyndale with some admixture from Wycliffe'.

However famous his writing, Tyndale himself is another matter. His work classified him as a heretic. As a result, he was chased and hunted – like Oldcastle, though for much longer – and his need to lie low means that our sightings of him are laced with *perhaps, possibly, most probably*.

It is in keeping with his life, and terrible death, that we can identify the date of his birth no better than as *in or about* 1494, at a place said by his contemporaries to be '*about* the borders of Wales'.

We arrive at the date by working back from a fixed point, his award as a Bachelor of Arts at Oxford. A better idea of the place comes from the careers of his brothers Edward and John. The Tyndales were prosperous yeomen – Edward became a receiver of crown rents and a person of substance in the county, and John a London merchant – living where the western part of Gloucestershire falls from the Cotswold uplands into the Vale of Berkeley. The farmland of the vale borders the banks of the Severn, with the Welsh hills beyond.

Two houses that survive here have links with the family. Hunt's Court stands outside the village of North Nibley, on a lane that runs up to the ancient Black Horse Inn, beneath the steep pastures and stands of beech and chestnut that tumble from the crest of Nibley Knoll. The house is rendered white, concealing its great age. The lintels in the ground floor rooms reflect its changing fortunes. In hard times, and during the period of the window tax from 1696, doors and windows were bricked up and the recesses used as cupboards, to be reopened as prosperity returned. It is a solid and utilitarian house, built on two sides of a farmyard, and facing old barns of stone patched with concrete breeze blocks. The grounds are now a garden centre with a nursery specialising in roses. A rambler is named for William Tyndale, red, with violet flush and gold stains.

Tyndales lived in the house from early Tudor times until 1784. The original heiress of Hunt's Court, Alice Hunt, married Thomas Tyndale during Henry VII's reign. They had a son, William. The mid-Victorians, the first (and largely the last) generation to wish to honour the man who had brought them the scriptures in English, thought this William to be him. They built a cenotaph 111 feet high on Nibley Knoll, the high point of the escarpment above Hunt's Court, and adorned it with carvings of the milestones in his life: the farewell to the Cotswolds, the betrayal at Antwerp, the martyrdom. The monument was completed at a cost of £1550 in 1866. Each workman was given a fine bound volume of the King James as a keepsake.

This would be a fitting memorial, and a compensation for the centuries of obscurity, had it been in the right place. It was not. Alice and Thomas could not have married before 1505, it was later established, and their son William was found to have been alive fifteen years after the translator had been executed.

The other candidate for our William's birthplace is four or five miles to the west, in the village of Slimbridge, which lies in flat farmland close to a wild fowl sanctuary and the high banks of the Severn. Hurst Farm, a later plain brick-fronted house with flashings above the windows, is on a bend of the road beyond the high-steepled parish church of St John the Baptist. It is still a working farm, with barns, a cattle yard and looseboxes. Edward Tyndale, William's brother, lived at Hurst Farm for many years, and he was buried in the Slimbridge churchyard in 1546.

This prosperous wool and cattle country has a special resonance because its dialect was Tyndale's mother tongue. The Gloucestershire in him is only noticeable now in the odd word that has failed to gel into general English; in 'toot-hill', for example, in Genesis 31, 'and this toot-hill which the Lord seeth', meaning a lookout hill. But he wrote for simple folk, for the ploughboy, he said, and the local sayings and idioms he used have passed through his writing into the language as a whole.

The family used two names, Tyndale and Hutchins, in a wide variety of spellings: Tindale, Tyndal, Hychyn, Hewchyns. A family tradition has it that they came originally from Tyndale in Northumberland, and adopted the name Hutchins to hide their northern origins during the Wars of the Roses. William was born only nine years after Richard III was killed at Bosworth Field and the violent flux of plots and rebellions had ended. One of the battles had been fought at Nibley Green in 1470; the dead were buried in the grounds of the parish church of St Martin, and the victors built a south aisle for the church in thanksgiving.

Henry VII, the new king, was a 'a sad prince, full of thoughts', his eyes 'small and blue, his teeth few, poor and blackish, and his hair thin and white'. Two of his four immediate predecessors had been murdered, one had been killed in battle, and the fourth had been driven in humiliation from his realm in mid-reign; Richard III had murdered, or was suspected of involvement in the murder of his brother, his wife, the king, Henry VI, and two nephews, the little princes who disappeared in the Tower of London in 1483. The dead princes were brothers of Henry VII's wife, Elizabeth of York, and Henry's natural and overriding ambition was to make his new Tudor dynasty stable and long lasting.

Two pretenders challenged him. Lambert Simnel, the son of an Oxford tradesman but put forward as a surviving nephew from the Tower, was proclaimed king in Dublin in 1487, but his forces were defeated in battle at Stoke later in the year. Shortly after William Tyndale was born, another pretender, Perkin Warbeck, claimed to be the Tower's second surviving prince; he was hailed by the Irish earls, and the king of Scotland gave him his cousin in marriage, before he landed in the West Country, failed to make progress, surrendered and was hanged in 1499.

Even after that, the dynasty hung by a single life. Henry VII's sons Arthur and Edmund died young, though only after Arthur had married Catherine of Aragon. The future Henry VIII was left as the only male heir, a fact that, together with his later marriage to Catherine, his brother's widow, was greatly to influence the adult life of William Tyndale and the future of English religion.

As a boy, Tyndale may have attended the grammar school at Wotton-under-Edge, the nearest large town. The school claims to be the eleventh oldest in England, and survives as Katharine Lady Berkeley's School, though it moved from its old site in the town in the 1950s, and its buildings have been converted into apartments. The town's motto is 'Strong by Stream and Staple', and its water-powered cloth mills flourished from the sixteenth century until they were put out of business in the nineteenth by the more efficient mills in the valleys around Stroud and by the giant works in Yorkshire. Its weekly cloth market flourished in Tyndale's day, attracting many 'tolseys', or 'foreigners', from other parts, who paid a toll to attend it.

Tyndale was an eager and talented child, and he was sent to Magdalen School in Oxford at the age of about twelve, in 1506. A turreted fragment of the school's Grammar Hall still remains; besides this school-room, the original building had little more than the chambers of the master and the usher, and a kitchen. Shortly after, he entered Magdalen Hall – then adjacent to Magdalen College but later moved and established as Hertford College – where he began the seven-year course that led to a BA degree.

Most undergraduates were from middling families – the great Thomas Wolsey was the son of an East Anglian butcher – and the nobility had yet to send their sons to Oxford in any numbers. The Tudor beau, with his florid languor, was still a generation distant. In Tyndale's day, students were forbidden to keep sporting dogs, ferrets or hawks for hunting, though some went poaching in the

Tyndale went to Oxford in 1506, when he was about twelve. He graduated as a Bachelor of Arts in 1512, and Master of Arts three years later. He scorned the academic sophistry of the day, but he improved himself 'in knowledge of tongues and other liberal arts'. His study of rhetoric helped to lay the rhythm and cadence that underpinned his translating genius. A later spell at Cambridge probably cemented his radical religious views.

(Bridgeman Art Library/National Portrait Gallery)

royal forests at Shotover and Woodstock; they were not allowed to gamble or to own dice or playing cards, or to carry arms unless travelling. Taverns and brothels were off limits. For legal amusement, students staged morality plays and pageants, and comedies by Plautus and Aristophanes, and sang and played the lyre and lute.

Board and lodging were cheap. Undergraduates were housed two or three to a chamber, with cubicles or 'studyes' partitioned off for reading, and an individual's room rent was no more than sixpence a year. His share of commons, the basic food and drink bought each week for members of the hall or college, amounted to less than a penny a day. A contemporary wrote of Oxford dinners as a 'penye pece of byefe amongst iiii, hauying a few porage made of the brothe of the same byefe with salte and otemell'. Each student provided his own bedding, knives, spoons, candlesticks, a lantern, a pair of bellows and a coffer for his books.

The chancellor of the university maintained his own court, with powers to deny a student a degree, or to expel, excommunicate or imprison in serious cases. Fines were the most common punishment. They were imposed for climbing in and out of college after the gates were shut, for bringing an unsheathed knife to table, for disorder, drunkenness, gaming and fighting. If blood was shed during a brawl, the fine was doubled. Scholars and fellows sometimes wore distinctive liveries and fur-trimmed cloaks, but undergraduates were required only to wear decent clerical garb, which varied in colour and style and differed little from ordinary dress. It was only later that they were obliged to wear black gowns, as they still do on formal occasions, thus making it possible for the university officers or proctors to distinguish 'town' from 'gown' in brawls.

Some one thousand young scholars attended the colleges, semi-monastic institutions of the regular and secular clergy, and the self-governing halls of the university. A small hall like Magdalen might have no more than twenty students, living in shared chambers with a central hall for meals and disputations. They were up at 5.00 for divine service before the first, 6.00 a.m. lecture. They ate together in commons, with a bell or horn announcing dinner at 10.00 or 11.00 a.m., and supper at 5.00. Before retiring to bed, they chanted the *Salve Regina* or some such antiphon to the Virgin together. The atmosphere was one of family, as well as church; to this day, colleges refer to themselves as 'domus', or 'house', as in 'house and home'.

Tyndale's schooling gave him a thorough grounding in Latin. Boys learnt to speak and write elementary Latin in the early forms. Classes then progressed from Aesop and Terence in the third form to Horace's epistles and Ovid's *Metamorphoses* in the seventh, by way of Virgil, Cicero's letters and Caesar's history. In the eighth class, the science of grammar was studied in depth. Verse was rendered into prose, and vice versa, translations were made, and, though Ovid's lascivious *De arte amandi* was strictly off the menu, Virgil was read out '*voce ben sonora* to bring out the majesty of his poetry'.

The Latin diet remained at the university. English had such lowly status that undergraduates were forbidden to speak it within the precincts of the hall, except at feasts and on holidays. It was compulsory for them to use Latin, although French was tolerated as an alternative in some colleges. Tyndale's love of English – 'our mother tongue', he said, 'which doth correspond with scripture better than ever Latin may' – was eccentric. It was spoken by only three million people on their foggy island; and the English themselves largely governed, educated and prayed in Latin. A foreign scholar or cleric, such as Erasmus, lived for several years in England, and followed a lively social and academic life, without speaking any English.

The MA course began with the *trivium*, the 'liberall artes', a trio of grammar, rhetoric and logic. Tyndale will have read the *Rhetoric* of Aristotle, Boethius's *Topics,* Cicero's *Nova Rhetorica* and some works of Ovid and Priscian. His insight into rhetoric was greatly to influence his prose. The mark of all Tyndale's writing is its brilliant resonance when read aloud. From the *trivium,* he moved on to the *quadrivium,* of arithmetic, music, astronomy and geometry. Whether Tyndale was musical or not, we do not know, though singing and playing music were a favourite student pastime; but the sense of rhythm and cadence that floods his work shows that he had a sensitive ear. He did not write poetry either and was somewhat sour to colleagues who did, and yet his images and his gift for the mood of words reveal a poetic temperament.

Public teaching was by lecture and disputation. The master took a set text and expounded on its meaning. His students had to provide interpretations and glosses on it, and to launch *quaestiones,* or investigations, into its aspects. Formal debates and oratory were held on *dies disputabilis.* In front of the young scholars, or sophisters, masters and bachelors argued on either side of an interpretation or proposition – usually one proponent and two opponents – until the presiding master gave his determination or final judgement.

Oxford was known as the Vineyard of the Lord for its learning and its beauty – 'a place gladsome and fertile, suitable for a habitation of the gods' Wycliffe had written of it – but Tyndale found its teaching sterile and antiquated. He improved himself 'in knowledge of tongues and other liberal arts', laying the basis of his translating genius. He devoted much attention to theology, and, so the Protestant martyrologist John Foxe recorded, 'read privily to certain students and fellows of Magdalen College some parcel of divinity, instructing them in the knowledge and truth of the scriptures'. He found the Oxford theologians, however, to be 'old barking curs . . . beating the pulpit with their fists for madness'.

The great enemies in his life – Sir Thomas More, Cardinal Wolsey, and two bishops of London, Cuthbert Tunstall and John

Stokesley – were between fifteen and eighteen years older than him. Thomas More, for example, had gone up to Oxford in 1492. They were closer to the swirling anarchy, intrigues and assassinations of the dynastic wars; they were more conservative, more fearful of change than Tyndale. In 1515, while Tyndale was still at Oxford, More was on a diplomatic mission to Antwerp. Here he had begun to write *Utopia*, his evocation of a magical island of happiness and fair play, where reason and justice reign; but Utopia means a 'non-place', as the name of its great city, Amaurotum, comes from the Greek for 'darkly seen', and for More this ideal was an irony reflecting on the brutishness of reality.

Tyndale's generation had less reason to fear change and disorder. He was restless at Oxford and scornful of the status quo. He found the student to be crushed by tradition and censorship: 'he is sworn that he shall not defame the university, whatsoever he seeth', he said, 'and when he taketh his first degree, he is sworn that he shall hold none opinion condemned by the church; but what such opinions be, that he shall not know.'

The influence of Scholasticism, with its attempts to reconcile classical learning with Christian revelation, was all-pervading. It involved the minute examination of the Bible as the source of the absolute truth of God, against which human knowledge must be reckoned. Elaborate glosses were built on verses, sentences and individual words. Some of these glosses touched deep issues of faith, but many were ludicrous; the number of angels who could be gathered on the point of a needle was discussed in one example, while another, cited by Erasmus, posed the question of whether Christ could have taken on the likeness of a mule, and, if so, whether a mule could be crucified. Tyndale himself attended a degree ceremony for doctors of divinity at which a formal disputation was heard over whether the widow has more merit than the virgin.

This was mere 'sophistry', Tyndale said, and he was at war with the Schoolmen and the tiresome armoury of 'their predicaments, universals, second intentions, quiddities, haecceities and relatives'. He had a particular interest in the Bible, and may have already thought of translating it; in the only reference to his childhood that he made, he remarked that he had heard as a boy 'how that king Athelstane caused the holy scripture to be translated into the tongue that then was in England, and how the prelates exhorted him thereto'. He said that the teaching of the scripture at Oxford 'is so locked up with such false expositions and with false principles of natural philosophy' that students could not enter into the true spirit of the Bible; instead, they were kept outside, and 'dispute all their lives about words and vain opinions, pertaining as much unto the healing of a man's heel as the health of his soul'.

He was, nonetheless, attentive to his studies. He graduated Bachelor of Arts, as William Hychyns, on 4 July 1512, and Master of Arts three years later. He had no reputation yet as a firebrand. Foxe says that his manners and conversation at this time were such that 'all they that knew him reputed and esteemed him to be a man of most virtuous disposition and of life unspotted'. It was a condition of his MA degree that he stay for a year at Oxford to teach in the Schools. At a date not before 1516, therefore, 'spying his time', as Foxe put it, Tyndale 'removed from thence to the university of Cambridge, where he . . . made his abode a certain space, being now farther ripened in the knowledge of God's word . . .'.

Cambridge was then more radical and more Lollard-influenced than Oxford. Erasmus had taught there from 1510 to 1514, and humanism was becoming rooted, fresh and open after the musty staleness of the Schoolmen. Erasmus had gone on to edit and publish a Greek New Testament in 1516 as a purer alternative to the Latin Vulgate, for the original was, of course, written in Greek. In 1518, Richard Croke gave the first public lectures on the Greek language at Cambridge. Tyndale thus acquired the necessary fundamentals for his future work on the New Testament: the original text and the fine-tuned Greek needed to translate it.

The Lollards kept reform ideas alive, and, despite the flames and pits that pursued them, they had undergone a revival since Tyndale's birth. Cells persisted in Buckinghamshire. In 1506, Bishop Smyth dealt with sixty cases at Amersham and twenty at Buckingham. Two were burnt. The others recanted and did penance. Bishop Fitzjames of London prosecuted more than forty Lollards in 1510, and a further thirty-seven in 1517. On each occasion, four relapsed heretics were burnt in the Lollard pit; the death sentence was mandatory for those who had recanted once and then resumed their heresy. Several Lollard cells were denounced to Archbishop Warham in Kent, particularly around Tenterden, Cranbrook and Benenden. In 1511 and 1512, the archbishop obtained fifty abjurations and handed five to the secular powers for burning. During the same period, Bishop Geoffrey Blythe of Lichfield dealt with seventy-four alleged heretics, a third of them women. Seven 'godly martyrs', including a widow, were burnt at Coventry in 1519.

This was as yet no great threat to the Church. Few or none were learned, so Foxe said, being 'simple labourers and artificers, but as it pleased the Lord to work in their knowledge and understanding by reading a few English books, such as they could get in corners'. Illiterates learnt Bible passages off by heart in English; some of the Buckinghamshire heretics could reel off the Epistle of St James and the Apocalypse.

But the Lollards persisted with the ideas for which Wycliffe had been cursed. The charges against them were generally a combination of the heresies condemned a century before at Constance: reading the scriptures in laboriously hand-copied English manuscripts, disbelief in transubstantiation, and mockery of pilgrimages, purgatory, saints' images and relics, and laughing at the notion that a cash payment to the Church or the pope could release a soul from purgatory. They laughed, too, at church bells, as peals of vanity. 'Lo, yonder is a fair bell, and it were to hang about a cow's neck in this town', one was accused of saying.

They had, too, a leavening of men whose time was coming, merchants, traders, prosperous shopkeepers, lively men with money and ambition. They travelled and spread their ideas. Four London heretics were found to have attended a Lollard meeting at Amersham; one was a goldsmith, another was Thomas Grove, a well-off butcher who was able to slip the large sum of £20 to Dr Wilcocks, the vicar general of the diocese of London, so as to avoid doing public penance, which might have ruined his reputation and his business. John Hacker, a water-bearer of Coleman Street in London, journeyed to Burford and to Buckingham and Essex to distribute heretical manuscripts. In London, he was associated with John Stacey, a prominent member of the Tilers' and Bricklayers' Company. Stacey kept a man in his house to 'write out the Apocalypse in English', the costs being met by John Sercot, a grocer.

A scholar like Tyndale, a university man, might seem on a different plane to these rougher and more practical men; but they shared ideas with him, they made up a natural constituency for reform, and they were very brave. 'Christ sitting at supper could not give his disciples his living body to eat,' John Badby, a tailor of Evesham in Worcester, said at his trial. In so doing, in front of two archbishops, eight bishops, a duke and the lord chancellor, he condemned himself to death. The Host was displayed to him by a prior as he was bound to the stake at Smithfield. 'It is the consecrated bread and not the body of God,' Badby cried, and the fire was lit.

It needed a bolt of spiritual lightning to fuse Tyndale and the Lollards into a new evangelical force and this was provided by Martin Luther. On 31 October 1517, about a year after Tyndale had gone to Cambridge, Luther nailed ninety-five theses attacking the Church to the door of the castle church at Wittenberg in eastern Germany.

The immediate cause of Luther's fury was a papal indulgence, a remission of the punishment for sins in return for a cash payment, which was being sold in Germany to raise money for the rebuilding of St Peter's in Rome. Luther denied that the pope had the power to remit any guilt, and that it was mere 'human doctrine' to preach that a soul flew out of purgatory at the moment that a coin rattled into a Church coffer.

The obscure Saxon raised a whirlwind. 'Nobody,' Luther boasted, 'will go to hear a lecture unless the lecturer is teaching my theology, which is the theology of the Bible, of St Augustine, and of all true theologians of the Church.' In fairness, he should have credited Wycliffe, for he went beyond the Lollards in only one major dogma.

In these final years of Catholic hegemony, popes and prelates reached the heights of magnificence. Nicholas V had summoned his cardinals to his deathbed in 1455, and told them that the loyalty of the 'uncultured masses' of believers was best obtained through giving them 'something that appeals to the eye'. Ideas and theology carried little weight; a popular faith 'sustained only on doctrines', he assured them, would 'never be anything but feeble and vacillating'. But if the Holy See was 'visible', if it was 'displayed in majestic buildings, imperishable memorials and witnesses seemingly planted by the hand of God himself', then belief could 'grow and strengthen like a tradition from one generation to another', and the Church would be 'accepted and revered by all the world'.

His successors were dazzling in their visibility. Julius II, pope when Tyndale went up to Oxford, laid the cornerstone of the Basilica of St Peter's, tapped the genius of Raphael and Bramante, and commissioned Michelangelo to paint the ceiling of the Sistine Chapel with a force and beauty that seemed divinely planted indeed. He also fathered three daughters, contracted syphilis, wore silver armour as he led papal armies in his vendetta against the Borgias, and launched the indulgence that drew Luther's wrath. He was succeeded in 1513 by Leo X, the son of Lorenzo de' Medici and the owner of a menagerie: Persian horses, a panther and two leopards accompanied his processions, together with an elephant, Hanno, whose portrait he had painted by Raphael. These men were indisputably great Renaissance princes, open to every manner of temporal vice and excess; but they were also Christ's vicars on earth, vulnerable to the spiritual assaults that Luther – and then Tyndale – were to heap upon them.

At home, Cardinal Wolsey was the grandest priest ever seen in England. He paid a visit of typical grandeur to Cambridge in 1520, a man of ordinary birth who combined the vast secular power of lord chancellor with the spiritual authority of a *legatus a latere*, the special envoy, of the Holy See. The university addressed him as Majestas, a fitting title, for he was plundering both State and Church to build a new foundation of exquisite grandeur on the Oxford water meadows, which he named Cardinal's College for himself,[1] and a palace at Hampton Court that outdid the king. Wolsey had attitudes to match his papal masters. 'How think you?' he said when criticised for flaunting his wealth. 'Were it better for me, being in the honour and dignity that I am, to make coins of my pillars and poleaxes and to give money to five or six beggars than to maintain the commonwealth as I do?'

This was anathema to a Bible-man like Tyndale, who believed that priests should share the poverty of the apostles. Tyndale dubbed him 'Wolfsee . . . this wily wolf, I say, and raging sea, and shipwreck of all England'. Wolsey was prey to 'all manner of voluptuousness, expert and exercised in the course of the world', Tyndale wrote in a racy character sketch, 'utterly appointed to semble and dissemble, to have one thing in the heart and another in the mouth . . . there was no man so obsequious and serviceable, and in all games and sports the first and next at hand . . .'

Thomas Wolsey, cardinal, lord chancellor and papal legate, was the grandest priest England had ever seen. His palaces, jewels, feasts and retinue spoke of a Church in which the worldly was overwhelming the spiritual. Tyndale mocked him as 'Wolfsee . . . this wily wolf, I say, and raging sea, and shipwreck of all England'. But he was a humane man, who preferred compromise with heretics to burning them at the stake.

(Popperfoto)

Beneath the brilliant display of the Church – the altar cloths of silk, velvet and sarcanet, the robes and vestments of damask and linen, the chalices and cups of jewelled silver – lurked a rottenness. Solemn warning had been given by delegates at the Church Council at Basle eighty years before. Henceforth, they had resolved, 'all simony shall cease . . . All priests shall put away their concubines [or] shall be deprived of his office, though he be the Bishop of Rome . . . The abuse of ban and anathema by the popes shall cease . . . The popes shall neither demand nor receive any fees for ecclesiastical offices. From now on, a pope should think not of this world's treasures but only of those of the world to come.' For their pains, the delegates were denounced as 'apostates, blaspheming rebels, men guilty of sacrilege, gaolbirds', and ignored.

Nepotism continued to flourish. Leo X was an abbot at the age of seven, a canon at eight and a cardinal at thirteen. Simony, the sale of office, accelerated and new bureaucracies were invented to extend the business. Leo X traded in 2150 Church appointments with a value of three million ducats. Forgery was rampant in the sale of relics, where demand far outstripped supply as private collectors vied with the clergy for trophies. A bishop of Lincoln, frustrated at his cathedral's lack of valuable objects, bit off a piece of the finger of St Mary Magdalene displayed at Fécamp. Erasmus pointed out that enough wood to build a battleship was said to have come from the True Cross; as well as its sliver of the cross, the abbey of St Denis outside Paris claimed to have part of the crown of thorns, a holy nail, the hand of St Thomas and the chin of St Mary Magdalene.

In Tyndale's own childhood diocese of Worcester, the bishopric was held successively by three Italians from 1512. They lived in Rome, on the fat of their Worcester stipends, and never set foot in England. The rector of Slimbridge, in whose parish Hurst Farm lay, was an absentee appointed by Magdalen College at Oxford. From 1509, the living was held by John Stokesley, whom we shall

meet later as a heretic-hunter; there is no record of his having visited it. Many English priests were so ill-educated that Tyndale
claimed that twenty thousand of them could not have translated
into English the line from the Paternoster: '*fiat voluntas tua sicut
in coelo et in terrâ*', 'thy will be done in earth as it is in heaven'.

Leo was little worried by the lack of reform, or by the professor
of theology at the obscure new university of Wittenberg. Luther
appeared to be a throwback to the old heresies for which Wycliffe
and Huss had been burnt. To a large degree, he was; but he had
arrived there by a different route. In his mid-thirties, the stocky
son of a prosperous and godly copper miner from Eisleben, he suffered a spiritual crisis. His life was earnest; he prayed, he fasted, he
carried out penances and made lists of his sins. 'And yet my conscience kept nagging,' he wrote. 'It kept telling me: "You fell short
there . . . You were not sorry enough . . . You left that sin off your
list."' Redemption, he feared, was denied him. He sought to ease
the pain in his soul with 'human remedies, the traditions of men'.
His efforts seemed only to increase his troubles. He read and
reread Augustine and Paul, until, of a sudden, six words of Paul –
'the righteous shall live by faith' – bit into his conscience 'as flashes
of lightning, frightening me each time I heard them . . .'.

A thought followed, of deep ill omen to traditional faith: 'If we
as righteous are to live by faith, and if the righteousness of faith is
to be for salvation to everyone who believes, then it is not our
merit, but the mercy of God.' Man was too steeped in vice and sin
to save himself. No penance, good works, fasting, pilgrimage,
indulgence or alms-giving – none of the traditional medicines of
the Church – could redeem him. Righteousness was a gift promised by Christ to all who had faith in him. It flowed directly from
God, without the priestly or institutional intercession of the
Church. The Christian was justified *per solam fidem*, by faith
alone. A mortal assault on the Church followed from this. Luther
rejected its 'human remedies'; its traditions, the papacy paramount

among them, were a cowl that concealed faith. Its greed and decadence, its shameless use of 'the threat of the stake and the shame of heresy' to terrify its critics, and the 'loose blabber' of its priests, prevented the faithful from understanding the manifest things of God.

As he pondered his insights, Luther 'felt as though I had been reborn altogether and had entered Paradise'. In the same moment, he wrote, 'the face of the whole of Scripture became apparent to me'. This immodest claim might have remained mere bravado without the printing press. The hand-copied book was an expensive and fragile rarity, prepared by a team of scribes and illuminators. Lollard tracts and their bulky Bibles were individual labours of love, not mass items sold at a profit. The press stood supply and cost on their head. Luther was a writer of verve and dash, a populariser and born pamphleteer who exploited it to the full.

The first documents printed with movable type were, ironically enough, indulgences published by Johann Gutenberg at Mainz in 1445. Fittingly, his next venture was the Vulgate Bible. Using a metal typeface designed by the professional scribe Peter Schoeffer, Gutenberg printed a run of three hundred copies on six presses. The technical quality was excellent from the outset. Experiments with colour printing began with the first dated book, a fine Psalter produced in 1457. Mainz was sacked in 1462, and fleeing print workers took the new technology with them. The wandering Germans were in Rome by 1464. By the end of the decade, they had set up at the Sorbonne in Paris, and, at Venice, had added lower case type and italic to the original Roman capital letters.

A measure of the fall in prices is given by printed volumes with hand illustrations. They cost eight times as much as those with plain printed text. By 1500, a Venetian artisan could buy four printed volumes for one week's salary. Bankers and merchants invested heavily in print shops and paper mills. Graduates from the new universities – two dozen were founded in Europe in the fifteenth century – provided readers as well as typesetters, proof-readers, editors, authors and translators. Controversial titles soon proved to be bestsellers. Erasmus's *Praise of Folly*, wounding to the papacy, ran to forty-three editions in his lifetime. Humble readers were snapping up copies of religious tracts and sermons. The major constraint, in an age of rapidly growing literacy, was the high price of paper, which made up two thirds of production costs. The humblest reader could afford religious tracts. A fraud investigation in Seville – indulgence printers were in the habit of running off extra copies and selling them on their own behalf – uncovered a single printer who held stocks of more than eighty thousand sheets of prayers, rhymes and devotional woodcuts.

Scores of thousands of pamphlets written by Luther came off the German presses, and they were soon flooding into England. By 1521, the English Church was so alarmed at the scale of smuggling that Wolsey presided over a grand burning of Lutheran books at St Paul's Cross in London. A few weeks later, another bonfire was lit at Cambridge.

Henry VIII himself was tempted into attacking Luther – Wolsey 'furnished the court with chaplains of his own sworn disciples,' Tyndale wrote, 'to be always present, and to dispute the vanities, and to water whatsoever the cardinal had planted' – and put his name to a treatise defending Catholic orthodoxy against Lutheranism. The English printer Richard Pynson published the king's *Assertio Septem Sacramentorum* in 1521. The actual author of this work, which won Henry the title of Defender of the Faith from the pope (the Latin abbreviation of *Fid. Def.* appears on English coins to this day), was Thomas More.

The battle lines of the coming conflict were being drawn up. More, humanist and author, but also rising lawyer and government officer – he was knighted in 1521 – appointed himself as the great lay champion of orthodoxy. Tyndale was coming to the end of his time at Cambridge. We do not know how or with whom he spent his time there. Foxe says merely that he was 'further ripened in God's word'. More wrote later that Tyndale at this time was known 'for a man of right good living, studious and well learned in scripture, and in divers places in England was very well liked, and did great good in preaching'. It was the only kind thing that More ever said of him. We do not know who was his informant.

We know that other reformers were Cambridge men, and that they were said to meet at The White Horse Inn: Hugh Latimer, Thomas Cranmer, Thomas Bilney and others whom we know that Tyndale met later – Robert Barnes, Miles Coverdale and John Frith. Perhaps Tyndale joined in their talks at The White Horse; perhaps not.

What is certain is that all of them, except Coverdale alone, were burnt for their beliefs; and that, at some time while he was at Cambridge, Tyndale was exposed to Luther's ideas and took his own first steps to the stake.

2

Decision

After he left Cambridge, Tyndale became tutor to the children of a Gloucestershire landowner. He arrived with the Walsh family in the midsummer of 1522. He was now aged about twenty-seven, and the months he spent in this rolling wool country set up the rest of his life. He discovered his vocation and he had the first warnings of the perils that went hand in hand with it.

His employer, Sir John Walsh, the future high sheriff of the county, was a good-natured ex-courtier who had served as ceremonial champion to the young Henry VIII at the coronation in 1509. The king remained fond of him, spending a night at his house with Anne Boleyn when a royal progress brought him nearby. Sir John was married to Anne Poyntz, an heiress from a leading county family, whom Tyndale affectionately recalled as 'a stout and a wise woman'.

The Walshes lived at Little Sodbury Manor, a rambling and friendly house of soft grey stone and mullioned windows that still stands in quiet splendour amid its lawns and ancient yews on a steep west-facing slope of the Cotswolds. Its buildings were grouped round a courtyard, now the west lawn, with one of the finest great halls in England set beneath a steep-pitched roof. 'Walche,' a chronicler wrote, 'is Lord of Little Sodbyri, and hath fayr place there in the syde of Sodbyri high hill and a park.' The manor was only a dozen or so miles along the lanes from Slimbridge and North Nibley, and the landscape of pasture and copses was familiar to Tyndale from his childhood. He worked and slept in a heavily beamed room under the eaves at the back of the house, so tradition has it, whose window looks out on to a steep hill. At the summit, where stumps of earth walls trace the remains of a Roman camp, the eye is drawn to Stinchcombe Hill and Nibley Knoll, and across the watery green of the Severn vale to the purple and black loom of the Welsh mountains.

The site was inhabited in the Bronze Age; it was mentioned as a border post against Welsh marauders by the Roman historian Tacitus at the end of the first century. Its name – Sod, or South, and Bury, or Camp – is derived from Saxon words. The manor house itself, one of only two definite homes that we know of in Tyndale's fugitive life, reflected some of the vicissitudes of English history. Its Saxon owner was expelled after 1066 by a conquering Norman, Hugo Maminot. It passed in time to Hugh le Despenser, an avaricious courtier created earl of Winchester by Edward II, and hanged at Bristol when his royal patron was deposed and murdered in 1327.

Unstable times had returned more recently. When the manor's great hall was built in the mid-fifteenth century, a spyhole, or 'squint', was set into a gargoyle on the wall to the left of the fireplace so that the room could be observed through it from an upper chamber. In the space of a fortnight in 1471, it witnessed the visits of the Lancastrian Margaret of Anjou, and her enemies Edward VI and Richard of Gloucester, as they billeted themselves in the house before riding on to clash at the battle of Tewkesbury. The house had passed to Sir John Walsh's father through marriage a few years later.

Sir John knew Tyndale's brother Edward well. The two men later served together on various commissions in the county. The young tutor was treated as a member of the family and his duties were light. The eldest Walsh boy, Maurice, was no more than seven (he was fated, as it transpired, to die of burns as an adult after a 'fiery sulphurous globe' rolled in through the parlour door and struck him as he sat dining during a thunderstorm) and he was only in the first stages of reading and writing and Latin grammar.

The tutor thus had time in plenty to indulge his passion for debate and preaching. A private chapel stood in the grounds of the manor. It was used as a parish church by villagers who did not attend the grand church of St John the Baptist three miles away in Chipping Sodbury, where Sir John Walsh lies in a side-chapel. The chapel fell into ruins and in 1859 its stones and simple pulpit were moved down the slope into the small hamlet and rebuilt as the church of St Adeline.

Tyndale roamed much further afield to find larger audiences. He went, so Foxe says, 'specially about the town of Bristol, and also in the said town in the common place called St Austin's Green'. This was a patch of open ground in front of the old Augustinian convent in Bristol, now called College Green, where wandering preachers gave al fresco sermons and harangued passers-by. In a tradition dating back at least a hundred years, preachers walked or rode round the country, speaking in fields, churchyards or on commons and greens, the public spaces in towns and villages. A licence was needed to preach in each diocese that the wanderer visited, at least in theory, but the rule was difficult to enforce and was frequently ignored.

Sermons were preached in English. They were the only part of an otherwise Latin service that most worshippers could understand; indeed, many priests had only a dim grasp of the meaning of the liturgy, and would have been hard pressed to compose half a sentence in Latin. In its core element, however, the English sermon relied on the Latin Bible. A preacher began with an *exordium*, or introduction. He passed to the text of the day, taken from the Bible, before completing the sermon with his peroration. This tradition of preaching a sermon on a text gave the single biblical verse, or part of a verse, a compelling power. One phrase, 'the righteous shall live by faith', was particularly popular with Lutheran preachers in 1522, as the encapsulation of the new doctrine of justification by faith; as one verse, 'thou shalt utterly destroy them; thou shalt make no covenant with them, nor show mercy unto them', was favoured by their enemies.

Worshippers thus knew that the Bible was a treasure chest, from which the preacher plucked a single gem of wisdom to flash before them each sermon time. But at all other times, except for the handful who could read Latin, the scripture was locked away in a dead language. As a preacher himself, Tyndale had special reason to resent the Church ban on translation into English.

Bristol was promising ground for a radical preacher. It was a great seaport, second only to London in the value of its trade, and ships' crews and travellers opened it to Continental thoughts and fashions. We cannot be sure whether Tyndale met Lutherans among the German and Dutch merchants and sailors in the city, nor how extreme he was in his open-air preaching over the winter of 1522–3. But there was already enough force and passion in his ideas to shock and anger the senior clergy of the Gloucester diocese. They did not, of course, compromise their dignity by mingling with unwashed laymen to hear him at St Austin's Green. He came to their ill-tempered notice over dinner conversations in the panelled hall at Little Sodbury. The Walshes kept one of the best tables in the county, and 'divers great beneficed men, as abbots, deans, archdeacons and other learned men' were regularly invited to dine. Tyndale sat with the guests.

The table talk often turned to Luther and the scriptures, and the young tutor 'did many times therein show his mind and learning',

arguing with his elders and winning points by producing a Vulgate
Bible and showing them the passage 'of open and manifest scripture' that proved them to be wrong. This did not endear him to
them. Divers and sundry times, Foxe reports, 'the great doctors of
divinity waxed weary and bare a secret grudge in their hearts
against Master Tyndall'.

They could not be openly hostile while they were enjoying his
employers' hospitality. A group of them therefore invited the
Walshes to a banquet, where they felt free to pour poison into their
ears. Lady Walsh was impressed that such rich and well-read men
found Tyndale to be a dangerous and misguided young man. She
tackled him when she returned home. 'There was such doctor, he
may dispend £200 by the year,' she said, 'another one hundred
pound, and another three hundred pound, and what think ye,
were it reason that we should believe you before them so great,
learned and beneficed men?' Tyndale was in no position to
answer – he was indeed inexperienced, and fortunate if the
Walshes paid him as much as £5 a year – and he did not try to do
so.

Instead, he won the family over by translating Erasmus's book
Enchiridion Militis Christiani into English. This, at least, is what
Foxe claims. Foxe's informant for this period in Tyndale's life was
probably one Richard Webb, a priest who grew up in Chipping
Sodbury. Webb knew Tyndale personally and he was living nearby
in his rectory at West Kingston at the time. No manuscript has
been found of what would have been Tyndale's first work as a
translator – the first known edition of the *Enchiridion* in English
was not printed for another ten years – but there is no reason why
Foxe should be mistaken. It was in character for Tyndale to set
himself such a project. He had a side that was bookish, vague,
naive, 'for in the wily subtleties of this world', it was said of him,
'he was simple and inexpert'. But he was also a doer, pragmatic and
alert, who saw a chance – a gift to the Walshes that was also a

dummy run as a translator – and took it. If he was scholarly, he was also bold and decisive.

The *Enchiridion* was an apt choice. Erasmus had written it in 1501 at the request of a Frau Poopenruyter, who wanted to reform her adulterous and dissolute husband, a German arms dealer. It took the form of a handbook for the good Christian soldier, advising him how to acquire and buckle on the spiritual armour of God. In it, Erasmus stressed that the great Christian weapons are prayer and knowledge of the scriptures, especially the New Testament, and above all the gospels and the epistles of Paul to the Romans and Corinthians. Erasmus also took some sideswipes at the state of the Church. He was sharply critical of the greed and superstition of the clergy, and flayed the Schoolmen for their dullness and casuistry. Their writing was unintelligible, he said, and Christians would find all they needed in the scriptures. 'Honourest thou the bones of Paul hid in a shrine,' he wrote of the cult of relics, anticipating Luther by more than fifteen years, 'and honourest thou not the mind of Paul hid in his writings?' Through study of the scripture, and personal faith and piety, the humblest soldier could open himself to Christ.

Tyndale agreed with this, ferociously so, and it seems that the Walshes were impressed enough with his translation to become reconciled to his ideas and to turn against his critics. After the Walshes had read the book, Foxe reports, 'those great prelates were no more so often called to the house', and when they did come they found that they were no longer greeted with the 'cheer and countenance' of past visits. They rightly sensed that this 'came by the means of Master Tyndale' and soon 'utterly withdrew' and came no more to the manor.

They planned their revenge, 'clustering together . . . to grudge and storm against Tyndale, railing at him in alehouses and other places'. They claimed that Tyndale was preaching heresy and denounced him secretly to the Gloucester chancellor, the chief administrator of the diocese, a harsh and ambitious man named John Bell. Bell had a reputation as a skilled interrogator of Lollards and other suspected heretics; four years later, he was temporarily drafted to London to examine German merchants accused of Lutheran sympathies.

Bell summoned Tyndale to appear before him in the early part of 1523. No formal charges were laid against him, only that unnamed accusers said that he was 'an heretic in sophistry, an heretic in logic, an heretic in his divinity'. Tyndale had no means of preparing for an examination that might turn into a staging post on his way to a Lollard pit. He was determined but frightened. He refused to deny his ideas and beliefs, but he never sought out martyrdom, either now or later, as some did. He may already have decided on his mission in life – he was within a few weeks of declaring it for the first time – and he wanted badly to survive to complete it. He told Foxe's informant that he had grave doubts about the 'privy', or secret, accusations made against him, 'so that he in his going thitherwards cried in his mind heartily to God, to give him strength fast to stand in the truth of his word'.

Local priests were present at the hearing, but, as in most heresy hearings, the accusers remained anonymous. None stepped forward when Tyndale demanded to face those who had given evidence against him. The chancellor 'thretened me grevously, and revyled me,' Tyndale recalled, 'and rated me as though I had bene a dogge'. Tyndale insisted that he had said nothing that was not justified by the New Testament. Bell had no witness to put against him, and was forced to let him go with a severe scolding.

The incident was not to be forgotten. As the examination was taking place in Gloucester, Thomas More was working in London on a polemic against Luther. He did so on behalf of Henry VIII in reply to a tirade Luther had written suggesting, among other pleasantries, that the king was a pig who should be rolled in his own dirt. More's *Responsio ad Lutherum* outdid the German in crudity

and frenzy. He wrote in Latin, and his command of its colloqui-
alisms underscored how familiar the language was to English
writers,[1] and how rarely they wrote in their own vernacular. More
described Luther as *merda, stercus, lutum* and *coenum*, respectively
shit, dung, filth and excrement; he said he was a drunkard, a liar,
an ape and an arsehole whom the Antichrist had vomited onto
earth.

This was more than the work of a civil servant – More was by
now a councillor attendant – eager to please his master. He was
obsessed by Lutherans. His loathing had an edge that, in the context of his other characteristics, in particular his usual calm and
kindliness, was abnormal. It was violent, vengeful and unbridled,
an aberration that he was starting to extend from Luther himself to
his followers. It was always likely that this fury would one day
attach itself to William Tyndale. When it did, More would dig up
the Gloucester affair, and fashion it into a weapon.

The Gloucester clergy remained the immediate danger. Tyndale
said that they continued to meet in alehouses to 'affirm my sayings
are heresy' and inventing others 'of their own heads which I never
spake'. He found them 'a full ignorant sort'. Many were incapable
even of reading their missals. The rest, he said, were only interested
in two books. One was a manual of female anatomy, over which
they would 'pore night and day' with the excuse that it was 'all to
teach the midwives'; the other was a tome that gave them tips on
gathering 'tithes, mortuaries, offerings, customs, and other pil-
lage'.

Tyndale was scarcely exaggerating. The county was known as
'God's Gloucestershire' for its supposed piety, but John Hooper, a
contemporary of Tyndale at Oxford, found 'inhospitable, non-
resident, inefficient, drunken and evil-living incumbents' in every
deanery when he later became bishop.[2] Hooper carried out a
survey of 311 of his clergy. Nine priests did not know that there
were Ten Commandments. Thirty-three did not recall where in

the Bible the commandments were to be found, most of them plumping for the New rather than the Old Testament, and 168 could not remember what they were. Ten could not recite the Lord's Prayer, and thirty did not know that Jesus Christ was its author. John Trigg of the parish of Dursley received a typical punishment. He was obliged to stand on a bench, wearing only a shirt, to declare: 'I suffer this penance because I cannot say one of the commandments of almighty God.'

At a meeting with a sympathetic 'ancient doctor'[3] who lived nearby, Tyndale was confident enough to open his mind. He had probably known the doctor at Oxford, and 'to him he durst be bold enough to disclose his heart'. Their conversation turned to Rome and the pope.

These were increasingly risky subjects. A few months before, in September 1522, Martin Luther had flouted the papal ban on translations by publishing the September Testament, his German New Testament. Luther was now writing furiously to the pope that the Roman See 'is more scandalous and shameful than any Sodom or Babylon . . . its wickedness is beyond all counsel and hope . . . under your name the poor people in the world are cheated and injured'. The papal legate in Germany was warning the pope that the whole country was in revolution. 'Nine tenths shout "Luther!" as their war cry,' he wrote, 'and the other tenth cares nothing about Luther, and cries: "Death to the court of Rome!"' The pope himself, Adrian VI, a Dutchman and the last non-Italian incumbent until 1978, had succeeded Leo X only a year before. He was already dying, however, worn out by the task of restoring some honour to an office so debased by Julius and Leo. 'For many years, abominable things have taken place in the Chair of Peter,' Adrian admitted wearily, 'abuses in spiritual matters, transgressions of the Commandments, so that everything here has been wickedly perverted.'

The Church in England knew well enough that the ceremonial

burning of Luther's works at St Paul's in 1521 had done nothing to contain the Lutheran infection. It continued to spread, with more books and pamphlets smuggled in from Germany and the Low Countries. Churchmen filled great offices of state – the lord chancellor, Wolsey, the grandest figure of all, was also the pope's legate and archbishop of York – and the Church's anxiety spread to government. The authorities were in a state of high alert for signs of Lutheranism. Attacks on the pope were a classic symptom of the plague.

Tyndale made some remark on the papacy critical enough for the doctor to respond: 'Do you not know that the pope is the very Antichrist, whom the Scripture speaketh of?' He added a word of warning to the young man. 'Beware what you say,' he cautioned, 'for if you shall be perceived to be of that opinion, it will cost you your life.'

In the late spring or early summer of 1523, Tyndale first mentioned his plan to translate the Bible. He was disputing with a 'certain divine, reputed for a learned man'. At one stage in their argument, Foxe wrote, the divine said: 'We were better off to be without God's laws than the pope's.' Tyndale blazed 'with godly zeal' at this blasphemy – 'God's laws' meant the scriptures, and 'the pope's' meant canon law – and he replied that he defied the pope and all his laws. 'If God spare my life,' he added, 'ere many years I wyl cause a boye that dryveth the plough, shall know more of the scripture than thou dost.'

The insult to the pope was at once reported around the diocese and there was talk of re-examining the young tutor for heresy. Tyndale found that he had become 'so turmoiled in the country where I was that I could no longer dwell there'. He feared that the Walshes would also become embroiled and he asked Walsh for permission to leave: 'Sire, I perceive that I shall not be suffered to tarry long here in this country, neither should you be able to keep me out of the hands of the spirituality,' he said, 'and also what displeasure might grow thereby to you by keeping me, God knoweth.'

Sir John gave him his blessing, and he left for London. The die was cast.

The 'causes that moved me to translate' the gospels, Tyndale wrote later, were so simple that he 'supposed it superfluous' to explain them. 'For who is so blind to ask why light should be showed to them that walk in darkness, where they cannot but stumble,' he wrote, 'and to stumble is the danger of eternal damnation?' Who could be 'so despiteful that he would envy any man so necessary a thing'? The word of God was the light, he said, and 'who is so bedlam mad to affirm that good is the natural cause of evil, and darkness to proceed out of light, and that lying should be grounded in truth and verity, and not rather clean contrary, that light destroyeth darkness, and verity reproveth all manner of lying?'

The months at Little Sodbury had given him a motive and a precedent for his task. He was convinced that the local clergy were too corrupt and foolish to lead their flocks to salvation; his dealings with them had shown him 'how that it was impossible to stablysh the laye people in any truth, except ye scripture were playnly layde before their eyes in their mother tongue, and they might se the processe, ordre and meaninge of the text'.

Luther's September Testament was a blueprint for him to follow. The book's earthy and vigorous German made it an instant bestseller. Luther had made it as colloquial as possible, visiting an abattoir to get exact German terms from the slaughterers, and rummaging through jewel boxes for the same purpose. 'I aimed to make Moses so German that no one would suspect that he was a Jew,' his friend Albrecht Dürer said of the woodcuts used to illustrate the new bibles.

The first edition of four thousand copies had sold out before Christmas and printers were already cashing in on the demand by running off pirate editions. 'Even the tailors and shoemakers, and indeed women and simple idiots . . . read it as eagerly as if it were the fountain of all truth,' Johannes Cochlaeus, a Catholic loyalist, reported with distaste in Germany. 'Some carried it in their bosoms and learnt it by heart.' This was bad for the Church – Cochlaeus complained that Bible readers 'without timidity . . . debated not only with Catholic laymen, but also with priests and monks' – but it was precisely the readership and the effect that Tyndale hoped for.

He knew that the Church would condemn him, but he had already been exposed to the malice of his fellow clergy in Gloucestershire, and he had survived. If the Church thought his ideas to be heresy, lay people like the Walshes had found them sympathetic. He had, too, put his talent for translation to the test. The *Enchiridion* was proof in itself of the colossal impetus that the printing press was giving to the written word; it had been through twenty-three Latin editions in the six years before Tyndale translated it. He had scholarship, and Greek and Latin, and he could learn Hebrew. He wrote a plain and powerful English, soaked with the cadence and rhythm he had learnt in his Oxford rhetoric classes. He was brave. Above all, he was inspired by the love of Christ and the gospels.

Tyndale and his age came to the Bible, and to Christ, with a raw hunger and amazement, as if the astonishing story of the brief passage of the Son of God on earth was new to them, and as if it was only when they were released from the Latin that the words of Christ's Passion struck home. 'What are these new doctrines? The gospel?' Luther's colleague Philip Melanchthon had asked the year before. 'Why, that is 1,522 years old.' But it was old only in the technical sense that it had been written long before.

In Latin, it was the priestly text of a religion whose true substance was the Church and its liturgy and tradition. Translated into a living language, devoured from cover to cover, read secretly in corners or aloud with trusted friends, its impact was wholly new; troubling, a cause of spiritual collapse and ecstasy, a divider of families, a breaker of kingdoms. 'We will try everything by the touchstone of the gospel,' Melanchthon said, 'and the fire of Paul.' Read in that light, the Bible was a force with the power of apocalypse.

What was not in it was quite as important as what was. Readers found that many powerful institutions and beliefs were not directly blessed by God at all, but only by tradition and the Church. The Bible made no mention of the papacy, or of bishops or hierarchies. It was silent on the celibacy of priests. It did not state that the sacramental bread and wine was 'transubstantiated' into the body and blood of Christ at communion. It did not encourage the cult of saints and relics, from which the Church derived much income and prestige; on the contrary, it warned that: 'Thou shalt not make any graven image, nor bow down to it, nor worship it.' It made no promise that a pilgrimage or a cash payment to a pardoner would result in the forgiveness of sins. The word 'purgatory' appeared nowhere in it; it was a twelfth-century invention. Yet, to escape its supposed clutches, men and women left large sums to chantry priests to perform 'trentals', series of thirty intercessionary masses for their souls. Henry VII had made special efforts to avoid purgatory; the old king ordered ten thousand masses for his own soul at 6d apiece, twice the standard fee.

Anyone who went through the scriptures in the 1520s was certain to remark on these and other omissions, all of which appeared to reflect badly on the Church. Radicalism was in the air – the English authorities cited 'the malignity of this present time, with the inclination of people to erroneous opinions' as an additional reason for banning translations – and readers knew what to look for. It was a fact, not a papal invention, that a widely read Bible was a danger to the Church. Serving Catholic priests – a category that covered both Luther and Tyndale – lost their faith simply by reading it. One such was Menno Simons, a twenty-eight-year-old who had 'never touched' the scriptures during his first three years as a priest. While handling the bread and wine in the mass, however, Simons had the troubling notion that they were not the flesh and blood of Christ. He attributed this to the devil trying to separate him from his faith. 'I confessed it often, sighed, and prayed,' he wrote, 'yet I could not come clear of the ideas.' He spent his time drinking, playing cards and brooding.

'Finally, I got the idea to examine the New Testament diligently,' he said. 'I had not gone very far when I discovered that we were deceived . . .' He was 'quickly relieved' to find that his doubts were justified, finding no evidence that the bread and wine were anything but mere symbols of Christ's passion. He heard of a new sect, the Anabaptists, who rejected infant baptism and were rebaptised as adults. 'I examined the scriptures diligently and pondered them earnestly,' Simons wrote, 'but could find no report of infant baptism.' He realised that his new beliefs on baptism and the sacraments now made him a heretic in the eyes of his Church. He had become so, he wrote, 'through the illumination of the Holy Spirit, through much reading and pondering of the scriptures, and by the gracious favour and gift of God . . .' The experience was overwhelming. Simons abandoned the lusts of his youth and his search for 'gain, ease, fame and the favour of men'; he was a hunted fugitive until his death. He thought it a bargain, for 'if I should gain the whole world and live a thousand years, and at last have to endure the wrath of God, what would I have gained?'

Tyndale had that same exhilaration. He wrote of being embraced by the light of 'Evangelion (that we call the gospel) . . . a Greek word and signifieth good, merry, glad and joyful tidings, that maketh a man's heart glad and maketh him sing, dance and leap for joy . . .' To translate it was an act of affection and rapture.

3

London

Tyndale needed a patron to support him while he worked on the translation. 'As this I thought,' he wrote, 'the bishoppe of London came to my remembrance, whom Erasmus praiseth exceedingly . . . for his great learning. Then thought I, if I might come into this mannes service, I were happye. And so I gate me to London.'

He arrived in the city to see Cuthbert Tunstall, the bishop, in or around July 1523. He was armed with a letter of introduction that Walsh had given him to a courtier he knew well, Sir Henry Guildford, the king's Controller of the Household, and until recently the Master of Horse.

Tyndale duly called on Guildford. The courtier was an amateur scholar, and Tyndale presented him with a translation from the Greek of an oration by Isocrates that he had recently finished at Little Sodbury. Guildford received him warmly and said that he would mention him to Tunstall. He evidently did so, because he then advised that Tyndale should write to Tunstall to beg for an appointment to see him. Tyndale delivered the letter to one of the bishop's servants and waited for a reply.

On the face of it, Tunstall was an admirable choice as a potential patron. He seemed to be the very model of a liberal scholar. After studying at Oxford, Tunstall had gone on to read law at Padua, where he was friendly with Aldus Manutius, founder of the famous Aldus publishing house in Venice. He knew Erasmus – who of importance did not? – and had helped the great man with the second edition of his Greek New Testament while he was on his diplomatic mission to the Low Countries. Tunstall had some Hebrew, as well as Greek, and a book he had written on arithmetic remained a standard work for students for many years.

His time in Italy had shown him that the pope as well as the Church would benefit from reform. 'I saw myself,' he recollected with some disgust, 'when Julius, then being bishop of Rome, stood on his feet and one of his chamberlains held up his skirt, because it stood not as he thought with his dignity that he should do it himself, that his shoe might appear, while a nobleman of great age prostrated himself upon the ground and kissed his shoe.' His friends found him generous and tolerant. More, to whom he gave a much-treasured piece of heart-shaped amber with a fly suspended in it as a keepsake, described him in *Utopia* as a man 'out of comparison'. Erasmus went further. 'Our age does not possess a man more learned, a better or a kinder man,' he wrote. 'I seem not to be alive now that he is taken from me.'

Above all, Tunstall met Tyndale's key criterion. As bishop of London, he had the power to lift the Constitutions of Oxford and authorise the translation of the scripture. Tyndale had high hopes. 'I was beguiled,' he said, that his approach to the bishop was 'the next way upon my purpose'. In fact, he had hopelessly misjudged both the man and the circumstances.

Tunstall was not solely a cleric. He was part lawyer, part diplomat and part politician, like his soul mate, Thomas More. The two men were bound together by friendship, political experience and a deep loathing for heresy. They displayed the latter in the Hunne

Cuthbert Tunstall, bishop of London and later Durham, whom Tyndale sought out when he arrived in London in 1523. The young tutor was foolish to think that Tunstall would aid him to translate the Bible. The bishop was a traditionalist, and a close friend of Thomas More, who found him a man 'out of comparison'. Thwarted, Tyndale left England for the Continent, cursing Tunstall as a 'still Saturn . . . a ducking hypocrite'.

(Bridgeman Art Library)

affair, and their views on this great *cause célèbre* should have warned Tyndale of the futility of approaching Tunstall.

Early in December 1514, the body of a rich London tailor named Richard Hunne had been found hanging by the neck in a cell of the Lollards' tower, the ecclesiastical prison maintained by the bishop of London in the west churchyard of St Paul's Cathedral. Three years before, Hunne's son Stephen had died at the age of five weeks. The infant's body was taken to St Mary's Church in Whitechapel for burial, where Thomas Dryfield, the priest at St Mary's, demanded a 'mortuary' for performing the service. By tradition, a priest could demand to be given a piece of property belonging to the deceased.

'Mortuaries' figured prominently in lay grievances against the Church. Wycliffe had condemned them in his day, as gouging the poor when they most needed the consolation of religion, and Londoners were notoriously anti-clerical, alert for any excuse to attack the clergy. Dryfield nonetheless insisted that Hunne give him the bearing sheet in which the baby Stephen had been wrapped for his christening. Hunne refused. He argued that, by English common law, a corpse cannot own property. He refused to let the sheet go.

The little scrap of cloth aroused passionate interest. If it was won by the priest, it would signify the continuing subservience of the laity to the priesthood and the Church. If Hunne kept it, common law would have triumphed over the canon law of the Church, for canon law had recognised the validity of mortuaries for centuries.

Dryfield sued Hunne for the sheet in the Bishop's Court, the ecclesiastical court where cases involving the Church were tried under canon law. The case was heard by Cuthbert Tunstall, then chancellor to the diocese, in May 1512. Tunstall ruled in favour of Dryfield. Hunne refused to part with the sheet. When he attended his parish church, St Margaret's in Bridge Street, Dryfield greeted him with the formula: 'Hunne, thowe arte accursed and thow stondist accursed.' Hunne was thereby excommunicated from the body of the faithful and his soul consigned to hell. Hunne retaliated by charging the priesthood with violating *praemunire*, a fourteenth-century statute upholding the rights of the common law courts and the king against the pope and the Church courts.

This development thoroughly alarmed Tunstall and senior churchmen. Bishop Fitzjames, Tunstall's predecessor as bishop of London, brought formal charges of heresy against Hunne. More was convinced that Hunne had Lollard friends 'that were wont to haunt those midnight lectures' at which manuscript copies of Lollard Bibles were read out. He accused Hunne of publicity seeking; the tailor was 'high-minded and set on the glory of a victory', he said, and 'he trusted to be spoke of long after his days and have his matter called Hunne's case'.

The case indeed became notorious, to the anger of More and Tunstall. Hunne was arrested and interrogated by the bishop and his officers on Saturday 2 December 1514. He was then locked away in the Lollards' tower for the weekend. In the early hours of Monday he was found hanging dead in his cell. A coroner's jury was summoned. It found there was no evidence that Hunne had killed himself. He could not have inserted his neck into the noose in which he was found; his wrists showed signs of having been bound, the only stool in the cell was too far from his body for him to have used it, and there were marks of manual strangulation around his neck. The jury declared that Hunne had been murdered.

The bishop declared the jurors to be 'false, perjured caitiffs' and continued with the heresy case against Hunne. Canon law, as in the case of Wycliffe, permits trials of the dead. An English translation of the Bible was said to have been found among Hunne's papers. More claimed that he had seen it, and that Hunne had written notes in the margin on the 'heresies' it contained, thus proving 'what naughty minds the men had, both he that so noted them and he that so made [the manuscript]'. More said that the prologue to the Bible contained a condemnation of the mass.

Hunne's corpse was charged with calling the pope 'Satan' and 'Antichrist', and with condemning papal indulgences and the veneration of images. The trial was held in the Chapel of Our Lady at St Paul's on 16 December, in the presence of More and Tunstall. Hunne was duly condemned and his property was declared forfeit to the crown, thus depriving his family and surviving children of a fortune More estimated at 100,000 marks. Four days after the trial, the body was burnt at Smithfield.

The coroner's jury was not easily cowed, however. The jailer of the Lollards' tower, one Charles Joseph, had fled from London to the countryside on the day Hunne's body was found. A warrant was issued for Joseph, and he was arrested two months later and brought to the Tower of London. Under interrogation, he admitted to the jury that at midnight on 3 December, on the direct orders of Dr William Horsey, chancellor to Bishop Fitzjames, he and the cathedral bell-ringer John Spalding had entered Hunne's cell. They found him lying in his bed and strangled him. The jury indicted Horsey, Spalding and Joseph for murder.

A few months before Hunne's death, Leo X had repeated the canon law principle that no layman had rightful jurisdiction over a clerk or cleric in any case of any nature. 'Clerk' was a broad term, covering any individual whom the Church deemed to be fulfilling a vocation. This included men with menial jobs on Church property, including bell-ringers and jailers. If a man had a tonsured head and read a little Latin, he was adjudged a clerk   and was safely beyond the reach of a coroner's jury and the gallows if he could mumble a few words from the Latin Bible.

Parliament, however, in anti-clerical mood in 1512, had passed a law against 'criminous clerks' that made unordained clerks subject to the common law courts in cases of murder committed in churches, in the home of the victim, or on the king's highway. Londoners, in increasingly angry mood, demanded that the accused men appear in a common law court. The bishop wrote desperately to Wolsey, asking him to intercede with the king on Horsey's behalf. 'For assured am I that if my chancellor be tried by any 12 men in London,' he wrote, 'they be so maliciously set in favour of heretical depravity that they will cast and condemn my clerk though he be as innocent as Abel.' The appeal worked. Horsey was kept in prison until London's anger died down; he then pleaded not guilty to the King's Bench, and was released.

In the face of the evidence, Tunstall and More continued to insist that Hunne was a suicide. More said flatly that Hunne 'hanged himself for despair, despite, and for a lack of grace'; he claimed that Hunne was frantic to find that 'in the temporal law he should not win his spurs' so that 'he began to fall in fear of worldly shame'. For good measure, More later cited an Essex carpenter who said that he had met Hunne at a conventicle of heretics in London. That the Essex man was a convicted felon and perjurer did not concern More in the least; all, to him, was fair in the war against heretics.

More may have discussed the morality of this with Tunstall while they were together in the Low Countries. More's humanism in *Utopia* has a strangely submissive streak when it comes to the Utopian priesthood. The secular authorities in his imagined island commonwealth let priests go free no matter what they might have done. 'Neither,' he wrote of the treatment of priests, 'do they think it right to touch with mortal hand anyone – guilty of whatever horrible deed – who has been set aside as a gift to God in such a singular manner.'

More's respect for the clergy was high, close to grovelling; Tyndale had none. Neither was More's friend Tunstall a better prospect. He, too, was deeply hostile to Lutheranism. While on a diplomatic mission to Worms in 1521, he had urged the king to ban the import of Luther's treatise *De Babylonica Captivitate*, which attacked the Church for subjugating the laity. The same year, Tunstall had collaborated with the violently anti-Lutheran bishop of Rochester, John Fisher, in the polemic *Assertionis Lutheranae Confutatio*.

Tunstall's reply to Tyndale's petition was some time in coming. The bishop was a member of the House of Lords and Convocation – both honours went with the job – and he also had personal and secular ambitions as the Keeper of the Privy Seal. High politics kept him busy over the summer. Parliament had met in London in April of 1523, in Blackfriars, the seat of the Dominican friars on a site between the river and Ludgate. Tunstall had delivered the King's Speech at the opening, to a splendid company of notables. Henry VIII himself had sat healthy and handsome on his dais, while below him were ranged the spiritual lords, the archbishops, bishops and abbots, and the temporal lords, barons and earls, with the judges sitting on their woolsacks between them, and, standing at the bar of the lower House of Commons, Tunstall's friend, Thomas More, the Speaker.

The members of the Commons were in sour and angry mood. Wolsey had squandered the funds carefully built up by Henry VII on feckless Continental wars, and was now looking to parliament for cash to fritter on another French campaign. He had taken the precaution of making sure that More, a most loyal servant of Church and crown, was elected as Speaker of the House. More allowed the cardinal to enter the Commons with a large and intimidating retinue, although several MPs had argued that he should have brought only a handful of retainers. Made bolder, Wolsey demanded the tremendous subsidy of £800,000, and, gaining much comfort when More clashed with his colleagues and supported the demand, declared that he would 'rather have his tongue plucked out of his head with a pair of pincers' than reduce it. The 'grettiste and soreste' arguments ensued, for none could remember 'that ever there was geven to any oon of the Kings auncestors half so moche at oon graunte', but Wolsey held out and won. He was delighted with More's soothing role as Speaker, and arranged for the king to give him a fee of £100 and a lucrative post as a collector of subsidies. More was duly grateful to the cardinal, assuring him that 'I shal be dayly more and more bounden to pray for your Grace'; he used the money to invest in land, buying twenty-seven acres on the Thames at Chelsea, where he was building a great house.

The subsidy was assessed at 4s in the pound on all the property in the kingdom. Convocation, the assembly of senior churchmen, balked at it as much as the Commons. The influence of Tunstall and the grander bishops was telling, and Convocation grudgingly granted a heavy tax on every benefice in the country. The laity conveniently forgot that clerics were as hard hit as themselves. The tax was being levied by the pope's cardinal, and the papal reputation took a further popular battering.

It was not until September that Tunstall found time to deal with the obscure young man from Gloucestershire who wished to translate the Bible. He was polite but firm. 'My lorde answered me,' Tyndale recollected, 'his house was full, he had mo then he coude well finde, and advised me to sek in London, wher he sad I coude not lacke a service. I . . . understode at the laste . . . that there was no rowme in my lorde of London's palace to translate the newe testament.'

Tyndale had arrived in London with a single letter of introduction and his grand project as an unemployed priest with no living, no means of support and no friends. His introduction had now failed him. He turned on the bishop – 'still Saturn,' he wrote, 'that so seldom speaketh, but walketh up and down all day musing and imagining mischief, a ducking hypocrite, made to dissemble' – as he turned on all who blocked him.

He was not fair, or reasonable, when he was crossed. Tunstall's palace may well have been full with provincial clergy who were in town for Convocation. Neither did it occur to Tyndale that his request was outrageous. The bishop of London was one of the most powerful men in the country. Tyndale, an unknown minor cleric whose last post was as a child's tutor, had asked if he could live in this awesome person's palace. Once installed, Tyndale had said, he intended to do something that had been punishable by death for more than a hundred years.

Tunstall might have ridiculed his plan, or had him flung into his episcopal dungeons for heretical intent. Instead, he was remarkably civil. But Tyndale's attack on him, however ill deserved, did not spring from spite or malice. It came from anger, from fury that the bishop would deny his countrymen the means of salvation, the Bible, in a language they could understand. It was, in its way, the wrath of God and it was, like Tyndale himself, righteous.

He had now to find another patron. While he was waiting for the bishop's decision, Tyndale had preached some sermons in the church of St Dunstan-in-the-West in Fleet Street. Among the congregation was Humphrey Monmouth, a kindly and wealthy cloth merchant living in the London parish of All Hallows at Barking. Monmouth was connected with the Christian Brethren, a loose and secretive ring of London merchants sympathetic to the new ideas in Germany, who imported and distributed the writings of the reformers and supported scholars and translators. Lollards helped them pass on books and ideas; Tunstall complained that to the Lollards' 'vast army of heresies new weapons had been added by their recent Wycliffite offspring' on the Continent.

Monmouth was to pay for his loyalty and friendship to Tyndale some five years later with an examination by Thomas More and a stint in the Tower. Here, in the presence of Tunstall, he signed a petition to Wolsey denying that he was a heretic, and begging to be released from the Tower before his business was ruined. In his petition, he explained how he had met 'a priest called Sir William Tyndal' – priests were often addressed 'Sir' as a courtesy – 'otherwise called Hotchens'. He said that he had heard Sir William preach two or three sermons at St Dunstan's, 'and after that I chanced to meet with him, and with communication I examined what living he had. He said he had none at all, but he trusted to be with my lord of London in his service; and therefore I had the better fantasy of him.'

On getting the bad news that Tunstall 'had chaplains enough, and . . . that he would have no more at that time', Tyndale had returned to see him. 'He besought me to help him,' Monmouth said, 'and so I took him into my house half a year; and there he lived as a good priest, as me thought.'

Monmouth seems to have become a 'scripture-man' who began to 'smell the gospel', the phrase used of Lollards, more than a decade before he met Tyndale. As a result, or so it was said, his Lollard-flavoured talk had offended a poor neighbour whom he liked well, lending him money and often having him at his table. The neighbour refused to visit him any more, cut him dead in the street and reported him to the bishop's officers as a heretic. Monmouth was deeply hurt and seized on a chance meeting in a narrow lane to find out what troubled him. The poor man tried to brush past but Monmouth caught his hand and stopped him. 'Neighbour, whence is this displeasure against me?' he said. 'What have I done to you? Tell me, and I will be ready to make amends.' Overcome by this gentle and loyal greeting, the poor man fell to his knees and begged Monmouth's forgiveness; and so, the story has it, they 'loved one another as well as ever they did afore'.

This kindness added to the unspoken obligation to look after kindred spirits that was shared by those who held dangerous beliefs. It was natural for him to have helped Tyndale. He drew a sober and scholarly picture of his young guest's lifestyle. 'He

studied most part of the day and of the night at his book,'
Monmouth said, 'and he would eat but sodden meat by his good
will, nor drink but small single beer.' Sodden meat was served
plain and without sauces, and small beer was thin and weak.
Tyndale was able to survive on very little indeed, a necessary virtue
for his project. Monmouth noted that 'I never saw him wear linen
about him in the space he was with me.' He made do with wool
even for his shirts, though it scratched his skin.

By his own account, Tyndale did not spend all his time in
London closeted with his books. 'And so in London I abode
almost a year,' he wrote, 'and marked the course of the world, and
heard our praters (I would say our preachers) how they boasted
themselves and their high authority, and beheld the pomp of our
prelates, and how busied they were . . .'

London showed how frail was Tyndale and how great his enemy.
The clergy were inescapable. They were the largest owners of property and the biggest employers in the city. The manor of Stepney,
one of the estates that Tunstall enjoyed as bishop, stretched clean
across modern London from the county of Essex in the east to
Barnes and Wimbledon in the south west. The canons of St Paul's
owned a further thirteen manors, running northwards from what
are now the office blocks of Holborn past St Pancras station and
on to the smart residential streets and shabby housing estates of
Islington.

London had more churches than any other city in Europe. Its
skyline was dominated by spires and towers, the houses meek
beneath them. There were more than 120 parish churches, sixteen
of them named for St Mary within the single walled square mile of
the old city, and thirteen grand conventual churches. A monastery
with a convent garden stood on almost every major artery; there
were sixteen priories, nunneries and friaries, and the same number
of charitable hospitals and refuges. The church bells made by the

Whitechapel bell foundry were famous; young bloods would ring them for hours to keep warm in winter, and lay bets on who could make them heard at the furthest distance. The city had several holy wells, Clerkenwell, Sadler's Well, Monkwell, guarded by hermits, where the sick took the waters in the hope of healing.

Beneath the orthodox surface – the chantries and shrines, and the teeming relics, Westminster Abbey displaying blood from Christ's wounds, milk from the Virgin, a hair of St Peter, pieces of the cross and a beam from the holy manger – were uneasy reminders of the fates reserved for heretics. London was almost as renowned for the number of its prisons as for its churches. Lambeth Palace, the residence of the archbishop of Canterbury on the south bank of the Thames, had a Lollards' tower built by Archbishop Chicheley a century before to hold suspected heretics during their interrogation and torture. The outer and inner doors were oak, and the cells were lined with wood, into which iron rings were driven so that prisoners could be suspended above the floor. Tunstall had cells available for the same purpose in his residence at St Paul's and at his other palace in Fulham.

The authorities could also dispatch religious suspects to sixty whipping posts, stocks and cages, and to a dozen common prisons, of which Newgate, the Old Compter in Bread Street and the Fleet were merely the most notorious. A viewing gallery stood outside the lowest and dankest storey of the Fleet, at the site where Farringdon Street now runs down to the Thames. From here the rich watched the antics of the inmates, while a prisoner rattled an alms box at the grating, crying: 'Pity the poor prisoners.' The Tower of London itself, built of alien, creamy Caen stone by William I, a symbol of Norman conquest that Londoners had resented ever since, penned heretics as well as traitors of sufficient note.

Burnings took place at Smithfield, open ground to the north of the priory of St Bartholomew the Great. This was home to the annual Bart's Fair, a fortnight of wrestling, bowling, archery contests, freak shows, dancing bears, and dancing people in canvas tents, acrobats, jugglers and miracle plays. Horses were sold there on Fridays, and whistling birds and puppy dogs, and herds of cattle, pigs and sheep were driven up from the country to be slaughtered. Then, as now, Smithfield was London's meat market, and in more ways than one, for the adjacent Cock Lane was the haunt of prostitutes, a place of 'bawdy-house keepers, night-walkers, robbers, women of ill-fame'.

An open field, in front of St Bartholomew's hospital, played host to the condemned. It had been the ritual place for duels and ordeals by battle in medieval days and it remained the home of the stake. Condemned heretics were chained to the stake by heavy irons at the feet, waist and chest. Bundles of faggots made of kindling wood interspersed with dried reeds were piled up around them to waist height or above. Large crowds circled the stake, and were sometimes held back by men with halberds or on horseback. Benches were put up for people of quality who wished to watch the spectacle. The senior official cried 'Fire the faggots! . . . *Fiat justitia!*' as the signal for justice to be done. At these words, the executioner tested the direction of the wind with his torch, and then lit the reeds on the windward edge of the pyre.

It was rare for a victim to die swiftly of asphyxiation or smoke inhalation, since the fire was set in the open air and the smoke and fumes were dispersed on the wind. Death was by multiple burns and shock, and it was often prolonged. Foxe recorded that a later heretic took forty-five minutes to die, noting that 'when the left arm was on fyre and burned, he touched it with his right hand, and it fell from his bodye, and he continued to pray to the end wythout moving'.

For the moment, the Smithfield ashes were cold. Wolsey was not a man-burner. Tyndale knew full well, however, that 'greater excommunication', or the fire, was the penalty demanded by the English Church for translators of scripture.

Even were he not betrayed while working on the Bible, he could not have published it. London had no more than seven printers, all of them tightly controlled, and none would have considered printing it. In 1524, Tunstall summoned the London printers and booksellers to meet him. He warned them of the penalties for handling heretical books and issued the first licensing order for imported books. No book was to be brought into the realm without episcopal permission. No new work could be published without the consent of a board of censors. Its members were the cream of the English Church: Wolsey, Archbishop Warham, fierce Bishop Fisher and himself. Foreign printers had the lion's share of London publishing. They relied on a statute of 1484 which had specifically exempted printers and booksellers from the ban which prohibited other foreign craftsmen from working in the city. This privilege was justified by the slow development of the trade, and the scarcity of English-born printers. It could be withdrawn at any time, however, and the Stationers' Company was lobbying hard for the removal of the exemption. The big foreign printers were careful to behave.

Lutheran books and tracts were thus coming into London from Germany and the Low Countries, and on a rising scale, as Tyndale saw. The printing industry across the Narrow Sea was flourishing. Cologne had double the number of printers as London, and Antwerp five times as many. Parts of Germany were Lutheran, and welcomed English exiles, and printers in Catholic areas were willing to publish Lutheran material for profit.

Monmouth, who had travelled as far as Rome and Jerusalem, had excellent contacts with merchants from the print-rich regions. He introduced Tyndale to Lutheran Hanseatic merchants at the Steelyard. Since Henry III in 1259, these 'merchants of Almaine', or Germany, had enjoyed a monopoly on the import of foreign corn and other valuable privileges. They were permitted to 'bring hither as well wheat, rye and other grain, as cables, ropes, masts, pitch, tar, flax, hemp, linen cloth, wainscots, wax, steel and other profitable merchandise'. They made loans to the crown and Londoners were obliged to show them a respect they rarely wasted on foreigners. Each Christmas and Easter, the Steelyard men paid a token toll of two grey cloths and one brown, with 10 pounds of pepper, five pairs of gloves and two vessels of vinegar. They were otherwise free of all subsidies to the king.

The Steelyard itself was a large complex situated where Cannon Street station now stands on the north bank of the Thames, with a quay, warehouses and a great stone hall with arched gates. Here, the traders worked, dined and entertained. They were, for Tyndale, heaven-sent. They knew bankers, printers and shippers throughout northern Germany and the Low Countries. They were experienced in the transfer of funds. They were also sympathetic to his cause. The Steelyard was at the centre of illegal Lutheran book imports and its members were adept at book smuggling.

A small group of Monmouth's friends raised some initial money for Tyndale's project: we do not know who or how much. When he was in the Tower, Monmouth admitted that 'I did promise him £10'. He added that this was 'to pray for my father and mother their souls and all Christian souls'. This was untrue – Tyndale was notorious for his attacks on chantry priests and all who made money through prayers for the dead – but Monmouth claimed it to distance himself from the financing of the Bible. Monmouth added that 'afterwards [Tyndale] got of some other men £10 sterling more', and that funds were transferred to him in Germany by a Steelyard merchant named Hans Collenbeke.

In any event, Tyndale felt himself ready to set out from London in the early spring of 1524. 'I understood at the last,' he wrote, 'not only that there was no room in my lord of London's palace to translate the new testament, but also that there was no place to do it in all England, as experience doth now openly declare.'

He sailed for Hamburg in, or close to, April 1524.

4

The New Testament

From the moment he arrived at Hamburg, Tyndale is elusive. For a controversialist who was recklessly brave in print, Tyndale had an extraordinary ability to fade into a background.

His writing was savage, taunting and awash with brilliant energy. He had wit and the Tudor love of puns. He wrote of bishops as 'bishaps', half-man, half-mishap, and of popery as 'popetrie', or puppetry; he invented the word 'divininite', half-divinity and half-ninny, to describe the bishop of Rochester. He had Tudor vulgarity, too, reminding bishops that 'to preach is their duty only and not to offer their feet to be kissed or testicles to be groped'. He was no timid, shrinking scholar. We already know that he wrote of Wolsey as Wolfsee, the wolf among the flock, and he wrote too of his 'shitten death' – the cardinal was to die after his physician gave him a purgative – and gloried that 'for al the worship of his hat and glories of his precious shoes when he was payned with the colicke of an evel conscience havynge no nother shifte bycause his soule could funde in nother issue toke hym selfe a medicine ut emitteret spiritum per posteriora'.

This is not the sort of prose – even if he dressed up 'and farted his spirit through his backside' in Latin – expected from the translator of the Bible. But to Tyndale, the Bible was a living book, with all the crudeness and vigour of everyday life. It excited him; it was a page-turner. He poured the same enthusiasm into his dangerous and public duel with his enemy Thomas More.

He was preserved by a ruthlessly purposeful and practical streak rare in a man so proud and noisy in debate. He was in self-exile on the Continent for eleven years before his betrayal, and actively hunted for nine of them; for four of those years, it is not known what city or even what country he was in, and only once, for a period of a few months, do we have a definite address for him. This was a remarkable feat. Sixteenth-century cities were small and intimate – London had about forty thousand people in the 1520s – and strangers were easy to identify. Tyndale was particularly vulnerable. He had very little money and could not buy secrecy as Oldcastle had. He was constantly publishing his work and he had to negotiate with printers, who were notoriously hard drinkers and indiscreet. He was also obliged to raise funds, for the printing of banned books was expensive as well as dangerous.

No portrait or sketch was made of him during his lifetime, lest a likeness betray him. He had great business skills – some charity apart, books were his only source of income and every word he published was banned in its home market – and a natural instinct for the new art of publishing. He was his own publisher and distributor, copy-editing with the renegade friar William Roye, finding merchants and smugglers. He judged his print runs nicely; the Bible apart, he knew what other subjects would sell, playing brilliantly on the English loathing for priests and prelates in his original writing; and he had an eye for design and format. His New Testament was the first of its kind to be printed in modern pocket paperback size.

We cannot be sure where he translated it. Thomas More

thought that Tyndale went straight from the Hamburg docks to work with Luther at Luther's base in Wittenberg. He based this on interrogations of Bible-men he had seized in England. 'Tyndall, as soon as he gat him hence, got him to Luther straight,' he wrote, 'and the confederacy between Luther and him is a thing well known, and plainly confessed by such as have been taken and convicted here of heresy, coming from thence.' The Catholic militant Cochlaeus, who was the first to be able definitively to place Tyndale on the Continent, at Cologne in the autumn of 1525, described Tyndale as an 'apostate from England, who had learnt the German tongue at Wittenberg'. Tyndale denied it: 'And when he sayth Tindale was confederrat with Luther that is not trueth.'

Tyndale had every reason to be sensitive of revealing his whereabouts to anyone, and particularly to a man who wished him harm as earnestly as Thomas More. If he was not 'confederate' with Luther in the sense of actively working with him, it is likely that he at least visited him in Wittenberg, and that he completed his translation there. A copy of the register of the university of Wittenberg records that Matthias von Emerson matriculated in May 1524. Matthias was the nephew of the widow Margaret von Emerson, an evangelical sympathiser with whom Tyndale may have stayed on his arrival in Hamburg – there is strong evidence that he stayed with her at later dates – on the recommendation of the merchants at the Steelyard. The register shows that *Gillelmus Daltici ex Anglia* matriculated at the same time as young von Emerson. Tyndale's acute pre-war biographer, J. F. Mozley, suggests that reversing the syllables of *Tindal* makes *Daltin*, which an overworked copyist could render as *Daltici*; and that this *Gillelmus* is indeed our William. The amanuensis whom Tyndale somewhat tetchily used, William Roye, a Franciscan from Greenwich who had fled overseas, was certainly at Wittenberg – the register records *Guilhelmus Roy ex Londino* matriculating in June 1525 – and the city was, as duke George of Saxony wearily complained, the 'common asylum of all apostates'.

It had taken Luther just five months to complete his translation of the New Testament. Tyndale took perhaps twice that time. He had first to learn German, to make full use of Luther's work and German scholarship; he understood it well enough to translate Luther's glosses and prologues accurately within six months of arriving in Germany. He had no other Englishman – Roye arrived when the work was almost ready for the press – off whom to bounce phrases and idioms. *Unus vir nullus vir,* Luther said of the task of translation – one man is no man.

Tyndale's primary source was Erasmus's Greek New Testament, already in its third edition by 1524, together with the Latin translation and notes, which accompanied the Greek text. He also had the Latin Vulgate, and Luther's 1521 September Testament. He had no Lollard Bible with him. He said that he had no man to 'counterfeit' or imitate; 'neither,' he added, 'was help with English of any that had interpreted the same or such like thing in the scripture beforetime'.

His words seem timeless now – 'eate, drynke and be mery . . . the salt of the earth . . . the powers that be . . . gretter love then this hath no man, then that a man bestowe his life for his frendes' – but he wrote at the infancy of the written language. At this time it was common for people to read aloud, even when alone; and it is this habit, and Tyndale's studies in rhetoric at Oxford, that accounts at least in part for the charm and thunder that soar from the English Bible when it is spoken from the lectern. Tyndale's prose sounds as well as it reads.

The richness of his vocabulary, his use of verbs in place of nouns and adjectives, his free sentence constructions, his ear for vivid sayings – 'as bare as Job and as bald as a coot' – and his sense of rhythm profoundly affected the language of the English-speaking peoples – the global language, now – as his Testament, incorporated almost whole into the King James or Authorised Version of the Bible in 1611, deeply influenced the religion of England and her colonies.

He said that English gave the sense of the original Greek of the Testament better than Latin, and he was right. Latin puts its verbs at the end of sentences: it is a subject–object–verb language. Greek, and particularly the *koine*, or the common Greek of the NT, is flexible in its word order. Its verbs can be placed at the beginning or end of the sentence, or, as in English, in the middle. A subject–verb–object sentence is better balanced to the English ear, and Greek is easier and more natural than Latin to English speakers. Greek makes more use of verbs than Latin, which prefers nouns. Spoken English also chooses a verb instead of a noun where possible, making it simpler and more vigorous. Written English can follow the spoken word and use verbs, if it pleases; but more often – in business, the law, government and literature that strives to impress – it is heavy in nouns.

Tyndale used verbs where less flowing writers use nouns and adjectives. Thus in I Peter 1: 23, he writes of 'the word of God, which liveth and lasteth for ever'. The King James Version remains with Tyndale's verbs, although it drops the attractive alliteration of '*liveth* and *lasteth*' by changing '*lasteth*' to '*abideth*'. Modern committee translations replace the verbs with adjectives – 'the living and enduring word of God' in the New English Bible, 'the live, permanent word of the living God' in the Phillips Modern English, 'the living and eternal word of God' in Today's English Version – and strip out the cadence and the sense of immediacy that verbs bring to Tyndale's prose.

Three verbs create pace and urgency in a Tyndale passage in Mark's gospel: 'the uncleane spirite *tare* him, *cryed out* with a loud voice, and *cam out* of him . . .'. The New English Bible has two: 'the unclean spirit *threw* the man into convulsions and with a loud cry *left* him' (Mark 1: 26). As Peter heals the lame man in Acts, Tyndale writes that the man 'sprange, stode and also walked, and entered with them into the temple, walkynge and leapynge and laudynge god' (Acts 3: 8). The lack of clutter in Tyndale's prose is clear by contrast with the needless additions of a modern translation, Phillips Modern English: the man 'sprang *to his feet*, stood and *then* walked. *Then* he went with them into the Temple, *where* he walked about, leaping and thanking God.' How else could the man have sprung, but 'to his feet'? He could not have walked without first standing, nor have entered the temple without first walking; the dual use of 'then' is ugly and pointless. As to the temple 'where' he walked about, since he was in the temple, where else could he have been?

Tyndale preferred short words and short sentences. He wrote in the parable of the good sower in Matthew 13: 8 – Tyndale used 'similitude' for parable, an accurate translation of the Greek parable, meaning to place alongside – that some seed 'fell on goode grounde, and spronge up and bare frute, an hondred foolde'. These twelve words have perfect economy, and they entered the King James Version intact. The Phillips Modern English Bible needs seventeen words – the seed 'fell on good soil and grew and produced a crop – a hundred times what had been sown' – and achieves no better clarity. Tyndale used the shortest and most simple phrases to express the mysteries of the faith: 'Axe and it shal be given you. Seke and ye shall fynd. Knocke and it shal be opened unto you.' The cadence here is perfect: change '*unto*' into '*to*' – 'knock and it shall be opened *to* you' – and it is lost. King James runs this as a single sentence, its power diluted by commas and colons.

Where the King James strays away from him, Tyndale is often both more vivid and more plain. 'Thou arte my dear Son in whom I delyghte' is more intimate than the King James: 'This is my beloved Son in whom I am well pleased.'

The language used by the authors of the few books then printed in English had some bias towards words derived from French and Latin. A single meaning in English might be covered by words from three derivations: kingly from Anglo-Saxon, for example, royal from French, and regal from Latin. Tyndale reversed this to favour Anglo-Saxon words – 'freedom' in place of the Franco-Latin 'liberty', 'hang' for 'suspend', 'brotherly' for 'fraternal', 'folk' for 'people', 'foe' for 'enemy' – or to use both. Religion was itself a Franco-Latin word, of course, and so were many of its expressions – saint, miracle, pilgrimage, disciple, Trinity – though Bible was Greek and the Anglo-Saxon God had bettered the Latin Deity.

Where later translators of the New Testament stick slavishly to a single English word for a word from the original Greek, Tyndale used as many English expressions as he wished. Thus it 'came to pass' is followed by it 'happened, 'chanced', 'fortuned' and 'followed'. 'Lo' becomes 'behold', 'mark', 'see', 'look' and 'take heed'. He sometimes, indeed, mixed his words in the same passage: 'Give to every man therefore his duty; tribute to whom tribute *belongeth*, custom to whom custom *is due*, fear to whom fear *belongeth*; honour to whom honour *pertaineth*.' The brilliance of his phrases is matched by a peerless rhythm: 'take thine ese, eate, drynke and be mery', or the wonderful 'for we are made a gazing stock to the world'. The King James replaced '*gazing stock*' with the dull 'we are made a *spectacle*'. As unhappily, for Tyndale's: 'And the devil took him up into an high mountain, and shewed him all the kingdoms of the world, even in *the twinkling of an eye*', the King James committee substituted '*a moment in time*'.

Tyndale often used a polysyllable as a sort of full stop to round off a string of monosyllables. This is an example: 'lest they bid thee again, and make thee recompense'. The King James adds an unneeded 'also' and destroys the rhythm at the end of the sentence: 'lest they *also* bid thee again, and a *recompense be made thee*'. Read aloud, Tyndale almost always beats all comers, King James or more modern, and the Bible, of course, is God's blank verse, and intended to be read aloud. 'Blynded in their understondynge,' Tyndale has in Ephesians 4, 'beynge straungers from the lyfe which is in god.' In the King James – 'having the understanding darkened, being alienated from the life of God' – the pulse has gone.

In a key chapter, Matthew 7, which has many famous sayings – 'beware of false prophettes . . . nether cast ye youre pearles before swynne' – King James's men change very little, but then rarely to advantage. Tyndale has: 'Iudge not that ye be not iudged. For as ye iudge so shall ye be iudged . . .' King James alters and obscures the second sentence: 'For with what judgement ye judge, ye shall be judged . . .' The individual voice is not always clearer or the committee clumsy. In the tale of the foolish man who built his house on sand, Tyndale wrote: 'And aboundance of rayne descended, and the fluddes cam . . .' The *abundance* of rain is implicit in the flooding, and the King James rightly does without it: 'And the rain descended, and the floods came.' But Tyndale's usual edge returns at the end of the verse. He has: 'and the wynddes blew, and beet uppon that house, and it was overthrowen, and great was the fall of it'. The committee uses *smote* for *beat*, and 'the fall *of it*' is replaced by the laboured 'the fall *thereof*'. In Romans, Tyndale's readers are urged 'fassion not yourselves to the worlde', where the King James abstractly bids them 'be not conformed'.

It is the plainness of Tyndale that startles and that made the Word of God seem so raw and fresh to his readers. Esau sold his birthright 'for one morsel of meat' to the King James men; to Tyndale, he had sold it 'for one breakfast'. Only a few of Tyndale's New Testament words have disappeared: 'arede' for prophecy, 'unghostly' for profane, 'appose' for question. Most have been preserved simply by being in his Bible.

Expressions can be traced from the earliest Gothic translation of the gospels, in about 360, through Anglo-Saxon translations of the eighth century, and the Wycliffe Bibles of the end of the fourteenth century, to Tyndale and on to the present day. The Gothic has survived in the Codex Argenteus, a manuscript written on mulberry-stained vellum in silvered letters of such perfection that it was long believed that they were printed in the Chinese style with an individual stamp for each character, although minute differences in width and height, too subtle for the naked eye, show it to be the work of a copyist of rare talent.

The Anglo-Saxon translation, possibly the work of the Venerable Bede, has a charming habit of literal translation from the Latin. For the Latin *centurio,* or centurion, it has *hundredman.* Disciple is *leorning eniht,* or learning-youth. A man swollen with the dropsy is said to be a *waeter-seoc-man,* a water sack man. The Sabbath is the *reste-daeg,* the rest day. A scribe is a *boc-ere,* a book fellow. Treasury is the self-explanatory *gold-hord.* The Anglo-Saxons had a lovely word for heaven: *heofunum – 'Fader ure de eart on heofunum . . .* Our father that art in heaven . . .'.

The door in 'I am thata *daur*' in Gothic changes to gate in the Anglo-Saxon's 'Ic eom *geat*' before reverting to Wycliffe's and Tyndale's 'I am the *dore'.* The Gothic *leiticia wheila* becomes the Anglo-Saxon *sume hwile* and Wycliffe's *litel tyme* before settling into Tyndale's *lytell whyle.* The Goths' *yuka auhsne* is close to Wycliffe's *yokis of oxen* and Tyndale's *yooke of oxen;* the Anglo-Saxon *getyme oxena* seems the odd man out, until *getyme* is seen as a *team. Hardu hairtai,* the Gothic hard-hearted, progresses through Anglo-Saxon *heortan heardness* and Wycliffe's *hardnesse of herte* before becoming Tyndale's *harde herttes.* The *sibun brothruys* of the Goths change into the Anglo-Saxon *seofon gebrotho* and Wycliffe's *sevene britheren* before becoming Tyndale's *seven brethren.* At the Transfiguration, Jesus's rayment was *wheitus swe snaiws* to the Goths, *hwite swa snaw* to the Anglo-Saxons, *white ful moche as snow* to Wycliffe's Lollards, and '*very whyte even as snowe*' to Tyndale. The question Jesus asked the man tormented by evil spirits in Luke 8: 30 has changed scarcely at all since Uphilus, bishop of the Goths, wrote in 360: '*Wha ist namo thein?*' Bede wrote: '*Hwaet is thin nama?*', the Lollards '*What name is to thee?*' and Tyndale: '*What is thy name?*'

For all that, a great gulf opens up even in the 140-odd years between Wycliffe and Tyndale. 'Ioye zee swith yn forth, and gladre zee with out forth,' the Lollard Bible goes, 'for zoure meede is plenteuouse in heunes; forsothe so thei han pursued and prophetis that weren before zou.' It is almost unintelligible now. Tyndale is modern: 'Rejoice, and be glad, for greate is your rewarde in heven, so persecuted they the prophets which were before youre dayes.'

His New Testament was entirely new, too, in the sense that it was meant to be read through as a whole. For a thousand years, the Bible had been more pored over than read. Tyndale complained that orthodox theologians 'devide ye scriptures into iiii senses, ye literall, tropologicall, allegoricall, anagogicall'. Jerusalem was the classic example of the way in which varying depths of meaning were extracted from a single word. Literally Jerusalem meant the biblical city of the Jews. As an allegory, Jerusalem signified the Church of Christ. The tropological sense involved tropes, or figures of morality; here, Jerusalem stood for the human soul. The anagogical involved the elevation to future glory; anagogically Jerusalem was the heavenly city.

To Tyndale, the decay of the faith sprang from Origen and the early scholars who had obsessively searched for allegory 'till they at last forgot the order and process of the text, supposing that the Scripture served but to feign allegories upon'. As a result, 'twenty doctors expound one text twenty ways, as children make descant upon plain song'. And when the sophisters came with their 'anagogical and chopologicall sense', they took a text half an inch long and 'drew a thread nine days long'. Tyndale did not simply translate the Bible. In the sense of restoring its sweep and drama, he recreated it.

5

Printing

Tyndale and Roye arrived at Cologne in the high summer of 1525. The city was, on the face of it, an unlikely place to find a printer for the banned Testament.

It lay within the jurisdiction of the Catholic archbishop-elector of Cologne, a ruler with fresh and raw reason to persecute Lutherans. The peasants' war had swept through the Rhineland in the late spring, accompanied by a bloody rising against the archbishop. The lords had ridden to the archbishop's aid, peppering the countryside with gibbets of hanged peasants, and he had regained control of his territory by the end of June. An edge of tension persisted as the two Englishmen quietly entered Cologne some time in August.

The city abounded with the vanities and superstitions that Tyndale so mocked in the old religion. Its jewelled prince-prelate, whose claim to temporal and spiritual dominion made him a papal Antichrist in miniature to Tyndale, presided over a motley of relics, shrines, chantries, monasteries, pilgrims, mendicant friars and indulgence salesmen. The cathedral was a prodigy of Gothic intensity and a measure of the majesty of the Church that Tyndale presumed to challenge. Building had begun 277 years before.

Masons were still decorating its great shoulders with slender pinnacles and gargoyles of laughing demons; its spires were not finally to be completed until 1880, but the chief glories were already in place, and it hung high above the Rhine in brilliant stonebursts. The exquisite tracery of the chancel gave delicacy and air to the vast five-aisled basilica. Above oak choir stalls carved with dancers, musicians and lovers, the Adoration of the Magi was portrayed in a lustrous series of stained glass windows, suspending sunbeams of colour in midair, and hinting at the treasures behind the high altar. Here was the *Dreikönigenschrein*, the shrine of the Three Kings. The dim light of offertory candles reflected on solid gold sculptures of kings, prophets and scenes from the Nativity, masterpieces of the goldsmiths' art that had been forty years in the making. The supposed bones of the Magi, looted from Milan by Barbarossa's chancellor 350 years before, rested in the largest gold sarcophagus in Europe, with a frieze of kneeling and muttering pilgrims. The cathedral fulfilled Pope Nicholas's dictum. It was a place of awe, among the largest structures on earth; it seemed planted by the hand of God himself, a witness to the imperishable power and tradition of the Church, and from its heights the troublesome Englishman appeared no larger than an insect.

A means to snuff out Tyndale's Bible was in place. Theologians at the large university of Cologne were early to grasp the scale and speed with which printing could spread heresy. In 1475, at their request, the pope had granted them a licence, the first of its kind, allowing them to punish the printers, publishers, authors and readers of 'pernicious' books. A decade later, Archbishop Berthold of Mainz pioneered precensorship, in which a board of cathedral priests and learned doctors examined manuscripts before they went to press. For good measure, Berthold forbade laity and clergy alike to translate any book on any subject from Latin, Greek or other foreign tongue into German. He had a particular dislike of vernacular Bibles, fearing that the 'uneducated and inquisitive laymen' who read them would 'hold themselves to be cleverer than the clergy'. Since 1501, the papal bull *Inter Multiplices* had forbidden the printing of any book in Germany without Church authorisation. The three archbishop-electors and archbishop of Magdeburg were appointed to control publications. The archbishop of Cologne was a member of this quartet and, although the bull was widely ignored, he imposed it as rigorously as he could in his territory. In 1520 he had organised a great public burning of Lutheran books and pamphlets and cartoons in front of the cathedral.

Tyndale gambled that Cologne's advantages outweighed its obvious perils. It was a great trading city – the Neumarkt was the largest market square in Germany – and the appearance of a pair of Englishmen would excite little comment. Its membership of the Hanseatic League, and its links with the Steelyard, made it easy to transfer the funds needed for the print run from London. Ease of access to English ports was a priority and here the city scored high. Printing in Wittenberg would have involved the expense and difficulty of moving a large consignment of illegal books by land. Wagons were crude, roads mere channels of dust and mud, and books were heavy and vulnerable to inspection at frontiers; Paris printers paid more for paper brought cross-country from Angoulême in southwestern France than rivals in Antwerp who shipped it from Bordeaux. So many ships and barges used the Cologne quays that the church of St Maria, though hundreds of miles inland, had a Sailors' Madonna. The print works were set among gold and ivory workshops close to the cathedral, on the site of the old Jewish ghetto, destroyed in pogroms during the Black Death. Cargoes were regularly loaded for England on wharves a few yards away.

Almost a score of printers had presses in Cologne. William Caxton had learnt his skills here, before leaving to set up the first press in backward England at Westminster in 1476. A major local publisher, Hittorp, kept several printers busy with textbooks for students at the university; he also had presses in Leipzig, Paris and Prague. The Cologne bookseller Birkmann was one of the grandest in the business, with agents throughout Europe and a branch in London.

Though it was an offence for a printer to accept Tyndale's commission without first clearing it with the archbishop's censors, the fact that the text was in English made this a largely technical breach of the law. Trading cities were tolerant. Cologne left foreigners to their own devices, provided they did not disturb the peace, and Tyndale had every reason to remain anonymous. Some printers were men of deep faith who dealt only with texts that mirrored their beliefs. Nuremberg's Hans Hergot was shortly to become the first of a dozen and more printer-martyrs, executed at Leipzig in 1527 for publishing Luther. But others in Catholic cities, notably in Cologne and Antwerp, were willing to print evangelical texts, taking the precaution of either not identifying their work, or using a false colophon. Albrecht Dürer had passed through Cologne five years before Tyndale's arrival, returning home after attending the imperial coronation of Charles V in Aachen. 'I have bought a tract of Luther's for 5 weisspfennigs,' he wrote. 'And I spent another weisspfennig for the condemnation on Luther, that pious man.' Dürer also bought a pair of shoes for six weisspfennigs. Banned Lutheran work might be sharply marked up in price, but a reader in Cologne could keep up with both camps in the great drama for the cost of some footwear.

Tyndale struck his bargain with Peter Quentell, a second-generation printer who worked both sides of the fence. In 1522, John Fisher, wishing to take his battle against heresy into Luther's German heartland, had chosen Quentell to print his diatribe, *Assertionis Lutheranae Confutatio*, in Cologne. Thus, by a not unusual irony, Tyndale was to share his printer with the peppery

Tyndale opened his New Testament with a woodcut of an angel holding a pot of ink for St Matthew to use for his quill pen. Until now, in Cologne in 1525, no page of the scriptures had ever been printed in English. Before the printing of the first gospel was completed, however, drunken printers betrayed the contract to Cochlaeus, a correspondent of Thomas More and a Catholic propagandist. He informed Henry VIII and Wolsey, and Tyndale fled for his life southwards along the Rhine.

(Hulton Getty)

bishop of Rochester, whose violent attacks on his Testament were to be exceeded only by Thomas More.

The contract was at Tyndale's expense. Only a handful of creatives – artists, writers, propagandists – made money directly from the printing industry. Illustrated pamphlets and cartoons were immensely profitable, and illustrators were sometimes well rewarded. *Das Wolffgesang*, a woodcut showing the pope flanked by bishops and cardinals with wolves' snouts, catching laymen like geese in a net while a monk with a cat's head sang the wolves' song of the title, sold scores of thousands of copies in 1520 and enabled its artist, Adam Petri, to demand a high price from printers. Lucas Cranach the Elder's Whore of Babylon, the papal diadem on her head, rode side-saddle in perhaps a hundred thousand prints, on a many-headed dragon with writhing tail and claws, while friars on bended knee and the princes of the Church grovelled before her beneath a roiling sky.

Dürer, master of slashing and vigorous woodcuts, and delicate and almost photographic engravings, was tempted to give up oil painting altogether. 'No one could ever pay me to paint a picture again with so much labour,' he wrote after completing an altarpiece. 'Herr Georg Tausy wanted me to paint him a Madonna in a landscape with the same care . . . I flatly refused to do it, for it would have made a beggar out of me . . . I shall stick to my engraving, and if I had done so before I should today have been a richer man by 1000 florins.'

Books were a different business. The market was far smaller. Printers made their books as visually attractive as possible, using woodcut illustrations and sometimes saving money by reusing them in several different books, but they could of course only sell to those who could read. The number of literates in England began to rise strongly from the late 1530s, spurred by pamphlet printing, and inspired at least in part by the desire to read the English Bible. Before then, it was doubtful whether one in ten ordinary husbandmen could sign their names. Perhaps 40 per cent of richer yeomen farmers could do so, and churchwardens and constables might be able to read. Literacy jumped sharply in the towns, and many journeymen, craftsmen and apprentices had some reading; but the rate in the country as a whole was probably little better than one in fifteen.

If the book market was restricted, though growing, it was also slow. It might take a decade or more to sell out an edition, and during that time the main investment – the cost of the paper – was dead money. Printers did not begin to buy manuscripts from authors and translators until the end of the century. Before then, a handful of authors with proven sales records were able to pressure their printers into giving them free copies of their work, which they then sold on their own account, becoming in effect their own publishers. Erasmus fell into this rare category, as did Luther. The two had huge leverage – some 300,000 copies of Luther's works were sold in the three years to 1521 alone – and they were able to supply cost-free copies directly to their booksellers and agents. 'We have sold out all your books except ten copies,' Luther's man in Basle reported, 'and never remember to have sold any more quickly.'

Lesser authors were obliged to buy a proportion of the print run from the printer in advance, normally between two thirds and three quarters, and to act as unpaid proofreaders. This guaranteed profits for the printer but it made writers dependent on patronage for survival. Erasmus and Luther also sought patrons – Erasmus dedicated his Commentary on the Lord's Prayer to Thomas Boleyn, Anne's father, who sent him fifty gold crowns in gratitude – but this was icing on the cake. Poorer writers were obliged to preface their books with a flattering dedication to a powerful personage, who was expected to return the compliment by the gift of a benefice or a pension, and a contribution towards printing costs. Early in his career, for example, Thomas More had opened *Utopia* with the words: 'The most victorious and triumphant king of England, Henry the eighth of that name in all royal virtues a prince most peerless . . .' His reward came with promotions in government service.

Tyndale could scarcely dedicate an illegal book to an individual patron. Neither could he expect Peter Quentell to accept any of the risk in printing books that would have to be smuggled by sea to their final destination. As Bible-running became an established business, some printers agreed to indemnify booksellers against loss of the merchandise if books were 'seized from the purchaser by the enemies of the gospel' within three months of buying them. The Geneva publisher Laurent de Normandie signed such contracts with his French clients, twenty-one of whom found themselves arrested and their books confiscated; but Tyndale was too early to benefit from such commercial insurance.

It was, of course, true that his work was a potential bestseller. Luther had proved the vast appeal of vernacular scripture. The four thousand copies of the first edition of his September Testament had sold out in ten weeks. Posters warning that pope and emperor condemned the book seem only to have boosted sales. They were, in any event, soon countered by a forged bull of Clement VII that Lutheran wags pasted up, which claimed that the pope was eager to 'permit and enjoin the reading, re-reading and dissemination of Luther's works'. By 1525, the Testament had been reprinted fourteen times in Wittenberg, making the printer Melchior Lufft a very rich man, and in sixty-six pirate editions.

Tyndale faced obvious obstacles in repeating this triumph. German speakers outnumbered the English by more than four to one. The German book market was far larger and more sophisticated than the English; where England had little more than a dozen presses, Germany had several hundred printers, who promoted their books at the large annual fairs at Frankfurt and Leipzig. Nonetheless, Tyndale set his sights high. His contract with Quentell was illegal and was probably never written down. It was for a handsome, large-page quarto edition on good quality paper, with a lengthy prologue and marginal comment and glosses. The first gospel was prefaced by a full-page woodcut of St Matthew sitting in the shade of a tree, writing and dipping his pen into an inkpot held by a chubby angel; the chapter divisions had large illuminations. A compromise print run of three thousand seems to have been agreed on. Tyndale had originally wanted six thousand, but Quentell was worried that he would be left out of pocket if any incidents took place.

The cost is uncertain. The smaller format copies of Tyndale's Testament that eventually reached England were sold at retail for an average of 3s a bound copy; Luther's September Testament sold in Germany for one gulden, the amount a farmer expected for a pig ready for slaughter. The retail price was generally three or four times above the production cost, with bound copies substantially more expensive than unbound sheets. If Tyndale had contracted to pay Quentell 10d per set of unbound sheets, a reasonable sum, a print run of three thousand would have cost some £125.

That was an appreciable amount. Ten pounds bought a year's lodgings and fees for a law student at the Inner Temple, and many a country rector was expected to survive on less, though his parsonage and his glebe land were free. At the same time, it was a readily manageable sum for the sympathetic London merchants whom Sir Thomas More was convinced were providing the funds for Tyndale; indeed, as a price for bringing God's word to the English, it likely seemed a pittance. The accounts of one William Mucklow, a cloth merchant, show that he enjoyed a multi-thousand pound annual turnover. He brought five hundred bales of cloth each year to the spring and summer fairs of Bergen op Zoom and Antwerp, selling these for £1800, of which he invested a fifth in buying luxury goods in Flanders to sell on the English market at further profit. The close links between merchants in the Steelyard and Cologne made transfers of money a simple exercise.

*

The first words printed, towards the end of August 1525, were from the prologue. Tyndale addressed them to 'brethren and sisters most dear and tenderly beloved in Christ', and they were less innocent than they seemed.

'I have here translated,' Tyndale wrote, as if it were the most natural thing in the world, 'the new Testament for your spiritual edifying, consolation and solace.' He said that he had not translated it word for word – he had sought to 'interpret the sense of the scripture and the meaning of the spirit' – and he modestly insisted that others will have greater skills than himself. Readers may perceive that he had failed to capture the exact sense of the scripture, or had not given the right English word. If so, he says, they have a duty to amend his writing. The gifts of God are not for ourselves. They are for the honour of God and Christ, and for 'edifying of the congregation, which is the body of Christ'.

The use of the word 'congregation' was an alarm bell for any English speaker. Tyndale was using it in place of 'Church', as in the Testament itself he translated the Greek εκκλησια as 'congregation' and not as 'Church'. This was a direct threat to the Church's ancient – but, so Tyndale here made clear, non-scriptural – claim to be the body of Christ on earth. To change these words was to strip the Church hierarchy of its pretension to be Christ's terrestrial representative, and to award this honour to the individual worshippers who made up each congregation. It changed the religion. Tyndale reinforced this in the choice of three other words. Instead of priest, he used 'senior' or 'elder' for the Greek πρεσβύτερος, stressing the absence of any priestly hierarchy in scriptural times. He rendered the Greek μετανοειτε as 'repent' instead of 'do penance', which the Church, with its huge vested interest in the lucrative penitential industry of pardons and indulgences, insisted was the correct translation of the Vulgate's *poenitentiam agite*. So it might be, from the Latin, but Tyndale was working from the Greek original. He also translated the Greek ἀγάπη as 'love' – 'nowe abideth fayth, hope and love, even these thre: but the chefe of these is love' – rather than as 'charity'. While 'charity' was obviously close to the Vulgate's use of *caritas* – '*major horum est caritas*' – Tyndale was justified in finding that 'love', from the Old English *lufu*, was a more accurate translation of the original ἀγάπη. But this, too, was a notion dangerous to the Church, for the apparent downgrading of charity might undermine the lucrative donations, indulgences and bequests with which the faithful were persuaded to pave their way to heaven.

Tyndale mocked the fact that his Testament was illegal. Who could be 'so despiteful that he would envy any man so necessary a thing' as the scripture in English. Who was 'so bedlam mad' as to deny the reader, enslaved in the dark human ignorance and mendacity, the true light of God's word?

These simple words, and run of the mill thoughts, were the very stuff of heresy as they came off the Quentell press. It was, as his readers well knew, the Church itself that was 'bedlam mad' enough to deny them the gospels in their own tongue. Any English reader will readily have identified the principal 'despiteful' men as Cardinal Wolsey and the bishops of London and Rochester. The Church was sketched, with economy and force, as mad, envious and unloving. Against this, the reader had for the first time in English the joyful illumination of the gospel.

Jesus had said, as Tyndale translated in John, that: 'I am come a light into the world, that whosoever believeth on me may not abide in darkness.' The new book allowed the English speaker to abide in the light; there need be 'none occasion of stumbling in him'.

But not yet. Cochlaeus, Tunstall's friend and Bible-hunter, had arrived in Cologne from Mainz shortly before Tyndale. He was seeking a printer to publish works by Rupert of Deutz, abbot of the monastery on the opposite bank of the Rhine from Cologne four centuries before, and a writer on the Real Presence in the Eucharist. Cochlaeus arranged a contract with Peter Quentell. As part of it, he was obliged to edit the work himself. This brought him into daily contact with Quentell's printers and he got to know them well. They were a hard-drinking crew and when they were in their cups they boasted to him that 'whether the king and cardinal of England would or no, the whole of England would soon be Lutheran'.

He invited some of the printers back to his lodgings, where he plied them with wine. They told him that two English apostates were working with them on the New Testament in English. Their expenses were being 'abundantly supplied by English merchants', who were to convey the book secretly to England. The book was being produced in three thousand copies, they said; work had already advanced as far as sheet K. This meant that ten sheets had already been printed, making eighty pages in quarto format. Cochlaeus, putting on a show of admiration, admitted to be 'inwardly astonished and horrified . . . gloomily weighing the greatness of the danger'. To scotch Tyndale's 'abominable plan', Cochlaeus secretly visited Hermann Rinck, a Cologne senator who was known to Henry VIII. Rinck sent one of his agents to confirm independently that the printing was taking place at the Quentell press. He then arranged for the senate to issue a prohibition on further work and to confiscate the existing sheets.

Tyndale got wind of what was afoot. He and Roye fled southwards up the Rhine, taking with them the sheets at least to signature H, up to verse twelve of Matthew 22. The loose-tongued Roye may have prompted this near-disaster by encouraging the printers to prattle over what should have remained a secret contract. Tyndale, though he could bellow with rage in print, was discreet and secretive in his personal habits. He never spoke of Cochlaeus, despite the expense and danger he was put to. Roye, however, wrote a snide and catchy verse about him:

Cochlaye, A little praty foolish poad;
But although his stature was small
Yet men say he lacketh no gall,
More venomous than any toad.

Tyndale later made it clear that he suffered Roye because he had
to. He found him 'somewhat crafty when he cometh into new
acquaintance . . . As long as he had no money, somewhat I could
rule him; but as soon as he had gotten him money, he became like
himself again. Nevertheless I suffered all things till that was ended,
which I could not do alone without one both to write, and to help
me compare the texts together.' As soon as that task was ended,
and the Testament had been edited in Worms, 'I took my leave,
and bade him farewell for our two lives, and, as men say, a day
longer.'

Both Rinck and Cochlaeus warned that the affair was not finished. Cochlaeus wrote to Henry VIII, Wolsey and Fisher to advise
them to keep strict watch on all English ports, since the 'pernicious
merchandise' might reappear from another press. He also dedicated a volume of Rupert of Deutz to the king. He felt he had
already rendered Henry as great a service as Mordecai had to King
Ahasuerus when he warned him of the plot against him; whereas
Mordecai had been rewarded with a place next in rank to the
king, Cochlaeus complained bitterly, Henry had not even
acknowledged his help.

6

'Lyfe, love, faveour, grace, blessinge . . .'

Other rumours reached England that Tyndale had not abandoned his project. Edward Lee, the king's almoner and a future archbishop of York, heard them as he passed through Bordeaux on his way to become ambassador to Spain. 'I am certainly informed,' he wrote to the king on 2 December 1525, 'that an Englishman, your subject, at the solicitation and insistence of Luther, with whom he is, hath translated the New Testament into English, and within a few days intendeth to arrive with the same imprinted in England.' Lee added that 'I need not advertise your grace what infection and danger' an English Bible represented.

Lee's informant mislocated Tyndale and was a little premature. Tyndale and Roye had not returned to Wittenberg from Cologne. They had gone to Worms, the city in which Luther had braved the imperial diet in 1521. The diet was unimpressed – 'the devil in the habit of a monk has brought together ancient errors in one stinking puddle and invented new ones' – and it passed an edict outlawing Luther and banning the sale of his books. The city had gone over to the Lutheran cause in 1524, however, and the Englishmen were safe here. The cost of shipping the Testaments to

England was marginally higher than from Cologne, for Worms was further upriver, but it had a considerable literary asset for Tyndale. He had determined to translate the Old Testament from the original Hebrew, a field in which Europe still had few scholars. Worms had a noted Jewish community, whose stone synagogue on the Hintere Judengasse was the oldest in Europe; their reputation for learning had been founded by the great Talmudic scholar Rabbi Schlomo. With the break-up and expulsion of the sophisticated and erudite Jewish communities of Spain, Worms was as good a place to study Hebrew as any in Christendom.

Its leading printer was Peter Schoeffer, the son of the Mainz pioneer printer, and it was he whom Tyndale commissioned. Neither printer nor translator was identified, but the type and some of the watermarks and woodcuts were used in other books that bear Schoeffer's colophon. Tyndale could have completed a quarto edition by using the Cologne sheets he had brought with him for the opening chapters. It mattered little if Schoeffer did not have a type to match the Gothic black used by Quentell, for this was a book designed to be read in secret, not displayed in a collection. Instead, Tyndale chose to distribute the Cologne material as unfinished sheets, and to print an entirely new octavo edition, without prologue or glosses.

Haste, and cost, must have dictated this. A press was not in itself expensive, as we have seen, and creating type was time-consuming but needed little investment if the printer cast his own fonts. Paper accounted for at least two thirds, and sometimes more, of the production cost of a book.

The paper industry was sophisticated. The Le Bé family, with mills near Troyes, sold their famous 'B'-watermarked paper to Worms, Cologne and Leipzig, the Low Countries, and as far as England. But it was pricey. Vellum, usually shaven and treated sheepskin, was far too expensive to be used in the quantities needed for printing. Even a short book would use up a dozen skins per copy, so that a print run of hundreds of copies would devour many flocks of sheep. Paper had been invented two centuries before. It made printing viable but it was still laborious and costly to make. The raw material consisted of old rags, collected by specialist dealers, the 'rag and bone' men of nursery rhymes. Flimsy white rag was needed for quality paper. This was cut up into small pieces and left soaking in cellars to ferment. Fatty substances were forced out as the cellulose gradually separated into a raw stuff that the collector brought to the mill.

Most mills were water mills converted to paper-making from corn-grinding. Paper-making was an Italian technology that was often financed elsewhere in Europe by Italian bankers. In the manufacture of paper, small wooden mallets, some fitted with nails or small spikes, ran from the main shaft to strike up and down on the treated rags in beating troughs. A quantity of soap was then added to the beaten rags to produce a pulp, which was mixed in turn into a vat of warm water. Next, a form, a wooden frame encasing a lattice of cross wires, was dipped into the vat. These wires retained the pulp in the shape of a sheet as the water drained off, and the form was shaken to produce an even surface. The sheet was then pulled off the form and pressed between layers of felt to absorb more surplus water. The sheet was taken to a 'little' hanging room to air and was then coated with a 'size', a thin coating of wax and clay that would prevent the printing ink from soaking crudely into it. After further drying in a 'great' hanging room, the sheet was finished by rubbing it with a flint. It was delivered to the printer in reams of twenty-five sheets each.

Paper-making needed pure water in enormous quantities. The best mills were situated upstream of large towns on rivers with a low iron content, to avoid discolouring. A ready supply of rags, or old hemp rope for lower-quality paper, was also essential. The paper-making industry thus favoured sea and river ports, to which rags could be shipped, and linen-making and hemp-growing regions, such as the Vosges and Champagne. Carters from the Vosges roamed far and wide, paying for old clothes in cash, pins and crockery, driving their wagons to major fairs to sell their loads to wholesalers. Fortunes were being made in the 1520s; Antoine de Laugerière, the king of French collectors, was selling rags by the ten tons. German ragmen profiteered so audaciously that paper-makers in Germany lobbied town councils to declare zones around each major printing centre, in which they alone had collecting rights.

The difference in labour costs between quarto and octavo sheets was not great; the compositors had the same volume of words to set, and the pressmen, although they had more sheets to handle with the large format, would not earn substantially more. The paper cost of the Worms octavo edition was half that of the Cologne quarto, however; sixteen pages were printed from each sheet instead of eight, and the saving was immediate. By doing without the Cologne prologue and the glosses, Tyndale reduced both composition and paper costs, of course, and also saved much time. It was laborious to add marginal notes and glosses to each page. It required careful copy-editing to ensure that text references were correct, and for Tyndale there was the added complication that his compositors were German-speakers. A skilled man could set type accurately enough by sight alone, character by character, but the setting of glosses ideally required an understanding of what was being said, which the Worms compositors lacked.

Octavo was an ideal format for an illegal book. Copies were also pocket-sized, easy to conceal – in the sleeve or lining of a cloak, for practical pockets were not in fashion – and easy to smuggle.

It had taken four months to print Luther's September Testament at Wittenberg in an edition of five thousand copies in 1522, with two and latterly three presses working flat out. Tyndale's Testament was, of course, almost the same length; a trifle shorter, in fact, due to the economy of English over German, and the absence of glosses. He had Roye to help him, and the two must have spent their waking hours in the print shop, supervising the compositors and urging on the pressmen. The printers did them proud. Finished copies were being loaded on to Rhine barges by February 1526, less than six months after Tyndale arrived in the city.

He was as discreet and anonymous as his Testament. No word of what was afoot in Worms leaked out until after the event, and then only in a single diary entry by Spalatin, the Lutheran secretary of the elector of Saxony. During a supper party in neighbouring Speyer the following summer, Spalatin was told that six thousand copies of the New Testament had been printed in English at Worms. It was the work of 'an Englishman . . . who is so skilled in seven tongues, Hebrew, Greek, Latin, Italian, Spanish, English, French, that whichever he speaks, you would think it his native tongue'. Spalatin added that the book was likely to be a bestseller, 'for the English,' he was told, 'despite the opposition and unwillingness of the king, so long after the gospel, that they affirm that they will buy the New Testament, even if they must pay 100,000 pieces of money for it'.

No accurate figure can be put on the Worms print run. Only three copies survive, two in England and one newly found in Germany. The English have not always, it must be said, treated it with the respect that Spalatin suggested. The first copy, in the library of St Paul's Cathedral in London, is missing seventy leaves. The copy in the British Library, which lacks the title page, was bought by the collector Edward Harley, Earl of Oxford, for 20 guineas (£21). At his death in 1741, the manuscripts in his Harleian Library were to pass to the new British Museum. His books were sold off, and the Worms New Testament was bought for 15s (75p) by Joseph Ames, the Wapping ship chandler who founded English bibliography with his work *Typographical*

The title page of the first complete New Testament. Less elaborate than the abandoned Cologne edition, it was printed at Worms in 1526. A single copy with this intact title page survives. Long misdated, it passed through several libraries, including the Cistercian monastery of Schönthal, before it was correctly identified in 1996. As the work of a fugitive, the title page bore no name or identifying marks. But Tyndale's prose rings out in the sharp message it bears. 'Christ Jesus commaunded that they shulde preache it vnto al creatures,' he wrote of the Testament. Did not 'all creatures' include English speakers? Was it not Christ's command to give them God's word in their mother tongue?

(Württembergische Landesbibliothek, Stuttgart)

Antiquities in 1749. It was sold to John White, a collector of early English Bibles, for fourteen and a half guineas (£15.22). White sold it for 20 guineas in 1776 to the Rev. Andrew Gifford, a Baptist minister who was an early assistant keeper at the British Museum. Gifford bequeathed the Testament to Bristol Baptist College in 1784. It was acquired by the British Library for a little over £1 million in 1994.

The only complete copy was discovered recently in Stuttgart. It was originally in the library of the Elector Ottheinrich of the Palatinate. The Elector's bookbinder bound it in 1550, and stamped it with that date on the cover, rather than 1526 as the year of publication. It narrowly avoided being sent to nestle in the bosom of the enemy when the bulk of the Ottheinrich Library was transferred to the Vatican Library in Rome in 1623. It passed instead to the Cistercian abbey of Schönthal. From there it passed through the library of King Friedrich I and the university of Tübingen before reaching its present billet in the Württembergische Landesbibliothek in Stuttgart in 1935. It continued to be catalogued as a 1550 copy until it was realised six years ago that its true provenance is 1526.

Its title page has no identifying marks – no colophon, no translator's name – but it is an exercise in descriptive brevity:

> The newe Testament
> As it was written
> and caused to be written
> by them which her-
> de yt. To whom
> also oure Saveoure
> Christ Jesus
> commaunded that they shulde pre-
> ache it vnto al
> creatures.

It has a curious border, with columns embraced by youths and gar-
lands of flowers, and a pediment on which lie a bearded male
angel and a bare-breasted female.

It is nonetheless the original of the most fecund book printed in the
English language. Pirate editions were being printed in Antwerp
within a few months, and, repolished by King James's panel of
divines in 1611, it has echoed in the very crannies of the earth.
Tyndale brought simplicity and force, and he was faithful to the
Greek, without a trace of pedantry: 'When I was a chylde, I spake
as a chylde, I ymmagened as a chylde: but as sone as I was a man I
put awaye childesshness.' In the same passage, in I Corinthians 13,
he used plain words to sustain a lyrical beauty of language: 'Love
suffreth longe and is corteous. Love envieth nott . . . swelleth not,
dealeth not dishonestly, seketh not her awne . . . beleveth all thynges, hopeth all thynges, endureth in all thynges. Though that
prophesyinge fayle, other tonges shall cease, or knowledge vanysshe
awaye: yet love falleth never awaye.' This was the finest English
prose yet written, and it defined what was to come.

Tyndale transformed the Paternoster from a mumbled and ill-
understood Latin formula into the infinitely familiar:

> O oure father which arte in heven, halowed be thy name
> Let thy kingdom come; thy wyll be fulfilled as well in erth as
>   hut ys in heven
> Geve vs this daye oure dayly breade
> And forgeve vs our treaspases, even as we forgeve them which
>   treaspas vs,
> Leede vs not into temptacion, but delyvre vs from yvell . . .

Another passage stamped for more than four centuries into the
memory of every English-speaking Christian is from the Worms
book, too:

> Jesus toke breed, and gave thankes, brake it, and gave it to his
>   disciples, and sayde, Take, eate, thys ys my body.
> And toke the cuppe and gave thankes, and gave it them,
>   sayinge, Drinke of it every won
> This is my bloudde of the newe testament, which shalbe
>   shedde for many, for the foryevenes of synnes.

Its earliest readers afforded the book more than the value ascribed by Spalatin; although, in money terms, they acquired their treasure for two or three rather than thousands of shillings, they risked ending their lives at the stake for reading it.

Tyndale wrote a short epistle, simpler and more moving than the abandoned prologue from the Cologne edition, and ran it at the end of his work. Its words seem to catch the cadence of the Bible itself, for they flow from the same hand; their ring is familiar, demanding to be read aloud; and they hint, in their plain and affectionate intensity, at the deep-boned faith and spirit of vanished generations.

Publishers were already highly skilled at promoting their books, using strong graphics and eye-catching copy to describe the contents, with introductions and end-pieces in the role of the modern dust jacket. Tyndale's epistle is a masterpiece of the art. He was selling salvation itself to his readers and his opening appeal was irresistible. 'Geve diligence, Reder, I exhort the, that thow come with a pure mynde, and as the scripture sayth, with a syngle eye, unto the wordes of health and of eternall lyfe,' he wrote, 'by the which, if we repent and beleve them, we are borne anewe, created afresshe, and enioye the frutes of the bloud of Christ . . .' That blood 'cryeth not for vengeaunce, as the bloud of Abel'; instead, it 'hath purchased lyfe, love, faveour, grace, blessinge, and whatsoever is promysed in the scriptures to them that beleve and obeye God', and it was Christ's blood that 'stondeth betwene us and wrathe, vengeaunce, curse . . .'.

This was no ordinary book, he made clear; it was the very word of God, speaking now in English, and those who attended to it and committed themselves 'unto the deservynge of Christ' would find in its tightly printed pages a guide to this life, and God's promise of mercy and immortality in the next. 'Soo shalt thou nott despeare,' he comforted his readers, 'but shalt feale god as a kynd and a mercifull father; and his sprete shall dwell in the, and shall be stronge in the, and the promises shalbe given the at the last.' It was a necessary reassurance, of course, for the possession of a copy carried with it the threat of the fire.

For his own part, Tyndale prayed his readers to forgive him if his rude English offended them. He had no man to 'counterfet', or imitate; 'neither', he added, 'was holpe with English of any that had interpreted the same or soche lyke thinge in the scripture beforetyme', confirming that he had not used Lollard manuscripts. He stood by the honesty of his work. 'I am sure, and my conscience beareth me recorde,' he wrote, 'that of a pure entent, syngly and faythfully I have interpreted it, as farre forth as god gave me the gyfte of knowledge and understondynge.' How well he had succeeded was demonstrated by James's divines, who incorporated almost nine tenths of him verbatim in their Authorised Version, despite the intervening eighty-five years of biblical scholarship.

Inevitably, there were revisions to be made – Tyndale mentioned the 'cumbrances' under which he laboured, not detailing them lest they help to identify him – and he warned his readers that the book was like a premature child. He caught seventy-two of the 'errours comitted in the prentynge' – 'for hegged, rede hegged . . . Noses rede Moses . . . anzareth rede nazareth' – but many others got through. 'Count it as a thynge not havynge his full shape, but, as it were, borne afore hys tyme,' he said, 'even as a thing begun rather than fynnesshed.' If God gave him time, he would fill it out, to give it more light, and 'to seke in certane places more proper Englysshe'. He wanted, he said, to make it simpler for ordinary folk to read – 'more apt for those with weke stomakes' – by including a table to explain words which were not commonly used, and to 'shewe howe the scripture useth many wordes which are wotherwyse understonde of the commen people'. He appealed to the educated to 'helpe thereunto, and to bestowe unto the edyfyinge of Christ's body (which is the congregacion of them that beleve) those gyftes whych they have receaved of god for the same purpose'.

It was at the few words in brackets that Catholics most bridled. They reaffirmed the Cologne prologue, and showed that the author's translation of εκκλησια as congregation, and of πρεσβύτερος as elder, was not accidental. The man believed Christ's body not to be the Church, but the sum of believers. The same aberration showed, too, in the way he bade his readers farewell, blessing those who had faith: 'The grace that commeth of Christ be with them that love hym. Praye for us.'

This was the work of a heretic.

7

Auguries

Two events – auguries, for they defined the future – took place in London as Tyndale had the first completed copies of his Testament collated and bound in Worms. At Shrovetide, in February 1526, Henry VIII appeared in the tiltyard wearing a jousting dress embroidered with the words 'Declare I Dare Not'. It was the first visible sign that the king was wooing Anne Boleyn, a young lady of the queen's household, an infatuation that changed the religious loyalties of England. (The religion itself was another matter. 'Our king has destroyed the pope,' a canny reformer was to note, 'but not popery.')

Anne was twenty-four. Catherine of Aragon, the queen, worn out by miscarriages, was forty-one. Her only living child was a daughter, Mary, and she was too old now to bear another. The king was six years younger than his wife, still fit and handsome, and eager for a son to shore up his dynasty. Talk already had Anne as Henry's mistress, but she was not. Her virginity was her trump card to become queen; it guaranteed the king's continuing lust for her and set him off on his seven-year quest for an annulment of his marriage to Catherine. The king's 'great matter' – his pursuit of the annulment and remarriage to Boleyn – weaves in and out of

Tyndale's life almost to the end. From the outset, 'Mistress Anne' was hostile to Cardinal Wolsey and to the Church, which treated her as the king's whore, and nourished a sympathy for reforming ideas.

In her portraits, Anne's face is pale and oval, her lips thin and pursed. They cannot do her justice for she had a vivacity that captivated men. 'The lively sparks that issue from those eyes,' the poet Wyatt wrote, 'sunbeams to daze men's sight.' She played cards and dice, sang, danced and hunted; she was graceful, with a quick wit and easy conversation. Above all, she knew her own mind, and the period she had spent at the French court as a girl had taught her the guiles and stratagems that she needed to meet her own expectations, and those of her ambitious father, Sir Thomas Boleyn, the Treasurer of the Royal Household. Her grandfather had been knighted by Henry VI, and had bought himself Hever, a moated castle that still stands in Kent. He had made his money in trade, however, as a successful mercer who had become Lord Mayor of London in 1457.

The family were upwardly mobile, but they retained the radical views of London merchants and were sympathetic to reformers. It is likely that Margaret de Valois, Francis I's evangelical sister, influenced Anne while she was in France. One of her chaplains, William Latimer, says that she was 'very expert in the French tongue, exercising herself continually in reading the French bible and other French books of like effect, and conceived great pleasure in the same'. She ordered her chaplains 'to be furnished of all kind of French books that reverently treated of the holy scriptures'.

Anne's first English suitor was Henry Percy, the young heir to the earldom of Northumberland. Such a marriage would have been glorious. The Percys had sailed with William the Conqueror; they were one of the most powerful families in the land, and the mercer's granddaughter would have become the chatelaine of their great seat at Alnwick Castle. Wolsey disapproved of the match, however, as indeed did young Percy's father when he heard of it. Wolsey discussed the matter with the king, whose permission was needed for a marriage at this level of nobility. The king is said to have confided his 'secret affection' for Anne to the cardinal. It seems that he was already planning to take Anne as a mistress, as he had taken her sister Mary; certainly, he instructed Wolsey to break off the engagement. Wolsey summoned Percy to his London palace at York Place. He gave him a public dressing down, telling him not to involve himself with 'that foolish girl yonder in the court'. This was reported back to Anne Boleyn, who neither forgave nor forgot the remark. 'His Highness intended to have preferred Anne Boleyn unto another person,' Wolsey added, 'although she knoweth it not.' This mystery person transpired to be the king.

Wolsey now had an enemy at court and Tyndale a potential friend.

The other augury – this one an ill omen for Tyndale – was a penitential procession that passed through the London streets to St Paul's on Shrove Sunday 1526. This marked the emergence of Thomas More as an active heretic-hunter.

Booksellers had been warned off Tyndale's Testament well in advance. The Bible translation itself ran foul of the 118-year-old anti-Lollard Constitutions of Oxford, which remained in force. The blanket ban on reforming books in general was based on a legatine commission issued by Wolsey on 14 May 1521. This was directed with papal authority to all the bishops of England and Wales, and was read out in every church in the land at mass. It said that 'many and diverse pestiferous and pernicious propositions and errors of Martin Luther' were in circulation, 'setting forth both Greek and Bohemian heresies'. The Bohemian reference covered John Huss, and thus embraced Wycliffe and the Lollards; the Greek Orthodox, among their other heresies, permitted the clergy to marry and the laity to take the cup at communion. Any person with such writings was to surrender them to the bishop or his agents within fifteen days.

Mindful of Tunstall's warning, in 1524, of the perils of handling heretical books, the printers also paid heed. The industry was small and easily coerced; 550 books were printed in England between 1520 and 1529, where Paris alone was producing three hundred different titles a year. The foreigners who dominated the trade – two thirds of the printers, booksellers and bookbinders in England were foreigners, men like the Norman Richard Pynson, and Wynkyn de Worde, an Alsatian, using French and German printing equipment – were in no mood for adventures. They relied heavily on the crown and the Church both for business and for protection from the jealous native Stationers' Company. Three English printers, John Gough, Thomas Berthelet and Robert Redman, were briefly in trouble, but these were merely technical offences in failing to obtain episcopal licences in advance. Indeed, one of the books was a translation of Erasmus by Thomas More's daughter Meg, which the printer had not thought to clear; a second edition, with Wolsey's arms and the permission, *cum privilegio a rege indulto*, was hastily published. English publishing remained heresy-free.

Imports were another matter. Lutheran books and pamphlets were shipped across the Narrow Sea, largely from Antwerp, in defiance of the ban. Robert Barnes was charged with heresy for a supposedly Lutheran sermon he preached at Cambridge at Christmas 1525. He was brought to London for interrogation, his friend Miles Coverdale travelling with him to help in his defence. He was given the standard choice between recanting and the stake. He was fortunate to survive an exchange with the bishop of Bath, his principal judge. When Barnes maintained that any man was a martyr who 'was persecuted, and dyed for the worde of God', the bishop snapped that 'he wolde make me frye for this'. He was, however, allowed to read out his revocation. His public penance was set for Shrove Sunday, 11 February 1526.

At the end of January, Thomas More led a raid with armed men on the Steelyard. He burst in on the merchants as they were about to dine in their hall on a Friday evening. More said that he had been informed that some among them were importing Lutheran books and tracts, which caused grievous errors to the Christian faith of the king's subjects. He named three merchants, who were arrested on the spot, and left with them. More was back the next day, with a squad of searchers who went carefully through each merchant's chamber, confiscating suspect books. A further eight merchants were marched off to Westminster, where Wolsey spoke to them severely of the dangers of heresy.

Four of the German merchants accompanied Barnes on the penitential procession to St Paul's, seated backwards on donkeys and wearing pasteboard mitres on which pages from the offending books were pinned. They were led into the church and obliged to kneel in the aisle with symbolic faggots tied to their backs. As a fiery preacher, Barnes had damned 'the gorgyous pompe and pryde of all exteryour ornamentes'. He was now forced to regard the elevated scaffold that Wolsey had ordered to be built for the ceremony, with 'six and thirty abbots, mitred priors and bishops . . . the Cardinal sat there enthronised, his chaplains and spiritual doctors in gowns of damask and satin, and he himself in purple, even like a bloody Antichrist'. Wolsey conducted the mass, and Bishop Fisher of Rochester delivered a searing sermon against Luther. Though it was difficult to hear the sermon 'for ye great noyse of ye people within ye church', Fisher later wrote it out and had it printed in Germany, so that Tyndale and the exiles might read it. During the ceremony, Barnes and his fellow penitents were made to kneel on their own platform, and at its end they publicly begged forgiveness.

Baskets full of the heretical books were now carried outside to the rood, the cross that soared by the north tower, to be burnt. A great fire was lit, despite heavy rain. Barnes and the others carried their faggots round the flames three times, and then hurled them into the fire, as a reminder of what would happen to their own bodies half a mile away at Smithfield should they lapse back into gospelling and Luther-reading.

On 3 March, the Steelyard merchants in London wrote to warn their colleagues abroad that More and Wolsey were on the hunt for heretical books, and that care must be taken with imports.

The first copy of the Testament was landed within a few days. We do not know the time and place that this pioneer arrived on its native coast, of course, for it slipped ashore furtively, but copies were certainly being sold in the early spring of 1526. In March 1528, Bishop Tunstall interrogated John Pykas, a Colchester baker and gospeller, in the same chapel where Tyndale had vainly asked for Tunstall's patronage. Pykas confessed that 'about two years last past he bought in Colchester, of a Lombard of London, a New Testament in English and paid for it four shillings'. To Tunstall's irritation, he added that he 'read it through many times'.

A steady flow of Testaments was maintained by the skills and mercenary instincts of the smugglers. The nearer an Englishman was to the North Sea coast, the closer he was to the genius of Tyndale. The diocesan records of Lincoln show that crews of Hull seamen, after visiting Protestant Bremen, spoke with awe of how 'the priest and all that were in the church, old and young, would sing after their mother tongue'. Bishop Nix of Norwich complained in 1530 that 'the gentlemen and the commenty [commonality] be not greatly infect, but merchants and such that hath their abiding not far from the sea'.

Englishmen had traded freely until 1275, when Edward I imposed a duty on export of wool and hides. In 1303, the system was expanded, and merchants had to pay special duties on imported wines as well as exported cloth, with a 'custom' of 3d in the pound value on all other goods entering or leaving the country. Permanent staffs of customs officials were established. Geoffrey Chaucer, whose poetry made him the most significant figure in the English language before Tyndale, had been appointed controller of the Customs and Subsidy of Wools, Skins and Tanned Hides in the port of London in 1374; the father of the man who would betray Tyndale had recently been made 'customer' at Poole in Dorset.

Smuggling had thrived since the imposition of duties. The first great smuggling fortune had been made by the Lombard Nicholas Sardouche 150 years before Tyndale; he specialised in the illegal export of wool to Italy and the Netherlands, but also made a turn from Venetian cloth of gold and Cornish tin. The customers were in permanent warfare with smugglers and with their own black sheep. Controllers were appointed to watch over collectors. Each kept a half of the seal of the port, so that a ship could not be cleared from customs without the say so of both men, and each rendered a separate account to the exchequer. That was the theory. In practice, corruption was so common that a third set of officials – 'surveyors' – were brought in, to little avail. Venice regularly voted a sum for the admiral of the state galleys to use to bribe English officials on the annual visit of the fleet to England and Flanders. Florentine merchants favoured landing their cargoes on the quays at Southampton, where their bribes enabled them to escape most duties throughout the century.

Merchants smuggled high duty cloth and wines, of course, but also more humble goods: brushes, felt hats, playing cards, pins, tennis balls, fans, bridles, girdles, swan feathers, leather buckets, pepper, spices, and treacle.

Books, however, were exempt from customs duties. An Act of 1483, imposing widespread duties on imports and restricting the immigration of foreign craftsmen, expressly allowed free entry and sale for 'any Books, written or printed'. Foreign printers, mainly

Dutch and Belgian, set up agencies in London and staffed them with their fellow countrymen. Large quantities of textbooks, primers and missals were printed in Antwerp and Paris for the English market. The flourishing Antwerp printers Christoffel van Ruremund and Johannes Hillen produced little else. There was thus a flourishing and legitimate trade in imported books that served as cover for those dealing in banned works by Luther and Tyndale.

Londoners were notoriously hostile to foreigners, and fretted at the freedoms given them. An Italian visitor noted that, though in Bruges he had been welcomed and complimented by all, Londoners treated foreigners 'with the utmost contempt and arrogance . . . they look at us askance by day, and at night they sometimes drive us off with kicks and blows of the truncheons . . .'. The constant pressure to repeal the 1483 privileges, backed up by sporadic rioting against immigrant craftsmen, was resisted until 1533. An Act was passed acknowledging that 'a marvellous number of printed books had and still do come in . . . whereby many of the King's subjects be destitute of work'. From Christmas 1533, anyone importing books for resale, or buying them, was to forfeit the books and be fined 6s 8d per copy. Only people granted a special licence were allowed to import books printed in English, or to sell, give or publish such books. The penalty was imprisonment during the king's pleasure, and the forfeiture of all possessions, thus reducing the malefactor's unfortunate family to penury.

Bible smuggling was made particularly dangerous by the heresy legislation. Detection involved a lengthy and sometimes lethal stay in a damp and unhealthy cell. At least one Flemish printer–bookseller died in a London prison, as we shall see, after his arrest for running pirate Tyndale editions. But it continued apace. Flat printed sheets were hidden in the inbound cargoes of woad, madder and alum for cloth-making, iron and steel tools, cannon, glassware, and luxuries, wines, raisins, figs, and 'all manner paper and parchment'. Books were stacked in barrels and casks which false cargo manifests declared to contain wine or oil; they were carefully wrapped and hidden in the meal in sacks of flour or slipped into boxes of furs. Correspondence from Tyndale's supporters in London, and the cash and letters of credit from his backers for which More searched long and fruitlessly, were carried in chests with hidden compartments. Bales and cases with contraband were marked with a dab of colour or a twist of cloth, identifiable to the smugglers. This could make a consignment vulnerable – More seized a large shipment, after breaking a prisoner under interrogation, and extracting from him 'the shipman's name that had them, and the marks of the fardels [bundles]' – but most cargoes got through.

London was the major destination. Wharves and warehouses ran along the north bank of the Thames from St Katherine's in the east, downriver from the Tower, through to Westminster. There were other quays and depots on the south bank, from Bermondsey as far as the archbishop's palace at Lambeth. The long estuary of the Thames abounded with creeks and quiet anchorages, at Deptford, Greenwich and Tilbury. Smugglers frequently offloaded contraband into small boats as they lay at anchor in the estuary waiting for the tide or wind to turn. Canvey Island provided a bleak and muddy depot for storing such cargoes. The customs men employed 'tide-waiters' who joined ships as they anchored off Gravesend, staying aboard as the tide carried them up to London to prevent cargo being run ashore, but there were more ships than tide-waiters.

The Essex, Suffolk and Norfolk coasts had many isolated creeks and 'dries', where a boat was left high and dry at low water and her cargo could be walked ashore. Inland from the coast were discreet tracks, 'cart gaps' and 'drove roads' and 'padders', used for driving cattle and sheep, which kept clear of villages and hamlets.

Flemings had the lion's share of the business. They ran cloth and wool out of England, and beer; the crews had a taste for English beer, and scarcely a cargo was seized that did not include barrels of beer, which the crew had tried to pass off as drinking water. They avoided the large ports, berthing at Drypool rather than Hull, and in Norfolk they regularly used Brancaster, Cromer and Happisburgh, a huge expanse of coast that had only a handful of customs searchers. There were English ships, too, most commonly of 30 tons burden, overmanned by Dutch standards with crews of ten and more. Walberswick in Suffolk had five masters capable of taking a ship to Iceland, the Low Countries and France, and eighty ordinary seamen of whom eighteen could navigate the coastal waters as far as London. The usual pay for a voyage from Yarmouth to Antwerp and back was 10s. Crewmen were allowed to engage in trade on their own account, and shared in the profits of any smuggling, piracy or wrecking that was done.

Losses were high, with ships wrecked on the shifting sandbanks and treacherous harbour entrances of the east coast. The lodesmen, or coastal pilots, were a professional body, whose members had to pass examinations held in Newcastle, Hull and Bristol; their Guild of the Holy Trinity and St Clement, later, as Trinity House, to be responsible for the navigation marks in British and colonial waters, was founded a dozen years before its pilots guided the first Bible cargoes to land.

The East Anglian coast was taxing. Haisborough Sand lies eight miles off the north Norfolk coast, steep-to with heavy breaking swells, an evil place if there is any north in the wind. The seas build up quickly over the bars at the river mouths. Further south, there are shoals and tide rips on the approaches to Great Yarmouth; dangerous shoals lie well offshore to the east of the Thames estuary, the Galloper, Gabbard, Drill Stone, the Falls. Informers were an additional peril. A new system of rewards was introduced in Henry's reign, which gave informers half the fines levied on the smugglers they betrayed. A London haberdasher named George Welplay employed his servants to spy on the Suffolk coast.

The governor of the Merchant Adventurers Company nonetheless told the statesman Thomas Cromwell that smuggled cargoes went to and from Antwerp on every tide. The skippers of herring busses and hoekers from the cod fishery, pinks and smacks, often ran cargoes when fish were hard to find, slipping between the sandbanks into the many rivers of the coast, the Stour, Blackwater, Crouch, Orwell, Deben. The local fishing communities supported the smugglers, who gave them work as dockers, carters, lookouts and draymen. A customs searcher based at Lynn in Norfolk would be spotted long before he made his way to Heacham, Burnham, Wells or Cley; the Suffolk smuggling ports, Walberswick, Southwold, Aldeburgh and Woodbridge, were equally remote from officialdom. In theory, a vessel with smuggled goods was seized and sold off with its cargo to the benefit of the crown. In practice, it was often sold back to the smugglers for a fraction of market value.

Risks were offset by the handsome profits on offer. It cost the London merchant Sir John Fulford less than £50 to built a coaster, the *Dorothy Fulford*; he expected the vessel to pay for herself within nine months. Smuggling Testaments was good business.

Thomas More convinced himself that the evangelicals had formed a great conspiracy and were distributing some Tyndale copies free of charge. 'I was by good honest men informed that in Bristol,' he wrote, 'there were of these pestilent books some thrown into the streets and left at men's doors by night, that where they durst not offer their poison to sell, they would of their charity poison men for naught.' Catholics in France made the same claim. A city ordinance at Laon in France a little later required all ventilation shafts giving on to the street from basements to be sealed off. This was because 'there come men secretly sent from the city of Geneva, carrying little books . . . These men throw these books secretly by night into the cellars and basements through the air vents . . . [S]hortly after, a fair number of inhabitants who were avid for novelties abandoned the Catholic religion and adopted the new one, which was called Lutheran, and all because of these little books.'

This was wishful thinking. The unpalatable fact was that people paid, and paid handsomely, for the Testament. John Tyball of Steeple Bumpstead in Essex confessed that he had bought his copy of Tyndale for 3s 2d. His friend Thomas Hilles paid 3s for the volume he bought at Whitsun in 1526. Tyball also had a copy 'of the gospel of Matthew and Mark in English', the rare sheets surviving from the aborted Cologne printing, as well as 'certain of Paul's epistles in English after the old translation', meaning hand-copied Lollard manuscripts.

We do not know whether Tyndale had completed Matthew's gospel and had started on Mark before Cochlaeus uncovered him in Cologne. Robert Ridley, Tunstall's chaplain, complained that 'M William hichyns, otherwais called M W tyndale, and frear William roy, manifest Lutheranes heretikes and apostates', were doing great damage 'by their commentares and annotations in Mathew & Marcum in the first print . . .'

The wholesale price, landed in England, was around 2s 8d for a bound copy. This corresponds to the eight groats apiece for five copies paid by one William Furboshore in the Suffolk town of Stowmarket. He marked them up to the retail price of between 3s and 4s charged by most bookrunners. This was a very reasonable amount – hugely so, compared with the £2 10s or more needed to buy a hand-copied Lollard Testament – and well within the pocket of a skilled craftsman. Spanking profits were made, nonetheless. In 1528, John Raimund – the English spelling of Ruremund – was denounced in London for 'causing 1500 of Tyndale's New Testaments to be printed at Antwerp, and for bringing 500 into England'. Raimund was an alias of Hans van Ruremund, also known as van Endhoven, who had printed a pirate edition at Antwerp to have smuggled on to the English market. A judgement was later secured on van Ruremund's behalf against the Antwerp bookseller Francis Byrkman for £25, the amount still outstanding from a bill of £28 17s 3d for the supply of 729 copies of Tyndale. The wholesale price in Antwerp was thus 9½d a copy. Once shipped to England, readers paid up to 4s a copy, a mark up of 500 per cent.

They did so willingly.

8

'A filthy foam of blasphemies'

A drought-spoilt harvest increased shipping movements and the opportunities for Bible-running. Wheat was so scarce that Wolsey feared that rioting would break out – 'either the people must die from famine,' he was warned, 'or else they, with a strong hand, will fetch corn from them that have it' – and he encouraged the Steelyard merchants to import grain from the Continent.

By late August of 1526, the inflow of Tyndale Testaments was so alarming that an emergency meeting of bishops was convened. No account of the conclave has survived, but the king referred to the recommendations it made to him. 'With deliberate aduyse of the Cardynall,' Henry announced, 'and other reurende fathers of the spyrytualtye determyned the sayde corrupte and vntrue translatyons to be brenned with further sharppe correction & punisshment against the kepars and reders of the same.' He spoke of 'certayne prefaces and other pestylent glosses in the margynes'.

London was the worst affected and Tunstall issued a proclamation on 23 October 1526. 'Many children of iniquity,' he said, 'maintainers of Luther's sect, blinded through extreme wickedness and wandering from the way of truth and the catholic faith, craftily have translated the New Testament into our English tongue, intermeddling therewith many heretical articles and erroneous opinions . . .' The following day, he formally warned his archdeacons that the translator of the Testament had 'profaned the hitherto undefiled majesty of holy scripture with cunning perversities and heretical depravity'. The bishop deplored the increasing sales of the Testament, 'of which translation there are many books imprinted, some with glosses and some without, containing in the English tongue that pestiferous and most pernicious poison, dispersed all throughout our diocese of London in great number . . .'. All copies were to be confiscated within thirty days under pain of excommunication and suspicion of heresy to the owners.

In fact, the bishop did not wait a month. Rumours that there was to be a grand conflagration of Tyndale's work had been current since early September, when an evangelical made the prediction in a letter to an English merchant in Antwerp. The burning took place at St Paul's Cross, most probably on Sunday 28 October 1526. Tunstall preached a fiery sermon, dismissing the Testament as *doctrinam peregrinam*, strange doctrine, and denouncing it for containing 'errours three thousand and more'. When he had finished, every copy of Tyndale's translation that had been seized was burnt.

Humphrey Monmouth, Tyndale's old benefactor, was at the burning. It seems that he owned one of the copies that was consigned to the flames, having dutifully passed it to his confessor, who in turn handed it to Tunstall. Though the Testament was anonymous, the bishop had no doubts of authorship. 'When I harde my lord of London preach at Pawles Cross,' Monmouth wrote later, after More had sent him to the Tower, 'that sir William Tyndal had translated the N. Testament in English, and was naughtilie translated, that was the first time that ever I suspected or knew any evil by him.' The gospeller John Lambert, later to be burnt himself, was also in the crowd 'when the newe testament, imprinted of late beyond the sea, was first forfended'. He said that 'truly my heart lamented greatly to hear a great man preaching against it, who showed forth certain things he noted for hideous errors to be in it, that I, yea and not only I, but likewise did many others, think verily to be none. But (alack for pity!) malice cannot say well. God help us all, and amend it.'

On 3 November, Archbishop Warham adopted Tunstall's declaration as his own, and instructed his suffragans to hunt down copies in like manner. Cardinal Campeggio wrote to Wolsey from Rome on 21 November, saying that he was pleased to hear of the burning of 'the sacred codex of the bible, perverted in the vernacular tongue, and brought into the realm by perfidious followers of the abominable Lutheran sect; than which assuredly no holocaust could be more pleasing to Almighty God'.

Many felt that heresy and shame lay not in the translation but in the burning of God's word. Tyndale naturally attacked Tunstall. '[F]or what service done in Christ's gospel came he to the bishoprick of London, or what such service did he therein?' he wrote. 'He burnt the New Testament calling it *Doctrinam peregrinam*, "strange learning". Yea, verily, look how strange his living, in whose blood that testament was made, was from the living of the pope; even so strange is that doctrine from the pope's law, in which only, and in the practice thereof, is Tunstall learned . . .'

Thomas More was acutely aware that people thought that the burning was to 'put euery man to silence that woulde anye thinge speake of the fautes of the clargye'. He found that 'men mutter amonge them selfe, that yt boke was not only faultles, but also verywel translated, & was deuysed to be burned, bicause men should not be able to proue that suche fautes (as were at Poules cross declared to haue ben found in it) wer neuer founde there in dede . . .'.

As his obsession with Tyndale grew, More reviewed the body of

*Sir Thomas More's hatred for Tyndale – 'a hell-hound in the kennel of the devil' he
described him – was fierce and all-consuming. It unhinged him. Lord chancellor of
England by day, More devoted his nights to penning half a million poisonous words
attacking his great enemy. He celebrated the burning of Tyndale's fellow evangelicals
with rapture – 'Tyndales bokes and theyr owne malyce maketh them heretykes,' he
wrote. 'And after the fyre of Smythfelde, hell doth recyue them where the wretches
burne for euer' – and yearned for nothing more than that Tyndale should join them.*

(Mary Evans Picture Library)

evangelical books and had no hesitation in placing 'fyrst Tyndales new testament father of them all by reason of hys false translatyng'. He saw a symphony of heresy in which Tyndale was 'the basse and the tenour whereupoon [others] wold singe the trouble [treble] wyth mych false descant'.

More said that 'no good Christian manne hauing any drop of witte in his head' should marvel that the New Testament had been burnt, for it had not. What had been consumed in the fire at St Paul's Cross was Tyndale's Testament, 'for so hadde Tyndall after Luthers counsayl corrupted and chaunged it from the good and wholesome doctrine of Christ to the devilishe heresyes of their own, that it was cleane a contrarye thyng'. Tyndale was 'a hellhound in the kennel of the devil . . . discharging a filthy foam of blasphemies out of his brutish beastly mouth'. The work was as 'full of errors as the sea is of water', More said, and much of it was 'wilfully mistranslated .. to deceive blind unlearned people'.

The 'pestilent glosses' in the margins of the Cologne sheets, referred to by the king, were clearly Lutheran and partisan. The text itself, however, was judged to be almost wholly accurate by the committee of divines later appointed by James I to produce the Authorised Version. They amended words and phrasings, of course, but Tyndale has never been found to deliberately alter the sense and meaning of any passage. Though they did not admit it, the wrath of Tunstall and More rested on the translation of three words.

Tyndale wrote, as we have seen, of 'the congregation', rather than the Church, 'which is the body of Christ'. The Greek εκκλησια is a word of particular importance to the papacy. It appears only three times in the gospels, each time in Matthew. The only biblical justification for papal power over the Church lies in a claim made in a single verse in Matthew 16 and nowhere else. Popes claim to be the successors of St Peter. Tyndale translated Jesus in verse eighteen as saying: 'And I say also unto thee, that thou art Peter: and upon this rock I will build my congregation. And the gates of hell shall not prevail against it.' To use 'congregation' in place of 'Church' was to strip the papacy of its claim to have inherited the leadership of the Church from St Peter.

More flayed him for this, and for the two other supposed mistranslation. Tyndale, he said, 'chaunged comenly this worde chyrche in to this worde congregacyon, and this worde preste, into this worde senyour, and cheryte in to loue [love] . . . and penaunce in to repentaunce'; in this, 'Tyndale dyd euyll [evil] in translatynge the scrypture in to our tonge'.

This was not hair-splitting. When King James's divines came to the Authorised Version, they made two changes to Tyndale's verse eighteen. One was to replace Tyndale's 'gates of hell' with the weaker 'gates of Hades'. The other was to substitute 'church' – 'upon this rock I will build my church' – for 'congregation', since the Protestant Church of England was itself now established, powerful and hierarchical enough to claim the same authority over its worshippers that Rome had enjoyed. Some Protestants continued to support Tyndale's definition. Robert Browne was the most prominent, claiming in *A Book which sheweth the Life and Manners of all true Christians* that individual congregations, bound under God by covenant, should govern themselves independently of the State. From this the Congregationalists spring, while, deriving from Tyndale's translation of πρεσβύτερος as 'senior' or 'elder', the Presbyterians developed a polity in which Anglican and Catholic bishops are rejected and the Church is governed by presbyters, or elders. Congregationalists and Presbyterians now number in the tens of millions.

The King James version also changed Tyndale's 'love' into 'charity'. More had demanded this. 'What nede was it to put the indyfferent loue [love] in place of the vndowted good worde cheryte?' he asked. 'I saye that euery loue is not cheryte, but onely suche loue as is good and ordynate'. He did so for the same reason.

Charity is linked in meaning to good works, and it was in the interests of the established Church – Catholic in More's day, Anglican under James I – to promote good works, donations and charity, of which it was either the direct beneficiary, or in whose moral glow it basked. To Tyndale, as he wrote in a thirty-two page *Compendious introduccion vn to the pistle off Paul to the Romayns*, much of it translated directly from Luther and which he published late in 1526, all good works that are unaccompanied by faith are 'vnprofitable, lost, yea and damnable in the syght of God'. Goodness did not exist in itself – if it did, men would 'be taken as Christe, yea and above christe and sytt in the temple of God' – but only as a natural adjunct of faith.

The real horror of Tyndale's Testament to the Church was not so much the words in themselves, however, but that they were English words. As heretical polemic moved out of Latin and into the vernacular, the whole of English society was open to the infection; and one book, passed from hand to hand, read out aloud by a literate to a company of illiterates, and spread by them in turn, could infect a multitude.

Already, More was using four fresh expressions to describe the Bible-men: 'newe men', 'newe named bretherne', 'evangelycall fraternyte' and the 'new false sect of our evangelycall Englysshe heretykes'. On 18 December, while attending the king at Greenwich, he wrote to Erasmus, his 'dere derlynge' friend, urging him to fight the evangelicals with 'strength of spirit up to your dying breath, even if there were a disastrous catastrophe'. As a lawyer, More was careful to accuse the evangelicals of sedition as well as heresy, since it enabled a dual attack to be made on them. They 'lyttle care in ded of hel or heauen,' he was to write, 'but would in this worlde liue in lewd libertie, and have all runne to ryot . . . that they may be able to tourne the world up so down, and defende theyr foly and false heresye by force'. In Luther's Saxony, he said, they had not only polluted the churches, despised the saints, and 'ioyned freres and nunnes together in lechery'; they had also 'abhorred all good gouernance, rebelled agaynst all rulers . . .'.

The profits to be made from the Testament soon attracted printers in Antwerp, who were already major suppliers of books in English. Pirate copies started arriving in England in November 1526. They were printed in Antwerp by Christoffel van Ruremund (brother of Hans van Ruremund), poorly proofread, perhaps, on cheap paper, but issued in quantity.

Pirate editions were known on the Continent as *Nachdruck*. It is estimated that five times as many pirate Luther works sold as originals. Luther was resigned to it as inevitable – he suggested that pirates might wait at least a month 'out of Christian charity' – but it irritated. 'Some rogue steps in, a compositor who lives off the sweat of our brow, who steals my manuscript before I have finished it, takes it away, and has it printed somewhere else, ignoring our expenses and our labour,' Luther complained. He said he could tolerate this if they made a decent job of it; he might even forgive their trick of printing 'Wittenberg' on the title page of books that had never been near the town. But the pirates filled them with so many mistakes, misspellings and mismeanings that 'when they reach me I do not even recognise my own books'.

He arranged for two 'marks of quality' to be printed in authorised editions of his work. One was the Lamb with the Chalice and Flag, in which wine flows from the breast of the lamb into a chalice beneath the flag of the Cross, as a symbol of the sacrifice of Christ; it was adapted for the signs outside 'Lamb and Flag' inns and hostelries. The other was the 'Luther Rose', an armorial device he had inherited from his father, bearing the letters 'ML' and the legend: 'Let this sign be a guarantee that these books have passed through my hands, for wrong printing and corrupt books now abound.'

Those who pirated Tyndale's work used satirical colophons; one, poking fun at More, claimed to be 'Printed in Utopia'; another claimed that it was 'Printed in St Peter's at Rome *cum privilegio apostolico*', while a third was 'Printed in Basle by Adam Anonymous'. All were set in the familiar Gothic bastard type – Gothic came in three main types, 'accounting', 'breviary' and 'bastard' – in octavo on poor quality paper. Tyndale objected only when alterations were made to his text.

He found his recompense, no doubt, in the zeal of his readers. The experience of reading God's word was perilous, exciting, intoxicating, and illegal. 'It is proved lawful of God, that both men and women lawfully may read and write God's law in their mother tongue,' an anonymous pamphleteer wrote, 'and they that forbid this show themselves heirs and sons of the first tormentors, and worse, and they show themselves the very disciples of Antichrist . . . in stopping and perverting of God's law.'

By the 1580s, people were already looking back to 'the fervent zeal of those Christian days' with awe and nostalgia. The old generation seemed 'much superior to these our days and times'; they manifested this by 'sitting up all night in reading and hearing, also by their expences and charges in buying books in English . . .' The readers included barrel-makers, weavers, tailors, monks, curates, journeymen, nail-makers, pewter-workers, furriers and carpenters, and their wives, sisters and daughters. 'It is a religion of the little people,' a chronicler said.

The greatest person in the realm remained utterly opposed to the new doctrine. Henry VIII made it clear that he remained a traditionalist in dogma, hostile to Tyndale and his translation. In his *Reply to Luther*, he castigated the German for associating 'with one or two leude persons borne in this our realme for the translatyng of the Newe testament in to Englysshe as well as with many corruptions of that holy text as certayne prefaces and other

Henry VIII, ominously for Tyndale, was immensely proud of his title of Fidei
Defensor, *Defender of the Faith. This was his reward from the pope in 1521 for
writing a defence of the Catholic sacraments against Luther. In Church politics,
in his break with Rome, and the subordination of the clergy, Henry was a revo-
lutionary. In theology, however, he was intensely conservative and his rage against
'abhomynable heresyes' made him highly dangerous to Tyndale.*

(Popperfoto)

pestylente gloses in the margentes for the advancement and set-
tynge forthe of his abhomynable heresyes entendynge to abuse
the gode myndes and devotion that you oure derely beloved
people beare towarde the holy scripture'.

In particular, the king shared with his people a deep belief in
Christ's real presence in the sacrament, and a loathing of those, like
Tyndale, who denied it. Thomas Ashby, an Augustinian canon of
Bridlington, wrote of this credence in his commonplace book:

> The bread is flesh in our credence
> The wine is blood without doubtance.
> They that believe not this with circumstance,
> But doth thyemself with curious wit enhance,
> To hell pit shall they wend,
> There to torment without end.

Ashby wrote, too, of his belief in miracles, of Hartlepool sailors
rescued by the saints, and of the Gascon pilgrim who came to the
shrine of St John of Bridlington and, overcome with curiosity,
opened the reliquary containing the saint's head. Angry at being
disturbed, the saint afflicted the wretched pilgrim with terrible
pains in his head and arms as he travelled south to Huntingdon.
Here, he turned back to Bridlington to beg the saint's forgiveness,
and was restored to health.

Books on the saints outnumbered any other type. Of fifty-odd
books published by Wynkyn de Worde around the turn of the century, thirty were of this type. Between 1490 and 1530, at least
twenty-eight editions of the *Hours of the Blessed Virgin* were
printed in England. The chief English collection of pious legends
and miracles, John Myrc's *Liber Festialis*, went through nineteen
editions between 1483 and 1532. The *Golden Legend*, a collection
of lives of the saints by the Italian archbishop and hagiographer
Jacob of Voragine, went through successive editions after Caxton

first printed it in 1483. Wynkyn de Worde also published John of Tynemouth's *Sanctilogium Angliae* in 1516 with lives of the English saints. The last great English hagiography, the *Martiloge*, by the Bridgettine monk Richard Whitford, was published in 1526.

Bible-women, and Bible-reading artisans, roused a particular horror. 'Even silly little women want to pass judgment on the Bible as they might on their needle and thread,' one traditionalist wrote. Cochlaeus and More both noted the eagerness of women readers. 'Despicable women, proudly rejecting the supposed ignorance of men,' Cochlaeus wrote, were looking to the Bible rather than the Church for evidence of God's purpose; some of them 'carried it in their bosoms and learnt it by heart' and within a few months thought themselves so well versed in scripture that 'without timidity they debated not only with Catholic laymen, but also with priests and monks'.

Even after English Bibles had been legalised and officially distributed, in 1543, social and sexual misgivings remained. Noblemen and gentlemen were allowed to read the scriptures aloud in English to all in their households. Noblewomen, and burghers, could 'read for themselves but for no one else any text in the Bible'. A statute was enacted to ban the reading of the English Bible absolutely to 'women, artisans, apprentices, and companions working for those of an equal or inferior rank to yeomen, farmers and manual labourers'.

Wolsey thus had royal and popular support when he tried to attack the Testament traffic at source. The cardinal sent instructions to Sir John Hackett, the English ambassador in the Low Countries, to take legal action against printers, booksellers and shipping agents involved in the trade. Hackett received the letter on 21 November 1526. By January 1527, he had collected up enough copies to provide for book burnings in Antwerp and Bergen-op-Zoom. Hackett also forwarded a request from Wolsey to Margaret, the regent of the Low Countries, to have van Ruremund arrested and his presses destroyed.

But Hackett ran foul of local law. Imperial officials pointed out that heresy was not an extraditable offence under the treaty signed between England and the Low Countries in 1506. Treason and sedition were another matter, and the English made frequent requests for the return of traitors and rebels who had fled to the Continent. But the local courts were competent to deal with heresy, and any English heretic who was detected could be tried and burnt on the spot. Van Ruremund's lawyer denied that his client had printed any book with heresies. He added that the emperor's subjects should not be judged by the laws of other countries, and demanded that van Ruremund be set free.

Hackett wrote to Wolsey on 12 January 1527 to say that he had become so frustrated at the legal wranglings that he thought of buying up all the Testaments and sending them to London; but, 'when my choler was descended', he decided to consult the regent herself first. Van Ruremund was found guilty, perhaps through her pressure, but his stocks of books were not confiscated. Hackett asked Wolsey for evidence of treason by evangelicals so that he could produce documentation for the local courts.

Hackett went on with his uphill task. He received intelligence of a cargo of testaments, only to arrive at the port in Zeeland a few hours after the ship had sailed for Scotland. He was told that two thousand English books were being offered for sale at the April 1527 Frankfurt Book Fair but was too late to intervene. On 21 May 1527 Hackett heard that 'some new printers' in Antwerp were taking new pirate editions of the Testament to the Bergen market. He hastened to Bergen. A copy of the king's statement and a warning that all Tyndale works should be delivered up was read out to the Englishmen in Bergen by the deputy of the English Nation, the association of English traders and agents resident in the Low Countries.

In England, Archbishop Warham was discreetly buying up 'all the boks of the Newe Testament translated into Englesshe and pryented beyonde the Sea, aswel those with the gloses ioyned vnto them as th'oder withoute the gloses'. He was confident that he was blocking both the Cologne fragments with their glosses and the Worms volumes. On 26 May 1527, Warham wrote to the bishops of his province, asking them to share his current expenses of £66 9s 4d. Some of the money was no doubt spent on informers, and the cost of buying bound copies will have been at least double that of the printed sheets. Even if he laid his hands on fewer than five hundred copies, however, he amassed enough for impressive bonfires. The fierce Bishop Nix of Norwich pledged ten marks, or £6 13s 4d, in his reply, and congratulated Warham for his 'gracious and blessed deed'.

In Germany, Tyndale was parting – on bad terms – with William Roye.

9

The Fish Cellar

Roye had left Tyndale in Worms after the completion of the Testament. 'He went and gat him new friends,' Tyndale wrote. 'And there when he had stored him of money, he gat him to Argentine [Strasbourg] . . .' In May 1527, while Hackett roamed further to the north looking for him, Tyndale was visited in Worms by Jerome Barlow, a renegade friar from the same Franciscan monastery at Greenwich as Roye. He said that he wanted to 'get his living with his own hands', and to feast no longer on the sweat and labour of the laity, whom the clergy had 'taught not to believe in Christ, but in cut shoes and russet coats'. Tyndale warned him of Roye's 'boldness' in drawing attention to himself and Jerome promised to have nothing to do with him. 'Nevertheless, when he was come to Argentine,' Tyndale recollected, 'William Roye (whose tongue is able not only to make fools stark mad, but also to deceive the wisest, that is at first sight and acquaintance) gat him to him, and set him a-work to make rhymes, while he himself translated a dialogue out of Latin into English, in whose prologue he promiseth more a great deal than I fear me he ever will pay'.

Some time after his meeting with Barlow, Tyndale moved from

Worms. He may have felt that Hackett was getting too close to him, or Cochlaeus may have disturbed him. Marburg, the city eighty miles to the north west to which he is thought to have moved, was certainly safer for a Bible-man. It was ruled by Philip the Magnanimous, landgrave of Hesse, a Lutheran who was actively seeking a defensive league of Protestant princes and cities. Hesse was emerging as a sovereign state with a Lutheran university, churches and schools.

In England, high-profile arrests were being made to try to staunch the flow of Testaments. Wolsey first attacked a group of Cambridge scholars, and 'little Bilney' was the most prominent victim. Thomas Bilney was a fellow of a Cambridge college, Trinity Hall, a trained lawyer and an ordained priest who was licensed to preach in the flat and fenny diocese of Ely.

He was, so the future martyr Hugh Latimer wrote, 'meek and charitable, a simple good soul, not fit for this world'. Bilney criticised the Schoolmen for their drab theology, and delivered 'many sermons against prayers to saints and image worship'. He had a way with people. Under his influence, Latimer, originally 'as obstinate a papist as any', found that 'I began to smell the word of God, forsaking the school doctors and such fooleries.' Bilney was 'of but little stature and very slender of body', but his evangelism and work for the poor and sick had made him much loved. He was 'very fervent and studious in the Scriptures, as appeared by his sermons [and] his converting of sinners', so much so, indeed, that he was twice physically removed from the pulpit in Norwich while in full flow.

His description of reading the First Epistle to Timothy shows the extraordinary impact the Bible could make on people who, in an age steeped in the ancient religiosity of the Church, now came across the word of God itself. The Bible was, of course, more ancient than the Church, but its effects were wholly new, and devastating, and his rapture would ultimately cost little Bilney his life. 'It did so exhilarate my heart, being before wounded with the guilt of my sins, and being almost in despair,' he wrote of his discovery of St Paul and justification by faith, 'that immediately I felt a marvellous comfort and quietness, insomuch that my bruised bones leaped for joy.'

The fears of those who wished the Bible to remain locked away – Tunstall, More, the pope – were confirmed by this experience. Here was another instance of an ordained man who lost his old faith by reading it. Scripture, Bilney continued, became 'more pleasant unto me than the honey or the honeycomb, wherein I learned that all my travails, all my fasting and watching, all the redemption of masses and pardons, being done without trust in Christ, who only saveth his people from their sins, these, I say, I learned to be nothing else but even . . . a hasty and swift running out of the right way'.

Bilney laboured for 'the desperates'; he was a 'preacher to the prisoners and comfortless', and particularly for lepers. Leprosy was a disease of Old Testament terror. The consequences were so appalling – the leper was banished from society, marooned on an island of sickness until he died – that a whole chapter of Leviticus is devoted to the accurate diagnosis of the disease. Tyndale translated it with simple but vivid and clear terms. 'The Lord spake,' Tyndale wrote, 'saying: when there appeareth a rising in any man's flesh either a scab or a glistening white: as though the plague of leprosy were in the skin of his flesh . . . let the priest look on the sore'. If it 'be waxed blackish and is not grown abroad in the skin' it was simply a 'scurf', and the person was clean; but if 'there be therein golden hairs and thin, let the priest make him unclean'. As Tyndale's prose showed with brutal finality, the penalty was harsh: 'And the leper in whom the plague is, shall have his clothes rent and his head bare and his mouth muffled and shall be called unclean . . . and shall therefore dwell alone.'

Christian lepers were bound by these Old Testament regulations. They gave a warning cry – 'Unclean! Unclean!' – as they walked, or sounded a horn, and wore cloaks marked with the letter L. They were forbidden to talk to anyone unless they were downwind. They were cast out of the community in a ritual dating from 1179. The penitent leper stood by an open grave with a black cloth on his head. 'Be dead to the world, be reborn in God,' the priest said. 'Jesus, my Redeemer,' the leper responded, 'may I be reborn in Thee.' The priest then read out a proscription: 'I forbid you to enter church, monastery, fair, mill, marketplace or tavern . . . I forbid you ever to leave your house without your leper's costume . . . to live with any woman other than your own . . . to touch a well, or well cord, without your gloves . . . to touch children, or to give them anything . . . to eat or drink, except with lepers.'

St Francis had shamed cities into building leprosariums or lazarhouses outside their walls, and Bilney preached 'at the lazar cots, wrapping them in sheets, helping them of that they wanted', hoping to convert them to Christ. He had been warned not to preach Lutheran doctrines in 1526, however, and in November 1527 he was seized and charged with heresy. He denied it, and described Luther as a 'wicked and detestable heretic' during his questioning. Indeed, Bilney was not a Lutheran, in the full-blown sense that Tyndale was. Bilney's views on the sacraments and the primacy of the pope were orthodox, but his acceptance of justification by faith was evidence enough for Tunstall, who refused to hear defence witnesses before declaring him a heretic. Bilney recanted and was taken to the Tower in December 1527, where he remained for a year until Wolsey let him return to Cambridge.

In February 1528, Tunstall began a six-month campaign to arrest Lollards, Lutherans and Tyndale's Bible readers. By the middle of March, the ecclesiastical prisons in London were full and suspects were held with common criminals in the Fleet,

Newgate, the Old Compter and the Poultry Compter near
Bucklersbury. A London friar was found to have sold a copy of
Tyndale's Testament for 3s 2d to some Lollards from Essex; a
Gloucestershire priest exchanged one for a load of hay; a law student at Gray's Inn distributed them from his rooms. It was now
that the Essex men Pykas, Hilles and Tyball were seized and interrogated. Tyball admitted that he had shown his books to the curate
of Steeple Bumpstead, Richard Fox, confirming that Tyndale was
a peril to ordinary country clergymen as well as to university
trained hotheads.

Tunstall did not want blood on his hands. He did not drive suspects to the sticking point, but left them space to repent without
too much damage to conscience. The penitent was required to sign
a confession listing his 'damnable and erroneous opinions', which
he swore that 'he now utterly abjures and renounces, desiring to do
penance for the same, and promising never to return to them'.
John Hig of Cheshunt was found to have a 'boke of the Gospels'
which he expounded in alehouses. He was brought in front of Dr
Geoffrey Wharton, Tunstall's vicar general, and abjured in March
1528. The document listed his heresies. Hig had said that all men,
including laymen, could preach the gospel; he claimed that Martin
Luther was more learned than all the doctors in England, and
that the Church was blind; he had mocked those who went on pilgrimages, and called them fools; he had preached against
purgatory, saying that prayers and alms were of no value to the
dead; at mass, he 'had not done reverences at the elevation of the
Host, but kept reading his Dutch book of the Gospels'. He
abjured these beliefs, which were typical of evangelists, by signing
a formal document.

The vicar general laid down the penance. Hig was ordered to
head the procession to St Paul's Cathedral on Palm Sunday 1528,
bareheaded, shoeless and carrying a faggot on his left shoulder. He
was to remain in the custody of the apparitor, the chief officer of

the ecclesiastical court, until Good Friday, when he was to stand at St Paul's Cross, again bareheaded and carrying his faggot, throughout the preaching of the sermon. On Easter Sunday, Hig was to head the procession at his parish church in Cheshunt, bareheaded and with his faggot. He was to hear the mass on bended knee but he was not to receive communion until the following day.

As additional punishment, Hig was forbidden ever to leave the diocese of London without the permission of the bishop. He was also commanded to wear a silken faggot embroidered on his sleeve for the rest of his life. Hig pleaded for dispensation from this, on the grounds that no one would employ him if he was compelled to wear it, and he would be reduced to beggary. His abject petition for forgiveness – 'Honourable Master Doctor, I desire you to be good master to me, for I do knowledge myself that I have offended in learning the Gospels . . .' – was accepted by Dr Wharton, and the stipulation of the silken faggot was dropped. The petition was signed '*Johannis Hig, scripta manu ejus propria in turri vocata Lollards Towre*'. His incarceration in one of the most forbidding places in England no doubt made an impression on him.

Thomas More, now chancellor of the duchy of Lancaster, was increasing his activity. He had attended the Bilney trial and he was sending out informants and listeners to pry about London, hoping to come on what he called 'nyght scoles' of heresy, where small groups met behind locked doors to read Tyndale's Testament and other forbidden texts. He and Tunstall had some success; a tailor, a merchant venturer, a scrivener's servant and a shoe-maker were arrested and forced to abjure.

Hans van Ruremund, the brother of the Antwerp pirate Christoffel van Ruremund, was imprisoned in the Fleet and abjured. Tyndale's own brother John was arrested, for 'sending five marks [£3.33] to his brother William Tyndale beyond the sea, and for receiving and keeping with him certain letters from his brother'.

More personally searched Humphrey Monmouth's house in May 1528. He came too late: Monmouth confessed that 'al the lettres and treatyes that Tyndale sent me . . . I did burne them in my howse'. After witnessing Tunstall's bonfire at St Paul's Cross, Monmouth had gone straight home and burnt every piece of paper that linked him with Tyndale, letters written by Tyndale to him from Germany, a copy of Tyndale's translation of the *Enchiridion,* a collection of the sermons that Tyndale had given at St Dunstan's. 'I did burn them,' Monmouth admitted, 'for fear of the translator more than for any ill that I knew by them.'

It is a loss to history, for the letters might have cast light on the elusive translator's movements in Germany, but it was a wise precaution. More thought that Monmouth was Tyndale's chief supporter and treasurer and had the unfortunate draper imprisoned in the Tower. He was accused of multiple heresy. 'Good, sadde and discrete persons in the Citye of London,' the accusation said, a reference to More's secret informers, attested that Monmouth 'wast privy and of counsail, and diddest ayde . . . with mony . . . that the new testament translated into English by Sir William Hochin, or Tyndal, and Friar Roye, was printed and brought into this realm . . . [A]fter they were openly forbodden, as being full of errors thou hast had, red, and kept them . . . Thou hast eaten flesh in the lent season . . . hast said, affirmed and beleved that faith onlie is sufficient to save a man his sowle, without any works . . . that pilgrimages be not profitable for man's sowle and should not be used . . .' At this point, the compiler of the list became weary and concluded with the catch-all: 'Briefly, for being an advancer of all Martin Luther's opinions, etc.'

On 19 May 1528, rightly thinking that the cardinal would be more sympathetic than More, Monmouth petitioned the king through Wolsey from the Tower. 'They examined me,' Monmouth wrote, 'what exhibition I did give to anybody beyond the sea. I said, None in three years past . . .' Monmouth confirmed that he had promised Tyndale £10 while Tyndale was staying with him in London – claiming, as we have seen, that this was for saying prayers for the dead and not to finance the Bible – and that this had been sent out to him in 'Hamborow', or Hamburg. Since then, Monmouth said, 'I never sent him the value of one penny, nor never will.' Monmouth said that he was innocent of heresy, and begged to be released from the Tower before his business was ruined. More had no hard evidence against him and he was freed to restore his fortunes. He returned to the Tower one day in 1535, not this time as a prisoner but as a sheriff of the City of London to escort Thomas More, his old tormentor, to the scaffold. Monmouth was perhaps too kindly a man to have relished the irony.

The net was cast beyond London. More wrote to Oxford to have 'Henry the mancypull of White Hall' arrested and escorted to London. He was particularly concerned that suspects might learn of his interest, and have time to suspend their meetings and hide their books. He therefore asked the Oxford authorities to 'handle the matter so closelye that ther be of hys apprehension and sen-dyng upp as lytyll knowledg abrode as may bee'. A manciple was lesser fry, a college steward responsible for buying supplies, but larger names were soon forthcoming.

Thomas Garrett, a London priest and bookseller, most intrigued the heretic-hunters. He had first appeared in Oxford at Easter in 1527. He sought out Greek and Hebrew scholars, pre-tending that he wished to study their subjects, and 'distributed a great number of corrupt books among them'. He had most success at Cardinal's College. Wolsey had brought a group of eager young scholars from Cambridge to his lavish new college at Oxford. Several of them were zealous reformers, as Cambridge remained the great breeding ground of Lutheran scholars. Garrett was back in Oxford on Christmas Eve 1527, lodging with one Radley, a 'singing-man', or choirmaster, at Cardinal's College. Garrett was helped in spreading his message and his books by other members of the college, whose names included Clerke, Dalaber and Sumner.

Evidence of this 'neste of heresye' reached Dr John Loudon, the dean of New College. He noted that Garrett 'has been privily doing much hurt' ever since his arrival, and that the Cambridge graduates Clerke and Dalaber were leading others astray. The 'most towardly young men in the university' were being infected with Bible-men's ideas. Loudon found it 'clearly proved that Clerke read in his chamber Paul's Epistles to young men and those who were of two, three or four years standing in the University'. The dean said that he wished Wolsey had not invited any Cambridge men to Oxford. 'It were a gracious deed if they were tried and purged,' he wrote, 'and restored unto their mother from whence they came, if they be worthy to come thither again.' The scholars of Cambridge complained at Oxford's 'calumny which has been circulated of their being favourable to Lutheranism'; the fenmen protested that they 'have done nothing more than practice their old scholastic disputations'.

Wolsey was informed of the goings on and he gave 'secret commandment' that Garrett should be arrested. Dr Loudon reported on 24 February 1528 that the wanted man had been seized the previous Saturday, but he had escaped when the episcopal officer, Dr Cottisford, had left him locked in his rooms to attend evensong. Garrett had taken a secular scholar's coat to disguise himself; the unfortunate scholar was promptly interrogated, 'confessed his books of heresy' and was thrown into prison. Cottisford was in a state of 'extreme pensiveness' as he contemplated being disciplined for his slackness in allowing his prisoner to escape. He consulted an 'expert in astrology' who divined from the stars that Garrett had 'fled in a tawny coat south-eastward, and is in the middle of London'. In the meantime, Radley's lodgings were searched, and some of Garrett's books were found. It was reckoned that Garrett had sold as many as 350 banned books, and Dr Loudon asked that Wolsey should be warned 'what poison these booksellers bringeth into England'. He prayed God that Garrett should be caught, and that after his trial 'the University may be clear for many years'.

Garrett did not flee south east, as Cottisford's astrologer claimed, though the ports of Dover, Rye and Winchelsea were alerted, but westward. John Flooke, the vicar general of Bristol, broke the news of his arrest to Cottisford on 1 March. Garrett had abandoned the scholar's jacket and was wearing a courtier's coat and a buttoned cap. He was caught by chance, on the suspicion of a Bristol man whose son-in-law was a proctor at Oxford and had mentioned the escape. Flooke reported that he was held securely in a cell at Ilchester, the common jail of Somerset.

The fierce bishop of Lincoln, John Longland, wrote to Wolsey saying that he suspected that Garrett had corrupted the monastery at Reading, whose prior was said to have bought sixty books from him. Garrett, he said, was 'a very subtyll, crafty, soleyne and an untrewe man'. He suggested that the prior should be put in custody and the monastery searched. He also warned the cardinal that the parson of Honey Lane in Oxford, Dr Farman, and his servant John Goodale, had dealt in Garrett's books and that the names of 'many infected persons' might be learnt from them if they were imprisoned. Longland also mentioned a London bookseller, John Gough, as a prime suspect.

Gough was promptly arrested and questioned by Tunstall. The bishop reported to Wolsey on 5 March that Gough said he did not know Garrett, 'and has never dealt in forbidden books with him, or anyone at Oxford . . . He has only had a shop of his own for two years, and, before that, was servant to another.' Gough claimed that he was the victim of mistaken identity. 'The bringer of these books this year past was a Dutchman from Antwerp, named Theodoryke,' Tunstall quoted him as saying, 'who was for some time in London and has brought many books . . .' The Dutchman had 'many New Testaments in English of the little volume'; Gough said that he was careful not to 'be aknowen of them' except to those he thought would buy them and be silent. Tunstall concluded that Gough was innocent, but nonetheless he committed him to the Fleet, 'as all his other prisons are full of persons from the furthest parts of the diocese'.

Tunstall also interviewed Goodale and Dr Farman. Goodale admitted that Garrett had sent two heavy fardels, or crates, to Oxford before Christmas last, but denied that he knew what was in them. Farman for his part confessed to buying banned books, but said that he did so 'to see what opinions the Lutherans had, and be the more ready to defend the Church'. He also claimed that Wolsey had given students at Cambridge a licence to read Lutheran books. Tunstall had sent informers to listen to the sermons that Farman gave at Honey Lane, and reported to Wolsey that he 'cannot find out that he preached otherwise than well'.

John Higdon, the dean of Cardinal's College, reported to Wolsey that he was keeping 'in ward' six men – Clerke, Sumner, Betts, Frith, Bayley and Lawney. In fact, since the college was still under construction and lacked suitably secure rooms, they were 'cast into a prison, within a deep cave under the ground of the same college, where the salt fish was laid'. Radley and several others were not imprisoned, on the grounds that they were young and 'unlearned'. Higdon wrote that many members of the college were excommunicated because of contact with Garrett; he asked Wolsey to absolve them, since Easter was near and they were denied the sacrament. Garrett himself wrote to Wolsey imploring the cardinal to release him, 'not from the iron bonds which he has so justly imposed upon him, but from the more terrible bonds of excommunication, and receive the wandering sheep back into the fold . . .'.

The accused scholars were kept in the stinking fish cellar

throughout the summer. They were thus much weakened and in poor condition to withstand an outbreak of fever that swept through Cardinal's College in August. On 1 September 1528, a priest named Thomas Byrd wrote to Thomas Cromwell, Wolsey's ambitious aid and able general factotum. Byrd begged for his pension to be paid, and included intelligence he felt would be useful. He reported that Clerke and Sumner had died a few days before. 'Jesus pardon their souls!' he wrote. 'They were buried in Christian sepulture, but the Sacrament was denied them by the dean.' The others remained in the cellar – 'the university is little infect but there, our Lord preserve it!' – and Byrd reported that he had heard that they would soon be released. This proved to be accurate. Wolsey, a humane and often kindly man, was shocked by the deaths and ordered that the survivors should not be 'so straitly handled'. John Frith, a man of singular charm and courage, was let go, and soon crossed the Narrow Sea to join Tyndale.

An interesting intervention was made during the affair: Anne Boleyn took up the cause of one of the booksellers. 'I beseech your grace with all my heart,' she wrote to Wolsey, 'to remember the parson of Honey Lane for my sake shortly.' Honey Lane is a street in Oxford in which stands All Hallows Church. The rector was Thomas Farman, whom Tunstall had arrested and interviewed. Whether Anne's plea was answered is not known. Farman died a little later in 1528, having been, according to Foxe, one of those who was 'troubled and abjured'.

Two others who were implicated were later patronised by Anne. William Betts, a survivor of the cellar, returned to Corpus Christi College in Cambridge. Anne chose him as one of her chaplains in 1533. Nicholas Udall, another survivor who recanted, stayed at Oxford, although his heretical views were thought too pronounced for him to be granted his Master of Arts degree for some years. Anne commissioned him to write verses for her coronation.

Anna Bollein Queen

Henry VIII's long infatuation with Anne Boleyn – the king's 'great matter' – was of great good fortune to the evangelicals. The pope's refusal to annul Henry's marriage with Catherine of Aragon led to the break with Rome, and undermined Wolsey and More. Anne was herself reform minded. She had a copy of Tyndale's banned New Testament, and she marked passages, with her fingernail, in his book The Obedience of a Christian Man *that she wished Henry to read, and 'besowght his grace moste tenderly to reade them'. But Tyndale failed to make use of her sympathy.*

(Mary Evans Picture Library)

Anne's confidence was waxing in 1528. At the start of the year, her present to Henry was a likeness of a ship on which a 'lonely damsel' was tossed about, a mirror of her own position. The king responded with the promise that his motto for the year would be *Aut illic aut nullihi*, 'Either there or nowhere'. He wrote to her 'assuring you that henceforth my heart will be dedicated to you alone, and wishing greatly that my body was so too, for God can do it if He pleases'.

In order to ginger up God's representative on earth, Henry dispatched two envoys to Rome in February 1528 to pressure the pope to put the question of the divorce before a decretal commission that would sit in England. They took a letter from Wolsey with them, which praised the 'purity of her life, her constant virginity, her maidenly and womanly pudicity, her soberness, chasteness, meekness, humility . . .'. It added the essential dynastic rider of her 'apparent aptness for the procreation of children'. Henry wrote to Anne of his trust that, thanks to the mission, 'shortly you and I shall have our desired end, which should be more to my heart's ease, and more quietness to my mind, than any other thing in this world'.

The optimism was misplaced. Wolsey half expected as much. 'If the pope is not compliant, my own life will be shortened,' he rightly surmised, 'and I dread to anticipate the consequences.' The pope could make minor concessions, and procrastinate; but he could not close the king's 'great matter' as Henry wished. Clement VII was no longer caught between Henry and Charles V, Queen Catherine's unforgiving nephew; he was now in the latter's hands. A rabble of Spanish soldiers and German mercenaries had broken into Rome the year before. They did so in the service of Charles V, whose devotion to Catholicism was compromised by the loom of his vast possessions. He was emperor of Germany and the Low Countries, and thus numbered Tyndale among the aliens living in his territory, and he was also king of Spain and her rapidly growing lands in the New World. The excursion by his forces to Rome was part of a squeeze he was applying to the papal states, which lay between others territories of his, in Lombardy and Naples.

Some of the German mercenaries were Lutherans. Thomas More claimed that the whole force was made up of 'fierce heretiques' who were so cruel that 'they haue taught ye deuill new tormentes in hell', and whose idea of 'sporte and laughter' was 'to take the childe and bynde it to a broch [spit] and lay it to the fyre to rost'. He exaggerated – most of the Germans were Bavarian Catholics and Charles V was a notably devout Catholic himself – but they did delight in humbling the pope and his priests. Blasphemers in the Eternal City, they wore cardinals' robes, drank from sacred chalices, stabled their horses in St Peter's and the Sistine Chapel, daubed Luther's name on paintings, stole jewels and offerings from shrines, and, tearing the bones of saints from reliquaries, threw them for dogs to devour. Cardinal Giovanni del Monte, the future Pope Julius III, was hung by his hair until a ransom was paid for him. Clement VII took sanctuary in the Castel del'Angelo, a purple robe thrown over his white papal vestments to disguise him as he fled.

The sculptor, goldsmith and gloriously immodest autobiographer Benvenuto Cellini served as a volunteer bodyguard for the pope. To 'an accompaniment of blessings and cheers from a number of cardinals', Cellini claims to have felled the imperial commander with his arquebus from the castle walls. He then cut a Spanish officer in two after his shot struck the man's sword. The pope was so 'astonished and delighted', Cellini wrote, that he made the sign of the cross above Cellini's head and 'forgave me all the homicides I had ever committed and all those I ever would commit in the service of the Apostolic Church . . .'

Looting and revelry by the imperial forces was unchecked for eight days. The pope's ransom was set at 400,000 ducats. Cellini claims that Clement summoned him to a room in the castle. Here he was told to remove the gold settings from tiaras. He also took jewels from the Apostolic *camera*, or treasury, and sewed them into the linings of the pope's vestments. Cellini then built a little brick furnace and melted down the gold. It weighed some 200 pounds. 'Harassed from within and without, completely in despair', Clement used the gold to negotiate a peace. Half the population had fled and Rome was a bruised shadow of itself. That a Catholic monarch had done this added to the humbling of the Church, for, as Erasmus wrote in shame, Rome was 'not only the fortress of the Christian religion and the kindly mother of literary talent, but . . . indeed the common mother of all peoples'.

If he accommodated Henry, Clement would humiliate Queen Catherine and, by extension, Charles, her nephew. Henry was the king of a distant and sea-girt realm. Charles was the most powerful man in Christendom and his writ ran to Rome. Clement was a Medici, a cousin of the flamboyant Leo X, a most cunning diplomat and a man of the world. The prospects of him agreeing to the divorce were negligible. In two years' time, indeed, Clement was to crown Charles as Holy Roman Emperor at Bologna, the last time a pope was ever to do so, an arrangement that enabled Rome and the papal states to be restored to him.

Henry's disaffection from the papacy – though not from Catholic dogma, to which he remained firmly attached – gave Tyndale and the reformers material to work. It also strengthened Anne Boleyn's existing sympathy with reform, which she had acquired during her time at the French court. She had a handsome copy of the *Pistellis and Gospelles for the LII Sondayes in the Yere* in French, given to her by one Francis Denham, who had spent time in Paris with 'pestiferous followers of Luther', before he died of plague in 1528. The daughter of an evangelical mercer, who supplied the court with fabrics, recalled that her father used to 'go beyond the sea' because Anne 'caused him to get her the gospels and epistles written in parchment in French together with the psalms'.

Anne had no hesitation in reading banned books. It is likely that she had already bought a copy of Tyndale's New Testament. Her copy of his later revised Testament survives in the British Library, with her name and title on the edges of the leaves, and Tyndale's ragingly Lutheran prologue tactfully removed. Certainly, she had a copy of Simon Fish's *A Supplication of the Beggars* in 1528, the year that it was printed in Antwerp, where Fish was in voluntary exile. This was a violent attack on the inventions – fees for masses, dirges, hallowings, indulgences, tithes and so on – that were used by the 'ravenous wolves' of the Church to gouge ever-increasing amounts of money from the laity. A meticulous man, Fish calculated the amount to the nearest penny, as '43 thousand pounds and £333 6s 8d sterling' per year. Foxe says that Anne showed her copy to Henry, at the suggestion of her pro-evangelical brother George, and that the king was so delighted with it that he gave protection to Fish and his wife. This may well be so. Henry clearly had a professional interest in seeing the detail of how the Church parted the laity from its money, being in the same business himself; and Fish and his wife indeed benefited from a royal safe-conduct that allowed them to return to England in 1530.

10

Wicked Mammon

In Germany, Tyndale had begun work on revising his New Testament and translating the Old. He was also writing *The Parable of the Wicked Mammon*, the first work that bore his name as an author. The colophon said it was 'printed the viij day of May Anno Mdxxviij', 8 May 1528, and named the printer as 'Hans Luft of Marburg'. This was false. A printer named Hans Luft existed, certainly, but he was happily making his fortune publishing the works of Luther in Wittenberg, and he did not work for Tyndale. Neither was the actual printer in Marburg, or 'Marlborow' or 'Marborch' as the English also called it.

Mammon was printed in Antwerp, though not by Christoffel van Ruremund, who as, the pirate van Endhoven, was continuing to print copies of the New Testament. The type, paper, woodcuts and style used in this and later Tyndale books shows the true printer to be Johannes Hillenius van Hoochstraten.

Antwerp was huge, bustling, known simply as 'the Metropolis', and ideal for Tyndale. It had expanded at breakneck speed since its rival, Bruges, was cut off from the North Sea by the silting up of the River Zwin. The population, 20,000 in 1440, had reached 75,000 and was soon to peak at 125,000, more than double that of London. The Fuggers of Augsburg, the great banking dynasty, had moved their trading house to Antwerp from Bruges in 1505, and others had followed, with buildings of late Gothic bravado topped by soaring watchtowers from which to espy the shipping on the Scheldt.

It was a cosmopolitan place. Thomas More had visited the city with Erasmus, and set the opening scene of *Utopia* in an Antwerp inn; more to Tyndale's liking, Albrecht Dürer had stayed in a house on the Wolstraat. Large contingents of foreigners lived there – Englishmen, Portuguese, South Germans, Hanseatic men and Castilians – who were organised into Nations, enjoying some immunity from local legislation. A stranger with Tyndale's skills at cloaking himself could pass unnoticed.

The city had no bishop and no university. This was to Tyndale's advantage. No senior churchman was on the spot to bully the city authorities into arresting heretics, and there were no radical university teachers and students to catch the repressive attention of the Church. He had no shortage of kindred spirits, however. The first Lutherans to be spotted by officials in the Seventeen Provinces of the Low Countries were in Antwerp. The Augustinian prior in the city was identified as a supporter of Luther very early on, in 1519, and two of his fellow Antwerp Augustinians, Hendrik Voes and Johannes Esschen, became the first martyrs of the Reformation when they were burnt in Brussels. The city magistrates, however, were proud of their autonomy and conscious that religious intolerance would sit badly with the trading freedoms on which their prosperity was founded.

The printing industry was outranked only by Venice and Paris. It was perfect for Tyndale's needs. Antwerp printers published work in Dutch, English, French, Spanish, Italian and Latin, and in the biblical languages, Greek and Hebrew. They were the leading printers of English language books, outstripping the small London printing trade. Books were a heavy cargo, but it was no problem to find a merchant ship to carry them across the Narrow Sea. Wharves ran along the bank of the Scheldt for more than a mile, making Antwerp the greatest port in northern Europe. Scores of ships served the English trade, carrying Flemish cloth, Rhenish wines, Venetian velvets and silks and glassware, and pepper and cinnamon transshipped from Portugal.

Censorship was an irritant to the evangelical book trade with England but it failed to stop it. Antwerp became a phenomenon, a Catholic city that was a centre for Lutheran, and then Anabaptist and Calvinist, propaganda. The theological faculty at Louvain university, the heart of ultra-Catholic feeling in the Low Countries, did its best to prevent this. It condemned Lutheran works in November 1519, seven months before the pope did so, and ten months before Charles V banned their publication in the Low Countries. The first public book burnings in Antwerp were held in July 1521 and were swiftly followed by three more. Printers merely took precautions – false colophons and bills of lading, aliases, bribes, the use of smuggling skippers – and continued publishing. The big printer Michael Hillenius van Hoochstraten, probably a relative of Johannes, was typical in simultaneously publishing works by Luther and attacks on him by Fisher and Henry VIII. Profit came before theology.

At least ten Antwerp printers were producing heretical material in 1528, in French, Danish, Dutch, English and even Spanish. The pirate Christoffel van Endhoven, or van Ruremund, was one of them; the most daring was Adriaen van Berghen, who was to be sent on a penitential pilgrimage to Cyprus, only to be executed when he relapsed and was again found trading in banned books. Tyndale chose well with Johannes van Hoochstraten. He was 'as wise as a serpent', discreet, avoiding arrest by publishing orthodox books bearing his own name, and using aliases and false addresses for his heretical output. His colophons gave Basle and 'Wittemberch', 'Argentorati' and 'Marborch' and 'Marlborow', respectively Wittenberg, Strasbourg and Marburg, as the place of publication, and 'Adam Anonymous', 'Peter Congeth', 'Joannes Philoponos' and 'Steffan Rodt' as the printer. For his work with Tyndale, he used 'Hans Luft' and 'Marburg'.

Tyndale was almost certainly in Antwerp while *Wicked Mammon* was printed, a slim octavo volume in Gothic black-letter type, with no title page or marginal notes. He identified himself as a heretic in the first line of the introduction. 'That faith the mother of all good works justifieth us, before we can bring forth any good work,' he wrote, 'as the husband marrieth his wife before he can have any lawful children by her.' He felt himself to be in some peril while the book was being produced, and was clearly relieved to have finished it at all. It was rushed, with many printing errors. In his apology below the colophon, he asked the reader not to be offended by the apparent negligence in printing, 'for verily the chance was such, that I marvel it is so well as it is'.

The preface was headed 'William Tyndale otherwise called hychins to the reader'. The game of his anonymity was over, and he explained why 'I set my name before this little treatise, and have not rather done it in the New Testament'. He said that Christ had exhorted men to do their good deeds in secret, and to be content with a good conscience and the knowledge that 'God seeth us'. But he felt obliged to dissociate himself publicly from a book of scurrilous doggerel attacking Tunstall and Wolsey, which people assumed that he had written, but which was in fact the work of William Roye and Jerome Barlow.

Barlow had ignored Tyndale's advice and had gone straight to join Roye at Strasbourg. Here Roye published a translation of a short Lutheran instruction book for children, *Brief Dialogue between A Christian Father and his Stubborn Son*, which was printed at the end of August 1527. Introducing it, Roye wrote that some of his readers would know 'how this last year, the new testament of our saviour, was delivered unto you, through the faithful and diligent study of one of our nation'. He identified this as 'William Hitchyns', to whom, he added, he was 'help fellow, and partaker of his labours'. Much to his irritation, Tyndale had now been named in print as the translator.

Worse, Roye and Barlow had jointly produced a rhyming satire that they called *Rede me and be nott wrothe*. It opened with a cartoon of Wolsey with six axes. Red ink was used for his cardinal's hat and for the drops of blood that fell from the axes. The poem was in the form of a conversation between Jeffrey and Watkin, the two servants of a priest, who discuss the burning of Tyndale's Testament:

JEFFREY:	They set not by the gospel a fly
	Didst thou not hear what villainy
	They did unto the gospel?
WATKIN:	Why? did they against him conspire?
JEFFREY:	By my troth they set him afire
	Openly in London city.
WATKIN:	Who caused it to be done?
JEFFREY:	In sooth the bishop of London
	With the cardinal's authority;
	Which at Paul's Cross earnestly
	Denounced it to be heresy . . .

Though the verse was primitive compared to his prose, Tyndale had himself attacked the bishop and the cardinal in more savage terms. It was the crudely expressed theology, and the claim that another hand had helped him write the prologue to his Testament, that most angered Tyndale in these lines:

JEFFREY:	In a certain prologue they write,
	That a whore or open sinner,
	By means of Christ our redeemer,

Whom God to repent doth incite
Shall sooner come to salvation
By merits of Christ's passion
Than an outward holy liver.

The prologue had not been written by 'they', Tyndale and Roye, but by 'him', Tyndale alone. He went on to lambast Roye and Barlow for failing to 'suffer the evil with meekness' – a charge that could as easily be made against himself – and for not making their points peacefully and rationally. He was also angry that they should treat the saving merits of Christ's Passion, a central part of Lutheran dogma, in frivolous verse. 'It becometh not then the Lord's servant to use railing rhymes,' he wrote, 'but God's word; which is the right weapon to slay sin, vice and all iniquity.'

With Roye thus rubbished in the prologue, *Mammon* then drove home the Lutheran message that a Christian is justified by faith alone. Faith is 'mighty in operation, full of virtue and ever working . . . and it setteth the soul at liberty and maketh her free to follow the will of God'. Good works are subsidiary to faith, for 'deeds are the fruits of love, and love is the fruit of faith'. Mary Magdalene washed Jesus' feet with her tears and anointed them through the love that came from faith; she 'did inflame and burn in love, yea was so swollen in love, that she could not abide nor hold, but must break out . . .'. Lyricism and tenderness cascade through Tyndale when he writes of faith and love. The crabbiness and tantrums that cloud his prose at the mention of pope or priest are dispelled; Mary is 'overcome and overwhelmed with the unspeakable yea and incomprehensible abundant riches of the kindness of God', and, kneeling before Christ, would 'have run into the ground under his feet to have uttered her love toward him, yea would have descended down into hell . . .'.

He saw the gospels as a part of that love; he adored them, in the religious sense. When we hear the gospels, he wrote in *Mammon*, we believe in the mercy of God, and through that we receive the spirit of God, and then, why – we 'are in the eternal life already, and feel already in our hearts the sweetness thereof, and are overcome with the kindness of God and Christ and therefore love the will of God, and of love are ready to work freely'. The Bible, and the faith that flowed from it, 'reneweth . . . and begetteth afresh', so that a man 'hath power to love that which before he could not but hate'. To Tyndale, it poured into the soul as 'health doth unto the body, after that a man is pined and wasted away with a long soking [consuming] disease'. The vernacular Bible had an intensity that could never be repeated. Lollards had willingly paid a wagon load of hay for a few hand-copied scraps of Paul's Epistles; but now the New Testament burst out in living English in the still new and vivid medium of print. With its explanatory glosses and marginal notes and prologues, it was a complete route-map to salvation.

Tyndale's sarcasms returned the moment he dealt with the Church. It had taught for centuries, of course, that it was itself the pathway to heaven. Tyndale ridiculed this claim. No salvation could come from the Church, he said. Popes, cardinals and bishops differed only in name from the Pharisees and Antichrists who had taken Jesus in front of Pilate. 'They do all things of a good zeal, they say, they love you so well,' Tyndale warned, 'that they had rather burn you than you should have fellowship with Christ.'

Good works flow naturally from faith. From lack of faith, he wrote in homely fashion, comes the man who looks to 'buy as good cheap as he can, and sell as dear as he can, to raise the market of corn and victuals for his own vantage, without the respect of his neighbour . . .'. Not to help a brother or a neighbour was to rob Christ, for 'every Christian is heir annexed with Christ'. And Christ was all: 'Our Redeemer, Saviour, peace, atonement, and satisfaction to Godward for all the sin which they that repent . . . do, have done, or shall do. So that if through fragility we fall a thousand times in a day, yet if we do repent again, we have always mercy laid up for us in store in Jesus Christ our Lord.'

Only the blood and merit of Christ can save. Without it, the reader was doomed, even 'though thou hast a thousand holy candles about thee, a hundred tons of holy water, a ship-full of pardons, a cloth-sack full of friar's coats, and all the ceremonies in the world, and all the good works, deservings, and merits of all the men in the world, be they, or were they, ever so holy'. All works are good that are done within the law of God. This includes pissing and breaking wind, for 'trust me if either wind or water were stopped thou shouldest feel what a precious thing it were to do either of both, and what thanks ought to be given God therefore'. By the same token, he said, a kitchen page was as pleasing to God as an apostle: 'if thou compare deed to deed there is a difference betwixt washing of dishes and preaching the word of God', but 'as touching to please God none at all'.

This held true for all his readers, and his description of them – 'whether brewer baker tailor victualler merchant or husbandman' – showed all too clearly to worried churchmen that Tyndale had indeed set his sights on the common man as a recipient of scripture.

He added that to pay a priest to pray for the dead was absurd, a statement that made a mockery of Monmouth's claim that he had given Tyndale £10 to pray for the souls of his parents. 'If thou give me £1000 to pray for thee, I am no more bound than I was before,' Tyndale wrote. 'I am bound to love the Turk with all my might and power – yea, and above my power – even from the ground of my heart, after the ensample that Christ loved me; neither to spare goods, body or life, to win him to Christ. And what can I do more for thee, if thou gavest me all the world?'

Tyndale was rightly confident that *Mammon* would share the fate of his Testament. Some would ask why he had written it, he said, 'inasmuch as they will burn it, seeing they burnt the gospel'. If that was God's will, he welcomed it: 'not more shall they do,' he added, 'if they burn me also'.

Tyndale was wrong, however, to presume that life would be made 'joyful' when its every aspect was referred to the Bible. The Swiss reformer Huldrych Zwingli was already creating the high-handed, snooping and self-righteous prototype of the Protestant pastor-prig of future caricature.

Zwingli had been elected priest of Zurich's Great Minster a decade before, in 1518. He prided himself on studying the Greek and Latin philosophers 'day and night', believing that this toil 'tames and perhaps extinguishes unchaste desires'. He preached at great length on the New Testament books, starting with Matthew and slowly working his way through the Acts and the Epistles. He accompanied his sermons with diatribes against papal superstition and vice, rebuking his congregation for their idleness, gluttony, rich clothing and suppression of the poor. This was not appreciated by all. Drunks mobbed his house and 'threw stones, broke windows, shouted, scolded and raged . . .'.

The reforms in place in Zurich by 1528 far exceeded those of Luther. Relics and images were stripped from churches and sold or smashed. Altars were bared of decorations. Organs were dismantled. Hymns were replaced by the singing of metrical psalms. Ministers wore ordinary clothes and faced the congregation. Worship was daily with a plain liturgy and interminable sermons. People 'spend the time of the sermon voluptuously in inns', the city council complained. '[S]ome of them even ridicule and abusively insult the Word of God and its proclaimers . . . Everybody is to be obediently present at the third ringing of the bells. Nobody is to evade this.'

But of course they did. They were found wandering on the bridges, along the moats and down alleys at sermon-time. It was decreed that all sermons should begin at the same time to make it easier to enforce attendance. The death sentence was imposed on heretics. The Zwinglians did not burn. They drowned. The year before, in 1527, a young Anabaptist had been led to the fish market and taken aboard a boat with his hands tied. As he 'sang with a clear voice "*In manus tuas, domine, commendo spiritum meum*"', the executioner pushed him into the waters of the Zurich lake.

The Bible could be quoted to elevate misdemeanours and simple pleasures into 'intolerable crimes'. Drinking, card-playing, singing, 'dancing and like dissolute behaviour', the wearing of slashed breeches – all these were to be censored by elders appointed to 'keep watch over the lives of everyone, to admonish in love those whom they see erring and leading disorderly lives and, whenever necessary, to report them to the body which will be designated to make fraternal correction . . .'.

And there was a joy in English Catholicism that Tyndale wilfully overlooked. The hundreds of religious guilds in towns and villages were societies of real spirituality. They maintained schools and almshouses, and gave their members a dignified funeral and intercessionary masses. Tyndale mocked their collective chantries and their mystery plays, but the plays brought colour and entertainment to the living, and the chantries reassured even the poorest that their souls would be prayed for after their death. He ridiculed the building of St Peter's at Rome, too, as papal pretension, but the villagers of Louth had just completed the building of a 300-foot steeple of soaring grace that pierced the skies above the Lincolnshire flatlands like a sword of faith. It took them fourteen years, and £305, a small fortune. They held a ceremony when the weathercock was lifted into place. The parish priest, Will Ayleby, 'hallowed the said weathercock and the stone that it stands upon . . . and the kirkwardens garte ring all the bells, and cawsed all the people to have bread and ale, and all to the loving of God, Our Lady and All Saints'.

It was no doubt nonsense, as Tyndale said, for people to raise their eyes to look at the Host during the Eucharist. Many did so because they believed they would prosper and avoid blindness and sudden death that day. But it gave them comfort. Long after its monks had been dispersed, secret pilgrimages were made at night to the site of Mountgrace Priory in the oakwoods beneath the windwracked Cleveland Moors by 'divers and sundry superstitious and popishly affected persons' who found a haunting spirituality amid the crumbling cells of its departed solitaries.

There was Tyndale's love of the gospels; but there was Catholic love, too, of long tradition, of the scented beauty of the mass and the cadence of Church music, of the colour and pomp and circumstance of Church processions, of the consolation of confession and the companionship of pilgrimage, of all those things – cherubims and seraphims, gargoyles and grotesques – that, as Pope Nicholas had said, held the eye.

Mystic hermits like Richard Methley, who died in 1528, found the same rapture in the damp English woodlands that Tyndale found in the Bible. 'In the beginning thou shalt feel some penance or pain, but ever after thou shalt live like a throstle-cock or a nightingale for joy, and thank God,' Methley wrote of his solitude. 'God visited me with great force, for I languished in such love that I almost expired . . . As men in peril of fire are only able to ejaculate the single word "fire", so, as the language of love grew stronger, I could scarce think at all, but merely formed in my spirit the words "love, love, love"; and at last, ceasing even from this, I wondered how I might wholly breathe out my soul, singing in spirit through joy . . .'

11

Manhunt

It took *Mammon* only a few weeks to get from Antwerp to England – Tunstall was picking up copies by June 1528 – and More denounced it as 'a very *mammona iniquitas*, a very treasury and wellspring of wickedness . . . by which many have been beguiled and brought into many wicked heresies'. It was promptly added to the list of banned books.

Wolsey moved directly against the evangelical exiles on 18 June. He ordered Sir John Hackett to secure the arrest and delivery of Tyndale, Roye and an English merchant named Richard Herman. Hackett was instructed to make a formal application for extradition to Margaret, the regent of the Low Countries and, like Queen Catherine, an aunt of Charles V.

The information about Herman came from one of Tunstall's best catches. He had arrested Robert Necton, a major bookseller in London and East Anglia, in March 1528. Necton had confessed that he had 'bought at various times many of the New Testaments in English' from a Mr Fyshe, who lived at Whitefriars in London, and who in turn had them off 'one Harmond, an Englishman, beyond the sea'. Harmond was otherwise known as Herman. Necton said that he had been introduced to Fyshe by 'vicar

Constantyne'. He had sold five Testaments to one William Furboshore, a 'singing-man' in Stowmarket, for 'seven or eight groats apiece', or between 2s 4d and 2s 8d. He implicated the unfortunate Thomas Farman of Honey Lane, saying that he had bought 'eighteen New Testaments of the smaller size' from the rector's servant, and adding that he had 'much resorted' to Farman's sermons. Necton went on to say that 'about Christmas last a Dutchman, now in the Fleet, offered to sell him 200 or 300 English testaments, at 9d each; but he did not buy, only sending him to Mr Fyshe'. Necton said that he had first obtained 'the chapters of Matthew', referring to the sheets that Tyndale had salvaged from Cologne. He then spoke of two sizes of Testaments, 'great' and 'small' volumes, referring to the original Worms copies and the van Endhoven pirate edition.

Hackett wrote to Wolsey on 14 July 1528. He said that 'my Lady [the regent] has caused great diligence to be made for the apprehension of the three heretics', but Tyndale and Roye 'could not be found'. Another English priest was taken, a mass priest from St Botolph's in London called Akyrston, whom Hackett was told 'has born a fagot at home, but for all that cannot refrain his tongue from evil speaking'. Of the big fish, there was no trace.

He had done better with the bookseller. Hackett went on to say that he had 'caused Ric. Harman to be arrested at Antwerp . . . and his wife, as suspected of the same faction'. Herman's goods and books 'are inventoried in the emperor's hands'. Hackett said that it was vital to have him extradited, 'for he is the root of great mischief'. He said that it would be best if the king or Wolsey 'write for his delivery as a traitor'. They would then have 'two strings to our bow'. Hackett feared that Herman would 'escape with a slanderous punishment' if he was charged with heresy, because he would be able to recant. 'But they cannot pardon him for treason against the King,' he wrote, 'in consequence of the statutes of intercourse dated 1506.' This was the extradition treaty between England and the Low Countries, which obliged each country to return the other's traitors where the evidence warranted it. He advised Wolsey that it 'would be a good thing if Lutherans were included with traitors', so as to make extradition easier. He argued that they were traitors anyway, 'for as soon as they have passed the sea they know neither King nor God'.

Hackett wrote a personal note at the end of the letter. 'As for myself,' he said, 'my heart is much better than my purse.' He was paying out large amounts of cash to try to pick up Tyndale's scent.

At the end of August 1528, Wolsey sent another hunter over the sea, John West, a friar observant from Greenwich. He had been in the same monastery as Roye and Barlow. It was wrongly thought that Roye was still with Tyndale, and that, when West tracked down his former Greenwich colleague, he would lead them to Tyndale.

West lodged himself in the Franciscan monastery in Antwerp and set to work. He first asked Sir John Style, the ranking expatriate Englishman, to get into Herman's house and look at his correspondence and books. Style told Hackett when he wrote to him on 2 September 1528 that he was at first faced with 'crafty delays'. When he finally got permission to search the house, he found that the seals placed on it when Herman was arrested had been broken. As he started searching, local people came and said that it was shameful that the king of England's lackey should be allowed to rummage through an Antwerp merchant's house. There were no books in the house. Style presumed that they were in the custody of the court.

He did, however, find four letters in English which were relevant to the case. One was from a Richard Halle, a London ironmonger, asking for two copies of Tyndale's New Testament. A letter from John Sadler of London, dated 3 September 1526, warned of news that English Testaments were to be 'put down and burnt'. Thomas Davy, of Cranbrook in Kent, urged Herman to keep his faith in Christ, and told him that none could speak of the New Testament in English 'on pain of bearing a fagot'. A final letter from another Cranbrook man, John Andrews, dated 20 February 1527, asked about the supply of Testaments. Style added a postscript to his letter. 'Harman's wife is a mischievous woman of her tongue,' he wrote, 'and as ill of deeds.'

West confirmed this account in his own letter to Hackett, written the same day. He noted with satisfaction that John Andrews had already been arrested and was in the Fleet prison in London. He also advised Hackett that 'I trust to catch another priest, come out of England, called Constantinus, who dresses like a secular.'

His main news was of a promising lead on Tyndale. West said that he had spoken with a local bookbinder and bookseller called Francis Byrkman who told him that Roye and Barlow, with 'Hucthyns otherwise called Tyndale', had written the book that had recently so angered the king and Wolsey. This referred to *Rede me*. West's bookbinder was wrong to think that Tyndale had a hand in it, but he was right to say that 'one John Schott, a printer of Strassburg, printed them' and that there is 'yet another whole pipe of them at Frankfurt' waiting to be sold at the autumn fair.

Byrkman was, in fact, actively trading in pirate copies of Tyndale's work on his own account. After his death two years later, as we have seen, a judgement was secured in Antwerp against his heirs over an unpaid balance owed by Byrkman for the delivery of more than seven hundred pirate Tyndale Testaments. Byrkman thus had firsthand knowledge of illegal printing; he had made money from the evangelicals' books and he suggested a way of snaring them to make more. He wanted West to write him a letter commissioning him to buy up copies of *Rede me*. 'If he buyeth them,' West wrote, 'he intended to send Roye with the other two to receive there the money for the books, and then I and Mr Herman Ryng of Cologne shall take them there.' 'Ryng' was Hermann Rinck, the senator who sold his services to the English crown, and who had aborted Tyndale's Cologne print run in 1525.

Another friar observant, named Flegh, was sent out from London to provide back-up for West. The two friars set out from Antwerp for Cologne in mid-September, changing out of their monastic dress so that their quarry would not recognise them. Wolsey commissioned Rinck on 21 September to 'buy up everywhere books printed in English and to seize Roye and Hutchins'. Rinck replied to the cardinal accepting the proposition on 4 October 1528. The heretics had not been at Frankfurt since Easter and the fair next to Lent, he said, 'nor is it known whither they have gone, and whether they are alive or dead'.

Their work, on the other hand, was all too evident in books that 'are crammed with heresy, offensive to your grace, and make the king odious to all Christians'. He was referring primarily to *Rede me*, thinking it to be written jointly by Tyndale and Roye. Something could be done about them, but Rinck warned that it would be expensive. He said that he had learnt that 'those very books had been pawned to the Jews at Frankfurt for a certain sum of money', and he had been thinking of buying them up 'on my own account' even before he had heard from the cardinal, doubtless to sell them on to English agents at a good profit. But the printer – Rinck confirmed that it was John Schott of Strasbourg – insisted that interest must be paid to the Jews, that he himself wanted to be compensated for his labour and the cost of the paper, and that he would sell them to the highest bidder.

Rinck said that he had 'spared no labour or expense' – after almost five hundred years, the whiff of the gravy train in his letter is as fresh as ever – in distributing 'gifts' to 'the consuls of Frankfurt and some of the senators and judges' in return for authority to collect books by Tyndale and Roye wherever he could find them. All the books were now safely in his hands, he said, with the exception of two copies which he had given to West to take to Wolsey. Rinck claimed that, unless he had intervened, the books were to have been bound and concealed in paper covers, packed in bundles of ten, and then covered with flax. They were then to have been 'craftily and without suspicion transported across the sea to Scotland and England', there 'to be sold merely as blank paper'. Rinck claimed that the printer had been forbidden to print any more copies, and that he had taken an oath to obey 'and also to send me the original written copy'. Rinck assured Wolsey that he 'will make the most strenuous efforts to arrest the aforesaid Roy and Hutchins . . . and find out where they live'.

Someone, Rinck or the printer Schott, was lying. Perhaps each of them was, for there was money in it for both of them. Rinck told Wolsey of a ceremonial oath in front of the consuls at Frankfurt. Here, 'using my papal and imperial mandates', he compelled Schott to swear how many copies of *Rede me* and *Brief Dialogue* he had printed. 'He confessed on oath,' Rinck claimed, 'that he had only printed a thousand books of six sheets and a thousand of nine sheets, and this at the order of Roy and Hutchins.'

But Hutchins–Tyndale had not ordered these two little works, which he loathed as heartily as he despised Roye. The scene is pure fiction. It is conceivable that Schott misled Rinck, though barely so, since the printer will have not have known the deep interest that Rinck's well-heeled patrons in England were taking in Tyndale. Rinck had every reason to involve Tyndale, by fraud if necessary; it was what his paymaster, Wolsey, wished to hear. And by inventing a scene in which the printer confirmed on oath the numbers of sheets he had printed, Rinck was able to show how brilliantly he had scotched their distribution. 'I have therefore bought almost the whole,' he wrote in a purr of self-satisfaction, 'and have them in my house in Cologne.' That left one last detail – to get a price from Wolsey. 'Will your grace inform me,' Rinck concluded, 'what you wish to do with the books thus purchased?'

Rinck sent Wolsey a bill for £63 4s for his services. It was still unpaid the following spring. Wolsey had other things on his mind. The divorce of Henry from Catherine had seemed to be set fair a few months before, but now it was haunting him more than ever. The hopes of the king, and of Anne Boleyn, were constantly being raised and then dashed, a cycle that infuriated the hot-tempered Henry.

Matters had seemed much more promising in the spring. The envoys sent to Rome – Stephen Gardiner, Wolsey's secretary, and Edward Foxe, an expert in canon law – had been granted an audience with the pope. Clement said that he had heard that the king's wish for an annulment was motivated by his personal lust and 'vain affection and undue love' for an unworthy lady. Gardiner replied that Anne was 'animated by the noblest sentiments', that 'all England do homage to her virtues', and that Queen Catherine suffered from 'certain diseases' which meant that Henry could not treat her as his wife. This was nonsense. The queen was too old to have any real hope of producing a male heir, but she was otherwise healthy enough, and the English had a warmth and respect for her that sharpened the public contempt for Anne. She was called 'Nan Bullen the naughty paikie', or 'the King's whore', which meant the same.

Gardiner's counterattack, and his bullying of the pope, were nonetheless effective. The pope agreed to send Cardinal Lorenzo Campeggio to try the case for an annulment with Wolsey in England. Campeggio had first visited England a decade before, to whip up support for a crusade against the Turks. Henry had later made him bishop of Salisbury, a position he combined with the archbishopric of Bologna and residence in Rome. He was the preferred candidate to hear the case and Henry greeted the news with 'marvellous demonstrations of joy'. Wolsey was less optimistic. 'I would obtain the decretal bull with my own blood if I could,' he said.

The harvest in 1528 was poor, the weather foul and mortality high with bouts of sweating sickness. This plague killed most of its victims on the first day, sometimes within an hour or so of the first appearance of the symptoms, a 'profuse sweat which devours the frame' accompanied by a foul smell with a 'great and strong savore' and thirst and delirium. Thomas More believed the hunger and sickness to be punishment from God for the import of Tyndale's heresy into the realm through 'the receypte of these pestylente bokes'. Henry ascribed it to the Almighty's vengeance for his efforts to divorce Catherine. His guilty conscience and hypochondria kept him in her company through most of May and June, as he moved his court from house to house ahead of the plague.

In mid-June, one of Anne's waiting ladies caught the sickness. Anne was sent home to her father's castle at Hever. 'I implore you, my entirely beloved, to have no fear at all,' Henry wrote to her from a safe distance. 'Wheresover I may be, I am yours.' Wolsey took advantage of Anne's absence, and Henry's renewed companionship with the queen, to urge him to drop his annulment suit. The French ambassador witnessed the scene when Henry opened the cardinal's letter. 'The king used terrible words, saying he would have given a thousand Wolseys for one Anne Boleyn,' he reported. 'No other than God shall take her from me . . .'

God came close to doing so. Anne caught the sweating sickness in late June, on the same day that her brother-in-law died of it. Henry sent Dr William Butts, a royal physician, post-haste to Hever. Anne had only a mild case of the sickness and she was soon fully recovered.

Butts, as it chanced, was an evangelical and he funnelled her grateful support and patronage to his fellow believers. Butts was a graduate of Gonville Hall at Cambridge, a centre of the 'evangelycall fraternyte', and so notoriously radical that the reactionary Bishop Nix of Norwich fumed: 'I heare not clerk that hath come out lately of that college but savoureth of the frying pan, though he speak never so holily.' Anne was generous, and the contact with Butts enabled her to pass on money to support poor students with Lutheran sympathies. One fortunate scholar was given the handsome sum of £40 to study abroad for a year; another recalled years later that she had 'employed her bountiful benevolence upon sundry students, that were placed at Cambridge'.

The love of the king's life was increasingly sympathetic to Tyndale and his sort, while Henry himself was maddened by the pope. Cardinal Campeggio did not leave Rome until the end of July 1528. He did not arrive in London until 8 October, travelling at a snail's pace. The pope had instructed him to try to 'restore the mutual affection between the king and queen', and if this proved impossible to 'protract the matter for as long as possible'. Campeggio used his painful bouts of gout as an excuse for his tardiness. The following day he met with Wolsey. Rinck's letter from Cologne arrived at this time, together with pleas from Hackett asking for evidence linking Herman with sedition and treason, without which the Antwerp court would not proceed with the prosecution. But the Tyndale affair played second fiddle to Wolsey's discussions with Campeggio on Henry's 'great matter'.

Campeggio suggested that the best solution was for Henry to become reconciled with Catherine. It was no surprise that, as he reported back to the pope, he had 'no more success in persuading the Cardinal than if I had spoken to a rock'. He spoke with the king on 22 October. He made the mistake of showing Henry a decretal bull, which the pope had secretly signed for use if the marriage could be honourably annulled – if, for example, Catherine could be persuaded to enter a nunnery. Though Campeggio told the king that it was 'not to be used, but kept secret', Henry naturally assumed that he would have it. Nothing would satisfy the king short of papal confirmation that his marriage was invalid. 'If an angel was to descend from heaven,' Campeggio thought, 'he would not be able to persuade him to the contrary.'

Catherine was as uncompromising as the king when she met Campeggio and Wolsey. She swore that she had never consummated her first marriage to the king's dead brother, and said that she 'intended to live and die in the estate of matrimony to which God had called her'.

12

Obedience

On 2 October 1528, Tyndale published *The Obedience of a Christian Man*. It was also paperback size, closely printed in Gothic black letter type. It laid out in thrusting prose the two great principles of the English Reformation: the supremacy of the scriptures over the Church, and of the king over the State.

Tyndale made the first point in one of the marginal notes that peppered the book like newspaper crossheads. 'Christ is all to a Christian man', he wrote. Rome's claims were dismissed as pithily: 'The pope's dogma is bloody.' The monarch, a point Henry VIII did not overlook, was invested with absolute authority: 'A king is a great benefit be he never so evil.'

A false colophon claimed that *Obedience*, like *Mammon*, was printed 'at Marlborow in Hesse . . . by me Hans Luft'. The ten copies that survive suggest that Tyndale changed printers to work with Martin Lempereur in Antwerp. Lempereur was a Frenchman who settled in Antwerp in 1525, where his name was translated as De Keysere, or Caesar. He printed humanist works, school texts and historical writings in his legitimate business. For his heretical books, however, he falsified the colophons to show that they were

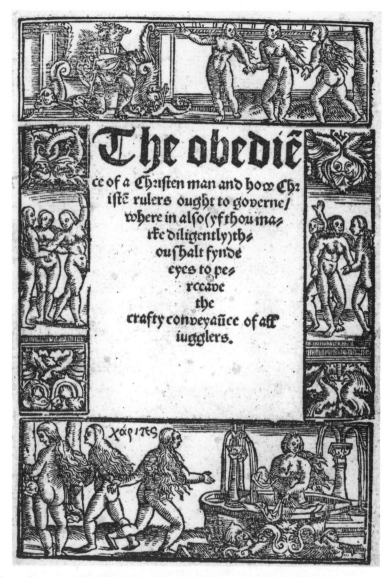

The title page of Tyndale's Obedience, *which he had printed in October 1528. The border was a job lot of woodcuts already used in two books printed in Cologne. The content, however, was a fresh and brilliant argument in favour of the authority of kings over popes. More called it 'a holy boke of disobedyence'. The first copies were smuggled into England within a few weeks. It was banned, and soon joined the New Testament in the flames at St Paul's Cross.*

(British Library)

printed by 'Iacobum Mazochium' at Tiguri or Zurich, 'at Argentine by me Francis Foxe', or 'at Straszburg by Balthassar Beckent'. For *Obedience,* Lempereur continued with van Hoochstraten's Luft identifier.

Where Tyndale wrote it is not certain. He knew that he was being hunted, and he may have been especially vigilant, for he referred with feeling in the book to the spies that the Church employed in every parish, 'in every great man's house and in every tavern and ale house. And through confession know they all secrets, so that no man may open his mouth to rebuke whatsoever they do, but that he shall shortly be made a heretic.' He was able to preserve the secret of his own whereabouts, despite the searching made by the ambassador, Hackett, by Style, the leader of the English expatriates, and by at least three commissioned agents, West, Flegh and Rinck.

Obedience was relatively free of printing errors, a sign that an English-speaker had watched it into the page, and Tyndale was most probably in Antwerp to oversee its printing in September and October 1528. While it was coming off the presses, Rinck and West were chasing red herrings in Cologne and among the bookstalls at the autumn Frankfurt Fair. But Style and Hackett were in Antwerp and will have visited the streets around the Onze-Lieve-Vrouwekathedraal, where the print shops were. Neither man knew Tyndale, however, and whatever description they had been given from London was four years out of date by now.

Tyndale began his preface by acknowledging that the reader as well as the writer of the book was putting his life in danger. 'Let it not make thee despair, neither yet discourage thee, O reader,' he wrote, 'that it is forbidden thee in pain of life and goods, or that it is made breaking of the king's peace, or treason unto his highness, to read the word of thy soul's health . . .' His prose has a melody that pleads to be read aloud, as indeed it was, of course, in meetings of fearful men and women – with an eye on the window, and an ear for the footfall of a bishop's officer – who gained strength from that salving phrase 'the word of thy soul's health' and from the call to courage that followed it. 'But much rather be bold in the Lord, and comfort thy soul,' Tyndale went on. 'Christ is with us until the world's end. Let his little flock be bold therefore, for if God be on our side, what matter maketh it who be against us, be they bishops, cardinals, popes or whatsoever names they will?'

He wrote of endurance with the striding rhythm and resonance of his New Testament. 'If God provide riches, the way thereto is poverty,' he warned. 'Whom he loveth, he chasteneth; whom he exalteth, he casteth down; whom he saveth, he damneth first. He bringeth no man to heaven, except he send him to hell first.' The notion of God working with the existing Church was dismissed with the vivid disdain of a simple metaphor. 'He is no patcher. He cannot build on another man's foundation,' he wrote of God. 'We are called, not to dispute as the pope's disciples do, but to die with Christ, that we may live with him, and to suffer with him, that we may reign with him.'

This was English that could growl, or slash and burn, or float as lightly as dandelion down, steeped in a liveliness that had died in Latin. It was a language able to meet every demand made of it. Tyndale said that it was nonsense to pretend that English was 'too rude' to express the scriptures. 'Has not God made the English tongue as well as others?' he asked with pride and affection. Greek and Hebrew, he said, 'go far more easily into English than Latin'. The Church allowed people to read of Robin Hood, or Hercules, or 'a thousand other ribald or filthy tales' in English. It was 'only the scripture that is forbidden', and it was clearer than the sun that this forbiddal 'is not for love of your souls, which they care for as the fox doth for the geese'.

The Vulgate was itself a translation, he pointed out, made from the Greek and Hebrew into Latin by St Jerome. Tyndale said that he had read as a child how King Athelstan had 'caused the Holy

Scripture to be translated into the tongue that then was in England', and how the prelates then had encouraged him to do so. Now, he said, the clergy prayed, christened, blessed and gave absolution in Latin. 'Only curse they in the English tongue,' he said, and he made another rare reference to his childhood, recalling how a man who had an ox or cow stolen on the Welsh borders would ask the curate to pronounce a solemn curse on the thief.

He mocked the Church's attempts to justify the ban on translating the scripture for the common man. The churchmen said that reading the Bible needed a pure and quiet mind, and that laymen were too cumbered with worldly business to understand it. 'This weapon strikes themselves,' he retorted, 'for who is so tangled with worldly matters as the prelates?' They said that laymen would interpret it each in his own way. 'Why then do the curates not teach people the right way?' For the most part, he claimed, the clergy had no more idea of what the Vulgate Bible meant than the infidel Turks; all they did was to 'mumble up' so much every day, as 'the pie and the popinjay' – the magpie and the parrot – 'speak they know not what, and fill their bellies withal'.

His conclusion was dangerous to the Church, for the readers of *Obedience* would be sure to pass it on to friends whom they trusted. 'They tell you that scripture ought not to be in the mother tongue,' he wrote, 'but it is only because they fear the light, and desire to lead you blindfold and in captivity.' This, he said, had a shocking consequence. By suppressing Christ's gospel, the Church was making of Christ 'not the light of the world, but its darkness'.

In this, the Church blasphemed. 'We do not wish to abolish teaching and to make every man his own master,' Tyndale warned, 'but if the curates will not teach the gospel, the layman must have the scripture, and read it for himself, taking God for his teacher.'

If the book urged defiance to the clergy in the preface, however, it moved on to encourage submission to the ruler. *Obedience* was

Tyndale's response to the blame that 'our holy prelates and our
ghostly religious' meted out to the reformers for making men to
'rise against their princes . . . and to make havoc of other men's
goods'.

The Church and its apologists were having some success in
linking reform with anarchy. Thomas More argued that the apparent *libertas* of Luther led to *licentia*. The blood and atrocity of the
Peasants' War in Germany had claimed at least seventy thousand
lives. More blamed this 'cruell insurreccyon' on the 'heretykes of
his [Tyndale's] own secte'. In fact, Luther had condemned the
uprising. He wrote a powerful tract *Against the Murdering Thieving
Hordes of Peasants*, and urged the princes to 'stab, smite and slay' all
the rebels they could, saying that the times were so extraordinary
that 'a prince can win heaven more easily by bloodshed than by
prayer'. Nonetheless, More claimed that it was Tyndale's Lutheran
friends who 'bare awaye all that euer they founde', and 'dyspyghted
the sayntes images'.

Tyndale retorted that the damage did not stem from reformers
preaching the word of God. How could it, when God 'is not the
author of dissension and strife, but of unity and peace and of
good order'? No, he said, it was 'the bloody doctrine of the pope
which causeth disobedience, rebellion and insurrection'. In their
greed, and their lust for power, churchmen were sucking the laity
dry, and usurping the authority that God had given on earth to
kings and princes.

Each day, more prelates, more priests, more monks, friars,
canons and nuns were 'sprung out of hell' to the ceaseless 'pattering of prayers'. They did not take away sin; on the contrary, 'sin
groweth as they grow'. In a brutal passage, using five verbs for the
same purpose, he said that the Church exploited the laity like animals. 'The parson sheareth, the vicar shaveth, the parish priest
polleth, the friar scrapeth, and the pardoner pareth,' he wrote.
'We lack but a butcher to pull off the skin.'

He turned the famous sermon given by Bishop Fisher of Rochester at St Paul's Cross in 1521 against the Church. Fisher had argued that Luther, having burnt the pope's bulls and decretals, would have burnt the pope himself if he had him in his power. 'A like argument,' Tyndale replied, 'which I suppose to be rather true, I make: Rochester and his holy brethren have burnt Christ's Testament: an evident sign verily that they would have burnt Christ also, if they had him.' As to the pope, and his claim to be the heir to the powers of St Peter, Tyndale snapped that the apostles 'preached not Peter but Christ'. The pope had authority to do no more than preach God's word. In any event, Tyndale said, St Paul was greater than Peter, 'in labours more abundant, in stripes above measure, in prison more plenteously'. This was an important claim to establish, since the evangelicals' theology rested fair and square on Paul; and Paul had proved his apostleship with preaching and suffering, where the pope and his bishops proved theirs 'with bulls and shadows'.

It was the king, Tyndale stressed, and not the pope, whom God had ordained to have no superior on earth. The king 'is in this world without law and may at his lust do right or wrong and shall give accompts but to God only'. Kings and governors must be obeyed, because God has chosen to rule the world through them. 'Who soever resisteth them resisteth God,' Tyndale insisted. This obedience was demanded even in the extreme case of the Christians who had fallen under Turkish Muslim rule, a fate that was befalling the Hungarians as he wrote. 'It is not lawful,' he wrote, 'for a Christian subject to resist his prince though he be an heathen man.'

The one restraint on the king was that he must govern by God's laws. If he commands anything that breaks divine law, his Christian subjects must neither rebel, nor go against God. This was a form of passive resistance and Tyndale applied it to his own translation of the Bible and consequent heresy. Ideally, he said, a king would judge heresy cases himself, instead of relying on the verdict of priests. He accepted that reality was different. 'Emperors and kings are nothing nowadays but even hangmen unto the pope and bishops,' he wrote, 'to kill whom soever they condemn without any more ado, as Pilate was unto the scribes and pharisees and the high bishops, to hang Christ.' A Christian faced by this terror must disobey ungodly commands, but he must not resist by force. If the king, at the bidding of his bishops, made the reading of the English Testament a treason against the State, and punished it by prison and the fire, the true believer must stand firm and accept every penalty for Christ's sake. This principle of Christian obedience, Tyndale said, ran throughout the family and society. The child owed obedience to the parent, the wife to husband, the servant to master, the subject to ruler.

Sudden gentleness, and affection, often breaks through the black gales of Tyndale's argument, and it did so here. 'Be as fathers unto your tenants,' he urged landlords, 'yea, be unto them as Christ was to us, and show unto them all love and kindness . . . For even for such causes were ye made landlords; and for such causes paid men rent at the beginning.'

He wrote with the same tenderness of 'matrimony or wedlock'; typically, he used the shorter Old English word as well as the Latin. He said that the Church was wrong to treat it as a sacrament, because it did not 'signify any promise that ever I heard or read of in the scripture'. But it was a fine and noble state, 'ordained for a remedy and to increase the world', and it was an equal partnership, 'for the man to help the woman and the woman the man with all love and kindness . . .'. Husbands must love their wives, 'as Christ loved the congregation', and 'be courteous unto them . . . and overcome them with kindness'.

Misogyny was part of the age – a much reprinted handbook to witchcraft, *Malleus Maleficarum*, or the *Hammer of the Witches*, described a woman as 'a foe to friendship, an inescapable punishment, an evil of nature painted in fair colours' – as was the view that a wife was the chattel of the husband. Tyndale was free of this, and free of the sense of guilt that had attached itself to sex and marriage at least since Augustine 1100 years before. Wedlock 'hath a promise that we sin not in that state, if a man receive his wife as a gift given to him of God, and the wife her husband likewise'; sex was like 'all manner meats and drinks', in that there is no sin in their enjoyment, if 'we use them measurably with thanksgiving'.

It was a rite of passage for ordained reformers to marry. Luther had most famously married a nun, so that both husband and wife broke their original Catholic vows of chastity, a betrayal Thomas More thought so obscene that he wrote that Luther '*volutatur incestu*', 'writhes in incest'. Tyndale was rare in remaining unwed. As a hunted creature, he may have felt it unfair to ask a wife to endure his perils and rootlessness, although other exiles like Frith were married. We do not know; the only certainty is that he wrote of women with fondness and respect, and that, sharp as ever, he made a fool of the Church by posing its dogma of a celibate priesthood against its insistence that matrimony is a sacrament. 'If wedlock be holy,' he asked of the clergy, 'why had they lever [rather] have whores than wives?'

Obedience arrived in England in the autumn of 1528, at much the same time as Cardinal Campeggio, by now in London, received a message from the pope urging him to find any excuse for delaying the decision on the divorce. Anne Boleyn was unaware of this setback, but she was quick to see that *Obedience*, with its message of the authority of kings over popes, might appeal to Henry VIII.

She obtained a copy of *Obedience*, which Foxe says she lent to her waiting woman, Anne Gainsford, after she had read it. The girl's suitor, George Zouch, snatched it from her hands in play. The young man found it interesting, too much so, because he was caught reading it during a service by Richard Sampson, the dean of the King's Chapel. The dean was shocked that a heretical work had reached court, and confiscated the book and gave it to Wolsey.

Told of the loss, Anne Boleyn vowed that 'yt shalbe the deerest booke that ever deane or cardynall tooke away'. She begged Henry on her knees to have it restored to her. She then marked passages in the margin with her fingernail, and 'besought his grace most tenderly to read' them. This he did, supposedly saying 'thys booke ys for me and all kynges to reade'. The story was corroborated in a biography of Anne written at the end of the century by the grandson of the poet Sir Thomas Wyatt, who knew and may have been in love with Anne. She must have chosen her passages well. Parts of the book will have pleased Henry, but he was doctrinally conservative and other aspects were certain to infuriate him. A section of the book – 'how they which God made governors in the world ought to rule if they be christian' – was aimed directly at the king. It urged him to count the money that the pope and clergy had cost him since he was crowned. 'I doubt not but that will surmount the sum of forty or fifty hundred thousand pounds,' Tyndale estimated. 'The king therefore ought to make them pay this money every farthing, and fetch it out of their mitres, crosses, shrines and all manner treasures of the church, and pay it to his commons again . . .' Henry was later to follow up this suggestion.

For the moment, however, he retained a proprietorial interest in the validity of the seven sacraments. He had, after all, received his title of Defender of the Faith from the pope in honour of *Assertio Septem Sacramentorum*, the book he had written – or had ghost-written by Thomas More – in defending the orthodox dogma. A slyer and foxier man – a 'juggler' as it was put then – would have recognised this well-known fact, and avoided any mention of the sacraments. Had he touched up *Obedience* to please the king, Tyndale might at the least have expected the hunters to be called off the chase. Wolsey, more vulnerable each day to royal anger over the papal foot-dragging on the annulment, would not have dared pursue him on his own initiative.

But Tyndale was incapable of compromise. It was his prime virtue, for from it came his persistence and the implacable honesty of his translation; a man who ducks and weaves in his life might shift and trim in his prose. He sailed straight into the dispute on the sacraments, and sank any prospect of royal favour with thunderous and heretical broadsides. He accepted only the Eucharist and Baptism as genuine sacraments blessed by the scripture. The other five – confirmation, penance, extreme unction, orders and matrimony – were given short shrift as clerical inventions not to be found in the Bible. 'Penance,' he wrote with hallmark brevity, 'is a word of their own forging to deceive us.'

The trawl for readers of the Testament continued. A suspect from Essex was examined in front of Tunstall on 15 October 1528. His was a typical case, although his name is missing from the record of the examination. His father-in-law had taught him the first chapter of James by heart in English, a standard Lollard practice. A butcher from Coggeshall taught him the second chapter. He met John Tyball, whom we have already encountered, at Steeple Bumpstead, who 'read Paul's epistles and the evangelists to him, and taught him heresy'. The reference to Paul indicates that Tyball was a Lutheran. A group met at a local shipwright's house to read Tyndale's Testament. The man gave six names, including two friars and the Steeple Bumpstead curate, Richard Fox. He admitted that he had gone to London at Whitsun the year before, in 1527, where he had bought a Tyndale Testament from a friar named Baron, whom he had found reading a Testament 'to a young gentleman with a chain round his neck'. He paid 3s for it. He gave five addresses where he had read it. Two of them were widows' houses, for women were quite as evangelical as their menfolk.

The Testaments had a startling multiplier effect. Here, a single copy had passed on the infection through readings in at least five places. Individuals were equally contaminating. Richard Fox was also named by one Robert Hemstede, who confessed and abjured his heresy on the sacraments. He said that it was Fox who had told him that Christ's body and blood were not physically present in the Eucharist. Hemstede said that he was afraid that Fox was leading him to the heresy that 'the men of Colchester be in', Lollardy, but the curate had scoffed at him. 'What, man, art thou afeard?' the curate retorted. 'Be not afeard. For those serve a better master than ever thou diddest.'

Robert's relative Thomas Hemstede confessed that his wife had taught him the Paternoster, Ave Maria and the Creed in English. Richard Fox then made him a churchwarden at Steeple Bumpstead, acknowledging him as a fellow evangelical by calling him 'brother in Christ' and 'a known man'. Fox taught him, and a ploughwright named William Boucher, that the sacrament of the altar 'is not the very body of Christ, but done for a remembrance of Christ's Passions', and that pilgrimages were to no effect. The proof of this, the curate said, was to be found in Tyndale's Testament. Hemstede named twelve lay persons, including his wife, his natural son, and three Augustinian friars. All, he said, had been taught by Fox.

Thomas More, and Tunstall and Wolsey, found Tyndale's *Obedience* to be every bit as alarming as his Testament. It was, More wrote, 'a holy book of disobedience', one 'whereby we were taught to disobey Christ's holy catholic church'. The efforts to track down its author continued.

On the Continent, meanwhile, Hackett was having little luck with Richard Herman. From his prison cell in Antwerp, the bookseller demanded to be given the names of the Lutherans whom he was supposed to have succoured, and the dates and places where he had done so. The ambassador wrote a stream of letters to Wolsey, pleading to be given some hard evidence that he could produce in court. It was not until 22 January 1529 that the prosecution supplied names: 'the one was named Willem Tandeloo', they claimed, and the other was 'the son of Petit Roy, being a runaway monk of the observant order'. Roye's father, Petit Roy, had been born in Antwerp but had later moved to London, where he had been 'denizened', or given English nationality.

A pair of names, with no other detail, hardly made a case. Herman petitioned Charles V for release, on the grounds that the Testaments had no obvious Lutheran content, and that they had done no harm within the emperor's realm since they had been shipped directly to England. He testified that 'a merchant out of Germany sent to the petitioner certain New Testaments in English without any gloss which books the petitioner received, and sold them to a merchant out of England, and the latter conveyed them over to England'.

Herman was duly released on 5 February 1529. He was, however, tainted with the heretic's brush. He was expelled from the English House in Antwerp, at the instigation of Hackett or Style, and fell on hard times. Anne Boleyn remembered him when she became queen, as we shall see, asking that he be readmitted to the House after the 'great hurt and hindrance' he had suffered on behalf of the English Testament.

West had by now returned to his monastery at Greenwich, but he still kept an ear to the ground. In December 1528, he heard that Roye had sailed secretly to England to see his mother at Westminster. The tip came to nothing, but in February 1529 he asked for a meeting with Wolsey to urge the cardinal to allow him to return to Germany, since 'the tyme drawyth nere of the Frankford Markte', and he half hoped to seize Tyndale at the Fair. Frankfurt lay in the diocese of Mainz, and a letter was drafted calling on the bishop of Mainz to arrest and hand over 'William

Roye and William Hutchyns, otherwise Tendalle, traitors and heretics'.

It is uncertain whether West set off for Frankfurt, or whether the hunt at the book fair was left to Rinck and the bishop of Mainz. In any event, they drew a blank. West was in England in June, searching in East Anglia for Roye and a red-haired man, whom he thought to be Barlow. A schoolmaster from Yarmouth told West that he had spoken and drunk with Roye at 'Lestoe', or Lowestoft. It was difficult to look for a man whose face was a blank, a fact that must have helped Tyndale to stay out of the clutches of West and the others. But the schoolmaster had good sight of Roye, and he told West 'the features and secret marks of his face, the manner of his speaking, his apparel, and how he does speak all manner of languages'. West followed the fugitive's tracks to 'Attellbryge', or Aldeburgh, but found that 'Roye and the other took ship for Newcastle'. West told Wolsey that he would try to follow – 'great as the labour is, we endure it for Christ's sake' – provided that the cardinal sent him funds. But from here both West and Roye disappear from sight. No more is heard of them, except for a note in Foxe that said that Roye was burnt in Portugal in 1531.

In fact, Tyndale had left Antwerp for Hamburg in December 1528 or early in the New Year. He was seeking a quiet place to complete his translation of the Pentateuch, the first five books of the Old Testament. Worry over those searching for him may also have prompted him to move. He had already completed the translation of Deuteronomy when he sailed for Hamburg. It proved a wasted effort. His ship was caught in a winter gale and wrecked on the Dutch coast. He lost all his books and manuscripts, but he arrived at Margaret von Emerson's house in Hamburg to restart work on the five books of Moses. Thomas More was also writing furiously. Tunstall invited him in the late winter of 1528 to defend the Church against 'certain sons of iniquity' who were 'trying to infect the land with heresy' by translating and printing Lutheran books. The bishop told More that he feared that the Catholic faith would 'perish utterly' unless 'good and learned men' met the danger by 'quickly putting forth sound books in the vernacular on the catholic side'. He urged More to do this 'holy work' himself, 'since you, dearest brother, are distinguished as a second Demosthenes in our native language as well as in Latin'. Tunstall gave More a special licence to read heretical works, some of which he enclosed with his letter. 'I am sending you their mad incantations in our tongue along with some of Luther's books,' he wrote, so that 'you will understand more easily in what hiding places these twisting serpents lurk.' In his Chelsea house, More began writing *A Dialogue Concerning Heresies*, an account of 'thyngys touchyng the pestylent secte of Luther and Tyndale'. It became known as his *Dialogue Concerning Tyndale*, for Tyndale, a 'very treasury and wellspring of wickedness', was its main concern.

A great feud, that would consume five years and three quarters of a million words, was under way.

13

The Flight to Hamburg

ore was now writing his first book in English, but he used a Latin tag – *simplicibus et ideotis hominibus*, the ordinary simple soul – to describe the readers he wished to warn of the evils of the doctrine of 'Luther and Tyndale, by the one begun in Saxony and by the other laboured to be brought into England'.

A Dialogue Concerning Heresies was in four books, and its author, fully absorbed by the law and politics in the day, drove himself into the early hours to complete it by night. A man must 'wryte by candellyght whyle he were halfe a slepe' if the need were urgent enough, More said, and nothing was more pressing than the war against heretics. Exhaustion did not drain the venom from his onslaught.

He described Tyndale as 'a hell-hound in the kenel of the dyuy' who discharged blasphemies 'out of his brutyshe bestely mouth', and a 'drowsy drudge' who 'hath drunken depe in the dyuy's dregges'. When his anger courses directly from his heart on to the page, More's other facets – the cool and temperate lawyer, the humanist author of *Utopia*, the discreet diplomat, the measured politician, the courtly servant of the king – are eaten up by his hatred, and vanish. He claimed that Tyndale was so full of evil, so crammed with pus like a boil in a biblical plague, that he must burst; but this also describes the malice that More himself bore Tyndale. His enemy 'is the beast who teaches vice, a forewalker of Antichrist, a devil's limb', More scribbled. 'He sheweth himself so puffed up with the poison of pride, malice and evil, that it is more than a marvel that the skin can hold together.'

The book's purpose was clear from one of its marginal notes, which read with Tyndale-like brevity: 'The Lutherans are the worst heretics that ever sprang in Christ's church.' More cast the book in the humanist style made fashionable by Erasmus of a dialogue between the author and 'the Messenger', a young man, bright and 'nothynge tonged tayed', who knows his Tyndale and who has fallen among Lutherans at university. The Messenger scorns learning, and apes Tyndale, saying that logic is mere 'babbling' since man 'hath no light but of holy scripture . . . which he said was learning enough for a Christian man'.

More chats to him in the study of his Chelsea house, and slowly persuades him to stay within the 'comen fayth and byleve of the ole chyrche'. Doctrinal questions, of the sacraments, pilgrimages, images, relics, are treated as individual rounds in the contest between them, all of which are won by More as he easily outpoints his opponent. More's arguments are, in their essence, those of Pope Nicholas. The Church was founded by the apostles, he says. It is a visible and majestic body, whose traditions date back fifteen hundred years, and which stands for order and stability. Its decisions are blessed by time and common beliefs, and 'so comen downe to our dayes by contynually successyon'. Miracles and relics and pilgrimages reinforce its divine purpose.

There had been heretics before, of course, who had 'lefte the common fayth of ye catholyke chyrche preferrynge theyr owne gay gloses.' But More said that the times were now more dangerous than ever. Modern heretics – he referred to 'new named bretherne', 'evangelycall fraternyte', 'our evangelycall Englysshe heretykes' – had become too pernicious to be left unburnt. They mocked the mass, denied the sacraments, scorned the Eucharist and insulted the saints; they wished to destroy the Church and replace it with their own vileness. Even their interest in the Bible condemned them. 'Of all wretches,' More wrote, 'worst shall he walk that, forcing [caring] little of the faith of Christ's church, cometh to the scripture of God, to look and try therein whether the church believe aright or not.'

More flew at their immorality. The Messenger remarks that 'it would do well that priests should have wives'. This sparks off a sentence so long and full of fury that it is almost unreadable: 'For Tyndall [sic] (whose books be nothing else in effect but the worst heresies picked out of Luther's works and Luther's worst words translated by Tyndall and put forth in Tyndall's own name) doth in his frantic book of obedience (wherein he raileth at large against all peoples, against all kings, against all prelates, all priests, all religious, all the laws, all the saints, against the sacraments of Christ's church, against all virtuous works, against divine service, and finally against all things in effect that good is) in that book I say Tyndall holdeth that priests must have wives.'

He relied on sarcasm to mock the case for married priests. For 'this fifteen hundred years', he said, none had the 'wit or grace to perceive that great special commandment' until God had revealed 'this high secret mystery to these two godly creatuyres Luther and Tyndall'. This was done, he said, lest the 'holy friar', Luther, 'should have lost his marriage of that holy nun, and Tyndale [sic] that good marriage that I think him toward . . .'. There is no evidence that Tyndale considered marriage, although we have seen that he wrote of it with striking gentleness. But many reformers had wives, some ex-nuns like Katherine Luther, and envy may have mingled with More's spleen when he wrote of them. He thought it to be a personal failing in himself that his yearning for a wife had outweighed his youthful desires to become a priest. In his own eyes, he was a failed celibate and a failed clergyman, and he seemed specially tormented that these heretics should have their cake and eat it, as it were, by combining ordination and matrimony. Lutheran 'harlots' were turning the Church into a brothel, he said. He wrote savagely of Luther's 'open lyvyng in lechery wyth his lewd lemman the nun'.

Tyndale was worse. He had 'sucked out the most poison he could find' in Luther's books, and 'in many things far passed his master', running so madly with malice that he 'fareth as though he heard not his own voice'. More claimed that Tyndale's translation was 'too bad to be amended'. The faults were so many, and so spread throughout the Testament, that it should be cast aside, as it 'were as soon done to weave a new web of cloth as to sew up every hole in a net'. He said that Tyndale had 'wilfully mistranslated' the scripture and deceived 'blind unlearned people' by 'teaching what he knows to be false'.

The mistranslation claim was bogus. More repeated the arguments over 'congregation', 'senior', 'love' and 'repent' for church, priest, charity and penance. 'These names in an English tongue neither express the thing he meant by them,' he wrote, 'and also there appeareth that he had a mischievous mind in the change.' In particular, More said, 'senior' in English 'signifieth nothing at all, but is a French word used in English more than half in mockery'. Tyndale agreed to this when he wrote his *Answer to More*. 'Of a truth senior is no very good English, though senior and junior be used in the universities,' he wrote, 'but there came no better word in my mind at that time.' Howbeit, he said, 'I spied my fault since, long ere Mr More told it me, and have mended it in all works which since I made, and call it an *elder*.'

Other than this dispute, More made little real attempt to justify the claim of inaccuracy. It was as well, for when he came himself to translate a chapter of the New Testament, his meaning was identical to Tyndale's. More translated John 6 in his polemic *The Answer to a Poisoned Book*, written in 1533 to oppose an unsigned tract on the sacraments, *The Souper of the Lorde*. More used the chapter as proof that the communion bread is the literal body of Christ. The nub of the argument is in verse fifty-one, which More translated as: 'and the bread which I shall give is my flesh, which I shall give for the life of the world'. Tyndale's translation differs only in that he uses 'will' instead of 'shall': 'and the bread that I will give, is my flesh, which I will give for the life of the world'. The other differences between them in the chapter are also matters of style and not of sense. Tyndale tends to use Anglo-Saxon words in preference to Latin. He has '*came down from*' and '*wilderness*' where More has '*descended*' and '*desert*'. Tyndale reads more fluently than More, and seems less dated. 'The Jews then murmured at him,' he starts verse forty-one, 'because he said: I am that bread which is come down from heaven.' More writes, awkwardly: 'The Jews murmured therefore of that that he had said: I am the lively bread that am descended from heaven.'

It may not be fair to judge More's translation skills on this single piece of work, but it confirms that More had no right to query Tyndale's accuracy or skill with language, and it raises its own brutal question. If More could render John 6 into English for his readers, how could he press for Tyndale's Testament and its readers to be burnt? Why did he refer to them, as he did in his *Answer*, as a 'corrupt canker' whom honest folk should 'not so mych as byd good spede or good morow whane we mete them'?

Though he argued that Tyndale's botched work was fit only for the flames, More was careful not to condemn the principle of an English Bible outright. An acceptable translation might one day be made by 'some good catholic and well learned man', he agreed, provided that the Church approved it. But only bishops should be allowed to buy copies, he said, and they should lend them only to the most trustworthy men. He suggested each bishop need not spend more than £10 on this; assuming a cost of 6s per complete copy, More was estimating that a diocese could get by on thirty or so Bibles. As an added precaution, he suggested that the bishops lend only a part of the Bible to each reader, so that one had John, but not Acts, and another Ephesians, but not Revelation, and so forth.

Simple Christians should be kept away from it. More said that the scripture was tricky – 'a fly may wade in, but an elephant can drown' – and would overtax uneducated minds. In particular, Paul's Epistle to the Romans, the key to the Lutheran doctrine of justification by faith, contained 'such high difficulties as very few learned men can very well attain'. Tyndale was wrong to claim that it was necessary to read the Bible, More said. Christ had revealed to his Church all that was needed to gain salvation. The pronouncements of the Church were the Word of God as surely as any verse in the scripture. In a largely illiterate world, it was natural and just that they should be passed on orally, 'bye onely wordes and prechynge . . . by mouth amonge the people'. In any event, More denied that Tyndale's Testament was the Word of God. 'If Tyndale's testament be taken up,' he wrote, 'then shall false heresies be preached, then shall the sacraments be set at naught, then shall fasting and prayer be neglected, then shall holy saints be blasphemed, then shall Almighty God be displeased, then shall he withdraw his grace and let all run to ruin . . . then will rise up rifling and robbery, murder and mischief, and plain insurrection . . . then shall youth leave labour and all occupation, then shall folk wax idle and fall to unthriftiness, then shall all laws be laughed to scorn . . .' Then, in short, society would suffer extreme breakdown; the Church, the fountainhead of law and authority, would be destroyed, and with it the continuity of the centuries would be shattered. Tyndale was guilty of a dual crime. Spiritually, he challenged Christ's true Church, and, in temporal terms, he was ruining the peace of the realm.

Tyndale was thus a heretic and a traitor, and, to More, the burning of heretics was 'lawful, necessary and well done'. Faint hearts might say that it was wrong to send heretics to the stake, because Christ had told Peter to 'put up thy sword'; but More reminded them that St Augustine and other Fathers of the Church had agreed that Christian princes 'have been constrained to punish heretics by terrible death'. Others might say that Christians, having themselves been persecuted by Jews and pagans, should not persecute others. 'That,' said More, 'is no reason to look that Christian princes should suffer the Catholic Christian people to be oppressed by Turks or by heretics worse than Turks.' It was wrong to make a 'covenant' with the heretics. They must be 'punyshed by deth in ye fyre'.

It may seem wrong, and perhaps it is wrong, that More should have been canonised in 1935, and it is, at the very least, bizarre that he should have been further elevated in 2000 to become the patron saint of politicians. Politicians persecute opponents readily enough without having More dangled in front of them as a role model.

In his diagnosis, however, if not in his cure, More was correct. He guessed accurately and very quickly that the 'evangellycalls' were a lethal threat to established order. The Christian religion had, over many centuries, come to mean the Church. Scholastic theology might be dull and nitpicking – More described it as 'milking a billygoat into a sieve' – but it remained a Church monopoly and it did not endanger civil peace. Scripture had become a priestly text submerged beneath more than a thousand years of Church traditions, and Church law and lore. More saw very clearly the dangers of blowing the dust off it, and promoting it afresh as the gauge of human conduct.

Tyndale and his fellow Bible-men, as More suspected, were indeed fuelling future wars of religion. These caused, in the regions

where they were most virulent, a carnage as great as that of the
Black Death, the bubonic plague of the mid-fourteenth century,
and infinitely more prolonged.

If Luther had not directly incited the German peasants to rebel,
his attacks on papal authority were certainly one of the triggers of
the uprising. The rebels made use of his September Testament to
attack serfdom – 'Here is neither lord nor servant', they quoted St
Paul in their pamphlets, 'We are all one in Christ' – and extended
his doctrine of the priesthood of all believers to make a naked call
to anarchy: 'True Christian faith needs no human authority.'

The notorious case of Thomas Müntzer showed how prone
evangelicals were to religious dementia. Müntzer was a young
chantry priest who fell under Luther's influence at Wittenberg. He
became the pastor of the small Saxon town of Allstedt in 1523.
Here, in classic reformer style, he married, composed liturgies in
German and translated Latin hymns into the vernacular. He fell
out with Luther, calling his old mentor the 'Pope of Wittenberg',
and took to signing himself 'God's messenger'. He believed that he
had been given the divine task of exterminating all priests and god-
less rulers. 'The living God is sharpening his scythe in me,' he
rejoiced, 'so that later I can cut down the red poppies and the blue
cornflowers.' In his sermons, he drew on the book of Daniel to
proclaim the coming apocalypse, and styled himself Jehu, after the
Lord's chosen executioner who had trampled the queen-whore
Jezebel to death beneath the hooves of his horse.

Expelled from Allstedt, Müntzer moved to Mühlhausen where
he hung a white sheet with a rainbow painted on it in his church,
as a sign of his covenant with God. Bodyguards carried a red cru-
cifix and a naked sword in front of him when he walked through
the streets. His sermons fed conservative fears of evangelically
inspired revolution. Müntzer spoke of lords stealing all creatures as
their property; the 'fish in the water, the birds in the air, the plants
on the ground have all got to be theirs . . . they oppress all people,

and shear and shave the poor ploughman and everything that lives'.

A peasant force of eight thousand had camped near Mühlhausen in May 1525 during the uprising. Müntzer agreed to lead them, while the princes raised an army against them. Reformers used biblical references as weapons, and Müntzer loosed one against the princes. 'God spoke of you and yours in Micah 3', he wrote, leaving them to look up the reference and see that they were rulers 'who hate the good, and love the evil . . . who eat the flesh of my people; . . . therefore it shall be night unto you, that ye shall have no vision'. After 1551, when the printer Robert Stephanus of Geneva introduced numbered verses, the process was refined so that specific verses – here Micah 3: 1–6 – could be used as ammunition. In their reply, the princes were careful to accuse Müntzer of being the 'perverter of the Gospel' who was rebelling, not against themselves, but 'against our Redeemer Jesus Christ with murder, fire and other disrespect of God . . .'. They offered to spare the peasants if they would turn over the 'false prophet' to them.

Müntzer persuaded the peasants that he was 'the sword of Gideon' and that he would 'catch all the bullets in his coat sleeves'. As the princes moved their artillery and cavalry on to the battle-field, a rainbow appeared. The peasants took it for a miracle. They appeared to be in a divine coma as the guns opened fire. A chronicler recorded that they sang 'Now we pray the Holy Spirit', and neither resisted nor fled, but stood still 'as if they were insane'. Five thousand were reported killed. Müntzer was found hiding in an attic. He signed a confession and a recantation, and was beheaded. His head was put on a lance and placed in a field as a warning of the perils of evangelism.

Luther was, as we have seen, quite as alarmed by these excesses as was More and dubbed Müntzer the 'Satan of Allstedt'. Tyndale, too, was careful to distance himself from rebellion by preaching submission to authority in *Obedience*. But More, a practising lawyer and politician who was deeply involved in maintaining law and order, was well aware of the powerful and destabilising forces that flowed from the evangelicals, with their vernacular Bibles and their contempt for tradition. The *Dialogue* was printed in July 1529, by his brother-in-law 'at the sygne of the meremayd' at Cheapside in London, at the moment when the word 'Protestant' was being coined. It was used to describe the Lutheran princes and cities who had signed a *Protestatio* opposing the Catholic majority at the diet or parliament of Speyer in April of that year. Reformers differed greatly in their own doctrines – already Lutherans, Zwinglians and Anabaptists were at one another's throats, and a score of new sects would soon arise – but the general term 'Protestant' was now applied to them all.

Fear of the 'newefanglede' Protestants joined with the advance of an old enemy to play on Catholic nerves. The Muslim forces of Sultan Suleiman, the Ottoman emperor, had conquered Christian Belgrade, Croatia, Rhodes and central and southern Hungary in the past decade. On 23 September 1529, two months after the *Dialogue* was published, Turkish horsemen reached the walls of Vienna, raising pikes with Austrian heads impaled on them. Churches tolled 'Turk-bells' in warning, and columns of smoke from burning villages rose 'like a forest from horizon to horizon'. The Viennese defenders were outnumbered by at least ten to one, but they were brilliantly led by the veteran soldier Count Nicholas von Salm, who had a fine view of enemy movements from the top of the spire of St Stephen's Church. The critical assault came on 12 October, when breaches were blown in the walls near the Carinthian Gate. Turkish beys and pashas were seen from the spire throughout the day as they beat their men forward with the flats of their swords, 'crying loudly to heaven and each other of the greatness of God and the glory of Islam'. It was a final effort and it failed. Two days later, the watchmen on the walls saw flames shoot up as the Turks fired their tents and slaughtered their prisoners, male and female, save those young enough to fetch a good price as slaves. The Muslims, venting their spite in the Christian villages along their line of retreat, created such revulsion that English parsons prayed each Good Friday for more than a century that 'all Jews, Turks, Infidels and Hereticks' should be punished as murderers of Christ and haters of God.

The Viennese were fortunate. It took the Hungarians 150 years to be rid of Moslem rule,[1] while, to the west, Catholics and Protestants played out Tyndale and More's verbal assaults in grisly reality. More's sense of Armageddon – he wrote breathlessly of 'domesday' – had much to feed it. He insisted in the *Dialogue* that the evangelicals must be 'oppressed and overwhelmed in the beginning'. It made perfect sense, from his standpoint. But he was late. The 'beginning' was now past.

Tyndale's name was mentioned in open court in England as a heretic and a rebel for the first time in January 1529. Hackett's point – that sedition was an extraditable offence, where heresy was not – had been taken. It was as well that Tyndale had taken himself to Hamburg.

The shipwreck on the Dutch coast had cost him 'both money, his copies and time', Foxe says. He lost all his books, and was 'compelled to begin all again anew', to the 'doubling of his labours'. The reference books he will have had to replace include the Hebrew text of the Old Testament, Hebrew grammars and the Septuagint, the ancient Greek translation of the Old Testament, said to be the work of seventy-two translators – hence 'LXX' or Septuagint – at Alexandria in the third century BC.[2] These were expensive books. He had also lost his money in the wreck, and had to pay for another passage to Germany. More and Tunstall personally interrogated those suspected of sending funds to Tyndale, his brother John Tyndale and Humphrey Monmouth included.

They established how £20 was sent over the sea to Tyndale – the two payments mentioned by Monmouth that went courtesy of the Steelyard merchants to Hamburg – but they failed to find out who was supplying the larger amounts he needed for printing contracts and to recover from the shipwreck.

Tyndale arrived in Hamburg early in 1529. It was safer than Antwerp. Johann Bugenhagen, whom Tyndale had known as a scholarly pastor in Wittenberg, had moved to Hamburg in October 1528 to organise the reformed church. The reformation was formally established by the city fathers in February 1529. Bugenhagen was a sympathetic figure who had helped Luther with the German Bible translation, and Tyndale had comfortable lodgings with the 'worshipful widow', Margaret von Emerson.

He spent most of the year working on the Pentateuch, the books supposedly written by Moses himself, Genesis, Exodus, Leviticus, Numbers and Deuteronomy.[3] His grasp of Hebrew was remarkable for a man who had learnt it while a fugitive. He knew none when he left England. There were no English Jews for him to learn from; hundreds had been hanged in violent pogroms in 1278, and the survivors were expelled from the kingdom twelve years later. The first professor of Hebrew was not appointed at Cambridge until 1524, after Tyndale had gone. It is most likely that he began studying it when he was at Wittenberg, and honed his skills during his stay at Worms.

Some books existed to help him in his task. Hebrew Bibles had been published in Italy for almost sixty years. The first great Christian scholar of Hebrew, Johannes Reuchlin, had published *De Rudimentis Hebraicis* in 1506. He added to this Hebrew grammar and lexicon with an edition of the seven penitential psalms in Hebrew and a treatise on Hebrew accents. Reuchlin, though he was tried for heresy, remained a devout Catholic, but his work was invaluable to a translator. The Complutensian Polyglot Bible, or *Complutum*, was financed by Cardinal Ximines de Cisneros, founder of the university of Alcala, and Inquisitor General of Spain. The Old Testament had the Hebrew, Vulgate and Septuagint text in parallel columns. Volume VI of this immense undertaking was a Hebrew vocabulary with a short Hebrew grammar published in 1515. The Italian scholar Pagnini, who was translating the Hebrew and Greek originals into an entirely new Latin Bible, compiled a Hebrew dictionary which was published in Lyons in 1529, possibly in time to benefit Tyndale. Luther's own German translation of the Pentateuch had been published four years earlier in a fine edition illustrated by Lucas Cranach the Elder.

A happiness floods through Tyndale's stay in Hamburg. He adored the Bible, as God's word, and it sparkled and refreshed him as writing, as a brilliant tale well told. 'This is a book worthy to be read in day and night and never to be out of hands,' he said of Deuteronomy. It was 'easy also and light and a very pure gospel' whose message is 'a preaching of faith and love', of deducing 'the love to God out of faith, and the love of a man's neighbour out of the love of God'. He found an utter freshness in the Bible. It was not musty, and it did not drone as the Vulgate did; it was a page-turner that danced and sang.

He loved both the Hebrew he was translating and the English he was writing. 'The properties of the Hebrew tongue agreeth a thousand times more with the English than with the Latin,' he wrote. 'The manner of speaking is both one, so that in a thousand places thou needest not but to translate it into English word for word.' Hebrew has a very simple sentence structure, which he caught in his translation. It coordinates clauses – 'and . . . and . . . and' – where Latin has a taste for complicated subordinate clauses. Where Hebrew flows into English, he said, 'thou must seek a compass in the Latin'. Even when the right phrase was found in Latin, it was difficult to translate it 'well-favouredly' so

that 'it have the same grace and sweetness, sense and pure understanding' of the English.

This lyrical joy sustained Tyndale, and saved him and his work
from the dourness often bred by intense faith and moral certitude.
A satirical pamphlet circulating while he was in Hamburg gave
instructions on how to be Lutheran: 'one should talk little, look
sour, and not cut off one's beard'. The portrait of Tyndale that
hangs in Hertford College at Oxford shows such a man. He is
dressed in black, with a black scholar's cap above a pale high forehead; he has a yellow-blond beard and moustache, and an eyebrow
is slightly raised with a glance of quizzical piety. This is a puritan,
aware that he is one of God's elect. But it is not Tyndale. It was
painted after his death, by an anonymous artist, commissioned to
produce an icon of a Protestant martyr. Beneath Tyndale's hand is
a Latin script that bears the propaganda message in translation:

> To scatter Roman darkness by this light
> The loss of land and life I'll reckon slight.

More was sketched and painted from life by Hans Holbein the
Younger, his face fine and energetic, but with a trace of cruel
melancholy to the lips. We do not know the cast of Tyndale's eyes,
the set of his mouth; his profession made him a man of the
shadows, and we know only, from his writing, that he was can-
tankerous, driven, and morally very self-assured, and that he was
also lively, a wit and punster, and that he knew what it was to be
happy.

While Tyndale was creating the English of the Old Testament, big-
mouthed and less delicately phrased than the New, the king's 'great
matter' was sliding badly. Campeggio, having run out of excuses
for delay, opened a legatine court with Wolsey to hear evidence
over the marriage on 31 May 1529. Catherine appealed to Rome

and refused to recognise the court, but she attended the first hearing in the great hall of the monastery of the Black Friars in London. She flung herself on her knees, and pleaded with Henry to let their wedlock continue. 'Sir, I beseech thee,' she cried in her thick Spanish accent, 'for all the loves that hath been between us, and for the love of God, let me have justice and right. Take of me some pity and compassion, for I am a poor woman and a stranger born of your dominion.' She repeated, as she had to the cardinals, that the biblical constraints on brother's wives did not apply to her, for she had come to Henry as a virgin. 'And when ye had me at the first,' she told the king, and the packed hall, 'I take God to be my judge, I was a true maid, without touch of man . . .'

Henry raised her to her feet. After she had left the court in tears, he gave a public explanation of his actions. 'As God is my witness, no fault in Catherine moved me,' he said. His concern was only for the succession. His sons by Catherine were stillborn or had 'died incontinent after they were born'. This was surely a punishment from God. The scriptures forbade a man to marry his brother's widow, and England had need of a male heir. This was his only motive in seeking the annulment, he lied; he was not in court 'for any carnal concupiscence or mislike of the Queen's person or age, with whom I could be well content to continue during my life if our marriage might stand within God's laws'.

Tyndale was one of very few people to believe the king's explanation. Passion for Anne Boleyn led Henry by the nose, a fact almost universally recognised. It was overwhelmingly in Tyndale's interest to attach himself to the king's cause. To do so was to submit to royal authority, the core dogma of *Obedience*. It would strike a blow at Rome, where the unhappy pope, compelled by Charles V to deny Henry his wish, was muttering that it was better 'for the wealth of Christendom if the Queen were in her grave'. It would bring the translator closer to Anne Boleyn, already an admirer of his work. And, of course, it would ingratiate him with the one man powerful enough in his own right to institute reform and license the English Bible.

No obvious biblical constraint prevented Tyndale from approving of the annulment. As so often, the Bible had two conflicting views on the relevent subject of marriage to a brother's widow. Tyndale translated both passages during 1529. Leviticus forecast that Henry would have no heir if he married dead Arthur's wife. 'If a man takes his brother's wife, it is an unclean thing,' Tyndale translated the verse, 'he hath uncovered his brother's secrets, and shall die childless'. Deuteronomy claimed quite the reverse: 'When brethren dwell together and one of them die and have no child, the wife of the dead shall not be given out unto a stranger: but her brother in law shall go in unto her and take her to wife and marry her.'

Tyndale took the king at face value. Henry had said that it was the scriptures alone that made him wish to cast off his wife of twenty years. Tyndale found that the scriptures did not in fact compel him to do so. Therefore the marriage should continue. Tyndale had a touching and gentle respect for married love. It was not that of a naïve bachelor. He was aware of sex, and thought it a pleasure ordained by God. 'Moreover as concerninge the acte of Matrimonye,' he wrote, 'as when thou wilt eate, thou blessest god and receavest thy dayle food of his hande . . . and knowelegest that it is his gyfte, and thankest him, belevynge his worde, that he hath creted it for thee to receave with thanks . . .' Henry claimed that he still loved Catherine; he should stay with her, then, Tyndale wrote, for marriage was a divine gift: 'Now is thy worke thorow this fayth and theankes pleasaunt and acceptable in the syght of God.'

Predictably, this verdict infuriated the king. The career of another reformer, Thomas Cranmer, shows how far Tyndale might have progressed with a more sanguine view of Henry's motives. In the summer of 1529, as an obscure fellow of Jesus College, Cambridge, Thomas Cranmer suggested that the king should canvass the universities of England and Europe for a judgement on the marriage. This proposal ingeniously bypassed Rome and the legatine court. Cranmer soon found himself a chaplain in the household of Anne Boleyn's father, employed in writing out his opinion of the marriage, a stepping stone on his way to becoming archbishop of Canterbury.

Where Cranmer rose, Wolsey subsided, dragged down by his monarch's unfulfilled lust. The cardinal pleaded with Campeggio to give him the decretal bull that authorised the annulment. Campeggio told him on 24 June that the pope had written to forbid its use. 'That will be my ruin!' Wolsey cried. At the beginning of July, fearful of Henry's 'inconceivable anxiety', the cardinal pleaded personally with the queen to compromise. 'Will any Englishman counsel or be friendly unto me against the King's pleasure?' she replied.

Campeggio proved a fine procrastinator. He was expected to announce his decision on the case in late July. These hopes were premature. He had already announced that he intended to adjourn the court for the summer, in keeping with the summer break enjoyed by the papal curia in Rome. On 17 July, the pope succumbed to pressure from Charles V and revoked Campeggio's legatine commission. Henry, knowing nothing of this, attended the court on 23 July. Campeggio announced that he had discussed matters with the pope, that no hasty decision could be made, and that he was returning to Rome and adjourning the case indefinitely. Dark red with anger, Henry stamped from the hall. 'By the mass,' the duke of Suffolk called from the gallery, 'it was never merry in England whilst we had cardinals amongst us!'

He meant Wolsey as well as Campeggio. The latter at once left London for Rome. As he sailed from Dover, word reached England that the pope had signed a treaty with the emperor that assured his freedom, on the condition that he never agree to the annulment unless Catherine wished it.

Wolsey's fate was sealed. Anne Boleyn accompanied Henry on a royal progress in August, meandering through Essex, Bedfordshire, Oxfordshire, Buckinghamshire and Berkshire. She complained that, through Wolsey, her youth was passing without Henry being permitted to enjoy it.

In that same month of August, the three leading Tyndale-hunters, More, Tunstall and Hackett, were in the Low Countries to negotiate a treaty at Cambra, tantalisingly close to the illegal presses of Antwerp. Tunstall tried to turn this to his advantage, so Edward Hall recounted in his *Chronicle* a few years later, by bulk buying New Testaments for burning at St Paul's. He contacted Augustine Packington, a London mercer who knew Antwerp well and who was sympathetic to Tyndale, but pretended otherwise.

Tunstall said that he would buy all available copies at a handsome rate. Packington assured the bishop that he was in contact with 'the Dutchmen and strayngers that have bought them of Tyndale, and have them here to sell'; he promised him that he should have 'every boke of them, that is imprynted and is here unsold'. Tunstall was delighted – he felt that 'he had God by the toe, when indeed he had (as after he thought) the devil by the fist' – and commissioned Packington to ship the stock to London for a grand burning.

Packington went direct to Tyndale. 'Willyam, I knowe thou art a poor man, and hast a hepe of newe Testamentes, and bokes by thee, for the whiche thou hast bothe indaungered thy frendes, and beggered theyself,' the merchant told him. 'I haue now gotten thee a Merchaunt, whiche with ready money shall dispatche thee of all that thou hast, if you thinke it so proffitable for your self.'

Tyndale asked who the merchant was. Packington told him that it was the bishop of London.

'O that it is because he will burne them,' Tyndale said. 'I am the gladder, for I shall get money of hym for these bokes, to bring myself out of debt, and the whole worlde shall cry out upon the burning of Goddes worde. And the overplus of the money, that shall remain to me, shall make me more studious, to correct the said Testament, and so newly to Imprint the same once again.'

Newly printed Testaments indeed soon came 'thick and three-fold over into England'. Tunstall sent for Packington for an explanation. 'Surely, I bought alle there was to be had, but I perceive they haue prynted more since,' Packington explained. 'I see it will never be better so long as they have letters and presses. Wherefore you were beste to buy the presses too, and so ye shall be sure.' At this, Hall recorded, the bishop smiled, and so the matter ended.

It is, of course, a suspiciously neat twist that Tunstall should thus have financed Tyndale's future projects – 'the bishop had the bokes, Packyngton had the thankes, and Tyndale had the money', Hall concluded – and it is highly unlikely that Tyndale was himself in Antwerp in August. It is probable that he did not leave Hamburg until later in the year, though, as ever with our skilful fugitive, this is no more than a best guess.

Even if Packington did not get his copies directly from Tyndale, but through van Hoochstraten or the pirate printer van Endhoven, Tunstall is known to have bought Tyndale Testaments for burning in London, and there is no reason why he should not have done so again in Antwerp. When More later arrested the Testament smuggler George Constantine, he brought him to his house in Chelsea and interrogated him over Tyndale's source of funds. The scene was described by Foxe.

'Constantine, I would have thee plain with me in one thing that I will ask, and I promise thee I will shew thee favour in all other things wherof thou art accused,' More said. 'There is, beyond the sea, Tyndale . . . and a great many more of you. I know they cannot live without help. There are some that help and succour them with money, and thou being one of them hadst thy part thereof and therefore knowest from whence it came. I pray thee tell me, who be they that help them thus?'

'My lord,' Constantine replied. 'It is the Bishop of London that hath holpen us, for he hath bestowed among us a great deal of money upon the Testaments to burn them. And that hath been, and yet is, our only succour and comfort.'

'Now by my troth,' More exclaimed, 'I think even the same, for so much I told the Bishop before he went about it.'

The fall of Wolsey was now imminent. In October, Henry had him charged with *praemunire*, the anti-clerical catch-all of falling under the influence of a foreign power, the papacy. Wolsey surrendered the Great Seal of his office on 18 October 1529. He wept in front of his household, telling his servants that he felt like an early Christian martyr. 'If I had served God as diligently as I have done the king,' he said, 'He would not have given me over in my grey hairs.'

Tyndale's slavering 'Wolfsee' was gone, but his departure added to the exile's perils. The cardinal was humane and compassionate. Three condemned men and women with halters around their necks had been led into Westminster Hall in the king's presence after anti-foreigner riots in London a decade before. Four had already been hung, drawn and quartered, and seven hanged. Wolsey 'besought his Majesty most earnestly' to grant the survivors grace, and when Henry at length agreed, Wolsey announced it to them with tears of relief flooding down his face, as they took off their halters and flung them in the air, jumping 'for extreme joy'.

Sir Thomas More had looked on, dressed in black, saying nothing. He was now told that he was to become the first lay chancellor of England for almost a century. He was sworn in at a ceremony in the lofty hammer-beamed Westminster Hall on 26 October. He gave his word that he would not 'suffer the hurte nor disherytyng of the king or that thye rightes of the crown be decreysed by any mean'. Henry reminded him at once that the great royal hurt was the failure to obtain the annulment. 'His grace moved me agayne,' More wrote, 'to loke and consydre his great mater.'

More was now the highest officer of the executive government, and the supreme figure in the law of England. He described the post as a gift from God. 'The more I realise that this post involves the interests of Christendom, my dearest Erasmus,' he wrote to his friend, 'the more I hope it turns out successfully.' He was Tyndale's greatest enemy, and he was a man-burner.

14

Eye for Eye, Tothe for Tothe

'In the begynnynge God created heauen and erth. The erth was voyd and emptie, and darknesse was vpon the depe, and the Spirete of God moued uponne the water, Then God sayde: let there be lyghte . . .' Thus, in the first English rendering to be made from the Hebrew, Tyndale opened Genesis.

The preface bore his initials, 'W. T. to the Reader', for it was pointless by now to disguise his identity. The colophon made the familiar claim – 'Emprented at Marlborow in the lande of Hesse, by me Hans Luft, the yere of our Lorde 1530 MCCCCC. xxx the .xvij dayes of Ianvarij' – but it was the work of van Hoochstraten in Antwerp. Van Hoochstraten had more reason than ever to falsify the book's origins. An edict issued by the imperial authorities in Antwerp on 7 December had warned that henceforth no one was to write, print or cause to be written or printed any new book 'upon what subject soever', without first obtaining letters of licence. The penalty was to be 'pilloried, and marked besides with a red-hot iron', or to have an eye put out or a hand cut off at the discretion of the judge, who was to see that sentence be 'executed without delay or mercy'.

Tyndale printed his translation of the Pentateuch, the Old Testament books of Moses, at Antwerp in 1530. A false colophon claimed that it was 'emprented at Marlborow in the lande of Hesse' to throw his pursuers off the scent. He could only afford to illustrate Exodus, using a secondhand woodcut of Aaron (above) dressed in the robes of a high priest, and others showing the ornaments of the tabernacle. He bought the woodcuts from an Antwerp printer who had used them before in a Flemish Bible.

(British Library)

Each of the first five books of the Old Testament was printed separately with its own prologue, so that the flat sheets could be shipped to England in parts for the reader to bind into a whole book. Genesis and Numbers were set in the Gothic bastard black-letter type, familiar to readers of the New Testament, *Mammon* and *Obedience*. The other books were printed in Roman type. Van Hoochstraten was probably using two presses simultaneously in order to finish the contract and to be rid of incriminating page formes as quickly as possible.

Only Exodus had illustrations, a woodcut of Aaron dressed in the robes of a high priest, and ten others showing the ornaments of the tabernacle. The woodcuts had been used before, by the Antwerp printer Willem Vostermann in the Flemish Bible he had published two years before. Vostermann happily printed large numbers of anti-Lutheran pamphlets, as well as evangelical works, but his secondhand woodcuts were doubtless cheap, and that counted for more than his dubious religious loyalties.

Tyndale had probably sailed back to Antwerp to supervise the printing in late November or early December 1529. An epidemic of the sweating sickness broke out in Hamburg then, and this may have helped to convince him that it was best to leave Germany. He was based in Antwerp from now until his capture, leaving the city at times when he felt threatened, though we do not know for where.

It did not take long for the Church, and the new lord chancel-lor, to discover that the heretic was at work again. A denunciation issued by Archbishop Warham at a meeting of divines on 24 May 1530 spoke of 'the translation of scripture corrupted by William Tyndale, as well in the Old Testament as in the New'. Informers must have spotted smuggled copies before then. A royal procla-mation the following month mentioned both Testaments as heretical works 'now in print'.

*

Tyndale had now written, financed, published and distributed four books in the six years since he had left England. He had produced the greatest body of work so far printed in English, and in doing so he had created a modern English prose that matched every emotion and nuance of thought in the New Testament, a book whose force and beauty changed the lives of many who read it. He had also remained a free man, an equally remarkable feat, able to cope with the strains of being hunted and rootless. He had grown greatly in confidence.

No longer did he submit his translation as unworthy and humbly beg forgiveness for his errors. His preface to Genesis recalled that he had 'desired them that were learned to amend if ought were found amiss' in his New Testament. This had no effect on 'our wily and malicious hypocrites'. They wished to 'keep the world still in darkness', and – here Tyndale galloped off on his moral high horse – to peddle their 'vain superstition and false doctrine', to 'satisfy their filthy lusts, their proud ambition, and insatiable covetousness', and to 'exalt their own honour above king and emperor' and, if that were not enough, 'yea, and above God himself'. He challenged 'our prelates those stubborn Nimrods' to 'burn this book' – Genesis – but only if 'it seem worthy when they have examined it with the Hebrew', so that they first 'put forth of their own translation that is more correct'.

The marginal notes alongside the immortal prose of the biblical text snap and fizz against the pope and clergy. When Moses says angrily to the Lord that 'I have not taken so much as an ass from them', Tyndale asks: 'Can our priests so say?' In Numbers 23, Balaam asks: 'How shall I curse whom God curseth not and how shall I defy whom the Lord defieth not?' Tyndale snipes from the margin: 'The pope can tell how.' Where Exodus 22 commands that 'ye shall trouble no widow nor fatherless child', he adds his own warning to heartless priests: 'Let all oppressors of the poor take heed to this text.'

Both More and Tyndale produced invective by the yard. More was more profligate, spraying it for page after page, sometimes rambling on as though his mind had fallen asleep in the early Chelsea hours, and his hand kept moving on some ghostly planchette; he was more malicious, too, and more personal than Tyndale. There were fewer constraints on More, of course; Tyndale had limited funds to pay his printing bills, and had to publish in secret, whereas More had a lord chancellor's income and a brother-in-law who was a printer.

There are wonderful words and phrases that run through their work and their disputes. Some, alas, have disappeared. A *gorbelly* was a fat man, often to be found in a *sottys hoffe*, a drinking den, where he became *sowe-drunke*, and a *nodypoll* was a blockhead who was often *apysshe*, or fantastically foolish. A *prym* was a pretty girl, and a *galyarde* a high spirited young man, with an eye for *caterwaywynge*, lechery. Some fine expressions have survived. *Huker muker* was the early form of hugger-mugger, or in secret, as a *iack an apes* was a ridiculous fellow. To *play mumme* was already to stay silent, while to be on *tenter hokes* referred to the hooks that kept the cloth under tension in a tenter, or press, and *aloufe*, soon to be aloof, came from *aluff*, to windward, unattainable. Tyndale has *brainpan* for head, and *goggle-eyed*, as well as the vanished *fainty* and *flaggy*; More has *out of a fryenge panne in to the fyre*, a *mone made of grene chese* and *as bare as a byrdys ars*. *Bychery* was ever bitchery, but some words have changed with time. A *Cokney* was not a Londoner, but a pet or a child who was tenderly brought up; *gossipes* were simply female friends, and *mynyons* were favourites.

More produced a list of the insults that Tyndale and his ilk hurled at Catholics: 'tormentours . . . traytours . . . Pylatys . . . Iudass . . . Herodys . . . Antecrystes . . . horemasters and sodomytes . . . iuglers . . . Crystekyllers . . . serpenters . . . scorpyons . . . meryre quellers . . . bloodsupers' who were 'abomynable . . . shameles . . .

pevysshe . . . faythlesse . . . and starke madde'. For all this, and its heroic, no-hold's-barred vigour, sixteenth-century vilification can pall. Tyndale knew a thousand ways to skin the pope, and More to flay the heretic, and they used them all, several times over, so that they penetrate the modern mind – free of the awe of those words, *pope, heretic*, and their terrible accoutrements, *inquisitor, stake, fire* – with the shrill inconsequence of a faulty burglar alarm.

It is when Tyndale gives the reader advice – 'as thou readest therefore think that every syllable pertaineth to thine own self, and suck out the pith of the scripture, and arm thyself against all assaults' – that his genius returns.

What, after all, is the Bible for? He tackles the 'use of the scripture' in a special prologue to Genesis. All of the Bible serves 'to strength thy faith', or, in darker mode, 'to fear thee from evil doing'; there is no story or gest in it, 'seem it never so simple or so vile unto the world', but that 'thou shalt find therein spirit and life and edifying', for this is God's scripture, 'written for thy learning and comfort'. A precious jewel, he says, is no more than straw to the man who does not know its value. We must thus desire God, to make us understand and feel why the Bible was given to us, so that 'we may apply the medicine of the scripture, every man to his own sores . . .'

The scripture is a true light that shows us 'both what to do and what to hope'; it is a defence from all error, and a solace and consolation. This comfort, Tyndale said, was to be found in the plain text and literal sense. 'Cleave unto the texte and the playne storye,' he advised his readers. This was a crucial point. For a thousand years and more, Christian congregations had heard the scripture only as a series of disconnected brief texts on which their priest hung his sermon. Long discourses were spun off a verse or a parable. Scholars argued on the meanings behind the apparent meaning – 'idle disputers and brawlers about vain words,' Tyndale said, 'ever gnawing on the bitter bark without and never attaining to the sweet pith within'. To Tyndale, the Bible is to be read as a whole, and the words accepted for what they are; for it tells a tale that any man or woman can understand, without being ordained, or studying theology.

Those who thought themselves great clerics, he said, saw many of the stories in the Bible as though they were mere inventions like 'a tale of Robin Hood' that had to be seen as allegories. But they were real to Tyndale; they were 'written for our consolation and comfort, that we despair not, if such like happens to us'. We are no better than Lot, and no holier than David, who 'brake wedlock and . . . committed abominable murder'; what happened to them was in the scripture as an example for us so that if 'we yet fall like-wise, that we despair not but come again to the laws of God and take better hold'.

Horrors abound in life. Virgins have been 'brought into the common stews, and there defiled'; martyrs have been bound up 'and whores have abused their bodies'. Why? The judgements of God are 'bottomless'. Tyndale says such things are 'chanced partly for examples, partly God through sin healeth sin'. Terrible events are needed to cure pride. Here Tyndale steers the reader into Protestant propaganda. Those of 'the pope's sect' rejoice 'fleshly . . .'. They think that 'heaven came by deeds and not by Christ', and that performing good works justifies them and makes them holy. But, he says in a classic statement of justification by faith, salvation comes from the 'inward spirit received by faith and the consent of the heart unto the law of God'.

He pumped into the reader the urgency and life that he brought to his own work of translation. Now, in a simple book, at an affordable price, the word of God existed in English for 'all men until the world's end'; such a thing had never happened before, and Tyndale's prologues tingle with the excitement of the new. 'Then go to and read the stories of the bible for thy learning and comfort,' he says, 'and see every thing practised before thine eyes . . .' In these pages, the reader can find the love and compassion of God, and His anger. 'All mercy that is shewed there is a promise unto thee, if thou turn to God,' Tyndale says, directly and intimately to the reader. 'And all vengeance and wrath shewed there is threatened to thee, if thou be stubborn and resist.'

His love for his great Bible project is palpable. Why does he work, at this most dangerous of labours? 'I answer that love compelleth me,' he says. 'For as long as my soul feeleth what love God hath shewed me in Christ, I cannot but love God again and his will and commandments and of love work them.' He does not think himself better for it, nor seek a higher place in heaven. He has 'prayed, sorrowed, longed, sighed and sought' to be of God, 'that which I have this day found, and therefore rejoice with all my might and praise God for his grace and mercy'.

From this devotion came phrases that still roll around the English-speaking world: 'an eye for an eye, a tothe for a tothe', 'the spirite ys willynge, but the flesshe is weeke', and the eternal blessing, 'The Lorde blesse the and keep the. The Lorde make his face shyne upon the and be mercyfull unto the. The Lord lift up his countenance uponne the, and give the peace.' So, too, a reminder of the savagery that some readers mined from the Old Testament, were the eight terrible words from Exodus 22 used in witch trials to justify the burning, hanging and drowning of more than a hundred thousand pitiful souls in Europe, and a handful at Salem in Massachusetts: 'Thou shalt not suffer a witch to live.'

Tyndale's Ten Commandments have travelled the centuries almost unchanged. 'Thou shalt have none other gods in my sight . . . Thou shalt make thee no graven image . . . Thou shalt not take the name of the Lord thy God in vain . . . Remember the sabbath day that thou sanctify it . . . Honour thy father and mother, that thy days may be long . . . Thou shalt not kill. Thou shalt not break wedlock. Thou shalt not steal. Thou shalt bear no

false witness against thy neighbour. Thou shalt not covet thy
neighbour's house: neither shalt thou covet thy neighbour's
wife . . .' King James's men, and the revisers almost four hundred
years after them, tweaked a phrase or two. They replaced '*in my
sight*' in the First Commandment with the less concrete 'no other
gods *before me*'. The sabbath day was to be '*kept holy*'; the unmis-
takable command not to '*break wedlock*' was replaced by the more
genteel and lawyerly '*commit adultery*'. But the essence is Tyndale's.

English was gelling while he was writing. He was, of course, a
prime factor in how it set. His Pentateuch was critical to the language. Hebrew narrative strings phrases together by the simple
insertion of 'and', where Latin and Greek use intricate clauses.
Tyndale's translation helped to set up the same flow of English narrative; the Hebrew use of the *noun* of a *noun* – 'the *fat* of the
land', 'the *beast* of the *field*' – was also confirmed in English. The
Old Testament struck readers with storm force; they might know
something of the New Testament, and the outline of Christ's life,
but the dramas, betrayals, murders, seductions, wars, plagues and
catastrophes of the Old were new and compelling. Evangelicals
combed it for the biblical forenames that became popular among
the English – Aaron, Jeremiah, Amos, Ezra, Joshua; its epic tales of
treks and wandering peoples soon inspired them to follow their
patriarchs across the Atlantic to the 'wildernesse among savages
and wild beasts' in America, a place so desperate that an English
pamphleteer said that 'divers malefactors have chosen to be hanged
than go to Virginia'. The settler Edward Johnson saw
Massachusetts in terms of Tyndale's Genesis, a place where 'the
Lord will create a new Heaven, and a new Earth'.

Tyndale very often had a choice between words of Anglo-Saxon
origins, and those derived from Latin and French. Had he stuck
with Latinisms – always virtue and never goodness, fidelity and
not faith, adoration and not worship – the existing Tudor appetite
for Latin neologisms would have grown. The Old Testament

would have a different ring, and so would English. 'The Lord is a *man of war*' he wrote in Exodus 15, but the Lord could have been a '*legionary*' or a '*martial man*'.

Or he might have rejected all Latin expressions and favoured or coined English words. The first Regius professor of Greek at Cambridge, Sir John Cheke, was a linguistic patriot of this sort in the 1540s. He held that 'in writing English none but English words should be used, thinking it a dishonour to our mother tongue to be beholden to other nations for their words and phrases to express our minds'. Cheke tried hard. He used 'mooned' for lunatic, 'hundreder' for centurion, 'bywords' for parables and 'crossed' for crucified. Some of his uses stuck, such as 'freshman' for proselyte. The overall effect was strained. Tyndale's 'O ye of *lyttle fayth*' becomes Cheke's 'Ye *small faythed* men'. When he translated an anglicised version – no doubt he would have used 'Englished' – of Matthew, Cheke described the tax gatherer or publican as a 'toller', and, rejecting the Franco-Latin expression of a house being 'founded' on a rock, was reduced to it being 'groundwrought'.

Those who bought the Pentateuch, either as separate books or as a set, were not used to reading anything so complex in English. English expressions could be as baffling as imports. Thomas Wilson recognised this more than eighty years later when he wrote a concordance of the Bible, an index of its words. He said that even English words so important that they carried with them the 'marrow and pith of our holy religion' strained the limits of under-standing; the vulgar reader jibbed at them 'as at an unknown language'.

A traditionalist, Stephen Gardiner, the bishop of Winchester, drew up a list of Latin words in 1542 that he wanted to be retained in the Bible because of their 'germane and native meaning and for the majesty of their matter'. Almost all of them were, in fact, well on their way to becoming anglicised. They included Baptizare,

Persevare, Apocalypsis, Pietas, Idololatria, Sacrificium, Gloria, Hospitalitas, Conscientia. Words ending in -'io' 'Religio, Satisfactio, Communio, Contentio, Confessio – needed no more than an 'n' to be added to pass muster as English; a 'y' in place of 'ium', 'ia' or 'as' did for Mysterium and Ceremonia and Pietas.

Tyndale's prose was not dominated by these so-called 'inkhorn' words, taken from the Latin. It was a natural process to avoid their overuse because he was not translating from the Latin Vulgate but directly from Greek and Hebrew. The temptation to translate '*scrutamini scripturas*' from the Latin as 'scrutinise the scriptures' is overwhelming; but coming from the Greek, 'search the scriptures' is more natural. He used inkhorn words when it suited, however. As in the New Testament, he varied the words he used in the Old as much as possible, so that the same Hebrew word was rendered by English word and Latin neologism, 'kindred' and 'relation', 'house' and 'habitation', 'acts' and 'deeds', 'aid' and 'help'. He also coined words: passover, scapegoat, mercy seat.

Accuracy was the only constraint on his language. Luther said that, in trying to produce a pure and clear German in translation, it often happened that 'for two or three weeks we have searched and inquired for a single word and sometimes not found it even then'. Tyndale had greater problems, for he was not in his home-land with university libraries and helpers at his beck and call. His translation of Hebrew was not as pinpoint as his rendering of Greek – in places he seems to have worked from Luther's German Bible and the Vulgate – but it was remarkable for the time.

Hebrew studies were transformed when the King James was published in 1611. The universities had professors of Hebrew, and the king's divines had the wisdom of two generations of Hebrew scholars to draw upon. Yet they made few changes to Tyndale's work, and when they did the original was often happier. In the Garden of Eden, Tyndale's serpent introduces himself with a cheery 'Ah, sir!' and reassures Eve: 'Tush, ye shall not die.' The

King James serpent says flatly: 'Ye shall not surely die.' Tyndale writes in Genesis 29: 'Then Jacob lifted up his feet and went toward the east country.' The king's committee added five words, and suppressed the wonderful image of Jacob's feet, all for no profit in meaning: 'Then Jacob went on his journey, and came into the land of the people of the East.' Tyndale's simple 'And when even was come' is made into the pompous 'And it came to pass in the evening.' Tyndale's cadence is clear when he is read aloud: 'And as he looked about, behold there was a well in the field, and iii flocks of sheep lay thereby, for at that well were the flocks watered . . .' The committee men destroy the lilt: 'And he looked, and behold, a well in the field, and lo, there were three flocks of sheep lying by it: for out of that well they watered the flocks . . .' For the most part, providentially, King James's men left well alone. Nine tenths of their Genesis 29 is taken word for word from Tyndale.

Tyndale included explanatory lists of words in his Pentateuch. He was thus the pioneer of English lexicography. It was an idea that took time to develop. The Elizabethan reformer and schoolmaster Richard Mulcaster compiled the first complete list of English words, or rather the eight thousand words that he knew and could recollect, in 1582. His book *First Part of the Elementarie* was based on teaching children English in the same disciplined way that they learnt Latin. 'I love Rome, but London better,' he wrote. 'I favour Italy, but England more. I know the Latin, but I worship the English.'

A more comprehensive book by a schoolmaster father and son, Robert and Thomas Cawdrey, was *A Table Alphabeticall, conteyning and teaching the true writing and understanding of hard usuall English wordes, borrowed from the Hebrew, Greeke, Latine, or French* of 1604. Progress was slow. The first dictionary for general use was *A New English Dictionary* of 1702. Its compiler, John Kersey the

Younger, was the first full-time English lexicographer. The process did not reach its first full flowering until Dr Johnson's two volume *Dictionary*, published on 14 June 1755, finally established standard English through the power of the printed dictionary. 'The English Dictionary,' the irascible doctor explained in the preface, 'was written with little assistance of the learned, and without any patronage of the great; not in the soft obscurities of retirement, or under the shelter of academick bowers, but amidst inconvenience and distraction, in sickness and in sorrow.' Yes; but Johnson did not write under the threat of the fire.

Tyndale, who did, included two 'Tables expounding Certain Wordes' between Genesis and Exodus. They were words that the reader might find difficult. He described them with simplicity in alphabetical order. Alb, he explained, is 'a long garment of white linen'. Ark is 'a ship made flat, as it were a chest or coffer'. Baptism 'now signifieth on the one side, how all that repent and believe are washed in Christ's blood: and on the other side, how the same must quench and drown the lusts of the flesh, to follow the steps of Christ'. Consecrate is 'to appoint a thing to holy uses'; Eden means 'pleasure'; firmament is 'the skies'; sanctify is 'to cleanse and purify'; reconcile is 'to make at one and to bring in grace or favour'; tabernacle is 'an house made tentwise, or as a pavilion'. Grace is 'favour: as Noah found grace, that is to say favour and love'.

He brings a vivid clarity to his mundane task. Vapour is 'a dewy mist, as the smoke of a seething pot'. Sacrament is 'a sign representing such an appointment and promises as the rainbow representeth the promise made to Noe, that God will no more drown the world'. Not that the waters would *recede*, or the flood *subside*, or the crisis *abate*; no, that God *will no more drown* the world.

Tyndale, like all others at the time, cared little for spelling. Noah was also Noe; God was often god. He spelt his own name

variously Tyndale, Tindall, Tindal and Tindale. 'Cain, so it is writ-
ten in Hebrew,' he noted. 'Notwithstanding whether we call him
Cain or Caim it maketh no matter, so we understand the meaning.
Every land hath his manner, that we call John, the Welshmen call
Even: the Dutch Hans.'

There was no mistaking that the lexicographer was a 'newe
man'. Under 'tyrants', he said that these had 'through falsehood of
hypocrisy subdued the world under them, as the successors of the
apostles have played with us'. By the successors, of course, he
meant the popes. Faith, he wrote, is 'the believing of God's promises and a sure trust in the goodness and truth of God. Which faith
justifieth Abraham and was the mother of all his good works
which he afterward did. For faith is the goodness of all works in
the sight of God.' This was the classic Lutheran dogma of the primacy of justification by faith.

A chilling ferocity then enters his definition. Faith, Tyndale
said, justifies evil acts as long as these are done at God's command. Murder can be divine. 'Jacob robbed Laban his uncle,' he
continued. 'Moses robbed the Egyptians: and Abraham is about to
slay and burn his own son.' All these, he claimed, 'are holy works,
because they were wrought in faith at God's commandment'. He
agreed that to steal, rob and murder are not holy works if they are
carried out by 'worldly people'. But crimes were transformed when
they were committed by 'them that have their trust in God', for
'they are holy when God commandeth them'. The 'worldly people'
who had no heavenly licence to sin were the pope, the bishops and
clergy, the chancellor, and all others with whom Tyndale was at
odds; the faithful few for whom crime can become holy work
were his fellow evangelicals. Slaying and burning were elevated
into religious deeds, with the proviso that they must be 'commanded' by God, acting through those who pinned their faith in
God.

*

Evangelicals' fury matched that of the Catholics. In Zwinglian Zurich, heretics were being drowned. The great evangelical Theodore Beza was to argue in Calvinist Geneva that it was wrong to spare a heretic because Christ had turned the other cheek. He said that 'true charity' lay in defending the flock against the wolf. It was the duty of the magistrate to protect his people against crime. Beza described heresy as a crime worse than murder, for that destroyed bodies, where the heretic assassinated souls and God's majesty. Calvin himself said wearily of heretics that 'an end could be put to their machinations in no other way than cutting them off by an ignominious death'.

Heresy was firmly established in Catholicism as the most mortal of all sins. 'In our charity towards God's sheep, who must all die some day, some way,' St Augustine, greatest of the Latin Fathers, had written in 430, 'we should be more afraid of a butchery of their minds by the sword of spiritual evil than of their bodies by a sword of steel.' He condoned the use of torture for heretics. 'We often have to act with a sort of kindly harshness, when we are trying to make unwilling souls yield,' he wrote, 'because we have to consider their welfare rather than their inclination.' It was good for a heretic to suffer, since 'nothing is more hopeless than the happiness of sinners'.

The principle of the 'just war' against heretics had been enshrined by the Bolognese monk and jurist Gratian in the *Decretum Gratiani* of about 1140. This passed into the *Corpus Iuris Canonici*, the chief collection of canon law, which laid down ecclesiastical rules on faith, morals and discipline in the Catholic Church for the next nine centuries. '*Ecclesiasticae religionis inimici etiam bellis sunt cohercendi*', Gratian wrote in his concise and unyielding Latin, 'the enemies of the Church and religion are coerced by war'. St Thomas Aquinas, known as 'Doctor Angelicus' for the divine inspiration that he was thought to bring to his teaching, had demonstrated to the satisfaction of the medieval

Church that heresy separates man from God more than any other sin. As an actual and physical emissary of Satan, the heretic was held to merit the fiercest punishment of burning alive. As the successor to St Peter, Catholics believed, the pope was God's representative on earth. He therefore had the right to establish the Inquisition, and to encourage and condone acts of repression that included the torture and burning of 'newe men'.

The evangelicals did not yet have the power to punish others in England and the Low Countries. Tyndale had no way of unleashing the 'holy work' of divine retribution against recalcitrant Catholics. For the moment, at least, Catholics remained in authority, and the English had in Thomas More a chancellor whose wrath with heretics was boundless.

The time of burnings had come.

15

The Shorte Fyre

There had been no burnings in England for eight years. More soon put a stop to that. He did not quite condemn his predecessors – 'I will not say that the Judges did wrong' – but he made it clear that he thought them lax. The heretic had been mollycoddled, allowed to escape through recantation and faggot-carrying, and in this the bishops and church officers were 'almost more than lawful, in that they admitted him to such an abjuration as they did, and that they did not rather leave him to the secular arm'. He concluded that 'in the condemnation of heretics, the clergy might lawfully do much more sharply than they do'.

The little phrase 'leave him to the secular arm' is very much less innocent than it seems. In legal terms, a prisoner was 'relaxed' after the Church had found him guilty of heresy. This did not involve a period of rest and relaxation for the unfortunate, of course, far from it. It meant that the Church authorities 'relaxed' their hold on him by transferring him to the secular authorities for execution. The ritual handing over was designed to preserve the principle that *Ecclesia non novit sanguinem*, the Church does not shed blood. It provided a form of ecclesiastical fig leaf, since laymen carried out the actual burning, but it was a singularly transparent one. No churchman exonerated the Pharisees for the death of Christ on the grounds that they had merely handed Jesus to Pilate for sentencing, and that Roman soldiers had performed the crucifixion.

A priest named Thomas Hitton was the first to suffer from More's new 'sharpness'. He was seized near Gravesend in January 1530 as he was making his way to the coast to take a ship for Antwerp. Hitton had fled to join Tyndale and the English exiles in the Low Countries after becoming a convinced evangelical. He returned to England on a brief visit to contact supporters of Tyndale and to arrange for the distribution of smuggled books. The first English psalter had been published in Antwerp in January, as well as Tyndale's Pentateuch, in a translation by George Joye that included a commentary 'declarynge brefly thentente and substance of the wholl psalme'.

Hitton was walking through fields by the coast, his mission completed, when he was stopped by a posse of men looking for a thief who had stolen some linen that was drying on a hedge. They searched him. He had no linen, but hidden pockets were found in his coat that held letters 'unto the evangelycall heretykes beyonde the see'. Unfortunately for the wretched Hitton, the new chancellor's strictures on heretics were fresh in people's minds. The men handed Hitton over to the archbishop of Canterbury's officers.

At his interrogation before the archbishop, Hitton refused to recant and remained true to his new beliefs. 'The mass he sayed sholde never be sayed', it was recorded of his answers. 'Purgatory he denyed ... No man hath any fre wyll after that he hath ons synned ... all the images of Cryste and hys sayntes sholde bde thrown out of the chyrche.'

Sentence was swiftly passed and executed: Thomas Hitton was burnt alive at Maidstone on 23 February 1530. He was the first of the Reformation martyrs. The English exiles in Antwerp were shocked. They had a new calendar printed with 23 February marked as the 'day of St Thomas'.

More gloated. He claimed that Hitton was arrested 'for pilfering certain linen clothes that were hanging on a hedge', which was untrue, and he indulged his strange obsession with married Lutheran priests. Hitton 'meant by likelihood that it was good enough to wed upon a cushion when the dogs be abed, as their [Lutheran] priests wed,' he wrote, 'for else they let not to wed openly at church, and take the whole parish for witness of their beastly bitchery'.

In fact, there is no evidence that Hitton wished to marry, although most evangelical converts in the priesthood did so. But More's speculation was bound up with his guilt at his own marriage, and his desertion of a Church career. He wore a hair shirt as an act of permanent though secret penance. Among his family, he told only his daughter Meg, although his daughter-in-law spotted it once in the summer as he sat at supper in his doublet and hose, wearing a plain shirt without ruff or collar to hide it. He whipped himself as well, though the Church had frowned on this since the excesses of the flagellants who had roamed Europe during the Black Death, beating themselves and murdering Jews, and singing the haunting words of the *Stabat Mater*:

> Wound me with his wounds
> Let me drink his cross
> For the love of thy son.

Meg used to wash the bloodstains from his shirt. 'He used sometimes to punish his body with whips, the cords knotted,' his son-in-law William Roper wrote, 'which was known only to my wife, his eldest daughter, whom for her secrecy above all other he specially trusted, causing her as need required to wash the same shirt of hair.'

More used the Hitton case to vent his spite against Tyndale. He wrote that Hitton had learnt his 'false faith and heresies' from 'Tyndale's holy books'. Under Tyndale's influence, the 'beggarly knave' had 'cast off matins and mass and all divine service' and had become 'an apostle, sent to and fro between our English heretics beyond the sea and such as were here at home'. And now, at Maidstone, More wrote with the murderous glee of a man possessed, 'the spirit of errour and lyenge hath taken his wretched soule with him strayte from the shorte fyre to ye fyre euer lastyng. And this is lo syr Thomas Hytton, the dyuyls stynkyng martyr, of whose burnynge Tyndale maketh boste.'

The wrath of the Church, and of More, had special qualities. They damned their victims twice. The *poena sensus*, the punishment of the senses, had been achieved by the earthly 'shorte fyre' at Maidstone. But the heretic was also condemned to the *poena damni*, the sentence of damnation that separated him from God for ever in the fires of hell. Tyndale had himself translated the biblical passages that would in time be used to condemn him. The justification for the first penalty came from Paul's First Epistle to the Corinthians: 'And the fyre shal trye every man's worke, what it is.' (I Corinthians 3:13) Christ himself was invoked for the second: 'Departe from me ye cursed, into ever lastynge fyre, which is prepared for the devile and his angells' (Matthew 25.41).

The dead man was no saint, More said, but a thief and a coward. Tyndale should not glory in him, but should scrape his name from the calendar, and 'restore the blessed bishop saint Polycarp', burnt in Smyrna in about 155.

The malice that drove More against Tyndale was a phenomenon, insatiable, galloping, morbific. It consumed his finer instincts, including his respect for the law. He was bound by oath as chancellor to abide by fourteenth-century statutes that required him to exert himself to the maximum in suppressing heretics. He was equally bound to obey the laws regulating their punishment.

The acts under which heretics were liable to persecution had been passed under Henry IV in 1401 and under Henry V in 1414. The bishops were obliged by the Act of Henry IV to bring offenders to trial in open court within three months of their arrest. If conviction followed, they could imprison the offender at their discretion. They were not at liberty to imprison any suspect except under these conditions. Under the Act of Henry V, a heretic who was first indicted in front of a secular judge had to be delivered to a bishop, 'to be acquit or convict' by a jury in the spiritual court, within a maximum of ten days.

A suspected heretic thus had some clearly defined rights. A secular judge could detain him for no more than ten days before delivering him to a bishop. The bishop could not imprison him for more than three months before trial. Neither judge nor bishop had the power to extend imprisonment if the trial was delayed. If the accused was acquitted, he could no longer be detained on the same charge. These safeguards were hardly onerous to the prosecution, and the chancellor, as the senior law officer in the kingdom, should have set an example in upholding them. Wolsey had done so.

More broke them within six weeks of coming to power. His first victim was a Londoner named Thomas Philippis, or Philips, a leather seller whom More took home to interrogate in Chelsea. 'Vpon certayn thynges that I found out by him,' More recollected, 'I sent for, and when I hadde spoken wyth hym, and honestly intreated hym one day or twayne in myne house, and laboured about his amendement in as harty louynge maner as I coulde: when I perceyued fynally the person suche that I could fynde no trouthe, . . . a man mete and lykely to do many folkie mych harme: I by endenture delyuered hym to his ordynary.' The 'ordinary' to whom More delivered his prisoner was Cuthbert Tunstall, the bishop of London, acting as the judge in the ecclesiastical case of heresy brought against Philips. Tunstall's vicar general, a man named Foxford, prepared the charges.

By rights, Philips should have been consigned to the bishop's prison. More feared a repetition of the Richard Hunne scandal, however. He said that Philips had 'a great spyce of the same spyryt of pryde that I perceyued beforc in Rycharde Hunne when I talked with him'; he feared that 'yf he were in ye byshoppes prysone, his gostcly cnymy ye deuyll myghte make hym there destroy hym selfe'. Whatever More thought of the 'hearty loving manner' in which he interrogated Philips, the example had certainly terrified a cousin of Philips, a 'barbour in Paternoster row called Holy Iohan', who, 'after that he was susspected of heresye and spoken to thereof', had drowned himself in a well. More said that he did so 'ferynge the shame of the worlde', but it is equally possible that the unfortunate Holy John killed himself in fear of the 'hearty loving manner' which More had brought to the examination of his cousin. Determined to watch his own back and ensure that no 'new besynes aryse agaynste master chauncellour', More arranged for Philips to be 'receyued prysoner in to the towre of London'.

The only evidence Foxford found against Philips was a 'general rumour' that he was a gospeller. Philips denied each separate charge in detail. The jury refused to convict him. He was 'found so clear from all manner of infamous slanders and suspicions,' Philips's petition to parliament later declared, 'that all the people before the said Bishop, shouting in judgement as with one voice, openly witnessed his good name and fame, to the great reproof and shame of the said Bishop'.

The case having failed, More was obliged by law to release Philips immediately. Instead, he called on the prisoner to confess his guilt by abjuring his heresy, 'as if,' Philips himself wrote, 'there were no difference between a nocent and an innocent, between a guilty and a not guilty'. In February 1530, the humane Tunstall had been elevated to the ancient bishopric of Durham, where he was to distinguish himself during the persecution of Protestants in Mary's reign by refusing to permit executions, though the fires burnt brightly in surrounding dioceses. He was replaced as bishop of London by John Stokesley, previously a chaplain to the king who had flattered his master by working hard for the divorce, a man altogether fiercer and suited to Thomas More's taste.

More and Stokesley sent for Philips from time to time, examining him in private, again illegally. They repeated their calls to him to confess, Philips complained, 'to save the Bishop's credit'. When they tired of his obstinacy, Stokesley declared Philips to be excommunicated. There was no appeal against this arbitrary sentence, except to the pope. It left the miserable Philips outside the protection of the law, and he was committed to the Tower, where he languished for three years.

John Petite was another of Tyndale's readers who 'cowght a swheetnes in Godes worde', and fell foul of More. Petite was a city burgess of London and one of its four Members of Parliament, a Grocer, an educated man well versed in history and the Latin tongue. He was also 'sore suspected of the lord chawncelor' of being a believer 'of the relegione that they called newe, and also a bearer with them in pryntyng of theyr bookes'. He lived in a house at Lion's Quay, on the river next to Billingsgate close to what is today the Swiss Bank building, a substantial property known as Petite's Quay.

More was unsure where Tyndale's Testaments were coming from; indeed, with the pirate editions, Tyndale himself cannot have been certain. Most doubtless came from Antwerp, but More did not rule out the possibility that some were being printed in England. He knew that Tyndale needed funds, for printing, for messengers and books and his daily life, and that the people supplying the money were most likely to be English sympathisers. Petite was a wealthy man, and More identified him as a Tyndale benefactor who had helped with printing operations.

More raided Petite's Quay in the early winter of 1530, with a lieutenant and armed guards, startling Lucy Petite who 'whypped in haste' to warn her husband – 'come, come, my lorde chawncelor ys at the dore, and wolde speake with yow'. The house was searched, while Petite attended to More with 'greate curtesy, thankyng hym that it wold please his lordship to visitt hym in his own poore howse'.

A copy of Tyndale's New Testament 'layc undernethe mr Petite's desk' as More searched his room, 'yet the chawncelor saw it not, by what meanes God knoweth . . .'. But Petite was not to escape so lightly.

As they were parting at the door, More asked him: 'Ye say ye have none of these newe bookes?'

'Your lordship sawe my bookes and my closett.'

'Yet, ye must go with Mr Lieutenante,' More said, and turned to the officer. 'Take hym to yow.'

Petite was led away to the Tower, where More had his prisoner 'layd in a doungeone apon a padd of strawe, in close prison'. It was only 'after longe sute and dayly teares' that Lucy Petite persuaded the chancellor to allow her husband the use of a bed.

An informant, described as 'a lytle old preest', was said to have made a statement incriminating Petite. In it, the priest claimed that Petite 'hadd Tyndale's testamente in Englyshe, and dyd helpe hym and suche other to puyblish theyre hertycall bookes in Englyshe'. Petite's health was undermined in prison – he 'caght hys dethe by so nawghty harbor of the lord chawncelor' – before he was allowed to face his accuser. The priest broke down, however, and withdrew his evidence: 'Mr Petite, I never saw yow afore this tyme; how should I then be able to accuse you?'

Petite could not be prosecuted without this key witness, and More had little option but to release him. Petite emerged from prison a sick man, with a 'payne came over his cheste lyke a barre of yron'. He died two years later, and More's wrath pursued him to the churchyard, where 'preestes powred sope ashes upon hys grave, affirmyng that God wold not suffer grasse to grow upon suchye an heretyckes grave'.

As we shall see, evangelicals claimed that More broke the law in his treatment of others whom he suspected of dealing or sympathising with Tyndale. In several cases, as with Philips, he illegally detained them at his house in Chelsea.

He was rightly proud of his estate. His friend Erasmus said that it was 'neither mean nor subject to envy, yet magnificent and commodious enough'. That More should have taken his work home with him, as it were, and imprison heretics in the bosom of his family, shows the extent of his obsession. Chelsea was very much a family home. He often had there with him his wife, his son, his daughter-in-law, his three daughters and their husbands, and his eleven grandchildren; Hans Holbein had rooms there for many months while painting his fine portraits of the family, and scholars, actors, divines and, on occasion, the king dined and debated at what Erasmus described as More's little 'Plato's Academy' in Chelsea.

The property ran from the present King's Road to the Thames, bordered by Beaufort Street to the west and Old Church Street to the east. The large gardens had apple trees, roses and a collection of herbs. The gatehouse had a flat lead roof, which More would climb for the views across the river to the fields of Battersea and the line of the Clapham hills. A landing stage allowed him to use his barge to travel to Westminster at any state of the tide.

He had a gallery, library and chapel built. On Fridays, when he had time, he retired to these buildings to spend the day in meditation and prayer. He assembled the family in the chapel morning and evening, to recite prayers and psalms, and he heard mass daily. He attended Chelsea Church by the river on Sundays. He paid for its communion plate, and for the building of its south aisle, and he sang in the choir, wearing a surplice like a common singing-man. The duke of Norfolk, visiting to dine with him during his chancellorship, was shocked to find him wearing his surplice. 'God's body, my lord chancellor!' he cried. 'What! A parish clerk! A parish clerk! You dishonour the king and his office.' More replied that his king could not be offended that he was serving his other master, God. Animals were a passion. Erasmus recalled that More kept many varieties of birds, and an ape, a fox, a weasel and a ferret in a little menagerie. He had different breeds of dog, and sat with his favourites on the gatehouse.

He was, of course, less fond of heretics. The garden had a 'tree of Troth' which More used as a whipping post. The porters' lodge in the gatehouse was fitted out with stocks, and with chains and fetters, to pinion suspects while he interrogated them.

More said that the flogging charges were the invention of a Cambridge book dealer, Segar Nicholson, whom he arrested and kept in his house for four or five days in 1530 for selling banned books by Tyndale and others. Nicholson claimed that he had been whipped at the tree in the garden, and that cords had been wound round his head and tightened until he fainted. More denied it. Nicholson 'neuer hadde eyther bodely harme done hym,' More wrote, 'or fowle worde spoken hym whyle he was in myne house'. He added that Tyndale claimed that while Nicholson was being beaten, 'I spyed a little purse of hys hangynge at his doublette . . . and put it in my bosome'; More said that he had never taken a groat – 4d – 'by all the theuys, murderers and heretykes that euer came in my handes'.

He claimed that only two heretics had been flogged at his orders. One was a boy in his service who came from a heretical family – the father had known George Joye – and who had denied the real presence of Christ in the sacrament. 'I caused a servant of mine to stripe him like a child before mine household,' More wrote, 'for amendment of himself and example of such other.'

The other was a local lunatic, 'which after that he had fallen into the frantic heresies, fell soon after into plain open frenzy beside,' More wrote mockingly; the man would creep up behind a woman in church, and lift up her skirts and throw them over her head. He was pointed out to More as he passed the Chelsea house. The chancellor had him seized, tied to the garden tree and publicly flogged. 'They striped him with rods until he waxed weary and somewhat longer,' More wrote with evident self-satisfaction.

He agreed that he had often sentenced men to be flogged for robbery, murder, or 'sacrilege in church, with carrying away the pyx with the blessed sacrament, or villainously casting it out'. But he denied that he had commanded any other heretics to be flogged, 'notwithstanding also that heretics be yet much worse than all they'.

This stretches the truth. Evangelicals often made off with the communion bread, or ground it underfoot, or committed other 'sacrilege in church' in protest against Catholic dogma. We shall see that three suspects close to Tyndale were flogged or racked in More's presence, that the use of the stocks in Chelsea amounted to torture, and that More made free with threats of violence. He never denied that he held prisoners at Chelsea, 'for suretie'; rather, he was proud of it.

In April 1530, More introduced a bill dealing with beggars and vagabonds. As a writer, in *Utopia* he had denounced cruelty and punishment as a way of dealing with vagrancy. As lord chancellor, he condemned any healthy man or woman found outside his native parish, who had no licence to beg or proof of how he earned his living, to be stripped naked, tied to a cart-tail and whipped publicly through the streets 'till his body be bloody by reason of such whipping'.

He acted to extend his powers to punish Tyndale's readers. The Testament, and now the Pentateuch, were circulating at a growing pace. Bishop Nix at Norwich was alarmed to hear rumours that the king secretly welcomed the success of the books. He therefore wrote to Henry to warn him that, unless these stories were scotched by a royal proclamation, his diocese would fall to the reformers, its long coastline being so handy to the smugglers across the North Sea.

Henry summoned a conclave of thirty bishops and divines to meet at Westminster. More attended as the only layman, and his 'dylygent and longe consyderacyon' were praised by the grateful clergy. On 24 May, Archbishop Warham and the others issued a Public Instrument for the 'abolishing of the Scripture and other Books to be read in English'. It listed the 'Heresies and Errors collected by the Bishops out of the Book of Tyndale named *The Wicked Mammon*'. The first was the reformers' touchstone – 'Faith only justifieth' – but the others were distortions. Tyndale was quoted as saying, for example, that 'Christ with all his works did not deserve heaven'; this apparently shocking claim was achieved by hiding half of Tyndale's sentence, for what he actually wrote in *Mammon* was: 'Christ did not deserve heaven (for that was his already).'

Three or four of the divines at the conclave favoured the publishing of an English Bible. Word reached Tyndale at Antwerp that More made sure that they were overruled. The bishops had 'disputed before the king's grace that it [translating] is perilous and not meet,' Tyndale noted, 'where Master More was their special orator, to feign lies for their purpose.' The conclave's decision was given visible force by the bishop of London, who caused 'all his New Testaments which he had brought, with many other books, to be brought into Paul's churchyard in London, and there openly burned . . .'.

The royal proclamation was printed in June. More's hand can be seen in its linking of heresy and treason. The king condemned *Mammon* and *Obedience* and other 'blasphemous and pestiferous

English books', adding that they had been brought into the realm for the purpose of sedition and revolt. Henry could hardly denounce his native tongue or the scriptures, and he paid lip service to the notion of an English Bible. He dealt first with Tyndale's work. He demanded that his people abandon 'all perverse, erroneous and seditious opinions, with the New Testament and the Old, now being in print'. Then, and only then, would he allow a translation to be made by 'great, learned and catholic persons'. Henry warned that, in the meantime, all books of scripture in English were to be surrendered to the bishops' officers within fifteen days.

By using a proclamation to ban heretical books, and by denouncing Tyndale's work as '*seditiosa dogmata*', so that the offence of ownership included sedition, More was able to deal with offenders personally in the Star Chamber. The *camera stellata*, a great chamber at Westminster with a starred ceiling, housed the king's council when it sat as a judicial tribunal to prevent abuses of the courts and to hear cases of public disorder, including riot, libel and sedition. More, as chancellor, was able to deal with offenders personally, bypassing the bishops' courts. He had several suspect booksellers arrested in the summer of 1530. Some he sent to the Tower, others he fined. He ordered Thomas Patner, for example, a London merchant, to be held in the Fleet prison on suspicion of distributing Tyndale's Testaments. Patner was eventually released for lack of evidence, only to be rearrested again on the instructions of Bishop Stokesley. A servant of Patner then drafted a petition to lay before parliament to ask for his master's release. When More heard of this, he warned the servant that he would prosecute him for contempt of court as a 'frivolous suitor' if he went ahead with the petition. Patner remained in prison throughout More's chancellorship.

More was fascinated by the game of heretic hunting. He perfected a web of spies and informers in London, and it excited him to know intimate details of those he had watched. He knew, for example, that a heretic met friends in secret 'at the sygne of the botell at Botolfes Wharfe'. This was an inn near London Bridge. He knew that the landlady, the 'good wyfe of the botell of Botolphs', walked wth a limp; he knew, too, that she had allowed two runaway nuns to sleep 'in an hygh garet' of the inn, smuggling in two men to lie with them. She was a garrulous woman, 'nat tong tayed'; he knew that because 'I have herd her talke my selfe'. He was aware that the good spy must be meticulous in his descriptions. He noted that the heretic living at Botolph's Wharf had been seen 'in a merchaunts gowne wyth a redde Myllayne bonet'.

A hothouse of fear and suspicion was thus created. As well as the glamorous suspects taken to the house at Chelsea, arrests took place at a humble village level. One Simon Wisdom of Burford was found with 'three bookes in English, one was the gospels in English, another was the psalter, the third was the Sum of the Holy Scripture in English'. A couple, John and Cecily Eaton, were denounced by 'certain in the parish' to John Longland, the fierce bishop of Lincoln, because they did not look up when the Host was raised during the sacrament, and for saying in a butcher's house when the church bells were rung, 'What a clampering of bells is here!' John Eaton was found to have 'Jesus's Gospels in English'. One James Algar had insulted the pope by following the biblical reference 'Thou art Peter' with another: 'Get thee after me Satan.'

Occasionally, as in 1530, one of the bigger fry was caught. 'Christopher, a Dutchman of Antwerp' was arrested 'for selling certain New Testaments in English to John Row aforesaid bookbinder, was put in prison at Westminster and there died'. This unfortunate was Christoffel van Ruremund, who was running unbound pirate copies of Tyndale into England. More had to wait for more senior men, but he had a stroke of good fortune with the arch-heretic in Antwerp.

Tyndale, with the best of intentions, was engaged in the high-risk enterprise of further irritating Henry VIII.

Over the summer of 1530, Tyndale was busy on a work he called *The Practice of Prelates*. It was printed in the late summer of that year. The false 'Hans Luft' colophon did not give a month of publication. Its main thrust was wholly favourable to the king and disturbing to the chancellor. Tyndale took a gallop through history to show how the papal lust for power had corrupted the Church and the clergy, and led to the humiliation of princes and the misery and ruin of the laity.

It was brilliant and lively propaganda. The Church had betrayed its roots and ceased to be the true Church of Christ, he said, at the time of Pepin, the eighth-century king of the Franks and father of Charlemagne. The popes used the Carolingian emperors to lift themselves from being mere bishops of Rome; then they separated the clergy from the laity, until they finally used canon law and their monopoly of the scriptures to become universal tyrants.

He compared the way 'oure holy father cam up' with the 'ensample of an ivytree: first it springeth out of the erth and then awhyle crepeth alonge by the grounde till it finds a great tree: then it joyneth itself beneth alow unto the bodye of the tre and crepeth upp a litle and litle fayre and softlyer. And at the beninninge while it is yet thyn and small that the burden is not perceaved, it seemeth gloriouse to garnysh the tre in the wyntre and to bere of the tempestes of the wether.' But then the 'foule stinckinge yvye waxeth mightye in the stompe of the tre and becomes a nest for al unclene birdes and for blinde oules which hauke in the darke and dare not come at the lyghte.'

This was how the pope crept up on kings and emperors, and fastened his roots in their hearts, and climbed above them; this was how the pope had 'perverted the ordre of the worlde' and 'put downe ye kingdom of christ and set up ye kingdome of the devell whose vicare he is'. This evil tradition was being continued in England by 'Wolfsee'. All bishops were vain and treacherous to their princes, being 'the pope's creatures'. Henry had been young and inexperienced when he came to the throne, and Wolsey, 'expert and exercised in the course of the world', had surrounded himself with placemen whose role was not to serve the king but 'to water whatsoever the cardinal had planted'.

When he moved on to day-to-day politics, however, Tyndale was as inept as ever. More referred to the 'frantic drifts . . . devised of his own imagination' that appeared in *Prelates*. This was not the result of distance, for a constant stream of people arrived in Antwerp from London, and kept the English expatriates up to date with events. Tyndale's views were coloured by his own naivety. He did not believe that Wolsey had been dismissed, for example, nor that papal influence in England was being broken. He was convinced that Wolsey had retired to his diocese at York merely as a ploy, and that More was a stopgap chancellor who was filling the office until the cardinal made his return, more powerful than ever.

This might be nonsense – 'Tyndale,' More wrote mockingly of *Prelates*, 'has weened to have made a special show of his high worldly wit, and that men should have seen therein that there was nothing done among princes, but that he was fully advertised of all the secrets . . .' – but most of it was harmless. The book had a sub-heading, however: *Whether the King's grace may be separated from his queen because she was his brother's wife*. Tyndale would not leave this question be. The divorce was damaging his enemies in fine style without any need for him to keep poking his nose into the king's great matter. It had ruined Wolsey, now a dying man, and it was poisoning relations between Clement VII and Henry. Campeggio had not returned to England – he was tactless enough to remind Henry of his existence by writing to him in June from Augsburg to congratulate him on the bonfire of Tyndale's books at

St Paul's Cross – and Rome was further than ever from settling the marriage in the king's favour.

The great universities of the Continent as well as England were debating the validity of the marriage. More had been made High Steward of Oxford in 1524, and of Cambridge the following year, but he wisely avoided taking part in the debate. The regents of the English universities were browbeaten into agreeing that God's law forbade a man to marry his brother's widow. Francis I, looking for alliance with England, coaxed the Sorbonne into making the same finding. Charles V ensured that the Spanish divines favoured his aunt's cause. The German Lutherans agreed that the marriage might be invalid, but said that it had been made, and so should stand. Sir Gregory de Casalis, Henry's agent in northern Italy, attempted to bribe the universities of Florence and Milan to back the king, with some success. In July 1530 the bishops, abbots and peers of the House of Lords signed a petition to the pope, asking him to give judgement in the king's favour. The chancellor did not sign the document.

Where More was too canny to venture, Tyndale felt compelled to plunge in. 'I could not but declare my mind,' he wrote, 'to discharge my conscience withal.' He said that 'neither can the king's grace or any other man of right be discontent with me', for even 'so vile a wretch' as himself had the right to see how a fellow Christian's conduct compared with God's law. The king did not see it like that, of course, as a man less uncompromising than Tyndale, and blessed with greater insight into the deviousness of human nature, must have realised. Henry was a ruler, whose power over his fellow mortals was summed up in the adage *Indignatio principis mors est*, 'the prince's wrath means death'. Tyndale was a mere heretic in exile.

All was not lost, nevertheless, provided that Tyndale now came down on the side of the lovers. He had every reason to do so. Anne Boleyn continued to support reformers through Dr Butts, the royal physician. She rewarded the Cambridge theologian Hugh Latimer for his support by making him one of her chaplains, and encouraging his elevation to the see of Worcester. She urged her household staff to read and discuss the scriptures, and asked her chaplains to teach her servants 'above all things to embrace the wholesome doctrine and infallible knowledge of Christ's gospel'. An admirer wrote to her at New Year 1530 that he had seen her at Lent 'reading the salutary epistles of St Paul, in which are contained the whole manner and rule of a good life'. The epistles were the mark of the evangelical.

With staggering simple-mindedness, however, Tyndale judged the matter solely by the Bible. He said that he 'did my diligence a long season' to find the reasons that the English bishops and universities supported the divorce, but 'I could not find them'. He had tried as best he could, he wrote in *Prelates*, but there was 'no lawful excuse . . . by any scripture that I ever read'. He had even consulted 'divers learned men of the matter', presumably among the other exiled priests in Antwerp, and that proved equally fruitless. There was no scriptural necessity for the annulment and common morality was against it. Having laid down that Henry must stay with Catherine, Tyndale then castigated the king for his sharp criticisms of Luther's marriage to the former nun. He advised Henry to fear lest God, angered by his wilful blindness, 'tangle his grace with matrimony (beside the destruction of the realm that is to follow) much more dishonourable than his Grace thinketh Martin's shameful'.

Tyndale expected Henry to return to Catherine, having seen the errors of his ways. But Henry was a boar in rut, lusting after Anne Boleyn more than ever – the Venetian ambassador was reporting that he was kissing her openly and 'treating her in public as if she were his wife', while the king himself wrote of 'wishing myself (specially an evening) in my sweetheart's arms, whose pretty ducks [breasts] I trust shortly to kiss' – and his response was to want Tyndale dead. Tyndale was also at pains to insult his natural allies, the reforming clergy who favoured the divorce. 'Let them remembre the wronge they have done to the quene,' he wrote furiously, 'and what frute they have cost him that neuer coude come to the right birth for sorow which she sofred thorow their false meanes.' It is touching that Tyndale should blame them for Catherine's failure to achieve the 'right birth' of a son and heir. It says much for his common humanity, and nothing for his political common sense.

More was delighted. The first copies of *Prelates* were smuggled in the early autumn and they were snapped up eagerly. The Milanese ambassador, who gave the author's name as 'Tindaro', a man '*magnae doctrinae*', of great learning, reported that three thousand copies were in circulation in England. Posters were displayed across London denouncing the book. The bishop of London arrested Tyndale's brother John, a merchant called Thomas Patmore, and a young man living near London Bridge, and handed them to More. The chancellor had them taken before him in the Star Chamber. They were charged with 'receiving of Tyndale's testaments and divers other books, and delivering and scattering the same' throughout London; in addition, John Tyndale was accused of sending five marks to his brother beyond the sea, and for receiving and keeping his letters. They pleaded guilty, and were sent to the Counter, a prison in Cheapside, before being paraded through the city the following market day.

The Venetian ambassador watched as they were led on horses, facing the tail, with pasteboard mitres on their heads, bearing an inscription '*Peccasse Contra Mandata Regis*', 'We have sinned against the mandate of the King', and copies of the offending books suspended from their necks; when they had completed their circuit of the thoroughfares, they cast the books into a great fire in Cheapside. This did William Tyndale's reputation nothing but good, of course. 'For one who spoke about these matters before,' the imperial ambassador, Chapuys, told his master, 'there are now a thousand who discourse of them freely and without fear.'

16

'My name is Tyndale'

Within a few weeks, Chapuys had startling news to report. The king, fearing that Tyndale would write 'still more boldly against him' and 'hoping to make him retract what he has already said' against the annulment, had 'offered him several good appointments and a seat in his Council if he will come over'. Chapuys claimed that a letter had already been sent inviting Tyndale to return. The royal proclamation and the placards condemning *Prelates* were removed.

The imperial ambassador exaggerated when he spoke of a government post being on offer. In the essentials, however, he was right. Peace feelers were indeed being put out to Antwerp by the end of 1530.

No doubt Anne Boleyn played her part in the royal change of heart. Her reforming instincts remained sharp and her frustrations with the papacy over the annulment continued. She was angry that Henry had relented towards Wolsey early in the year, granting him a formal pardon and confirming him in his archbishopric of York, so that he remained the second most important churchman in the realm. Anne rightly suspected that Wolsey was intriguing against her over the summer and autumn of 1530.

Charles V was still active on his aunt's behalf, and in July Wolsey had supported him when he had called on the pope to order Henry to estrange himself from Anne Boleyn. The following month, Wolsey wrote to Clement again to ask why the annulment decision was delayed, and the queen's cause not pursued with more vigour.

Having wind of this, Anne conspired with the duke of Norfolk, her uncle, to kill off the cardinal. Wolsey's physician was bribed to say that his patient was urging the pope to excommunicate Henry and to place the country under interdiction. These were extreme measures – the normal services and sacraments were forbidden in countries under interdict, though priests not personally responsible for the dispute could continue to perform rites in a low voice and in private behind closed doors – and the physician claimed that Wolsey was hoping to provoke an uprising in favour of the queen and himself.

Henry believed his lover, and on 1 November a warrant was made out for the cardinal's arrest. Henry Percy, Anne's old suitor who had now succeeded to the earldom of Northumberland, rode to the episcopal palace at Cawood in Yorkshire to charge Wolsey with high treason. The prisoner was already a sick man and he collapsed as he was being taken south to London. His escort, Sir William Kingston, the Constable of the Tower, took him to Leicester Abbey. 'Sir, I tarry but the will and pleasure of God, to render Him my simple soul into His divine hands,' the cardinal said as he was helped to his deathbed. He made a final statement. 'Well, well, Master Kingston,' he said. 'I see the matter against me, how it is framed. But if I had served God as diligently as I have the King, he would not have given me over in my grey hairs. Howbeit this is the just reward that I must receive for my worldly diligence and pains that I have had to do him service, only to satisfy his vain pleasures, not regarding my godly duty . . .' He spoke of the divorce: 'I assure you I have often kneeled before [the king] in his privy chamber on my knees the space of an hour or two to persuade him from his will and appetite [for Anne Boleyn]; but I could never bring to pass to dissuade him thereto . . .' He remembered Tyndale and the little band of heretics. He bade Kingston to ask the king 'that he have a vigilant eye to depress this new perverse sect of the Lutherans, that it do not increase within his dominions through his negligence'.

At that, he died. Kingston sent an express messenger to inform the king. As a sign of the dangerous times, Kingston thought it best that the mayor of Leicester and other local worthies should be summoned 'for to see him personally dead, in avoiding of false rumours that might hap to say that he was not dead but still living'. Wolsey, to general astonishment, was found to be wearing a hair shirt beneath his ordinary shirt of fine Holland linen. His corpse was laid out with all things 'appurtenant to his profession' – mitre, crosier, ring, pallium and vestments. He was kept all day in his coffin 'open and barefaced that all men might see him lie there dead without feigning'. That night, the canons sang dirges and devout orisons, with torches in their hands and wax tapers burning around the bier. At 4.00 a.m., they sang mass and interred the body. By 6 a.m., all 'ceremonies that to such a person was decent and convenient' were completed.

Anne Boleyn was delighted at Wolsey's death. She staged a masque for the court called 'The Going to Hell of Cardinal Wolsey'. Her self-confidence grew; Chapuys noted that she 'is becoming more arrogant every day, using words in authority towards the king of which he has several times complained . . . saying that she was not like the Queen who never in her life used ill words to him'. She told one of Catherine's ladies that 'she wished all Spaniards were in the sea' and boasted that she cared not a fig for the queen and 'would rather see her hang than acknowledge her as her mistress'.

In Antwerp, Tyndale rejoiced too, his words for once matching

More's in crudeness. The cardinal had died a 'shitten death', he wrote, having collapsed after his physician gave him a purgative, and it was now, as we have seen, that Tyndale revelled that 'for al the worship of his [cardinal's] hat and glories of his precious shoes when he was payned with the colicke of an evel conscience havynge no nother shifte bycause his soule could funde in nother issue toke hym selfe a medecine *ut emitteret spiritum per posteriora*.

A sea change was beginning for the reformers. Thomas Cromwell, by now the king's secretary, was the main influence, and it was he who instigated and took in hand the approach to Tyndale. One of the most far-sighted and brutal of Tudor administrators, Cromwell was a meticulous organiser with a contrary streak as adventurer and fortune-hunter. He was born at Putney, three miles upriver from More's great Thames-side house at Chelsea. He was a barrel of a man, with a strong jowl and close-set hawkish eyes. His father was variously described as a brewer, a fuller or a blacksmith. At nineteen, an age when Tyndale, and More and Wolsey, were refining their intellects at Oxford, Cromwell crossed the Channel to seek his fortune as a mercenary. He followed the French armies in Italy for eight years, also gaining book-keeping expertise as a clerk and business acumen as a trader.

He came back to England in his late twenties, setting himself up as a wool stapler, a dealer in raw wool. He married an heiress, and learnt some law, working as a scrivener, drawing up contracts and money-lending. After a year in London, he entered Wolsey's service. The cardinal was a good judge of men, and he recognised Cromwell's tenacity and ambition. By 1525, Cromwell was a Member of Parliament and Wolsey's dogsbody, supervising the endowment of the impressive new colleges Wolsey was founding at Ipswich and Oxford.

He stayed loyal to his master longer than most, and feared he would go down with the wreckage. Wolsey's gentleman usher and

Thomas Cromwell exercised immense influence as principal royal secretary after the fall of Wolsey and More. Though an earl when Henry VIII tired of him and had him beheaded, Cromwell was the son of a Putney brewer and blacksmith, and a radical who sympathised with Tyndale and tried to reconcile him with the king. His efforts foundered on Tyndale's refusal to pay lip service to the royal position on the divorce and the eucharist.

(Popperfoto)

biographer, George Cavendish, came across Cromwell reciting prayers to the Virgin and weeping. It was 'a very strange sight' to find so hard a man in such a state, and Cavendish asked him if he was distressed for the cardinal, who had been forced to resign a short time before. 'Nay, nay,' Cromwell said, 'it is my unhappy adventure, which am like to lose all that I have travailed for all the days of my life for doing of my master true and diligent service.' He was weeping for himself, and for his ruined prospects. Typically, however, he had a plan to take his fate by the scruff of the neck. 'I do intend, God willing, this afternoon . . . to ride to London and so to the court,' he told Cavendish, 'where I will either make or mar or I come again . . . I will put myself in the press to see what any man is able to lay to my charge of untruth or misdemeanour.'

Come again he did. He was too guileful, too competent and hard-working for the king to ignore. By the end of 1530 he was an influential member of the king's council. Though devious, a man who turned on old allies and drew blood when it suited, he was sympathetic to the reformers. It was in his interests to be so, for he was able to use Henry's fury with the pope to his own advantage, pressing the king to break with Rome, and making himself an indispensable part of the new doctrine of royal supremacy.

His views were close to those of Marsiglio of Padua, whose great work *Defensor Pacis* Cromwell paid to have translated into English for the first time. Marsiglio, a rector of the university of Paris, had argued against the temporal power of the pope and the clergy. He held the Church to be inferior to the State, which he saw as the power house and unifier of society. Clerics should have no privileges, he said, for 'all Christ's faithful are churchmen'. Marsiglio had been excommunicated for his pains in 1327. His ideas, though two centuries old by then, seemed raw and radical when Cromwell expressed them in terms of an English empire 'governed by one Supreme Head and King' to whom both temporality and spirituality 'be bounden and owe to bear, next to God, a natural and humble obedience'. Within three years, Cromwell himself was to become principal secretary with control of a range of affairs unmatched in the history of the realm. His leaning towards reform was personal as well as political. He was ultimately to be beheaded as an earl, but he had been born into the class of petty traders that was the breeding ground of Lollardy, and from which Tyndale drew his support. In religion, at least, Cromwell retained some of the adventure and free spirit of his youth. He was a natural ally of Tyndale.

Towards the end of November 1530, Cromwell sent an experienced merchant venturer named Stephen Vaughan to the Continent on a most secret and delicate mission. Vaughan was the king's agent, a sort of commercial consul, in the Low Countries. He was instructed to find Tyndale, and offer him a safe conduct back to England. Vaughan sent letters to Tyndale in Frankfurt, Hamburg and Marburg – 'Frankforde, Hanboroughe and Marleborughe' – the three cities where rumour located Tyndale. The exile was offered 'whatsoever surety he would reasonably desire for his safe coming in and going out' of the realm.

On 26 January 1531, Vaughan wrote to the king that, although he had not found Tyndale, he had received a reply to his letters 'written in his own hand'. Tyndale had refused the offer because he had heard the 'bruit and fame' of events in England, presumably the persecutions let loose by More and Stokesley, and suspected 'a trap to bring him into peril'. Vaughan found out that Tyndale had written *An Answer unto Sir Thomas More's Dialogue*. He did not know whether it had yet been printed, but assured the king that, 'as soon as it is, I will send it without fail'.

Vaughan succeeded in tracking down a manuscript copy of the new book in March. He wrote to Cromwell on 25 March from Antwerp to say that the copy was 'so rudely scribbled' that he was writing it out again in a 'fair book' to send to the king. Vaughan was uncertain whether Henry would like the *Answer* or not. 'I promise you,' he told Cromwell, 'he maketh my lord chancellor such an answer as I am loth to praise or dispraise.' He said that Tyndale had never written 'in so gentle a style' – a claim the clergy might have disputed, since Tyndale wrote of their 'dumb blessings, dumb absolutions, their dumb pattering, and howling, their dumb strange holy gestures, with all their dumb disguisings, their satisfactions and justifyings' – and that, if Tyndale heard that the king took the book well, it 'may then peradventure be a means to bring him to England'. Other than that, Vaughan admitted, it was unlikely that he would come, 'for as much as the man hath me greatly suspected'.

Then, remarkably, Tyndale broke cover. Vaughan wrote to Henry again on 18 April 1531. 'The day before the date hereof,' he said, 'I spake with Tyndale without the town of Antwerp.' A messenger had come to him, he reported, saying that a friend of Vaughan wished to speak to him. The messenger did not know the name of the friend, but said he would take Vaughan to him. Vaughan followed him to a field on the outskirts of Antwerp beyond the city gates.

A man arrived. 'Do you not know me?' he asked. 'My name is Tyndale.'

'But Tyndale!' Vaughan exclaimed. 'Fortunate be our meeting.'

'Sir,' said Tyndale, 'I have been exceeding desirous to speak with you.'

'And I with you.'

Tyndale said that he was upset and surprised that the king had disliked *Prelates*, 'considering that in it I did but warn his grace of the subtle demeanour of the clergy of his realm towards his person, and of the shameful abuses by them practised, not a little threatening the displeasure of his grace and weal of his realm: in which doing I showed and declared the heart of a true subject . . .'. He

This map of Antwerp shows the waterfront, where smuggled copies of Tyndale's works began their journey to England, and the walls of the great city. When Tyndale agreed to meet Stephen Vaughan, Cromwell's agent, he was careful to do so in a field outside the gates. He then scurried off along a road leading away from Antwerp, so that Vaughan could not follow to him to his secret lodgings. Such vigilance kept him alive; only once, fatally, did he drop his guard.

(Bridgeman Art Library)

said that he had suffered greatly for his work, through 'my poverty . . . mine exile out of my natural country, and bitter absence from my friends . . . my hunger, my thirst, my cold, the great danger wherewith I am everywhere encompassed'. He had warned the king to beware of Wolsey and the churchmen. How could the king feel that this did not show 'a pure mind, a true and incorrupt zeal and affection to his grace? . . . Doth this deserve hatred?' Tyndale went on to ask how Henry, as a Christian prince, could 'be so unkind to God' as to 'dare say that it is not lawful' for his people to have the scriptures in their own tongue. God had commanded that his word be spread throughout the world, to give 'more faith to the wicked persuasions of men'. Why were the king's subjects so dangerous that they were denied that word in a language they could understand?

After a long conversation, during which Tyndale confirmed that he had finished his answer to More's *Dialogue*, Vaughan 'assayed with gentle persuasion' to have him travel to England. 'But to this he answered,' Vaughan reported, 'that he neither would nor durst come into England, albeit your grace would promise him never so much the surety: fearing lest, as he hath before written, your promise made should surely be broken, by the persuasion of the clergy, which would affirm that promises made with heretics ought not to be kept.' Tyndale then seemed 'somewhat fearful' at being with the king's agent in an isolated and darkening field. Evening was coming and Tyndale scurried down a road leading away from Antwerp. Vaughan presumed that Tyndale had doubled back to Antwerp as soon as he was safely out of sight.

'Hasty to pursue him I was not, because I had some likelihood to speak shortly again with him,' Vaughan explained to the king. 'To explain to your majesty what, in my poor judgement, I think of the man, I ascertain your grace, I have not communed with a man—' At this point, the copy of Vaughan's letter is torn off. Henry himself may have ripped it across. The letter certainly angered him. Cromwell's notion of having Tyndale return to England was acceptable only if he came as a penitent, to whom the king could graciously extend his mercy and protection. Yet, far from being humble and contrite, the fellow complained that the king was 'unkind' to God and ungrateful for the support given to him in *Prelates*. Moral lectures were not the way to Henry's heart, but to the scaffold; that this did not occur to Tyndale shows once more his innocence, or blindness, to human frailties and vanity. He was more astute in matters of safety. He was right to fear that a safe conduct might be broken for a heretic. This was, as we shall see, More's exact opinion.

Vaughan met Tyndale twice more. He informed the king on 20 May that he had again urged Tyndale to return to England. He had shown the exile an extract from a letter he had received from Cromwell. In it, the royal secretary said that he hoped that Tyndale might be converted from 'the train and affection which he now is in', and disavow the 'opinions and fantasies sorely rooted in him'. If this happened, Cromwell continued, 'I doubt not but that the king's highness would be much joyous', so much so that the king would be inclined 'to mercy, pity and compassion'. Vaughan said that these words were of such sweetness and virtue 'as were able to pierce the hardest heart of the world'. When Tyndale read them, he said, he became 'exceedingly altered', tears stood in his eye, and he murmured: 'What gracious words are these!'

Tyndale proposed a deal, but it did not compromise his demand for the English Bible one jot. 'If it would stand with the king's most gracious pleasure to grant only a bare text of the scrip- ture to be put forth among his people,' Vaughan reported him saying, 'like as is put forth among the subjects of the emperor in these parts, and of other Christian princes, be it of the translation of what person soever shall please his majesty, I shall immediately make faithful promise never to write more, nor abide two days in these parts after the same: but immediately to repair unto his realm, and there most humbly submit myself at the feet of his royal majesty, offering my body to suffer what pain or torture, yea, what death his grace will, so this be obtained. And till that time, I will abide the asperity of all chances, whatsoever shall come, and endure my life in as many pains as it is able to bear and suffer.'

He thus offered never to write again, to return to England, to submit himself to torture and death at the king's pleasure, all this if only the Bible – in whoever's translation the king chose, and in 'plain text' without glosses or notes – could be given in English to the people. Henry was closer to permitting the English Bible than he himself realised; but he would not do so at the urging of a

Tyndale. And Tyndale, being Tyndale, could not resist a sting in the tail of his conversation with Vaughan. The king could be assured, he said, that whatsoever 'I have said or written in all my life against the honour of God's word, and so proved', he would utterly forsake and renounce 'before his majesty and the whole world', abhorring his errors and embracing the truth. He added a waspish rider. 'But if those things which I have written be true, and stand with God's word,' he said, 'why should his majesty, having so excellent gift of knowledge in the scriptures, move me to do anything against my conscience?'

On 19 June, after a further meeting, Vaughan reported to Cromwell that he had told Tyndale 'what the king's royal pleasure was, but I find him always singing one note'. Unless Henry authorised an English Bible, Tyndale would not budge. Vaughan added that Tyndale was publishing a translation of the prophet Jonas in English, and that it 'passeth any man's power' to stop it from being printed. Vaughan returned to England soon afterwards.

He was back in Antwerp in the autumn of 1531 and wrote two (unanswered) letters to Cromwell, one of which on 14 November contained a copy of 'another book lately put out by Tyndale, being *An Exposition upon the First Epistle of John*' which had been published in Antwerp in September. 'I have taken in hand to interpret this epistle,' Tyndale wrote in it, 'to edify the layman, and to teach him how to read the scripture, and what to seek therein.' It was not enough for a father and mother to beget a child, he said; they had to care for it until it could help itself, and 'even so it is not enough to have translated . . . the scripture, into the vulgar and common tongue, except we also brought again the light to understand it'. The exposition was mainly concerned with portraying God as love. 'Blind reason saith, God is a carved post, and will be served with a candle,' he wrote, 'but scripture saith, God is love, and will be served with love. If thou love thy neighbour, then art thou the image of God thyself . . .'

Jonas had already undergone its rites of passage. It appeared on a list of forbidden books proclaimed at St Paul's Cross in Advent 1531, and it was mauled by More. 'Jonas was never so swallowed up with the whale,' the lord chancellor wrote, 'as by the delight of that book a man's soul may be so swallowed up by the devil, that he shall never have the grace to get out again.' *John* received the same treatment. Had the 'blessed apostle' known what sense would be made of his work, More presumed on his behalf, he 'had liefer his espistle had never been put in writing'.

Momentous events had unrolled in England over the period of Vaughan's fruitless endeavours in Antwerp. Henry had summoned the Convocation of the clergy from Canterbury to Westminster on 21 January 1531. He said that the pope's delays and quibbles over his marriage had cost him £100,000. He demanded restitution, claiming that every bishop and priest who had submitted to Wolsey's authority had abetted the cardinal's *praemunire*, and was thus liable to life imprisonment and the forfeiture of their property to the crown. Convocation jibed at the huge sum for a few days, but submitted and prayed the king for pardon. In return, they asked for the traditional privileges of the clergy to be reconfirmed.

Cromwell advised his master to refuse. Instead, *praemunire* was extended to include the ecclesiastical courts, on the grounds that the king should govern his realm 'in concert with his lords and commons only'. On 7 February, Henry addressed parliament and demanded that he be recognised as the 'sole protector and supreme head of the English Church and clergy'. More remained silent over this body blow to Rome – though Chapuys reported that 'the chancellor is so mortified at it that he is anxious above all things to resign his office' – and it was left to John Fisher, the fierce book-burning bishop of Rochester, to fight the Church's corner. Royal supremacy, Fisher rightly argued, was 'a tearing of the seamless coat of Christ in sunder'. He said that it involved abandoning union with the see of Rome. 'We renounce the unity of the Christian world,' he warned, 'and so leap out of Peter's ship, to be drowned in the waves of all heresies, sects, schisms and divisions.'

The bishops had a clause added to the formula. The king was to be supreme head '*quantum per legem Dei licet*', 'as far as God's law allows', but this was mere face-saving and all knew it. When the title was put to it on 11 February, Convocation responded with angry silence. Archbishop Warham lamely announced '*Qui tacet consentire videtur*', that the silent were seen to agree, and the English Church, which had recognised the pope as its head since Gregory the Great had sent St Augustine to evangelise England almost 950 years before, fell under a new master.

Anne Boleyn was exhilarated that her lover was now, so to speak, both king and pope. Rome could now be bypassed over the annulment. 'The woman of the king,' Chapuys noted with disdain, 'made such demonstrations of joy as if she had actually gained Paradise.' Her father, now elevated as earl of Wiltshire, showed the family sympathy to reform by stating that the scriptures showed that 'when God left this world He left no successor or vicar'. When an attempt was made to murder the fractious Fisher, suspicion fell on the Boleyns, who despised him for his resistance to the royal supremacy and the annulment. The bishop's cook, one Richard Rouse, added a white powder to the soup served to Fisher and his household. Several men died, though Fisher drank only a small amount of the soup, and escaped with severe stomach pains. Henry made a point of having the wretched Rouse boiled to death; 'nevertheless,' Chapuys noted, 'he cannot wholly avoid some suspicion, at least against the Lady and her father'.

Tyndale did not share the Boleyns' excitement over the humiliation of the pope and clergy. 'Our king had destroyed the Pope,' the reformer John Hooper was to comment shrewdly, 'but not Popery.' It was never likely that Henry would approve of the leather-bound copy of Tyndale's *Answer* that Vaughan had forwarded to him. Henry remained theologically conservative in everything save papal supremacy. He was as sensitive as ever to any deviations in the dogma of the sacraments, and, though the pope had awarded it to him, still boasted of his title as *Fidei Defensor.*

The *Answer* had no truck with 'penance, pilgrimages, pardons, purgatory and praying to posts' – posts being the mocking word Tyndale used for crucifixes – and condemned the Church's 'dumb ceremonies and sacraments' out of hand. Henry's response, which Cromwell recorded in a letter to Vaughan, was predictable. 'His highness nothing liked the said book,' he wrote, 'being filled with seditions, slanderous lies, and fantastical opinions . . . to seduce, deceive and sow sedition among the people of this realm.' Tyndale, the king railed, lacked grace, virtue, learning, discretion and every other good quality; he was 'malicious, perverse, uncharitable and indurate'.

Though Tyndale had finished writing the *Answer* by the end of January 1531, it was not printed until July. A marginal note gave a crisp guide to the text: 'More, a lying papist.'

In his *Dialogue*, More had his questioner say that the reformers 'hath some that preach sometime, but ye will not suffer them; ye punish them and burn them'. To this, More replied: 'Nay, they be wiser than so; for they will rather swear on a book that they never said so.' This was, of course, a deadly insult. More was claiming that the reformers had no honour or courage; faced with the stake, they rolled over and abjured.

Tyndale punned on 'more' in his reply. 'And when he saith, he never found nor heard of any of us, but that he would forswear to save his life,' he wrote. 'Answer: The more wrath of God will light on them that so cruelly delight to torment them, and so craftily to beguile the weak.' He went on to point out that More's insult was untrue. More knew that he was lying, Tyndale said, because 'he hath heard of sir Thomas Hitton, whom the bishops of Rochester and Canterbury slew at Maidstone; and of many that suffered in Braband, Holland and at Colen, and in all quarters of Dutchland, and so daily. And when he saith that their church hath many martyrs, let him shew me one, that died for pardons and purgatory, that the pope hath feigned.' More had indeed heard of Hitton.

The war over the use of the word 'congregation' ground on. 'Wheresoever I may say a *congregation*,' Tyndale wrote, 'there may I say a *church* also; as the church of the devil, the church of Satan, the church of wretches, the church of wicked men, the church of liars, and a church of Turks thereto. For M. More must grant (if he will have *ecclesia* translated throughout all the new Testament by this word church) that church is as common as *ecclesia*. Now is *ecclesia* a Greek word, and was in use before the time of the apostles, and taken for a congregation among the heathen, where was no congregation of God or of Christ. And also Lucas [Luke] himself useth *ecclesia* for a church, or congregation, of heathen people thrice in one chapter . . . Let, therefore, M More and his company awake by times, ere ever their sin be ripe; lest the voice of their wickedness ascend up, and awake God out of his sleep, to look upon them, and to bow his ears unto their cursed blasphemies against the open truth, and to send his harvestmen and mowers of vengeance to reap it.'

Translating the Old Testament had given Tyndale a sonority of menace and insult – 'the harvestmen of vengeance' – that sweeps the reader along well enough. Some sharper blows accompanied the general pounding. 'But how happeth it that M More hath not contended in like wise against his darling Erasmus all this long while?' he asked. 'Doth he not change this word *ecclesia* into *congregation*, and that not seldom in the new Testament?' This was indeed true. Erasmus and More were the closest of friends or 'darlings' – it was Erasmus who had given More his lasting tag as a man '*omnium horarum*', a 'man for all seasons' – and translating from the Greek into Latin he had used *congregatio* for *ecclesia*.

The core of the *Answer* was a pithy rebuttal of More's placing of tradition above scripture. 'Judge therefore reader,' Tyndale wrote, 'whether the pope with his be the church, whether their authority be above the scripture, whether all they teach without scripture be equal with the scripture, whether they have erred . . .'

It was absurd, he said, for More to claim that ignorant laymen and women could not divine the truth in the scriptures without the help of the Church. Mankind was born with a spiritual sense. 'Who taught the eagles to spy out their prey?' Tyndale retorted. 'Even so the children of God spy out their lord, and trace out the paths of his feet and follow; yea, though he go upon the plain and liquid water, which will receive no step, and yet there they find out his foot; his elect know him, but the world knoweth him not.'

More had followed the classic Catholic position in his *Dialogue*. He said that scripture must be read or listened to with care. Only 'if we be not rebellious, but endeavour ourselves to believe, and captive and subdue our understanding to serve and follow faith', could it be properly seen. And even then the scripture was no more than an adjunct to Church tradition and doctrine; it merely gave 'fast and firm credence to the faith that the church teacheth, in such things as be not in the scripture, and to believe that God hath taught his church those things without writing'.

This, of course, skirted round the great issue of the Reformation. Tyndale and his like attached no credence whatever to Church teachings of 'such things as be not in the scripture'. On the contrary, they believed that what the Church taught outside the Bible was wicked and self-serving and inspired by the devil. They had the same contempt for the things that, as More put it, 'God hath taught his church without writing'. How had God managed this feat? The New Testament, as Tyndale had written on his title page, was 'written, and caused to be written, by them whyche herde yt', yt being the word of God. Who had heard these later things that God had taught? How had they heard? Why had they not written them down?

These taunts were to an extent mere goading by Tyndale. He knew well enough what Catholic apologists like More actually meant. For fourteen hundred years, the Church had been the guardian of the Christian spirit. It had distilled the thoughts of the great men of the past, the ancient Fathers and colossal figures like Augustine, Bernard, Gregory and Aquinas, into a tradition whose patina and polish, so laboriously acquired, sparkled like some antique altar of silver and ebony. The spiritual immensity of the Church seemed reflected in its gigantic constructions. A cathedral, with its chantries, baptistry, shrines, relics, stained glass, organ, gargoyles, tombs, pulpit, its spire and nave, had a sense of immortality to it. So, too, did the Church hierarchy, an equally magnificent edifice, with its popes, cardinals, bishops, chancellors, abbots, priors, legates, nuncios, prothonotaries, archdeacons, pastors, monks and friars, its canon lawyers and its church courts.

Compared to this, the Bible was no more than a relic of dusty parchment. To More, the Christian religion was so identified with the Church that it seemed natural that God should whisper truths into its collective ear. The Church had acquired God's word through osmosis, as it were, by a gradual and unwritten absorption over the centuries.

This view was entirely sensible, and it had long since proved its worth in sustaining the Church. It depended, however, as More admitted, on holding reason 'captive'. This was easy meat for Tyndale.

More 'peppereth his conclusion, lest men should feel the taste', Tyndale wrote, 'saying, "If we endeavour ourselves, and captive our understanding to believe."

'O how beetle-blind is fleshly reason! The will hath none operation at all in the working of faith in my soul, no more than the child hath in the begetting of his father; for, saith Paul, "It is the gift of God", and not of us. My wit must conclude good or bad, ere my will can love or hate. My wit must shew me a true cause, or an apparent cause why, ere my will have any working at all.'

It was a powerful point, but one that More retained the power to answer by the fire.

17

The Confutation

More read the *Answer* over the late summer of 1531. He was a proud man, and what he read stung him. He at once set to work on his reply, *The Confutation of Tyndale's Answer*. It was a work of devotion to the old religion, or of obsession, for he took all of Tyndale's points, one by one, and wrote of them at such rambling length that he seemed to be trying to smother them by the weight of words alone.

By day, More was chancellor, involved in the legal, diplomatic and parliamentary affairs of the realm, and snared in the royal pursuit of the annulment and the bending of the Church to the will of the king, approving of neither policy, but warned, so Chapuys wrote, that he would be 'thrown into the Thames' if he did not accept both. By night, after the brief respite of the river journey from Westminster to Chelsea, and a simple supper, he sat down to dash off page after page of his *Confutation* in furious storms of ink.

The first three volumes of the book were completed by the early months of 1532. The final six volumes appeared a year later. In all, the *Confutation* ran to half a million words. It was six times longer than the *Answer*, and More's biographer, Nicholas Harpsfield, noted a few years later how he had thrown everything into the hunt, so that Tyndale 'scuddeth in and out like a hare that hath twenty brace of greyhounds after her, and were afeard at every foot to be snatched up'.

The book was intended to stem the advance of 'Tyndales great Mayster Antecryst', and the odds appeared to be greatly in More's favour. Tyndale and his readers were a poor and hunted handful. More's side enjoyed all the strengths of a long-established Church – power and privilege, vast estates, income from rent rolls, tithes, legacies, indulgences, masses, dirges, hallowings – and the loyalty of the great majority of worshippers. Convocation had been forced to accept the king as its supreme head, but in the same month, February 1531, it showed that the clergy still had sharp teeth. The squire of Toddington in Gloucestershire, William Tracey, left a will in which he said that salvation came through Christ alone, and that none of his estate should be used to pay a priest to say prayers for his soul. Tyndale had known Tracey in his Gloucestershire days, finding him 'a learned man' who knew the works of St Augustine 'better than ever I knew a doctor in England'. Convocation, outraged at the Lutheran slant to the will, and at the danger it posed to clerical income, condemned it as impious and heretical. Tracey's corpse was duly dug up and burnt by the bishop of Worcester's chancellor.[1]

Yet the 'evangelycalls' survived, and their 'newfanglyncs' was proving to be a formidable foe. More's *Confutation* was prodigious, but its length, and the 'monotonous fury' of its thousand-plus printed pages of barbs, insults, ribaldries, carpings and cavils, revealed the author's uneasy intuition that it might serve as an obituary for England's old faith. More admitted that some people found that 'my writyng is over longe, and therfore to tedyouse to rede'. He explained that he had to hammer each point home, so that his audience 'shal not nede to rede over any chapyter but one,' but it should have worried him that Tyndale's message was so much briefer and plainer.

The *Answer* and the *Confutation* make war on all fronts. They pitch faith against works, the direct inspiration of the scripture against the traditions and teachings of the church, private prayer against the pomp of public worship, redemption through Christ against salvation through the Church and its sacraments.

More said that there was room for only 'one fayth in the howse of god', and that faith, blessed by tradition, made lustrous by the souls of the saints, resided in 'the comen knowen catholique chyrch'. The Church interceded between man and God; it contained all that was necessary for salvation; and its customs and usages had the force of God's truth behind them. Its purpose was secular as well as spiritual. More helped to govern the secular state. He knew how frail it was, how subject to plots, dynastic crisis, spoilt harvests, debts, plagues and riots. As the body of Christ on earth, the Church was universal and all-embracing. It gathered all ranks and conditions of men and women, and glued them into the common society and civilisation of Christendom.

Fear of apocalypse, and a collapse of the known world, haunted More. If the Church was broken, he warned, it would be the signal that 'the great archeheretyke Antycryste come hym selfe whyche as helpe me god I fere be very nere hys tyme'.

It was absurd and wicked, he said, for Tyndale and 'such fond fellows' to 'bid all the world believe them upon their bare word, in the understanding of holy scripture, against all holy saints and cunning doctors of fifteen hundred years passed'. These ignorant 'newe men' jested and railed against 'all good works, against all religion, fasting, prayer, devotion, saints, ceremonies and sacraments'. They 'praise lechery between friars and nuns' – More reminded his readers incessantly that, in marrying the Cistercian Catherine von Bora, Luther 'toke out of relygyon a spouse of Cryste' and that it was said 'that Antecryste sholde be borne betwene a frere and a nunne' – and made 'open shameless blasphemy'.

He was shocked that Tyndale had written that Sunday need not be the day of rest – 'we be lords over the Sabbath' – and that spoken confession to a priest was unnecessary and harmful. 'He that, after Tyndale's doctrine, repenteth without care of shrift, and dieth in a false heresy against his holy housel', More responded, 'such folk be finally reprobates, foreknown unto God before the world was wrought, that they would finally for impenitence fall utterly to nought'.

Tyndale had imagined a Christian woman shipwrecked on an island among people who knew nothing of Christ. In this emergency, he felt, she could act as a priest, preaching and saying mass. More was horrified. Not a sparrow falls to earth, he retorted, without it being part of God's providence. 'There shall be no woman fall a-lande in any so farre an Ilande where he will have his name preached and His sacraments mynystered,' he claimed, 'but that god can and wyll well inough provide a man or twayne to come to lande wyth her.'

More drew a veil over Henry's new position as supreme head of the English Church, preferring to remember the younger, slimmer and more devout figure who had written the 'most erudite, famous book against Luther' a decade before. The king 'nothing more effectively desireth' than the preservation of 'the true catholic faith', More said, and 'nothing more detesteth than these pestilent books that Tyndale and such other send into the realm, to set forth here their abominable heresies withal'.

He took care not to mention the pope at all in the sensitive context of the governance of the Church. 'For the avoiding of all intrickation whereof, I purposely forbare to put in the pope as part of the definition of the church, as a thing needed not,' he explained rather lamely, 'since if he be the necessary head, he is included in the name of the whole body . . .'

The king was 'fain for the while' to allow the English Bible, More said, because the onslaught of heresy meant that even good and innocent books were dangerous. 'Evil folk' would draw false morals from it 'to the colour and maintenance of their own fond fantasies', and, 'turnynge al hony into posyn', would do deadly hurt to themselves and 'sprede also that infec-cyone farther a brode'. Things had reached such a pitch, he said, that if anyone translated his 'darling' friend Erasmus's *Praise of Folly* in English, or 'some workes eyther that I have my selfe wryten ere this . . . I wolde not onely my derlynges books but myne owne also helpe to burne wyth my own hands'. His own *Utopia* was presumably among the books he was prepared to throw on the bonfire.

Tyndale himself had the devil's mark on his forehead, More said; he was worse than Sodom and Gomorrah, an abominable beast who wishes his followers 'to die in the quarrel for the defence of his glory'.

Time and again, More compared Tyndale's works to the plague. 'Our Lord send us now some years as plenteous of good corn as we have had some years of late plenteous of evil books,' he prayed. 'For they have grown up so fast and sprung up so thick, full of pestilent errors and pernicious heresies, that they have infected and killed I fear me more silly simple souls then the famine of the dear years have destroyed bodies.' Hunger and disease were signs of God's wrath with the nation for allowing heresies to be smuggled in and circulated.

He was at pains to establish that Tyndale was seditious, and a traitor as well as a heretic. Trained barrister that he was, More found the chink in *Obedience*. Tyndale had written that, if the prince orders the subject to violate God's law, the subject must dis-obey and meekly suffer martyrdom, though he must not resist the prince by force. More found this to be seditious, because Tyndale condoned disobedience to the ruler on the grounds of conscience. He added that it was seditious for Tyndale to protest that heretics were put to painful deaths. More said that princes were right to punish heretics 'accordynge to iustice by sore payne-fule deathe, both for ensample and for infectyon of other'.

At times, More's passion for heretic-burning runs almost out of control. 'There should have been more burned by a great many than there have been within this seven year last past,' he wrote. 'The lack whereof, I fear me, will make more burned within this seven year next coming, than else should have needed to have been burned in seven score . . .' The proffered regret – 'I fear me' – is false; More looked forward to the fires, and fantasised on the punishments he would inflict on Tyndale and Luther. 'If the zele of god were amonge men that shold be,' he wrote, 'such rayling rybalds that so mokke wyth holy scrypture, shold at every exposy-cyon have an hote iren thruste thorow theyr blasphemouse tonges.'

He gloried meantime in the death of Hitton and others of Tyndale's friends who had gone to the stake. 'Tyndale's bokes and theyr owne malyce maketh them heretykes. And for heretikes as they be, the clergy dothe denounce them. And as they be well worthy, the temporaltie dothe burne them,' he purred, and then added the terrible words, 'And after the fyre of Smythfelde, hell dothe receyue them, where the wretches burne for euer.'

The formula of direct dialogue, or question and answer, was used again in *Confutation*, with More replying to remarks made by Tyndale in his *Answer* and elsewhere.

'Marke whyther yt be not true in the hyest degree . . .' says Tyndale, while More butts in. 'Tyndale is a great marker,' he says. 'There is nothynge with hym now but marke, marke, marke. It is a pytye that the man were not made a marker of chases in some tenys playe.'

The reference to tennis is apt, because the author has complete control over the supposed conversation, scoring points effortlessly, able to write in his own clever lobs or, as here, a brutal smash:

Tyndale: 'Iudge whyther yt be possible that any good sholde come oute of theyr domme ceremonyes and sacramentes.'

More: 'Iudge good crysten reader whyther yt be possible that he be any better than a beste oute of whose brutyshe bestely mouth, commeth such a fylthye fome.'

A one-sided match like this soon becomes dull to watch. Tyndale was quite as tedious in the dialogue he inserted in his *Answer*, where, of course, it is More who is pummelled:

More: 'What harm shall he care to forbear, that believeth Luther, how God alone, without our will, worketh all the mischief that they do?'

Tyndale: 'O natural son of the father of all lies . . .'

There is a touch of the ayatollah to that response. Tyndale was more economical with his insults than More, but just as savage. He compared More to Judas in the *Answer*. 'But verily,' he wrote, 'I think that as Judas betrayed not Christ for any love that he had unto the highpriests, scribes and phariseehs, but only to come by the wherefore he thirsted: even so Master More (as there are tokens evident) wrote not these books for any affection that he bare unto the spirituality, or unto the opinions which he so barely defendeth, but to obtain only that which he was a hungerd for.' He later filled in what More's belly slavered for, 'to get honour, promotion, dignity, and money, by help of our mitred monsters'.

In his *Exposition upon the v, vi, vii Chapters of Matthew*, covering the Sermon on the Mount and published in Antwerp two years later, in 1533, Tyndale used his most purple prose to lash out at More's supposed greed. 'Covetousness,' he wrote, 'maketh many, whom the truth pleaseth at the beginning, to cast it up again, and to be afterward the most cruel enemies thereof . . . after the ensample of Sir Thomas More, knight, which knew the truth, and for covetousness forsook it again . . . Covetousness blinded the eyes of that gleering fox more and more, and hardened his heart against the truth, with the confidence of his painted poetry, babbling eloquence, and juggling arguments of subtle sophistry . . .'

This is nonsense. More was not covetous. He had amassed something of a fortune, but he had a large family to maintain, and his lofty office obliged him to keep up appearances. The frugal Tyndale once boasted that he would be happy to live on £10 a year, but he was neither a married man nor lord chancellor of England. When the clergy later offered More a huge sum to thank him for his support, he refused to accept it from them. 'Loke I for my thanke of god that is thyre better,' he said, 'and for whose sake I take the labour and not for theyres.' The young humanist who wrote *Utopia* had changed into a reactionary, it is true, at least as far as heretics were concerned, but Tyndale was wrong to think that greed had played any part in the process.

Ignorance, however, was a factor that did. For all his verbosity, More never truly understood or got to grips with the reformers. Tyndale distinguished between Catholicism, which he called 'an hystorycall fayth', and his own, 'a felynge fayth'. This intensity, and the belief in the 'sure felynge' that 'god shall wryte yt in theyr hertes wyth his holy spyryte', passed More by. He felt, intuitively and rightly, that Tyndale's ideas were immensely dangerous to the Church, but he failed to tackle the core doctrine of justification by faith. The issues into which More poured his energy – pilgrimages, relics, confession, fasting, even transubstantiation and good works – were sideshows compared to Bible-based faith.

Faith was Tyndale's engine. The Church, to him, was 'the whole multitude of all repenting sinners that believe in Christ, and put all their trust and confidence in the mercy of God, feeling that in their hearts God for Christ's sake loveth them . . .'. They have this faith 'without all respect of their own deservings, yea, and for none other cause than the merciful truth of God the father, which cannot lie, hath so promised and so sworn'. This faith is 'everlasting life, and by this we be born anew and made the sons of God'. It is 'the mother of all truth . . . the foundation laid of the apostles and prophets . . . the rock whereon Christ built his congregation'.

It was, too, a fortress. 'Against the rock of this faith can no sin, no hell, no devil, no lies, nor error prevail.'

A passage in Tyndale's *Answer* reads as though it is a primer for an evangelical about to face the interrogator. It begins by stating that it is a plain and evident conclusion, 'as bright as the sun's shining', that the truth of God's word does not rely on the truth of men or of the Church.

'And therefore, when thou art asked, why thou believest that thou shalt be saved through Christ, and of such like principles of our faith,' it continues, 'answer, Thou wottest and feelest that it is true.

'And when he asketh, how thou knowest that it is true; answer, Because it is written in thine heart.

'And if he ask who wrote it; answer, The Spirit of God.

'And if he ask how thou camest first by it; tell him whether by reading in books, or hearing it preached, as by an outward instrument, but that inwardly thou was taught by the Spirit of God.

'And if he ask, whether thou believest it not because it is written in books, or because the priests so preach; answer, No, not now, but only because it is written in thine heart, and because the Spirit of God so preacheth, and so testifieth unto thy soul.'

An accused who defended himself along these lines faced death, as Tyndale well knew. 'And thus good night and good rest!' he admitted. 'Christ is brought asleep, and laid in his grave; and the door sealed to; and the men of arms about the grave to keep him down with pole-axes . . .'

It was an apt lesson for More's harsh new age. Poor 'little Bilney', the comforter of lepers who had escaped Wolsey in 1527, and who had abjured in front of Tunstall in 1529, did not survive the new lord chancellor. Bilney had such black dog depressions after his abjuration that his friends at Cambridge feared to leave him on his own lest he harm himself. On a night early in 1531 he announced that he was leaving Trinity Hall to 'go up to Jerusalem', the words Jesus had used when he set out from Galilee on his final journey to the cross. Bilney began preaching in the fields of Norfolk to crowds who came out to listen to him. He gave out copies of Tyndale's Testament and *Obedience*. More was told that he gave one to a Norwich anchoress. Informers reported that Bilney had described how priests 'take away the offerings, and hang them about their women's necks; and after that, they take them off the women, if they please them not, and hang them again upon the images'.

These were the actions of a man who was seeking out death. As an abjured heretic, he was certain to be burnt if he relapsed. The urge to martyrdom was as old as the faith itself. To die in imitation of Christ was the noblest of all fates in itself, and it had long been observed that it also served to spread the dead man's beliefs among the living. Pliny the Younger, adopted son of the great natural historian and the Roman governor of Bithynia, had noted in about AD 112 that persecuting Christians for their 'depraved and extravagant superstition' was fine in theory, but in practice produced 'the usual result of spreading the crime'. Tertullian, one of the Fathers of the Church, confirmed this a century later. 'The blood of martyrs,' he said, in a famous adage that Thomas More ignored, 'is the seed of the Church.'

Bilney was duly seized in March 1531 and brought in front of Bishop Nix of Norwich. He was convicted of heresy and 'relaxed' to the secular power. Foxe says that More sent down the writ to burn him. Bilney practised for his martyrdom in his cell by burning his fingers in a candle, constantly repeating Isaiah's words: 'When thou walkest through the fire, thou shalt not be burnt.' It was nearing harvest time, and he compared himself to the straw in the fields. 'Howsoever the stubble of this my body shall be wasted' by the fire, he told himself, 'yet my soul and spirit shall be purged thereby: a pain for the time, whereupon notwithstanding followeth joy unspeakable.' While he was waiting to be bound to the stake, in the Lollards' sandpit at Norwich, on 19 August 1531, Bilney repeated the creed as proof that he died as a true Christian, and offered up a prayer: 'Enter not into judgement with thy servant, O Lord, for in thy sight no living flesh can be justified.'

The day, to his misfortune, was windy enough to damage the harvest crops. The executioner first set his torch to the reeds round the stake. These made a great flame in the breeze which disfigured Bilney's face. He held up his hands and cried 'Jesus!' and 'Credo!' The flame was 'blown away from him several times, the wind being very high', and 'for a little pause, he stood without flame, the fire departing and recoursing'. It was many minutes before the wood caught solidly afire, and, so More wrote with satisfaction, God 'of hys endles mercy brought hys body to deth'. Bilney's little body shrank as it burnt and roasted. Eventually the executioner struck out the staple holding the chains to the stake, so that the body fell into the bottom of the fire.

In the *Confutation*, More claimed that Bilney had recanted his heresy at his trial, falling to his knees in front of Dr Pelles, the bishop of Norwich's chancellor, begging to be absolved from the sentence of excommunication, and confessing that he deserved to die. On the morning that he was to be burnt, More said that Bilney asked to receive the sacrament in bread alone, rather than the bread and wine of Lutheran practice. Dr Pelles objected, thinking him insincere, but, 'finally perceiving him to be of a true, perfect faith', administered the sacrament. More claimed that Bilney took it reverently, reciting the collect '*Domine Iesu Christe*', beating his breast at the words 'peace and concord to thy church' several times, and crying to God for mercy for his grievous errors 'in that point'. He confessed that the 'false delyght of Luthers & Tyndales bokes' had brought him into their 'secrete secte and scatered congregacyon' until 'god of his goodnesse opened his eyes' and he saw that 'if he dyed in those heresyes' he was doomed for ever 'in the fyre of hell'. He then 'turned to the trewe fayth agayne, and exhorted them all vnto the same'.

This was, to More at least, brilliant proof of the efficacy of the fire in saving the soul of the heretic. He said that Bilney, having recanted, was able to suffer his purgatory at the stake. Christ 'hath forwythe from the fyre taken his blessed soul to heauen,' More surmised, 'where he now prayeth incessantly for the repentance and amendment of all such as have been by his means while he lived, into any such errors induced or confirmed'.

More's account was self-serving and false. It suited him, of course, to imagine Bilney in heaven praying for those he had led into heresy on earth. Criticism of the *ex officio* nature of heresy trials was growing; liberals thought it unjust that a man could be tried for his life on the evidence of anonymous accusers at a hearing that had no open witnesses. The Bilney case, as painted by More, showed the machinery of persecution to be in perfect order and even humane. The fire was no more than a prelude to heaven for the penitent heretic; Bilney's body might be destroyed, but his immortal soul was saved by his trial and by his admission of guilt.

This, as More knew full well, was not how those who had witnessed the trial and burning remembered events. Bilney had been well loved by people in Norwich, and there had been trouble at the trial. Bilney, far from being quiescent, had appealed for his case to be taken to the king, on the grounds that the supreme head of the Church of England was no longer the pope or his nominee, but Henry VIII himself. Members of the audience shouted that the appeal removed Bilney from ecclesiastical jurisdiction. They demanded that he be handed over to Edward Reed, the mayor of Norwich. Reed seemed willing to accept responsibility, but nobody was certain quite what the king's brand new title involved. The mayor asked Dr Pelles for an explanation; the bishop's chancellor replied that, whatever the title might mean, it did not justify the removal of a suspected heretic from the traditional jurisdiction of the Church. So the trial continued, and Bilney was judged a contumacious heretic, and relaxed to the secular authorities.

None of the Norwich laity who watched Bilney die saw anything that made them think that he had recanted. Their outcry was loud enough for More to summon witnesses to the Star Chamber for interrogations in the late autumn of 1531. The Norwich men were clearly intimidated by the venue and the lord chancellor; they suffered from convenient lapses of memory and difficulties of hearing, but they refused any suggestion of a retraction. James Curatt, an alderman, told More that he had walked with Bilney to the stake and had stood close by him. He had not heard Bilney say anything, beyond the cries of 'Jesus!'. This might be because he had stepped briefly away to tie his shoe, he said, but he had heard no strong words of recantation.

Reed was summoned before More on 1 December 1531 and again on 5 December. The mayor agreed that Dr Pelles had given Bilney a paper to read out at the stake. However, if Bilney had read it, he did it either silently or so softly that neither Reed nor anyone else heard him. Reed was asked if he had heard Bilney exhort the people to obey God, the ministers of the Church, and the law. He said he had not. After the execution, Dr Pelles had brought a paper to Reed. The doctor claimed that it was a copy of the one Bilney had read at the stake, and asked the mayor to notarise it with the town seal. Reed smelt a rat. He showed Pelles's paper to other aldermen. They said that it was not the one that had been thrust into Bilney's hand before the burning, and confirmed that Bilney had not been heard to read it out.

No hint of this appeared in More's account of Bilney in the *Confutation*.

18

'The Lord forgive
Sir Thomas More!'

More's abiding passion remained the taking of Tyndale and the destruction of his friends. When anyone who had been at Antwerp appeared before him, More 'most studiously would search and examine all things belonging to Tyndale, where and with whom he hosted, where-abouts stood the house, what was his stature, in what apparel he went . . .'.

The attempt to win over Tyndale had been abandoned before Vaughan returned to England in June 1531. Vaughan had no contact with the exile after he came back to Antwerp the following November. The plan was now for Sir Thomas Elyot, the new English ambassador at the imperial court, to have Tyndale seized by force and shipped to London for punishment.

More's greatest successes followed the arrest of the renegade priest and colporteur George Constantine, whom one of More's agents – 'a faythfull seruant of mine' – had located.

Constantine was a Cambridge canon lawyer who had fled to the Low Countries in 1528, where the friar John West had searched for him without success. He met Tyndale in Antwerp, returning to England on a trip to sell banned books in 1531. He was arrested and taken to More's house at Chelsea where the lord chancellor had him locked in the stocks in the porter's lodge, and interrogated him over several days. As a member of the royal council, More was able to use the statutes against Lollardy that authorised political officers who were not priests to interrogate heretics in the presence of a clergyman.

More recorded joyfully that Constantine 'uttered and dysclosed dyvers of hys companyons', and revealed details of the smuggling of 'those develkyshe bokes whyche hym selfs and other of hys felowes hadde brought and shypped'. More learnt the names of the shipmen and the secret marks placed on the fardels, or crates, of freight in which the Testaments were hidden. He wrote happily of 'Rycharde Necton whyche was by Constantynes deteccyon taken and commyted to Newgate'. Unless 'he happe to dye before in pryson,' More chuckled, Necton 'standeth in grete paryll to be [dead] ere long, for hys fallynge agayne to Tindales heryses burned'. More said that he was also 'fortuned to iuntercepte my selfe' a letter written to Constantine by the bookseller Johan Byrte, leading to the latter's arrest.

It is likely that Constantine also leaked details of an exile's life in Antwerp. He did not come to trial, however. He escaped, or so he and More claimed, by breaking the stocks and climbing over the Chelsea garden wall. On 6 December 1531, the fugitive made his way safely back to Antwerp.

More claimed that he was not even angry when he was told that his prisoner had gone. He simply told his porter to mend the stocks, and cracked a joke with him that he should lock up well 'lest the prisoner try to steal back in'. This is out of character for More, a man who never relaxed when it came to heretics, nor forgave those who outsmarted him. It is likely that More allowed Constantine to escape, as a reward for his betrayals, and it is probable that he had him followed as he 'fled' back to Antwerp.

Certainly, More was aware of the fugitive's movements. He

warned 'all good crysten folke . . . to forbere and etsyew hys company'. He had also unearthed the details of Vaughan's secret mission to Tyndale, again through Constantine, and he added a chilling rider about Vaughan. 'For that Englishman which shall be found to be familiar with him there,' he warned, 'may thereby bring himself in suspicion of heresy, and haply hear thereof at his returning hither.' It appears from this that More had agents watching Vaughan in Antwerp; they were instructed to inform on any who fraternised with him.

Vaughan wrote to Thomas Cromwell in a state of considerable fear on 14 November 1531. He reported that he had been informed that Constantine 'hath of late declared certain things against me before my lord chancellor'. He begged Cromwell to find out what Constantine had betrayed. 'Peradventure he hath declared that I spake with Tyndale,' he said. 'If so he have done, what hath he herein declared, that I myself have not signified to the king's highness?'

On 9 December, three days after Constantine had arrived back in Antwerp, spreading a tale of woe about his ordeal, Vaughan again wrote to Cromwell. He said that, if the fugitive had accused him of being a Lutheran, 'I do not thereat marvel'. He had been 'credibly informed' that More, in his examination 'of the said George and all other men', showed 'evident and clear desire in his countenance and behaviour to hear something of me, whereby an occasion of evil might be fastened against me.' As well as that, he said, George was afflicted by the 'imminent peril and danger wherein he was, abiding prisoner in my lord's house', and was also 'vehemently stirred' with the remembrance of his poor wife in Antwerp, 'remaining here desperate, bewashed with continual tears and pinched with hourly sorrow . . .'

The result of the pressure piled on Constantine in Chelsea, Vaughan said, had brought him 'to accuse whom they had longed for, rather than to be tied by the leg with a cold and heavy iron like a beast . . .'. Such perils and fears were enough to 'make a son forget the father which gat him', and to say whatever the lord chancellor wished him to. Vaughan begged that the king should put a stop to these 'tortures and punishments', because they forced his subjects to flee the realm and to 'inhabit strange regions' where their faults multiplied, 'so that in the end it shall cause the sect to wax greater'. Although he begged that the king 'shall fatherly and lovingly reform the clergy of his realm, Vaughan claimed that 'whatsoever the world babble of me, that I am neither Lutheran nor yet Tyndalin'.

He wrote of the 'dangerous occupations' of being a secret agent. His conversation had to be that of the men he was with; 'among Christians I have been a Christian, among Jews like to them, among Lutherans, a Lutheran also'. Yet, for all his loyalty to the king, he complained, 'I hear everywhere how diligently my lord chancellor inquireth of all those he examineth in cases of heresy, for me – what are my manners, my opinion, my conversation, my faith.' Why did More take such pains, he asked. What thought he to hear? He was a hunted man, like Tyndale, 'suspected above all men'; he was weary, and he wanted no more than that 'I might come to England, and live in a corner of the realm for the residue of my short time . . .'.

Vaughan wrote to Cromwell once more, on 30 December 1531. He repeated that more Lutherans, both men and women, were fleeing England for fear of punishment. He warned that 'by this means it is likely that new Tyndales shall spring, or worse than he'. He refused to inform on them – 'whose persons nor names I know not nor will know' – and said that he was 'utterly determined from henceforth never to intermeddle, or to have any communication with any one of them'. With that, this most decent of spies quit the Tyndale case for good.

More denied that Constantine had been tortured. He said that his prisoner had merely been set in the stocks, and was not struck so much as a tap on the forehead. It was obviously in Constantine's interests to claim that he had been tortured, as an excuse for his betrayals, but More is probably accurate in this case, and Constantine turned King's Evidence under the threat of the stake rather than actual torture.

Others were less fortunate. Richard Bayfield was a leading trader in the Testaments and the other Tyndale books, a Cambridge graduate and a former Benedictine monk at Bury St Edmunds, who had taken up evangelical ideas. He had abjured in front of Tunstall in 1528, thus exposing himself to the fire if he lapsed, and had then fled to the Low Countries. Here, he helped Tyndale and John Frith, the survivor of the Oxford fish cellar, who was now working with Tyndale. Bayfield 'brought substance with him', so Foxe recorded, and 'sold all their works and the works of the Germans, both in France and England'.

Bayfield ran at least three large cargoes of Tyndale's books into England. On his first trip, at midsummer in 1530, he landed illicitly on the east coast and brought the books to London by way of Colchester. The following November he shipped another consignment to St Katherine's docks, less than a thousand yards downriver from the Tower of London. More had wind of this operation and most of the cargo was seized. At Easter 1531, avoiding the Essex coast and the London docks, Bayfield landed in Norfolk and brought his books to London along graziers' roads.

Betrayed, he was seized and held in the Tower, shackled to the wall of his cell by his neck, waist and legs, in darkness. More's strange obsession with married heretics resurfaced. He falsely claimed that Bayfield, 'beynge both a preste and a monke, went about two wyves, one in Brabande [Brabant], a nother in Englande'. Bayfield 'fell to heresye and was abiured, and after that lyke a dog returnyng to his vomyte,' More wrote, 'and beyng fledde ouer the see, and sendynge from thense Tyndales heresyes hyther with many myschevouse sortes of bokes'. The previous abjuration made the sentence inevitable. On 4 December 1531, More wrote with brutal economy, Bayfield 'the monk and apostata' was 'well and worthely burned in Smythfelde'. He added: 'Of Bayfeldes burnynge hath Tyndale no great cause to glory', claiming that 'though Tyndales bokes brought hym to burnynge', the dead man was a coward who was 'well contente to have foresworen agayne' had he been given the chance.

Less than three weeks later, the London leather seller John Tewkesbury shared the same fate. He was also betrayed by Constantine. Tewkesbury was held in the porter's lodge at More's Chelsea house, so Foxe wrote, pinioned 'hand, foot, and head in the stocks', for six days without release. Foxe claimed that More had Tewkesbury whipped at 'Jesu's tree' in his garden, 'and also twisted his brows with small ropes, so that the blood started out of his eyes'. This was, of course, the torture also described by Segar Nicholson. Tewkesbury was then sent to the Tower and racked until he was nearly lame.

More led two public examinations of Tewkesbury. He found his prisoner very obstinate. 'He couvered and hyd yt [his heresies] by all the meanes he coulde make,' More wrote, 'and labored to make euery man wene that he had neuer holden any suche opynyons.' But the lord chancellor's informers had done their work well. 'In hys howse was founden Tyndales boke of obedyence, and hys wykked boke also of the wykked mammoma,' More gloated, noting that, after the discovery, Tewkesbury said 'at hys examyna-cyon, that all the heresyes therein were good and crysten fayth, beynge in dede, as full of false heresyes, and as frantike as euer heretyke made any syth cryst was borne'. How did More winkle that out of him? For later, 'when he was in the shyryffes warde, and at the tyme of his deth,' More remarked, 'he wolde not speke of hys heresyes any thynge but handled hym selfe as couertly as he coude . . .'.

As was now usual, More taunted Tyndale over Tewkesbury's

death. His agents had told him that 'Tyndale reioyceth in the burnyng of Tewkesbery', and he commented with malicious sarcasm that 'I can se no very grete cause why but yf he rekened it for a grete glory that the man dyd abyde styll by the stake when he was faste bounden to it.' The only reason that Tewkesbury did not recant, More said, was because, as the prisoner himself had said, 'I have abiured by fore, there uis no remedy wyth me but deth'.

Of the death itself, Tewkesbury was 'burned as there was never wretche I wene better worthy'. More – then the chief executive officer of England – rejoiced that his victim was now in hell, where Tyndale 'is like to find hym when they come together', with 'an hote fyrebronde burnynge at hys bakke, that all the water in the worlde wyll never be able to quenche'.

The next victim was James Bainham. A barrister of Middle Temple, Bainham had roused suspicions by marrying the widow of Simon Fish, author of the notorious *Supplication for the Beggars*, who had died in 1528. He came from a good Gloucestershire family, which Tyndale may have known. As a lawyer, he was said to be 'very diligent in giving counsel to all the needy, widows, fatherless and afflicted, without money or reward'; although this is Foxe's description, Bainham's acceptance of a terrible death hints at the selflessness of his soul.

Soon after his wedding, Bainham was arrested by a sergeant-at-arms in his chambers in Middle Temple on More's orders. He was charged with denying transubstantiation, questioning the value of the confessional and mocking the power of the papal keys. He was also accused of asserting that 'if a Turk, a Jew, or a Saracen do trust in God and keep his law, he is a good Christian man', a sentiment so tolerant that it was held to smack of heresy. He was taken to the Chelsea house in December 1531. When More saw he 'could not prevail in perverting him to his sect', Foxe claimed, he had Bainham whipped 'at the tree in his garden, called the tree of Troth, and after sent him to the Tower to be wracked'. Foxe says that More was present in the Tower as the racking took place, and that More continued the torture of Bainham 'until he had in a manner lamed him'. This was because Bainham refused to implicate 'the gentlemen of the Temple of his acquaintance, nor would show where his books lay'. More called him 'Baynam the iangler', the babbler whose talk meant nothing. When Bainham's wife denied that she and her husband had kept Tyndale Testaments at their house, she 'was sent to the Fleet, and their goods confiscated'.

Feeble with torture and fear for his wife, Bainham was brought before Stokesley and abjured. His shame proved unbearable. After a month, he attended a secret meeting of evangelicals at a warehouse in Bow Lane. He asked forgiveness 'of God and the whole world' for what he had done, accepting upon his shoulders 'the heavy burden of the cross'. The next Sunday, he attended mass at St Augustine's Church. He rose in his pew, with Tyndale's lethal Testament in his hand, and 'declared openly, before all the people, with weeping tears, that he had denied God'. He prayed to the congregation to forgive him, and to beware of his cowardice in abjuring; 'for if I should not return to the truth,' he told them, 'this Word of God would damn me, body and soul, at the day of judgment'. He then begged everybody 'rather to die than to do as he did, for he would not feel such a hell again as he did feel for all the world's good'.

He had, in effect, sentenced himself to death by appearing in a church with the English Testament. No mercy was possible for a relapsed heretic and Bainham did not seek it. Instead, he wrote a letter to Stokesley, telling the bishop what he had done. Like Bilney, he made no attempt to flee or disguise himself.

His interrogation in front of More and Stokesley illuminates the battle lines of the Reformation, and fascinates as an account of the courage that can stem from religious faith.

Bainham was asked if a person should honour and pray to dead saints. 'Jesus Christ the just is the propitiation for our sins,' he replied, 'and not only for our sins, but for the sins of the whole world.' To pray to saints thus had no purpose. What, then, did St Paul mean when he wrote: 'Let all the saints of God pray for us'? Paul, Bainham said, meant living saints, not the dead, because 'they which be dead cannot pray for him'.

Was it necessary for his salvation that a man confess his sins to a priest? 'Sins are to be forgiven of God,' Bainham replied, 'and a man need not go to any confession.'

What did he mean by saying that the truth of holy scripture had been hidden for eight hundred years until now? 'I mean no otherwise,' he said, 'but that the truth was never, these eight hundred years past, so plainly and expressly declared unto the people, as it hath been within these six years.'

What had happened in the last six years to make him say this? 'The New Testament now translated into English, doth preach and teach the word of God,' he said, 'and before that time men did preach but only that folks should believe as the church did believe, and then if the church erred, men should err too.'

This claim that the Church had purloined the Bible for its own false purposes was the very heart of the matter. Bainham added a comment that crackled and spat with the threat of the fire. 'Howbeit the church of Christ cannot err,' he said, 'and there are two churches. That is, the church of Christ militant, and the church of Antichrist, and that this church of Antichrist may and doth err, but the church of Christ doth not.'

To say this directly into the face of the lord chancellor was brave, or reckless, indeed. Bainham was now asked if he knew of anyone who had 'lived in the true faith of Christ' since the apostles. 'I knew Bayfield,' he said of More's recent victim. 'He died in the true faith of Christ.'

What did he think of purgatory? 'If any such thing as purgatory after this like had been moved to St Paul,' came Bainham's unyielding response, 'he would have condemned it for heresy.'

And what of vows on holy orders? On the celibacy of priests? 'Vows of chastity, and all godliness, is given of God by his abundant grace, which no man himself can keep, but it must be given him of God,' he replied. If a monk, friar or nun could not keep their vow of celibacy, 'they may go forth and marry . . . for there are no other vows, than the vow of baptism'.

Did he think that Luther, a friar, had done well in taking a nun out of religion and marrying her? Bainham was noncommittal on More's favourite topic. 'I think nothing of it,' Bainham replied. The interrogator persisted. Was it lechery by Luther, or no? 'I cannot say so.'

Were the bread and wine of the sacraments not the body and blood of Christ? The king was at his most sensitive on this point. Henry remained proud of his treatise defending the traditional view of the sacraments; he flew into a rage when evangelicals meddled with it, as Bainham did now. 'The bread is not Jesus Christ, for Christ's body is not chewed with teeth,' Bainham replied. 'Therefore it is but bread.'

He confessed that he had a copy of Tyndale's New Testament, but denied that he had offended God by keeping it and using it. He also admitted to having a full set of Tyndale's other works – *Mammon, Obedience, Prelates* and the *Answer to More's Dialogue* – but said he never saw any errors in them. He added that 'the New Testament in English was utterly good', and added that he did not know that Tyndale was a 'naughty fellow'.

Bainham could not be saved in this world, but More and Stokesley felt obliged to purge his soul before they had him burnt. He was taken first to the bishop's coal cellar at Fulham Palace, a place where many episcopal prisoners were kept. He was locked in irons, put in the stocks and left to reflect on his fate for several chilly March days. When this failed to produce any remorse, he was taken back to Sir Thomas More's house at Chelsea. Here, he was chained to a post for two nights, and whipped, before being returned to

Fulham to be 'cruelly handled the space of a week'. After a further fortnight of whippings in the Tower, Bainham remained unredeemed, and charity was deemed to have run its course.

Bainham was delivered to Sir Richard Gresham, the sheriff, who had him carried by his officers to a cell in Newgate. He was burnt on the last day of April 1532. Stokesley sent a Dr Simons to his cell in Newgate 'to convert him, and to wait upon him to the stake'. Simons feared the crowd might beat him, however, and slipped away, for Bainham was a popular man whose execution angered Londoners. There were many horsemen about the stake at Smithfield, indicating a well-bred audience. Bainham embraced the stake, and then stood on the pitch barrel, with a chain about his waist held by sergeants of the guard.

'I come hither, good people,' he said to the crowd, 'accused and condemned for a heretic, Sir Thomas More being my accuser and my judge.' He then spoke of the beliefs for which he was to die. Foxe claims that he ticked off all the main evangelical articles. 'First, I say it is lawful for every man and woman, to have God's book in their mother tongue. Second, that the bishop of Rome is Antichrist . . . there is no purgatory, but the purgatory of Christ's blood, for our souls immediately go to heaven and rest with Jesus Christ for ever . . .'

At this, the town clerk, Master Pave, said: 'Thou liest, thou heretic! Thou deniest the blessed sacrament of the altar.' Bainham retorted that he did not deny the sacrament of Christ's body and blood, but only 'your idolatry to the bread, and that Christ God and man should dwell in a piece of bread . . .'. At that, Pave ordered: 'Set fire to him and burn him.'

As the train of gunpowder came towards him, Bainham lifted up his eyes and hands to heaven, and said to Pave: 'God forgive thee, and show thee more mercy than thou showest to me. The Lord forgive Sir Thomas More! and pray for me, all good people . . .'

With that, the fire 'took his bowels and his head'.

The following week, Pave bought ropes, climbed into a high garret in his house and tried to hang himself.

Tyndale's friends and sympathisers could be burnt but the man himself continued to dance just beyond More's reach. In the autumn of 1531, Henry had asked the imperial authorities for his extradition to England, on the grounds that he was living in subterfuge in the imperial dominions, from where he was sending seditious books to England.

The appeal fell on deaf ears for Charles V had no reason to grant Henry favours. The humiliation of his aunt Catherine did not amuse him. Henry, too, had recently accused the emperor of forcing the pope to recall the annulment case to Rome. And, for good measure, it was an open secret that Tyndale had earned Henry's anger through his support for Catherine's cause.

The imperial reply was therefore curt. No proof had been tendered that Tyndale had committed an offence serious enough for him to be extradited. 'The general opinion', the letter noted tartly, 'is that Tyndale is only persecuted for his attachment to the Queen's cause, which it is thought all the best men in England favour.' If evidence did exist, it should be sent for the emperor to peruse. In its absence, Tyndale would stay put.

Private and illegal means – betrayal, kidnap – were now the only solution. The king ordered that Tyndale be seized and brought to England.

19

'Let not your body faint'

Sir Thomas Elyot, ambassador at the imperial court, was too intelligent to fool himself for long. He was a scholar as well as a lawyer and diplomat who had recently published *The Boke Named the Governour*, the earliest English treatise of moral philosophy. His time at Oxford had overlapped with Tyndale's and he may have known his quarry. Tyndale certainly knew of Elyot and his mission to trap him. The ambassador soon concluded that his task was near impossible.

He wrote to the duke of Norfolk, who was attending the opening of the imperial diet at Regensburg, on 14 March 1532. He said that the king had ordered him to remain in Brussels 'some space of time for the apprehension of Tyndale'. He complained that Tyndale was elusive and highly skilled at concealing himself, and that he had feared he had gone to ground. 'He is in wit movable,' Elyot added wearily, 'semblably so is his person uncertain to come by; and as far as I can perceive, hearing of the king's diligence in the apprehension of him, he withdraweth him into such places where he thinketh to be farthest out of danger.'

Elyot paid agents to loiter round print shops and keep their ears open for gossip. He lavished more than he could afford in bribes – his allowance was 20s a day, and he was spending twice that, and he was also losing on the exchange rate – but still to no effect. He resigned his post in frustration and returned to lick his wounds in Cambridgeshire in June 1532. By then he had spent eight months fruitlessly seeking to have Tyndale extradited or kidnapped. The crown was tardy in paying his expenses, and in November he asked Cromwell to intervene as he was heavily in debt. He said that the experience of looking for Tyndale 'is now grievous unto me', as he had incurred a serious debt of 600 marks beyond his allowance. To make matters worse, his failure meant that 'the King's opinion of me is diminished, for many are advanced to be councillors whose services were not as important as mine'. He asked that his losses be made good. 'I gave many rewards,' he explained, 'partly to the emperor's servants to get knowledge, partly to such as by whose means I trusted to apprehend Tyndale, according to the king's commandment.'

We can locate Tyndale in 1532 no better than could Elyot, a man with the advantage of being alive at the time, and with money and a king's commission behind him. It is significant that the ambassador was convinced that Tyndale knew that he was looking for him. Tyndale had been on the Continent for seven years by now. Local Lutherans had an effective intelligence system – their lives depended on knowing the identity of informers and anticipating the actions of the authorities – and Tyndale was also able to tap sympathetic expatriate merchants. Only once did Tyndale fail to identify a danger.

Whether, as Elyot suspected, Tyndale escaped by moving from place to place, we do not know. In his rare letters to England, he avoided using an address and dropped few clues as to his whereabouts; and even so, at least one of his correspondents in London, Humphrey Monmouth, took the precaution of burning the letters. It helped, of course, that writing was a solitary trade, and could be practised in hiding and in disguise. Martin Luther had begun his translation of the scriptures concealed in a room of the Wartburg Castle in Saxony, dressed as a country gentleman and renamed 'Squire George'. He was already well known, a bluff, beefy figure; but, though he became depressed at being cooped up – he imagined the cawing of the crows and rooks that gathered beyond his window to be the echoes of his soul, and on his sorties from the castle he saw hunters out for hare and partridge as priests trapping the souls of the poor – he escaped detection.

It is possible that Tyndale was in Antwerp for at least part of 1532, and likely that he wrote two expositions that year, one on *The Testament of W Tracie*, and the other *Upon the v, vi, vii Chapters of Matthew*. If, of course, we knew now through some document where Tyndale was lodging and writing, then Thomas More and Elyot and the others who sought him would probably have unearthed him too: his fieldcraft as a fugitive remained impeccable. It must have added to More's frustrations that he knew Antwerp so well himself. Seventeen years before, he had stayed with Pieter Guilles – or Petrus Aegidius, as he preferred to be known, in the Latin style then fashionable with the humanists – in the city; he had been inspired to write *Utopia* when he met Guilles and Raphael Hythlodaye, a young man just back from a long sea voyage, while walking back to his inn after attending mass at Onze-Lieve-Vrouwekathedraal. Guilles, who was secretary of the City of Antwerp, had bought a house that still stands at the end of a small alley known as the Spanjepandsteeg, off the Hofstraat. Tyndale must have lodged within a thousand yards or so of this place that More knew intimately, and from where Erasmus had sent More a famous double portrait of himself and Guilles as a token of his friendship. No such portrait existed to aid the search for Tyndale.

The exposition on Matthew shows how Tyndale survived the strain of his solitary and outcast life by welcoming it as a gift from

God. More's efforts to stamp out the evangelicals before they got a grip on English life foundered on their ability to see their sufferings as a reflection, however dim, of Christ's passion. Tyndale wrote on the verse in the Sermon on the Mount: 'Blessed are ye when they revile you and persecute you.' Here, he said, 'seest thou the uttermost, what a Christian man must look for'.

A man might preach and prosper long enough, he said, if he did not 'meddle with the pope, bishops, prelates and holy ghostly people'. He compared true preaching with 'salting', however, and said that all that is corrupt must be salted, and 'those persons are of all other the most corrupt, and therefore may not be left untouched'. This brought the true preacher persecution, and it was good for a man not to suffer lightly for righteousness. He must be flung into the nethermost depths, Tyndale wrote, so that 'no bitterness or poison be left out of thy cup'; he should be 'excommunicate and delivered to Satan', deprived of fellowship, cursed down to hell, 'defied, detested and execrate with all the blasphemous railings, that the poisonful heart of hypocrites can think or imagine', and brought to death. 'Yet let not thine heart fail thee neither despair, as though God had forsaken thee, or loved thee not,' Tyndale added, 'but comfort thyself with old ensamples, how God hath suffered all his old friends to be so entreated, and also his only and dear son Jesus; whose ensample, above all other, set before thine eyes, because thou art sure he was beloved above all other . . .': Christ was mocked as he hung on the cross – 'Save thyself, thou that savest others' – as the evangelicals were now. Yet he was beloved of God, and so is Tyndale's reader. 'His cause came to light also, and so shall thine at the last,' Tyndale wrote, 'yea, and thy reward is great in heaven with him for thy deep suffering.'

Writing on the seventh commandment, 'Thou shalt not commit adultery', Tyndale again showed his rare respect and gentleness for women. The 'true heart of his wife' is the 'preciousest gift that a man hath of God in this world', he said, 'to abide by him in wealth and woe, and to bear all fortunes with him.' The adulterer robbed the husband of this bounty, for 'after she hath once coupled herself to thee, she shall not lightly love him any more so truly, but haply hate him . . .'. By making the woman sin, too, the adulterer 'hast untaught her to fear God'. Every husband, Tyndale said, should think his wife 'the fairest and best-conditioned . . . for God hath blessed thy wife and made her without sin to thee, which ought to seem a beautiful fairness.'

Tyndale returned to the theme of the power of princes. *Matthew* is less generous to the ruler than *Obedience*, possibly as a result of Henry's renewed attempts to trap the author. Though 'every man's body and goods be under the king', Tyndale wrote as before, 'yet is the authority of God's word free and above the king'. He made clear his hostility to dictatorship – 'no king, lord, master, or what ruler he be, hath absolute power in this world' – and said that the authority of rulers 'is but a limited power' which obliged them to ask forgiveness of their people when they sinned against them. He also claimed that, in matters of conscience, the spiritual power – he was careful not to say 'the Church' – had primacy. The king 'is as deep under the spiritual officer, to hear out God's word what he ought to believe, and how to live, and how to rule,' he wrote, 'as is the poorest beggar in the realm'.

With his majestically poor sense of political timing, Tyndale wrote this at the moment when Henry VIII was subjugating the spiritual power in England to his command. Tyndale was still claiming that the clergy 'wax at once rougher than a hedgehog' when people threatened their perks and income, and 'consume them to powder'; but when it came to the king, the clergy flattened their quills and obeyed.

Parliament had met in session in mid-January 1532, and the legislation promoted by Cromwell ran strongly against the clergy and in favour of reform. More had said to his son-in-law that, 'high as we seem to sit upon the mountains treading heretics under our feet like ants', he hoped the time would never come when Catholics and Lutherans lived side by side and tolerated each other. The situation had become graver still than that. The Church as More knew and loved it was under fresh assault by the king and Cromwell.

The House of Commons, so the duke of Norfolk found, echoed with the 'infenyte clamor of the temporalyte . . . agaynst the mysusing of the spiritual jurusdiccion'. An Act was introduced restraining the payment of 'first fruits', or *annata* to the pope. These were the first year's revenues from an ecclesiastical benefice that the new incumbent traditionally paid to Rome. The bill was conditional and was first used to put pressure on the pope to grant the divorce. When this blackmail failed, it was put into effect and the revenue was paid to the crown.

It was now agreed in the Commons that 'all the griefes which the temporall men were greved with should be putte in writyng and delyvered to the kyng, which by great advyse was done'. The result was the Supplication of the Commons Against the Ordinaries. A petition was delivered to the king in mid-March 1532: it complained that the 'cruel demeanoure' of the clergy touched the 'bodyes and goodes' of the king's subjects, and implored Henry to use his jurisdiction and royal prerogative to put an end to clerical privilege. Convocation made no response other than reiterating the rights and responsibilities of the clergy.

More was deeply concerned, and tried to organise resistance to the Supplication. It was a forlorn task. Henry would not brook opposition to his will from parliament or the Church, associating it with hostility to the annulment. When Convocation produced a more detailed reply to the Supplication, Henry presented the document to the Commons with the provocative comment that: 'We think this answer will smally please you, for it seemeth to us very slender.'

A deputation of bishops implored the king on 8 May to defend their time-hallowed powers. Two days later, he replied disdainfully that he would indeed protect and favour them, but only on condition that all the legislative powers of the Church were ceded to the crown. On 11 May he showed Members of Parliament the oath by which bishops bound themselves to the pope when they were consecrated. 'Well beloved subjects,' Henry said, 'we thought that the clergie of our realme had been our subjects wholy, but now wee have well perceived that they bee but halfe our subjects, yea, and scarce our subjects.' The imperial ambassador recorded on 13 May that, 'The king also wishes bishops not to have the power to arrest persons accused of heresy.' This was perfect anathema to More; with Anne Boleyn constantly pleading to Henry for lenience, it could destroy the campaign against the reformers. 'The Chancellor and the bishops oppose the bill as much they can,' Chapuys added, 'at which the king is exceedingly angry, especially against the said Chancellor.'

Convocation surrendered to the royal demands on 15 May. Under the Submission of the Clergy, the clergy promised to make no new canon laws without royal licence. All existing canons were to be submitted to a committee of thirty-two, half lay and half clerical, and all chosen by the king. Effectively, the king was now the supreme authority in all ecclesiastical causes. A bishop was no longer the arbiter of heresy in his diocese. The ultimate sanction rested with the king and his commissioners.

It was too great a blow for More to bear. He put the Great Seal into a white leather bag and delivered it to the king in the garden at York Place in the early afternoon of 16 May 1532. 'Chancellor More,' a wag wrote, 'is no more.' A few days later, Henry replaced him with another layman and common lawyer, the malleable Sir Thomas Audley.

More's resignation was attributed in public to ill health and the heavy financial burdens of the office. In reality, More went because he was helpless to defend the Church. 'Our savyour sayth that ye chyldren of darkenes be more polytyke in theyr kynde then are the chyldren of lyght in theyr kinde,' he wrote. 'And surely so semeth it now.' There were 'traytors' at court, he thought, and the clergy in Convocation were 'of theyr dewty so neglygent'. He retired from active politics, passing his time in Chelsea.

He remained as busy as ever in the campaign against heresy. The first volumes of his *Confutation of Tyndale's Answer* were now published, and he wrote on as copiously and ferociously as before. He compiled his Epitaph, as was the custom of gentlemen of the time, which he intended to have carved and placed on his tomb in Chelsea parish church. It flattered the king – 'the defender of the faith, a glory afore not herd of' – and claimed that his own record over his years in office was such 'that his Excellent Sovereign found no fault with his service, neither did he make himself odious to the nobles nor unpleasant to the populace, but he was a source of trouble to thieves, murderers and heretics'.

He apologised for the heretic phrase in a letter to Erasmus. 'As to the statement in my Epitaph that I was a source of trouble for heretics,' he said, 'I wrote that just to show off. I find that breed of men absolutely loathsome, so much so that unless they regain their senses, I want to be as hateful to them as anyone can possibly be; for my increasing experience with these men frightens me with the thought of what the whole world will suffer at their hands.' Heretics, he said, 'have a passion for wickedness', and he pledged that 'all my efforts are directed towards the protection of those men who do not deliberately desert the truth, but are seduced by the argument of clever fellows'.

He had no intention, he told Erasmus in June 1532, of giving up the struggle against 'these newfangled sects' and those who were sending a stream of 'every brand of heresy into our country' from the Low Countries. He wrote the same month to 'my most excellent and most affectionate Cochlaeus', Tyndale's old adversary from Cologne days, thanking him for his letters, particularly one bearing tidings of the deaths of the reformers Zwingli, killed in battle in Switzerland in October 1531, and Johannes Oecolampadius, the first Protestant pastor in Basle, who died the following month. 'I was glad to hear the news of their deaths,' More wrote, adding that 'they have left in their wake many very real reasons for being sad, which I cannot mention without a shudder . . . Still, it is right to rejoice that such savage enemies of the Christian faith have departed from our midst, enemies that were so fully equipped for the destruction of the Church . . .'

Old Archbishop Warham died on 22 August 1532. As a fresh fillip to the reformers, the king arranged for Thomas Cranmer to be elected as his successor to the see of Canterbury. Cranmer was the Boleyns' man. He had been the family chaplain and his affection for Anne Boleyn reflected his hope that her influence would help him see through reforms. Chapuys warned of 'the reputation Cranmer has here of being devoted heart and soul to the Lutheran sect'. He confirmed to the emperor that Cranmer 'is a servant of the Lady's', his ironic term for Anne, and said that it was suspected that Cranmer 'may authorise the marriage in this Parliament'. Cranmer was, in truth, more Lutheran than the ambassador or indeed the king supposed. He had married Margaret Ösiander, the niece of Andreas Ösiander, an evangelical professor of theology, while on a diplomatic mission to Nuremberg shortly before the royal summons reached him. He sent his wife secretly to England before returning himself.

Anne was wholly confident that, with Cranmer as archbishop, nothing could prevent her becoming queen. On 1 September, Henry granted her a peerage in her own right, as 'marques' of Pembroke, using the male style of the title, an honour never before given to a woman in English history. It was, perhaps, the reward for at last sleeping with the king. Chapuys said that Henry's lust was now such that he 'cannot leave her for an hour', while the Venetian ambassador soon slyly reported that 'the King accompanies her to mass – and everywhere'.

It seemed safe, too, for reformers to assume that England was a safer place with the change of lord chancellor. It was not. Even out of office, More was as pitiless towards heretics as ever.

One of More's victims, an unconvicted suspect named John Field, appealed to the new chancellor, Sir Thomas Audley, to right his predecessor's wrongs. In his petition, Field described how he had been arrested and brought to More's house in Chelsea by the chancellor's servants. He was imprisoned there for eighteen days, eight days longer than was legal. When he was released, More bound him to appear in the Star Chamber a week later on the eve of Candlemas, 1 February 1530. From there, Field was sent to the Fleet prison, although no sentence had been passed against him or proof of heresy established. He languished in the Fleet for two years in clear breach of statute. Field complained that More often had him searched, sometimes at midnight, 'besides snares and traps laid to take him in'. No copy of the English Testament or of other Tyndale books was found. Among the books confiscated from him in the Fleet was a 6s Greek vocabulary and, ironically, a copy of More's own *The Supplication of Souls*, which More had dashed off as a response to Simon Fish's *Supplication for the Beggars*, in which, showing his characteristic obsession with the fire, he wrote how the souls of the dead 'in most piteous Wyse continually called' for prayers and intercession while 'the gay gere [clothes] burneth uppon our bakkys' from the fires of purgatory.

On Palm Sunday 1532, two warders at the Fleet transferred Field to the equally dank Marshalsea prison in Southwark, stealing his purse with 10s in it as they did so. He fell seriously ill in the Marshalsea, and was delivered to his friends on Whit Monday to see if it pleased God for him to recover. Field was well enough to be up and about on his feet within three weeks. Despite his resignation of the chancellorship, More arranged with Bishop Stokesley and the bishop of Winchester to have Field returned to the Marshalsea. Field assured Audley that More 'had neither word nor deed which he could ever truly lay to [my] charge'. At last, still uncharged, Field was bound over and released from prison the following St Lawrencetide, 10 August.

Ten men had burnt in England since More had first become chancellor. Tyndale knew three of them well, and may have met two more. Next to the stake went his closest and dearest friend, 'my dear son in the faith', John Frith, a young scholar with a charm and grace that beguiled all who knew him. In his pursuit of Frith, More revealed all the fieldcraft – the use of double agents, political intuition and the intricate manipulation of rulers and senior officials, the sowing of bribes, flattery, and inflexible and murderous intent – that he brought to bear on Tyndale.

Frith was a survivor of the Christ Church fish cellar, the son of a Kent innkeeper who had been at school at Eton, becoming an evangelical after he went up to King's College, Cambridge, as a nineteen-year-old in 1522. His first meeting with Tyndale seems to have been in London shortly before Tyndale sailed for Hamburg in 1524; they supposedly talked of the need for the scriptures to be 'turned into the vulgar speech, that thye poor people might also read and see the simple plain word of God'. Wolsey had Frith transferred to his new college at Oxford in 1525. After his release from the cellar, Frith joined Tyndale and the English exiles abroad.

He published a short translation of Martin Luther in 1529, *Revelation of Antichrist*, which he had printed by van Hoochstraten at Antwerp using the false 'Hans Luft of Marburg' colophon. He was briefly in England in 1531, returning to Antwerp before More could pick up his trail. He now wrote his *Disputacyon of Purgatorye*, a treatise in three books in which he argued against More and Fisher that purgatory was a recent invention of the

Church that had no foundation in scripture. As well as his own writing, he helped Tyndale to revise his New Testament and Pentateuch. George Joye, who found him 'ientle & quyet & wel lerned and better shuld have ben yf he had lived', said that Frith worked on 'tindals answers to More and corrected them in the prynte'.

Cromwell had mentioned Frith in his correspondence with Stephen Vaughan over Tyndale. The previous May, in 1531, after the king had abandoned his efforts to persuade Tyndale to return to England, Cromwell urged Vaughan to try to win over Frith in his place. He said that Henry had heard good reports of Frith's learning, and lamented that he should use it to further 'the venomous and pestiferous works, erroneous and seditious opinions of the said Tyndale and other'. The king hoped, however, that Frith was not 'so far as yet inrooted' in heresy that he could not be recalled to the right way. Indeed, Cromwell continued, the king instructed Vaughan to speak with Frith, if he was able, and to urge him to return to England where the king was minded to be merciful to him. If Vaughan got Frith to agree – and if he was careful 'utterly to forsake, leave and withdraw your affection from the said Tyndale' – then Cromwell assured him that 'you will win merit from God, and thanks from the king'. Vaughan promised to do his utmost, but added that he was told that Frith 'is very lately married in Holland, and there dwelleth, but in what place I cannot tell'. He feared that 'this marriage may by chance hinder my persuasions'.

So it proved. Frith did return to England, but a year later, in July 1532, and without the protection of a safe-conduct from the king. His luck seemed to hold out. He went to Reading, where the prior of the abbey was an evangelical who had been imprisoned for a year after the Oxford arrests of 1528, but subsequently released on the king's orders. Poverty, and disguise, belied Frith's status as an Old Etonian and Cambridge graduate. He was arrested at

Reading and put into the stocks as a vagabond under More's new vagrancy legislation. He refused to give his name, or explain what business had brought him to the town. As a result, he was not fed, and became starved with hunger. He pleaded with an onlooker to beg a Reading schoolmaster to come to him, so that he could prove that he was no beggar. Leonard Cox, a local schoolmaster and scholar, duly arrived and found to his astonishment that the ragged figure in the stocks was a fellow Etonian who could recite Homer's *Iliad* faultlessly in the original Greek. Cox reported this to the town's governors and Frith was released.

Stokesley and More got wind of this, and searches were made in Berkshire and Oxfordshire. Frith was in grave peril as he made his way through London and on to Essex to take a ship back to Antwerp. A reward was put on his head and the roads close to the coast were watched.

It was at this moment of greatest vulnerability that Frith, like Hitton before him, was taken in October 1532 by the sea at Milton Shore near Southend, in Essex. The arrest was made by servants of Stokesley, but neither he nor More had, as they hoped, custody of the prisoner. Cromwell arranged for Frith to be kept in loose detention, unshackled, in the Tower of London.

There was still every chance that Frith would remain safe. Cromwell wished him well. The king was impressed by reports of his learning and charming demeanour; the duke of Norfolk thought there was 'no fitter or better qualified man to send abroad on an embassy to a great prince'. Henry had sailed for France with Anne Boleyn on 10 October, at the time of Frith's arrest, for talks with Francis I on the annulment. The lovers stayed in interconnecting bedrooms in the Exchequer Palace in Calais, and the Milanese ambassador referred to Anne as 'the king's beloved wife', convinced by their intimacy that they had already married in secret. By December, Anne was pregnant; before dawn on 25 January 1533, a small number of guests assembled in the king's private chapel in Whitehall Palace to celebrate her wedding to Henry. Unofficial word was soon out. Chapuys heard Anne say that she had 'an inestimable wild desire to eat apples', which the king had told her was a sign of being with child; Anne denied it, but the ambassador noted that 'then she burst out laughing loudly'.

The royal couple needed every theologian they could muster to attack the pope and his refusal to grant the annulment. Frith was thus partly protected by events. He was treated with great favour at the Tower. He was released over Christmas 1532, and lodged by Stephen Gardiner, the bishop of Winchester, at his palace in Southwark, a 'fatherly favour', More said, as Gardiner had been Frith's tutor at Cambridge. A manuscript printed by John Strype, the eighteenth-century ecclesiastical historian, claimed that the underkeeper at the Tower, a man named Thomas Phelips, 'lett hym go at liberty in the nyght to consult with godly men'. Among them was More's old victim John Petite, who at first took his visitor for a ghost, so amazed was he that a man could walk out of the Tower.

Frith certainly received letters, from Tyndale among others, and he wrote freely. One short work was titled *The Bulwark against Rastel*, John Rastell being More's brother-in-law, and a printer, dramatist and pageant promoter. Frith wrote of the conditions in which he was held in the Tower. He had pen and ink and paper, though only 'secretly'. It was a nerve-racking business to write – 'for whensoever I hear the keys ring at the door, straight all must be conveyed out of the way' – and he begged his readers to pardon 'my rudeness and imperfection'. But materials were smuggled into the Tower, and his completed writings were smuggled out.

One of these writings was Frith's undoing, and it gave More the leverage he needed to destroy him. Frith was asked by a friend to write down his views on the Lord's Supper. This was a very dangerous subject indeed, and Frith knew it. 'Albeit I was loth to take

the matter in hand,' he wrote later, 'yet to fulfil his instant intercession, I took upon me to touch this terrible tragedy, and wrote
a treatise, which, besides my painful imprisonment, is like to purchase me most cruel death.' We do not know who this 'friend' was.
He may have been an *agent provocateur* directly employed by
More; he certainly knew one of More's agents intimately enough
to pass on to him the treatise that More used to send Frith to the
stake.

The Last Supper, of course, is the origin of the Eucharist and
the sacraments. Catholics believed – still believe – in transubstantiation. They hold that the communion bread and wine change
their substance into the very Body and Blood of Christ, and that
only their 'accidents' – their colour, taste and texture – continue to
be perceptible to the senses. Luther proposed consubstantiation, a
hybrid in which bread and wine, Body and Blood, coexist in
union. Luther gave the simile of iron put into a fire, in which the
two are united in red-hot metal. Zwingli denied outright the
bodily presence of Christ at communion. He believed that the
sacraments remain bread and wine, and that Christ is only spiritually present at communion in the hearts of the worshippers.
'The mass is not a sacrifice,' he wrote, 'but a remembrance of the
sacrifice and assurance of salvation which Christ has given us.'

Zwingli and Luther had held a bad-tempered colloquy at
Marburg in October 1529, which Frith had attended. It ended in
furious argument and bad blood. As in much else, both sides used
passages from the Bible to justify their differences. The Zwinglian
Johannes Oecolampadius cited Jesus from the passage in John 6,
which Tyndale had translated as: 'I am the living bread which
came down out of heaven. If any man eat of this bread, he shall
live for ever. And the bread that I will give, is my flesh, which I will
give for the life of the world.' This, Oecolampadius argued, was
purely symbolic, since Jesus had added: 'It is the spirit that quick-
eneth, the flesh profiteth nothing. The words that I speak unto

you are spirit, and are life.' The communicant does not partake of Christ's body in the bread, but shares in his spirit. 'You must prove that the body of Christ is not here, when the Word says, "This is my body"!' Luther shouted at Oecolampadius. 'I do not want to hear reason . . . God is above all mathematics. The words of God are to be adored and observed with awe. God commands: "Take, eat, this is my body."' He condemned the Zwinglians – 'your spirit and our spirit do not go together' – as blasphemers.

The sacraments set fellow reformers at one another's throats. The effect on Henry VIII, as More well knew, would be explosive. Tyndale recognised the danger from afar. In a letter from Antwerp that was smuggled into the Tower in January 1533, Tyndale pleaded with Frith to steer as far clear of the subject as possible. 'Mine heart's desire in our Saviour Jesus,' Tyndale wrote to his friend, 'is that you arm yourself with patience, and be cold, sober, wise, and circumspect; and that you keep a-low by the ground, avoiding high questions that pass the common capacity . . . Of the presence of Christ's body in the sacrament meddle as little as you can . . .' Tyndale's own view was that it was an 'indifferent thing' whether Christ was present in the sacraments or not. It 'hurteth no man' to believe that 'the body of Christ is everywhere, though it cannot be proved'. If he was required to do so in his interrogation, Frith could 'show the phrases of the scripture, and let them talk what they will'.

For his part, Tyndale said he taken steps to prevent the subject being raised by the exiles. 'George Joye would have put forth a treatise of the matter, but I have stopped him as yet,' he said. 'My mind is that nothing be put forth, till we hear how you shall have sped.'

The letter went on to give some news from Antwerp. Tyndale said that Stokesley had a servant called John Tisen, 'with a red beard, and a black reddish head', whom he knew because he had taught him at Oxford fifteen years before; Tisen 'was seen in

Antwerp, but came not among the Englishmen: whither he is gone, an ambassador secret, I wot not'. It was an affectionate letter. It addressed Frith as 'Brother Jacob, beloved in my heart' and assured him that 'there liveth not another in whom I have so good hope and trust, and in whom mine heart rejoiceth, and my soul comforteth, as in you'. He told Frith that he would give him any help he might need, for 'my soul is not faint, though my body be weary'. He was anxious that Frith should be discreet, and act 'in fear, and not in boldness . . . and not pronounce or define of hid secrets, or things that neither help or hinder, whether they be so or not so', because he would be lost without him. 'God hath made me ill-favoured in this world, and without grace in the sight of men, speechless and rude, dull and slow-witted,' Tyndale wrote. 'Your part shall be to supply that lacketh in me . . .' Then he cut himself short: 'Abundance of love maketh me exceed in babbling.'

It was too late to warn Frith to be silent on the sacraments. A copy of his little treatise, in which he denied the real presence of Christ, was acquired by William Holt. A London tailor, Holt was one of More's agents who often posed as a Bible-man, and he immediately took the copy to Chelsea. More boasted of receiving three copies in all, and a copy of Tyndale's letter as well. Though gone from office, he was keeping his network of informants well oiled.

More used all his skills to ensure that the treatise – a 'draught of dedely poysen' – would bring Frith to the fate he had planned for him. 'I fere me sore that Cryst wyll kyndle a fyre of fagottes for hym,' he wrote with demonic glee, '& make hym theirin swete the bloude out of hys body here, and strayte from hense send his soule for ever into the fyre of hell.'

More had to be circumspect. He was in no position to bludgeon Frith with an open and publicly circulated denunciation; he was no longer chancellor, and he had lost the king's favour. He had to target very accurately. To do so, he wrote *A Letter of Sir Thomas*

More, Knight, impugning the erroneous writing of John Frith against the blessed Sacrament of the Altar. It was circulated privately to leading figures in the realm. He claimed that Frith's theology was too perverse to reveal to the general public. 'I wolde wysshe,' he wrote piously, 'that the comon people sholde of suche heresyes never here so myche as the name.' This was not true, of course. More had already published volumes of material on heresy, and was continuing to do so with his *Confutation*.

More knew that Cromwell thought of Frith as a potential supporter of the Boleyn marriage. His task was to use Henry's loathing of unorthodox views on the sacraments to set the king against them both. A private letter was the most subtle way of achieving this. In it, More was careful to remind Henry of the title of Defender of the Faith that he had been awarded for his defence of the sacraments. He stressed that Frith's book was 'a false folysshe treatyce agaynste the blessed sacrament of ye aulter'. He flattered the king for being 'lyke a moste faythfull catholyke prynce for the avoydynge of suche pestylente bokes', reminding Henry that his duty to protect the realm against heresy was increased by his position as supreme head of the English Church.

The very mention of Luther still irritated the king beyond measure; More said that Frith was many times worse than the German. In the few pages of his treatise, More wrote, Frith had piled up all the poison spewed out by Wycliffe, Oecolampadius, Tyndale and Zwingli. Frith was not content to say that the sacrament was bread, as Luther had; he said, 'as these other beasts do', that it was nothing but bread. More's imagery of fire dances through his *Letter* like bloodlust; heresy is a fire that 'begynneth to reke oute at some corner . . . burneth up whole townes, and wasteth whole countrees . . . lyeth lurkynge sly; in some old roten tymber under cellers & celynges'.

It took some time for Frith to obtain a copy of the *Letter*, but he did so, and his reply to it was smuggled out to Antwerp and published after his death. For his part, More found out that Frith had seen the *Letter*, and that he had replied to it. 'Howbeit he got mine answere, I can not tel of whome,' More wrote, 'and since I have herde of late that . . . he hath begun and gone a grete way in a newe boke agaynst the sacrament.' The Tower was very porous.

In his *Answer* to More, Frith again ignored Tyndale's advice and plunged once more into the sacrament. He was wholly honest – 'I neither will nor can cease to speak,' he wrote, 'for the Word of God boileth in my body like a fervent fire' – and wholly self-incriminating. He repeated that the communion words '*Hoc est Corpus Meum*', 'This is My Body', were to be understood in the spiritual and not the literal sense. He treated the subject with gentle wit – 'for I have good experience,' he pointed out, 'that my body cannot be in two places at once, both in the Tower and where I would have it beside' – but he was firm that Christ could not be simultaneously on heaven and in earth.

He also defended his dear friend whom More had denounced as a beast. 'Tyndale, I trust, liveth,' he wrote, 'well content with such a poor apostle's life', existing on as many farthings a year as More had pounds sterling, and for all that 'more worthy to be promoted than all the bishops in England' for his learning and judgement.

He recalled how Tyndale had written to him to say of his Bible translation that, 'I never altered one syllable of God's word against my conscience, nor would do this day, if all that is in the earth, whether it be honour, pleasure or riches, might be given me.' Frith asked his readers to judge whether these words 'be not spoken of a faithful, clear, innocent heart'. He repeated the pledge of 'my brother William Tyndale and I', that, if the scriptures were published in English, he 'will promise you to write no more'. If this condition was not granted, 'then will we be doing while we have breath . . .'.

That little remark – 'while we have breath' – now seems the very stuff of boastful melodrama. It was not then, of course; it was a simple vow made the more poignant by the fact that Frith's final breath was likely to be an inhalation of smoke and flame.

Events outside the Tower continued to favour the reformers. The papal nuncio ordered Henry in the pope's name to recall Catherine to court. Henry refused, on the grounds of 'her disobedience and severity towards me'. Anne and Henry held a great banquet at Whitehall on 24 February 1533; Henry, like a boisterous young bridegroom, was lecherous and incoherent with drink by turns. Clement and Charles V agreed a new alliance, the pope promising the emperor that his aunt's case would be heard in Rome and not in England. On 7 April, Henry summoned his council and gave them the startling news that he had married Anne two months before, and that she was pregnant with the heir to the throne. More momentous news followed. On 12 April 1533, the eve of Easter Sunday, 'Anne Bulleine, Marques of Pembroke, was proclaymed Queene at Greenewych, and offred that daie in the Kinges Chappell as Queene of Englande.'

She was not a popular queen. A London congregation walked out in high dudgeon when the priest ordered them to pray for her; a man hauled into court for describing her as 'the scandal of Christendom, a whore and a harlot' was expressing the popular feeling. Catholic loyalists were deeply disturbed by the combination of Anne and Cranmer, who had given her elevation his blessing as archbishop. John Fisher, the fiery bishop of Rochester, secretly appealed to the emperor to invade England; Charles was too busy fighting the Turks to oblige.

A pro-Catherine lobby appeared in exile in the Low Countries. It included Fathers William Peto and Henry Elstow, two Greenwich Franciscans who had fled to Antwerp. They were a mettlesome pair. Peto had preached a sermon in the Chapel Royal in which he warned the king that the royal preachers were 'not afraid to tell of licence and liberty for monarchs which no king should dare even to contemplate'. He warned Henry to his face that, unless he took good heed, 'the dogs [will] lick your blood as they licked Ahab's'. When Elstow defended his colleague, the earl of Essex, sitting with the king, rebuked him: 'You shameless friar! you shall be sewn up in a sack and thrown into the Thames, if you do not speedily hold your tongue!' Elstow was defiant: 'Make those threats to your fellow courtiers. As for us friars, we make little account of them indeed . . .' From Antwerp they wrote a treatise on the validity of Catherine's marriage and distributed tracts supporting her cause. Cromwell reactivated Stephen Vaughan as an agent to find out what More was doing to support them.

'Master More hathe sent often tymes, and lately bookes unto Peto in Antwerp, as his book of the confutacion of Tyndale, and Frythe his opynyon of the sacrament, with dyvers other bookes,' Vaughan reported. 'I can no further lern of More his practises, but if you consider this well, you may perchance espye his crafte.' He confirmed that the friars 'be so much helpen out of England with money, but I cannot learn by whom'. It seemed that More might be sending the friars money through a London merchant, Antonio Bonvisi, a close friend of his who had recently been a sponsor at the baptism of his grandchild. Cromwell did not inquire further. More's connections with Antwerp did not yet seem significant.

Frith seemed in little danger in the Tower, but More's *Letter* and his own *Answer* still hung darkly over him. A royal chaplain named Dr Currein preached a sermon on the Eucharist in front of Henry. Whether More instigated it we do not know, but it is probable that Currein had read the *Letter*. In his sermon, Currein said that it was no marvel that errors abounded over the real presence in the sacrament when there was a prisoner in the Tower at that very moment who was 'so bold as to write in defence of that heresy, and no man goeth about his reformation'. The sermon struck the king's sensitive spot, and he ordered Cranmer and Cromwell to have Frith brought for trial.

On 1 June, Whit Sunday morning, Anne, clad in silver and red velvet, her hair spilling over her shoulders, was crowned queen by Archbishop Cranmer at Westminster. Chapuys thought the spectacle 'a cold, meagre and uncomfortable thing'; the crowds watched in silent hostility and few raised their caps or cheered.

The archbishop now had another duty to perform. He sent one of his gentlemen, and a Welsh porter, to bring Frith from the Tower to his palace in Croydon to be examined. As they started the journey on a boat to Lambeth, Cranmer's gentleman advised Frith to be prudent and non controversial, if only for the sake of his wife and children across the sea; while Cranmer and Cromwell wished him well, he had enemies who wanted him burnt. Frith replied that, if he had twenty lives, he would give them all for the truth.

As they continued their journey on foot, they passed the woods of Brixton. Cranmer's man suggested that Frith make off into the woods and travel home east to his native Kent, while he and the porter would first search the woods to the west towards Wandsworth before raising a general hue and cry. Frith refused the offer. He said he would simply walk on to Croydon and give himself up. Before he was taken on the Essex shore, he said, he had tried everything to escape; but now that he was face to face with his enemies, he felt he had to testify to his faith and remain true to God.

He was held overnight in the porter's lodge at Croydon. He held resolutely to his belief that the sacramental bread and wine were no more than symbols of Christ's Body and Blood. He added that he did not condemn transubstantiation, provided that the eucharist was celebrated 'without idolatry', meaning that no obeisance should be shown to the pyx or the cup. Cranmer saw him in private three times to ask him to 'leave his imagination', but he would not. On 17 June 1533, Cranmer wrote that: 'We had to leave him to his ordinary.' That meant that he was given over to the mercies of Stokesley, the bishop in whose diocese he had been taken. On 20 June, Frith appeared in front of Stokesley, Gardiner and Longland in St Paul's Cathedral. He again refused to abjure. 'The cause why I die is this,' he said, 'for I cannot agree . . . that we should believe under pain of damnation, the substance of the bread and wine to be changed into the body and blood of our Saviour.' He signed his heretical answers in his own hand: 'I, Frith, thus do think, and as I think, so have I said, written, taught, and affirmed, and in my books have published.' Stokesley declared him guilty for having denied that the doctrines of purgatory and transubstantiation were necessary articles of faith. He was relaxed to the secular power for execution on 23 June.

From Antwerp, Tyndale sent a last letter to his friend urging strength in facing the fire. 'Dearly beloved,' he wrote, 'fear not men that threat, nor trust men that speak fair: but trust him that is true of promise, and able to make his word good. Your cause is Christ's gospel, a light that must be fed with the blood of faith. The lamp must be dressed and snuffed daily, and that oil poured in every evening and morning, that the light go not out . . . If when we be buffeted for well-doing, we suffer patiently and endure, that is thankful with God; for to that end we are called. For Christ also suffered for us, leaving us an example that we should follow his steps, who did no sin. Hereby have we perceived love that he laid down his life for us: therefore we ought to be able to lay down our lives for the brethren . . .

'Let not your body faint. If the pain be above your strength, remember: "Whatsoever ye shall ask in my name, I will give it you." And pray to your Father in that name, and he will ease your pain, or shorten it . . . Amen.'

In a grim postscript, Tyndale gave details of the agony of other Bible-men: 'Two have suffered in Antwerp unto the great glory of the gospel: four at Riselles [Lille] in Flanders: and at Luke [Liège] one at the least hath suffered; all that same day. At Roan [Rouen] in France they persecute; and at Paris are five doctors taken for the gospel. See, you are not alone.'

There was one positive note. Tyndale recorded that George Joye had printed two leaves of Genesis, and sent one copy to the king and the other to the new queen, asking for a licence 'that he might so go through all the bible'. Hopes were high that Henry and Anne might permit translations to be sold in England, and 'out of that is the great seeking for English books at all printers and book-binders in Antwerp'. But this was rumour, and too late to save Frith. His wife might, as a last resort, have begged him to abjure. She did not. 'Sir,' Tyndale closed his letter, 'your wife is well content with the will of God, and would not, for her sake, have the glory of God hindered.'

The prisoner was held in Newgate prison, his neck bound to a post by an iron collar. On 4 July 1533, he was taken to Smithfield with Andrew Hewitt, a young tailor's apprentice who had also been betrayed to More by Holt. The rector who addressed the crowd forbade them to pray for the prisoners, no more than they would for a dog. At this, Frith smiled and asked God to forgive the rector. Foxe says that the wind blew the flames away from Frith, so that his dying was prolonged, but he showed no sign of pain.

More had said of Frith's work that he wished 'to plukke as I truste the moste gloryouse fetters from hys gaye pecoks tayle'. No doubt he felt that he had succeeded.

On 11 July, Clement declared Cranmer's validation of the new royal marriage to be void. The pope ordered Henry to put Anne away and warned that any child of the liaison would be illegitimate. He also excommunicated the king, though this was not yet put into effect. Matters were on the move.

20

'A fellow Englishman, who is
everywhere and nowhere'

To the burning of his dearest friend in England, Tyndale had now to add a sharp increase in the danger in Antwerp. Catholic loyalists were angry and militant at the headway that reform was making in the city.

The process was much the same in the Low Countries as in England. Converts were among merchants and skilled tradesmen. A list of early heretic suspects in nearby Bruges showed a cabinet-maker, a ribbon weaver, a miller, a shingler and a shoemaker, who met to read the Bible and discuss the scriptures. A fish seller, turning informer to save his neck, told how a butcher had led him into a field where he found a dozen young men and women. One of them preached that 'everyone should beware of evil and improve his life', a girl handed out black cherries and the little group dispersed. The informer agreed to allow his house to be used for meetings. Eight or nine people came and one of them preached 'evil unseemly sermons'.

A group of Antwerp Catholics sent a long and detailed letter to the chancellor of Brabant in 1533, giving details of local Lutherans and other heretics. They described renegade monks and nuns who spread reform and the officials who tolerated them. They also complained about the foreign exiles who lived in their midst, and who used local printers to produce their evil books.

In particular, the letter referred to a printer who lived in the Camerstraat, within the old gate and next to the Venne Henne, near the 'churchyard of our lady', of the Onze-Lieve-Vrouwekathedraal. The writers told the chancellor that, if he went into the printer's inner room and opened the chests stored in it, 'shall you find books full of heresy in the English tongue, and also others'. They added a note that most probably referred to Tyndale. 'And the printer will also show you,' they claimed, 'a great heretic and doctor, who for his heresy has been driven out of England.'

They insisted that the chancellor take action. 'We have given you material enough,' the letter concluded. 'Do as they have done in Spain. Purge the town. Strengthen the laws; make half-yearly searches after heretics. We write because our spiritual and lay heads have no care for these things.'

The letter was put in front of the council and Margaret, the queen-regent, asked for a report to be made. A priest named in the letter was arrested, taken to the state prison at Vilvoorde Castle, and burnt at Brussels the following year, in 1534. Two laymen, who had attended a church declared to be a nest of heresy by the informers, were beheaded in Antwerp. The printer Adriaen van Berghen was interrogated in 1533 but managed to extricate himself. Three years later, he was condemned for selling Lutheran books and was forced to make his penitential pilgrimage to Cyprus; returning to his old ways, he was later arrested at Delft and executed. Another Antwerp printer, Jacob van Liesvelt, was also later beheaded for printing Bibles in Flemish.

England, in contrast, was becoming more benign. From her coronation to her death, Anne Boleyn protected and promoted evangelicals, and favoured Tyndale's scriptures and other writing. The red-headed child she gave birth to on 7 September 1533 profited her little, for it was not the male heir that Henry longed for, and a hurried 's' had to be filled in after 'Prince' in the document read out by the chamberlain to proclaim the event; but, as Queen Elizabeth, the child was to become the most significant Protestant queen in history.

Anne had commissioned Nicholas Udall, a survivor of the Oxford fish cellar affair, to write verses for her coronation in June. Udall was no glum puritan but a racy man who wrote *Ralph Roister Doister*, the first comedy in English. He had abjured and stayed at Oxford, though his views remained heretical enough to prevent him from taking his MA until the following year, when he was appointed headmaster of Eton. William Betts, a former scholar of Gonville Hall at Cambridge (a college known for its evangelical streak) and another veteran of the affair, became one of Anne's chaplains in 1533. So, too, did the notoriously evangelical preacher Hugh Latimer, soon to be elevated to the see of Worcester.

Nicholas Shaxton had been forced to recant in 1531 by the cruel Bishop Nix after being found with heretical books in the Norwich diocese. Two years later, he found himself appointed treasurer of Salisbury Cathedral and Anne's almoner; by 1535, he was bishop of Salisbury. When Nix heard the news, he was appalled that a man so much more dangerous than little Bilney should find favour with the queen. 'Christ's mother!' he is said to have cried. 'I fear I have burnt Abel, and let Cain go!' Shaxton was another Gonville Hall man. 'I hear no clerk that hath comen out lately of that college,' Nix remarked grimly, 'but savoureth of the frying pan, though he speak never so holily.' First fruits were still payable on acquiring a bishopric, although they went now to the king and not the pope. As poor evangelicals, neither Latimer nor Shaxton had enough money, and Anne lent them £200 each for this.

She was so eager to have the reformer Matthew Parker at court with her that John Skip, another of her evangelical Cambridge chaplains, had to write to him twice in a day. 'I pray you resist not your calling, but come in any wise to know further her pleasure,' Skip wrote to him. 'Bring with you a long gown and that shall be enough until your return to Cambridge.' Parker, later to become the second Protestant archbishop of Canterbury, was duly appointed chaplain to the queen. Anne was to trust her infant daughter Elizabeth to Parker's pastoral care a few days before she was beheaded.

'I have carefully chosen you to be the lanterns and light of my court,' Anne told her chaplains, as Latimer recorded. She asked them to watch over the morals of her household staff and to teach them 'above all things to embrace the wholesome doctrine and infallible knowledge of Christ's gospel'. To keep them from frivolity, Latimer wrote, she kept an English Bible open on her desk in her chamber, which her servants were all encouraged to read. A copy of Tyndale's 1534 New Testament, with its preface discreetly removed, and with her name and title on the edges of the leaves, survives in the British Library. The daughter of William Locke, an evangelical mercer who supplied the court with fabrics, recalled that when her father 'used to go beyond the sea' in his youth, 'Queen Anne Boleyn caused him to get her the gospels and epistles'.

Anne was known as a protector of Tyndale's readers. An evangelical named Thomas Alwaye petitioned her after he was prosecuted for buying a Tyndale Testament. 'I remembered how many deeds of pity your goodness had done within these few years,' he wrote, 'and that without respect of any persons, as well to strangers and aliens as to many of this land, as well to poor as rich: whereof some looking for no redemption were by your gracious means not only freely delivered out of costly and very long imprisoning, but also by your charity largely rewarded and all things restored to the uttermost, so that every man may perceive that your gracious and Christian mind is everywhere ready to help, succour and comfort them that be afflicted . . .' Among the aliens she helped was Nicholas Bourbon de Vandoeuvre, a young French poet, 'very zealous in the scriptures', who was imprisoned for having 'uttered certain talk in derogation of the bishop of Rome and his usurped authority'. Anne 'did not only obtain by her grace's means the King's letters for his delivery but also after he was come into England his whole maintenance at the Queen's only charge'.

This did not, of course, mean that all England was now friendly. More had not forgotten 'the heretic Tyndale'. He described him, in a letter he wrote to Erasmus from Chelsea in mid-1533, as 'a fellow Englishman, who is nowhere and yet everywhere . . .'. More was receiving reports from Antwerp; the agent sought by Vaughan, who was giving money to the friars Peto and Elstow, may have been looking for Tyndale on More's behalf.

More was aware that Tyndale was not attending church, and taunted him for it. 'As they say that know him,' he wrote, 'he sayeth none at all, neither matins, evensong, nor mass, nor cometh at no church but either to gaze or talk.' It would have been more dangerous than ever for Tyndale to attend a service in 1533, when the local hue and cry against Lutherans was under way.

Tyndale kept himself well guarded in 1533 and deep into 1534. Stephen Vaughan, whose wife, interestingly enough, was one of Anne Boleyn's silkwomen, reported to Cromwell from Antwerp on 21 October 1533 that Tyndale had been approached by opponents of the royal divorce. He was asked to work on a treatise condemning the Boleyn marriage, a task suspiciously similar to the one that Peto and Elstow were working on. He refused, Vaughan said, saying that 'he would no farther meddle in his prince's matter, nor would move his people against him, since it was done'.

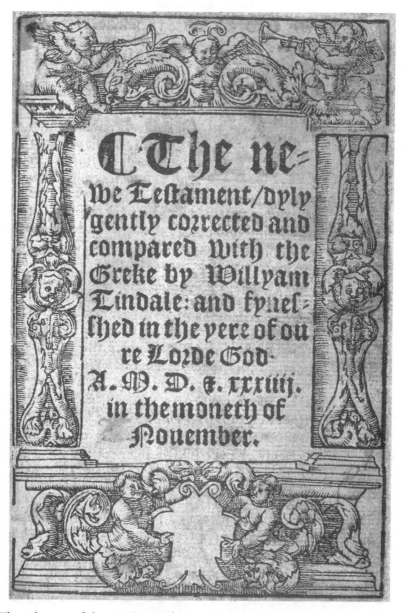

The title page of the 1534 revised New Testament. Tyndale was his own publisher, proofreader, editor, distributor and blurb-writer. He made more than five thousand changes to the 1526 edition. His description of the content is a gem of the copywriter's art: 'Here thou hast the newe Testament or covenaunt made wyth vs of God in Christes bloude.'

(British Library)

We know what Tyndale was doing at this time, if not precisely where he was doing it. He was revising Genesis and the New Testament. The new Genesis was printed in Roman letter rather than black Gothic. The glosses attacking the pope were removed, perhaps showing a greater confidence that reform might flourish in itself, rather than through the fury of its attacks on established Catholicism. The text was little changed from 1530, and it was sold bound into the other existing books of the Pentateuch.

The second edition of the New Testament was thoroughly revised, however, with more than five thousand changes. The new book had four hundred pages of black lettering with wide margins for references and comments. It was pocket-sized, 6 inches by 4, and comfortable to hold in the hand and read. This was not a lectern-sized tome designed to impress but a modern paperback-style book with vivid woodcuts that was intended to sell and to be read. The tales of apocalypse in Revelation, a favourite with readers, had twenty-two illustrations to increase their appeal.

The colophon was accurate, in order to distinguish it from a pirate revised edition that was in circulation. It read: 'Imprinted at Antwerp by Martin Emperor Anno 1534.' The printer was the Frenchman Martin Lempereur, whose main business was in French and Latin school texts and historical writings, and a series of French translations of Luther and Erasmus. He had became involved in English heretical writing from 1530. Although, as we have seen, he had a number of fake colophons, he was not fearful enough of the revised English Testament to use one of them.

The title page referred to the content as 'diligently corrected and compared with the Greek, by William Tyndale', and gave the date of publication as November 1534. All the books except Acts and Revelation had prologues. To a large extent, these were translations from Luther, although Tyndale added passages of his own which were sometimes at odds with the German. Luther felt that Hebrews and James were not apostolic. He had reason for doing so – the origins of Hebrews remain obscure to modern scholars, and James, which Luther found a 'right strawy epistle', has a grounding in Greek culture that raises doubts about its authorship – but Tyndale insisted that they 'ought of right be taken for Holy Scripture'.

The marginal notes were brief and explanatory. The pope and clergy did not escape scot-free. Where Paul urged the Thessalonians 'to meddle with your own business, and to work with your own hands', Tyndale could not resist a taunt from the margin: 'A good lesson for monks and idle friars.' In general, though, the usual ill-tempered assaults on the pope and clergy were missing.

At the back of the book Tyndale included forty passages from the Old Testament read out in services according to *Sarum Use*. This was the local medieval variation of the Roman rite used in the cathedral church of Salisbury, which became the standard for England. The reader thus had all the epistles heard through the year translated into English. For the most part, the Old Testament epistles came from the books that Tyndale had already translated. There was new material, however, from the Song of Songs, Zechariah, Joel and Malachi, and a haunting passage from Ecclesiasticus 24, lost to all those whose Protestant Bibles do not include the Apocrypha: 'As a vine, so brought I forth a savour of sweetness. And my flowers are the fruit of glory and riches. I am the mother of beautiful love and of fear . . . In me is all trace of life and truth . . . Come unto me all that desire me, and be filled with the fruits that spring of me. For my spirit is sweeter than honey . . . They that eat me, shall hunger the more, and they that drink me, shall thirst the more . . .'[1]

Tyndale described the book with a phrase worthy of any dust jacket. 'Here thou hast (mooste deare reader)', he began his introductory epistle, 'the new testament or covenaunt made wyth us of God in Christes bloude.' This was no dry priestly tome, but 'glad tydynges of mercie and grace, that oure corrupt nature shalbe healed agayne for Christes sake'; it was the guarantee of God's gift of love, 'loue overcomynge all payne, greffe, tedyousnesse or lothsomnes'.

He went on to claim that he had 'weded oute of it many fautes, which lacke of helpe at the begynninge, and oversyght, dyd sowe therein'. He was helped by the experience of Hebrew he had gained with the Pentateuch, because there were Hebrew patterns of speech and ideas beneath the Greek in the New Testament, and he could now 'consider the Hebrue phrase or manner of speche left in the Greke wordes'. For those who find faults, he declares, 'it shalbe lawful to translate it themselves, and to put what they lust thereto'. If he himself agrees with any correction, then 'I will shortlye after cause it to be mended'.

The row with More rumbled on. Tyndale explained why he would not change the words that were said to be offensive. 'Repentance' was right, he said, and the Catholic insistence on 'penance' was wrong. In the Old Testament, the Hebrew word *Sob* was generally used, meaning 'turn or be converted'. The Greek in the New Testament 'hath perpetually *metanoeo* to turn in heart and mynde, and to come to the ryght knowledge, and to a manne's ryght wyt agayne'. Saint Jerome's translation in the Vulgate, Tyndale insisted, should also be given as 'repent' in English. Jerome 'hath some tyme *ago penetenciam* I do repent: sometimes *peniteo* I repent: sometime *peniteor* I am repentant . . .'. The 'verye sense and significacion' of both the Hebrew and Greek word 'is, to be conuerted and to turne to God with all the hert'.

He said that repentance, 'if it be unfeigned', had four companions. Confession – 'not in the preestes eare,' he wrote of Catholic practice, 'for that is but manne's invencion' – must take place to God in the heart. Then contrition, 'sorrowfulness that we be such damnable synners'. Thirdly, faith, through which God for Christ's sake 'doth forgive us and receave us to mercie', but of which the doctors of the Church make 'no mencion at all in the description of their penaunce'. Finally comes 'satisfacion or amendesmakynge', which is done 'not to god with holye workes', as More and the Church insisted, 'but to my neyboure whome I have hurt, and the congregacion of God whome I have offended'.

The distinction between 'repentance' and 'penance' was more than wordplay. It was a matter of God's meaning. Repentance to the evangelical involved private confession to God, and making amends, not to the Church, but to the whole 'congregation of God'. It depended upon individual faith, for, as Tyndale wrote, 'Christ saith Iohn viii "except ye believe that I am he, ye shall dye in your sinnes"'. To the Catholic, penance was impossible without the Church, and involved physical actions: auricular confession to a priest, taking part in a penitential procession or pilgrimage, the purchase of an indulgence, the carrying out of good works that met with the Church's approval. To Tyndale, all this mattered nothing.

Tyndale was no pedant, and he did not mind what precise word was used. 'Whether ye saye "repent", "be converted", "tourne to God", "amende youre lyvynge" or what ye lust,' he said, 'I am content so ye understonde what is meant therby.' It was meaning that was important. The same applied to the non-use of 'priest' that More had criticised. Tyndale replaced the 'seniors' of the 1526 Testament with 'elders' in the revised edition. He explained that the Old Testament used the word 'elders' for the Jews who ruled over the laity. From this custom, 'Paule in his epistle and also Peter' – the mention of Peter being a sly dig at the pope, with his claim to be the apostle's successor – 'call the prelates and spirituall gouernors which are byshoppes and preestes, "elders"'. He said that whether his readers called them 'priests' or 'elders' was 'to me all one', but he put a sting in the tail of this apparent concession. These were 'offycers and servauntes of the worde of God' whom all Christian men must obey, but only for 'as long as they preache and rule trulye and no lenger'.

In the echoing passage of I Corinthians 13 – 'Nowe abideth fayth, hope and love, even these thre: but the chefe of these is love' – he refused to revise 'love' to 'charity'. To have done so would have reverted to the Latin Vulgate, '*major horum est caritas*', and to Wycliffe, 'the moost of these is charite'. The English charity comes from *caritas* by way of the French *charité*. The Latin word derives from *carus*, dear. In the New Testament sense, so Tyndale insisted, it means 'universal love' and not its alternative of 'good works', or gifts, to the needy. It was the perceived insult to Catholic good works that led More to consider the use of 'love' to be heretical.

In the revision itself, he made an effort to correct the 'errours committed in the prentynge' of the 1526 edition. The misprints were numerous and indicated that the Worms compositors had no English. Sometimes they used a German spelling, *gebe* as in *geben* instead of *gave*, for example. No standard spellings existed in English, and it was common for a word to be spelt differently in a single passage: blessid, blessd, blesste and blest coexisted with blessed.

Simple misprints were of little concern – although he was at pains to restore '*Gog*' to '*God*' in a verse in John 8 – and he concentrated on errors that changed the meanings of words. In the same passage, he corrected *soone* to *sonne*, or son, *thought* to *taught*, and *thought* to *though*, *stoppeth* to *steppeth*, *beloveth* to *beleveth*, *ynought* to *ynough*, *hat* to *hath*.

His main aim was to strengthen his writing, to clarify meaning and to bring it closer to the Greek. He chose his words with great care, and his delicate editing is well seen in the Sermon on the Mount in Matthew's gospel. He dropped the original '*blessed are the maynteyners of peace*' for the more direct '*blessed are the peacemakers*'. He was unhappy with: 'Ye are the salt of the earth; but and if *the salt be once unsavery*, what can be salted therwith.' This was replaced by 'if *the salt have lost her saltnes*', a charming phrase that assigns a gender to salt. The passage continues: 'It is thence-forthe goode for nothynge, but *to be caste oute at the dores, and that men treade it vnder fete.*' This was replaced by the simpler and more rhythmic: '*to be caste oute, and to be troden vnder foote of men*'.

He was unhappy with the next verse, on the light of the world: '. . . it lighteth *all them which* are in the house. *Se that youre light so shyne before men* . . .' In the revised version, it lighteth '*all that are in the house*', and readers were admonished: '*Let your light so shyne* before men . . .' The next verse starts awkwardly in the 1526 edition: 'Ye *shall not thynke* that I am come to *disannul the lawe*, or the prophets: No I am nott come to *disannul* them, but to fulfyll them.' Disannul was a legal, Franco-Latin term with little punch; 'ye shall not thynke' was a mouthful. Both went in the 1534 edition, replaced by: '*Think not* that I am come to *destroy the lawe*, or the prophets: no I am nott come to *destroy* them but to fulfill them.'

Where he had it right, as in the next verse, he left it be: 'For truely I saye vnto you, till heven and erthe perisshe, one iott or one tytle of the lawe shall not scape, tyll all be fulfilled.' *Not one jot or tittle* is in the language still.

To the Lord's Prayer he made the smallest of changes and an addition. The 1526 passage reads: 'O our father which arte in heven, halowed be thy name; Let thy kingdom come; thy wyll be fulfilled, as well in erth, as hit ys in heven; Geve vs this daye oure dayly breade; And forgeve vs oure treaspases, even *as we forgeve them which treaspas vs*; Leede vs not into temptacion, but delyvre vs ffrom yvell. Amen.' He changed 'forgeve them which treaspas vs' to '*forgeve other men theire treaspases*', and he added '*And*' before 'leede vs not into temptacion' to improve the flow. The 1534 addition came with the doxology, or glorification, before the Amen: 'For thyne is the kingdom and the power and the glory, for ever. Amen'

The Gospell of Sainte John.

The fyrst Chapter.

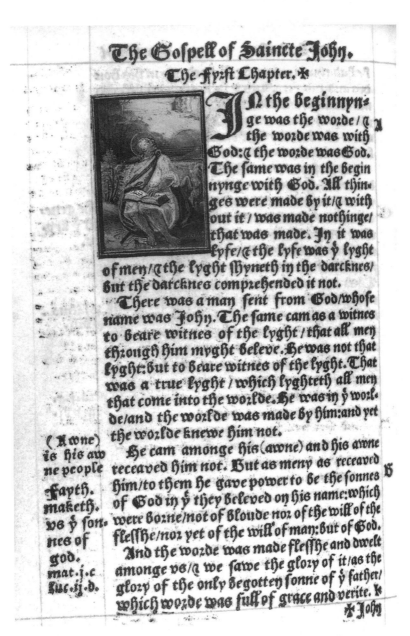

IN the beginnynge was the worde/ꝗ the worde was with God:ꝗ the worde was God. The same was in the beginnynge with God. All thinges were made by it/ꝗ with out it/was made nothinge/ that was made. In it was lyfe/ꝗ the lyfe was y lyght of men/ꝗ the lyght shyneth in the darcknes/ but the darcknes comprehended it not.

There was a man sent from God/whose name was John. The same cam as a witnes to beare witnes of the lyght/that all men through him myght beleve. He was not that lyght:but to beare witnes of the lyght. That was a true lyght/which lyghteth all men that come into the worlde. He was in y worlde/and the worlde was made by him:and yet the worlde knewe him not.

(Awne) is his awne people

He cam amonge his (awne) and his awne receaved him not. But as meny as receaved him/to them he gave power to be the sonnes of God in y they beleved on his name:which were borne/not of bloude nor of the will of the flesshe/nor yet of the will of man:but of God.

Fayth. maketh. vs y sonnes of god. mat.j.c Luc.ij.d.

And the worde was made flesshe and dwelt amonge vs/ꝗ we sawe the glory of it/as the glory of the only begotten sonne of y father/ which worde was full of grace and verite. ✳John

Tyndale's revision of his original New Testament in the 1534 edition was almost always for the best. 'In the beginnynge was that worde,' he had opened John's Gospel in 1526, 'and that worde was with God, and that worde was God.' He used 'the worde' in 1534, since 'that worde' begs the question of 'what word?' This happy change, passed down through the King James Version of 1611, is with us still.

(British Library)

He changed '*Beholde* the lyles off the felde, howe they growe' to the more thoughtful '*Consider* the lyles off the felde'. An awkwardness hangs to the 1526 advice to: 'Care not therfore for *the daye foloynge for the daye foloynge shall care ffor yt sylfe*; eche dayes trouble ys sufficient for the same silfe day.' This disappears in 1534: 'Care not thene for the *morrow, but lete the morrow care for yt silfe* . . .' The plodding 'O ye *endued with* little faith' of 1526 became the gossamer 'O ye *of* little faith'. The change in the opening verse of John's gospel is minimal – *that* becomes *the* – but the result is startling. 'In the begynnynge was that worde,' he wrote in the first edition, influenced by the Vulgate, 'and that worde was with god, and god was thatt worde.' A fresh drumroll comes with the revision: 'In the beginning was the word and the word was with God, and the word was God.' It is also clearer, for the instinct when confronted by '*that* Word' is to ask '*what* Word?'. A famous passage of 1526 – 'No man can serve two masters . . . ye can nott serve God and mammon' – he left unchanged.

When Tyndale had almost completed his work, an edition of a pirate revised Testament 'was spyed and worde brought me'. He had been beaten to the post at his own task. 'George Ioye secretly toke in hand to correct it also by what occasyon his conscyence knoweth,' he wrote, 'and prevented me, in so moche, that his correccyon was prynted in great nombre, ere myne beganne.' The edition was being printed in Antwerp by the widow of Christoffel van Ruremund, who had died in prison in London after being arrested for smuggling Tyndale Testaments.

Pirate copies of his work did not much bother Tyndale. He knew Joye and thought it dishonest that he had revised the Testament 'seeing he knew I was correcting it my selfe'; but that apart, 'I toke the thinge in worth as I have done dyvers other in tyme past'. He was prepared to let it go until, with his own edition at the printers, he saw a copy of Joye's work. He was 'astonyed' to

The Revelation of St John was a favourite with readers. Tyndale illustrated it with twenty-two woodcuts in the 1534 edition of his New Testament. They include this vivid block of the Four Horsemen of the Apocalypse.

(Bodleian Library)

find that it was 'in such wise altered' from his original that he wondered 'what furye hath dryven [Joye] to make socke chaunge and to call it a diligent correccyon'. He added a second foreword to his own revised edition – 'Willyam Tindale, yet once more to the Christen reader' – dissociating himself from Joye's work. He included the colophon of the pirate work, 'printed now again at Antwerp, by me widow of Christopher of Endhoven in the year of our Lord 1534 in August', so that his readers could recognise and avoid it.

He would not have minded had Joye brought out his own book with his own name on it. It was quite lawful, he said, for a man to translate a work, whether or not it had been translated before, provided he put his name to it. As 'the foxe when he hath pyssed in the grayes [badger's] hole chalengeth it for his awne', so it was acceptable for others to 'take my translacions and laboures, and chaunge and alter and corrupte at their pleasures, and call it their awne translacions, and put to their awne names'. But it was wrong 'to play boo pepe after George Ioye's manner and take another man's translacion and put out and in and chaunge at pleasure, and call it a correcyion'. Joye was stung by the criticism and published his own *Apology* to put his side of the affair.

Joye was a fellow exile who had fled to Antwerp after being investigated for heresy. He was a Cambridge man, a former Fellow of Peterhouse, who fell foul of the prior of an abbey near Bedford. The prior secretly informed John Longland, the rigorous bishop of Lincoln, that Joye harboured Lutheran ideas. Joye was ordered to London in the early winter of 1527 to be examined by Wolsey. He was in some danger – little Bilney was one of the other suspects appearing in front of Wolsey – but he seems to have been more concerned at the weather and the affront to his status. 'I got me to horse when it snowed, and was cold,' he complained of his journey to London. Worse, when he arrived at the cardinal's palace, no one knew who he was or why he was there; he was eventually told to go to Longland's palace, where he was given neither board nor lodging. 'I thought thus with myself, I am a scholar of Cambridge under only the vice-chancellor's jurisdiction and under the great God the Cardinal,' he wrote, 'and . . . I will take a breath ere I come to these men again.' So indeed he did. 'I got me to horse,' he continued, 'and conveyed myself toward the sea side.' He crossed the Narrow Sea in December 1527, settling in Antwerp.

Here he set to work as a translator. He produced the first printed edition of the Psalms in English in 1530. The following year, he translated the Book of Isaiah, which was printed for him by Martin Lempereur in Antwerp. His translation of Jeremiah was printed by van Ruremund's widow, using the van Endhoven alias, in May 1534.

Van Ruremund had set up his print shop in Antwerp in 1522. He and his brother Hans specialised in liturgical works and printed widely for the English market. It was natural for them to pirate Tyndale's Testament as a potential bestseller. Christoffel van Ruremund copied his first pirate edition from the 1526 Worms original in a small sextodecimo volume, adding a Calendar at the beginning, Concordances, or parallel references, in the margin, and a Table of Contents at the end. No Englishman was at hand to correct the setting, Joye said, and van Ruremund made 'many more faults than were in the copy, and so corrupted the book that the simple reader might ofttimes be tarried and stick'. Joye claimed that more than two thousand copies were printed in this edition. They must have made up a good proportion of the books burnt in Antwerp and Bergen-op-Zoom in January 1527, after Wolsey had instructed Sir John Hackett to act against the printing and distribution of English Testaments. Robert Ridley mentioned the following month that 'many hundreds' of them had been 'burnt beyond the sea'.

When it had sold out, a bigger volume with a larger typeface was printed, to make a total of some five thousand pirate copies.

Woodcuts were used to illustrate the Apocalypse, but Joye said that the printers produced it 'also without a corrector' and that the volume was 'much falser than their first'.

Tyndale had promised to revise his first translation, Joye said, but he 'prolonged and deferred' so much that a third pirate edition in small format was produced in Antwerp. It was 'much more false than ever it was before'. Joye claimed that he had been approached by the printer to correct it. 'I suppose that Tyndale himself will put it forth more perfect and newly corrected,' he said that he had replied, 'which, if he do, yours shall be nought set by, nor never sold.' Despite this, the printer had gone ahead and printed two thousand copies, and 'had shortly sold them all'.

Van Ruremund ventured to England to sell his editions and was picked up in More's wave of arrests. Foxe reported that in 1531 'Christopher, a Dutchman of Antwerp' was arrested 'for selling certain New Testaments in English to John Row bookbinder' and 'was put in prison at Westminster and there died'. His widow maintained the workshop in Antwerp. She continued to produce banned books for the English market until the end of the decade, including translations of Savonarola and Zwingli, when she changed to safer publications – almanacs and news-sheets.

The Tyndale Testament was a great money-spinner, and the widow prepared to print a fourth pirate edition in 1534. All the long while Tyndale slept, Joye said, 'for nothing came from him, as far as I could perceive'. He again said that if Tyndale amended his work, the pirate edition would not sell a copy. The van Ruremund printers did not agree. 'For if [Tyndale] print two thousand, and we as many,' they said, 'what is so little a number for all England? And we will sell ours better cheap, and therefore we doubt not of the sale.'

Joye realised, or so he wrote, that 'whether I had corrected their copy or not, they had gone forth with their work, and had given us two thousand more books falselier printed than ever we had before'. He was also confident that the market in England, with Anne Boleyn as queen and Cranmer as archbishop, was better than ever. 'Now there was given, thanked be to God,' he said, 'a little space to rest unto Christ's Church after so long and grievous persecution for reading the books.' In the absence of any news from the translator himself – 'what Tyndale doth I wot not, he maketh me nothing of his counsel' – Joye decided to go ahead and correct the Testament in the press.

The explanation in the *Apology* is so lengthy that it smacks of a guilty conscience. So, too, does Joye's pious attack on 'Tyndale's uncharitable and unsober pistle', and the self-righteous appeal to God to 'Deliver me from lying lips, and from a deceitful tongue'. He accused Tyndale of standing 'high in his own opinion', a man so arrogant and convinced of the perfection of his work that 'he must be the Almighty himself'. Tyndale had a party of supporters, Joye said, who looked on him as their master, and resented any who disagreed with him, while Tyndale himself was only 'patient when every man say as he saith, and look up and wonder at his words'. Joye accused Tyndale of plagiarism, saying that his Exposition of Matthew was written by Luther, with Tyndale only translating it and 'powdering it here and there with his own fantasies'. Malice and envy were Tyndale's 'two blind guides'; Joye added that Tyndale had attacked him because 'he has long nourished hatred and malice against me, though outwardly he has feigned to love me'.

Some of Joye's barbs strike home. He said that he preferred the scripture to be purely and plainly translated, with 'neither note, gloss nor scholia', so that the reader 'might once swim without a cork'; and it is true that the margins of Tyndale's work sometimes resemble a battleground in his war against the pope. But the overall portrait – of a crabbed, malicious and self-satisfied pedant – is devalued by Joye's own record, of persistently falling out with his acquaintances, and by the affection in which Tyndale was held by those close to him, such as Frith. It cannot be said, however, that Joye acted out of greed. Van Ruremund's businesslike widow paid him a pittance for his work – 4½d for every sheet of sixteen pages, or a total of 12s.

A copy survives in the British Museum, the earliest pirate copy known to exist. It is a well-printed enough little volume, without notes or glosses, and Joye's work was competent. He made few changes, though, when he did, he sometimes guessed wrong. Thus, in a passage in Matthew 6, where Tyndale's original read 'else he will *lene* the one and despise the other', Joye substituted 'else he will *love* the one'. Tyndale himself rectified his error in the 1534 edition: 'he will *lean to* the one'.

In one important respect, however, Joye wilfully changed Tyndale's meaning. Tyndale had claimed, in his controversy with More, that 'the souls of the dead lie and sleep till Doomesday'. Joye, in common with most others, believed that the soul passed on to a higher life at death. He had several arguments over this with Tyndale. 'As we walked together in the field', Joye wrote – an interesting detail which, together with Vaughan's similar meetings, suggests that Tyndale was careful to set up his meetings in the open air rather than at a particular address – Tyndale ridiculed his ideas by 'filliping them forth between his finger and his thumb after his wonted disdainful manner'. Joye took his revenge in print. Where Tyndale used 'resurrection', Joye substituted the phrase 'life after this', except where the passage clearly concerned the resurrection of the body. Thus, in Matthew 22, Tyndale wrote: 'in the *resurrection* they neither marry nor are given in marriage . . . as touching the *resurrection* of the dead, have ye not read?'. Joye altered these references: '*in the life after this* they neither marry . . . as touching *the life of them that be dead . . .*'.

The souls of the dead were not 'already in the full glory that Christ is in', Tyndale wrote; Christ had said that 'the time shall come' in which all that are in the grave shall hear his voice, but that time of resurrection had not yet arrived. Joye was premature to claim that those who have done good shall at the moment of death 'come into the very life'; and this flaw was so great that Tyndale would not accept it 'though the whole world should be given me for my labour'.

This preoccupation with the grave was timely. Tyndale's enemies would see to it that he did not have one.

21

Judas

Tyndale had been living in the English House at Antwerp since the middle of 1534. It is the first definite address that we have for him since he left Little Sodbury Manor and Humphrey Monmouth's London house a decade earlier.

The English House was a mansion that the city magistrates had given to the English merchants sixty years before to encourage trade with England. It served much the same purpose as the Steelyard did for the Hanseatic traders in London. It stood in its own alleyway in a block of streets, now bounded by the restaurants and lace shops of Zirkstraat and Oude Beurs, a few hundred yards north of the city's Grote Markt, the great market square, and the cathedral. A similar building survives today close by, a tall and gabled house built for the guild of archers. Known as Den Spieghel, The Mirror, it also stands discreetly at the end of a cobbled alley. It was well known to Thomas More, for it had been bought in 1506 by his friend Pieter Guilles – 'a very fine person,' More wrote of him, 'and an excellent scholar' – and More had described meeting Guilles and the adventurer Raphael Hythlodaye in the opening scene of *Utopia*.

The waterfront on the Scheldt was three streets away. Its

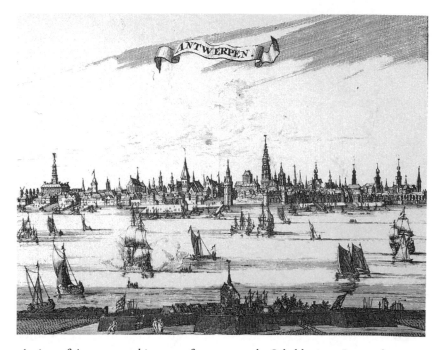

A view of Antwerp and its waterfront across the Scheldt river. It was the great-est commercial city in northern Europe in the 1520s and 1530s, a thriving port known simply as 'the Metropolis'. Though nominally a Catholic city, its printers and shipowners were willing to produce illegal Bibles and run them across the Narrow Sea to the Thames and the creeks of Suffolk and Essex. The English House, the only definite address we have for Tyndale in all his years on the Continent, lay in a narrow street close to the Cathedral, whose high spire is at the centre of this view.

(Mary Evans Picture Library)

skyline was webbed by the masts and rigging of bluff-bowed merchantmen with heavy leeboards and lighter galliots, which mingled with the spires, towers and belfries of a score of chapels, churches and monasteries. The English Quay, tucked downriver from the cannon and towers of the Steen Castle, handled most of the wool trade across the Narrow Sea, with other specialist quays and warehouses for wines, grain and spices. The world's first stock exchange opened in the city in 1531, in an elaborate

pinnacled building in the Flamboyant Gothic style close to
Tyndale's new home.

He was close, too, to the soaring beauty of the Cathedral of Our
Lady. Its graceful north spire, ninety-eight years in the building,
had recently been completed; at more than 450 feet it acted as a
landmark for shipping and as a symbol of Catholic extravagance to
puritan evangelicals. A fire a year before Tyndale took up residence in the English House had burnt out the roofs of the nave,
the transept and the south tower. The wooden trusses above the
nave had not yet been vaulted over with stone, and the timbers fell
in flames into the church, destroying some sixty altars and their
retables, a measure of the rich ornamentation that Tyndale and the
reformers so disliked. The English merchants had their own side-
chapel, presented to them in recognition of their importance to
the prosperity of Flanders, with an altar named for St Anthony,
and a stained glass window dedicated to Henry VII and bearing a
red rose in deference to his Lancastrian forebears.

The English House was run by Thomas Poyntz, a sympathetic
and, as events proved, courageous man who was a relation of
Lady Walsh of Little Sodbury. Membership of the House was
much valued. The citizens of Antwerp enjoyed several legal privileges, including freedom from arbitrary arrest and detention
without trial, and these were extended to the English merchants.
As a resident of the House, Tyndale could only be arrested within
the confines of the building for a grave crime for which evidence of guilt already existed. Richard Herman, the merchant
who had been arrested in 1528 on charges of helping Tyndale,
had petitioned Queen Anne to help him regain his membership
two months or so before Tyndale's arrival in the House. Anne
wrote to Cromwell in May 1534 to say that Herman had been
'expelled from his freedom and fellowship of and in the English
house' for his 'help in the setting forth of the New Testament in
English'. She urged Cromwell to see that 'this good and honest

merchant' should be 'restored to his pristine freedom, liberty
and fellowship'. It may be that the special vellum copy of the
revised New Testament that was sent to Anne from Antwerp,
inscribed *Anna Regina Angliae*, was a gift of thanks for her intervention.

Details of Tyndale's routine at this time were passed on to Foxe,
probably by Poyntz. Tyndale was 'very frugal and spare of body'.
He kept two days a week for what he called his 'pastime'. On
Mondays, he visited the Englishmen and women who had fled to
Antwerp, whom he 'did very liberally comfort and relieve', providing for the sick and diseased. On Saturdays, he walked round
the town, looking into 'every corner and hole' for the old and
weak, and families overburdened by children, whom he 'also plentifully relieved'. The English merchants at Antwerp had begun
giving him a stipend, so that he had a secure income for the first
time since leaving Little Sodbury; he gave 'the most part' of this to
the poor. On Sundays, he would go to an English merchant's
rooms, and 'read some one parcel of scripture' to those who gathered there. He also read for an hour or so after dinner, 'so fruitfully,
sweetly, and gently' that he brought 'heavenly comfort' to his audience.

The rest of the week was given 'wholly to his book'. He saw the
revised New Testament through the press in November 1534, and
started work on a third edition. He was also close to completing
the Old Testament historical books from Joshua to II Chronicles.
The three short books of Ezra, Nehemiah and Esther were then to
follow before he tackled Job – whose suffering innocence Tyndale
shared, if not his patience – and the mass poetry of the one hundred and fifty Psalms.

Tyndale had recently turned forty: he had every reason to look
forward to completing his life's work, in the comfortable and sympathetic surroundings of the English House in Antwerp. Or,
indeed, in England. The two men most in the ascendancy,

Cromwell and Cranmer, were favourable to reform. The first printed French Bible had recently been produced by the scholar Jacques Lefèvre d'Etaples, to join the translations already made in German and Italian. An English Bible was within a whisker of gaining official approval. Convocation, meeting on 10 December 1534, petitioned the king 'that the sacred Scriptures should be translated into the English tongue by certain honest and learned men for that purpose by his Majesty, and should be delivered to the people according to their learning'. No royal command was issued, but Miles Coverdale began to integrate Tyndale's existing translations into a complete Bible, dedicated to Henry VIII. Coverdale was a Cambridge reformer and renegade Augustinian friar who had fled abroad in 1528; Foxe says he joined Tyndale in Hamburg in 1529, staying with him in the house of the widow Margaret von Emerson, and 'helped him in the translating of the whole five books of Moses'. Coverdale based his work on Tyndale where he could; the missing books of the Old Testament he translated from the German versions of Luther and Zwingli, with guidance from the Vulgate and the translation from the original Hebrew into Latin completed by the Dominican scholar Pagnini in 1518.

Tyndale's great enemy was still writing furiously from Chelsea – warning of the 'corrupt cankar' of heretics, and advising his readers not to 'so mych as byd theym good spede or good morrow whan that we mete them' – but More was himself now in peril as the king's anger with papal loyalists grew apace.

The pope had already denounced the Boleyn marriage as invalid. In March 1534, after seven years of vacillation, Clement finally pronounced judgement in Henry's annulment suit. He declared that the marriage of Henry and Catherine 'always hath and doth still stand firm and canonical, and the issue proceeding standeth lawful and legitimate'. Henry was required to resume living with Catherine, and to treat her 'as becometh a loving husband and his kingly honour so to do'. For good measure, Henry was ordered to pay the legal costs of the suit.

Catherine had been redubbed the 'Princess Dowager', as the widow of Henry's brother Arthur, a title she refused to accept, maintaining that she was still the rightful queen; her household was removed from her, and she was sent to the damp and ancient palace of the bishop of Lincoln on the edge of the fens at Buckden in Huntingdon. Her daughter was downgraded from 'Princess' to 'Lady' Mary, as befitted her new status as a bastard, and she was separated from her mother. All this the pope required Henry to throw into reverse; the king was bidden to abandon his new wife and daughter Elizabeth, at a time when Anne was pregnant with a child who transpired in July to be stillborn, but who in March was expected to be the long-awaited boy.

The king was obliged to protect himself and the succession. The pope himself was denounced as a 'bastard, simoniac and heretic'. Cromwell saw More as the most prominent defender of the papacy and the old queen, and moved against him, trying to link him with Elizabeth Barton. This young woman – known as the 'holy maid of Kent' to the many who believed in her, and the 'mad nun' to those who did not – had become famous for the prophecies she made while swooning in mystic fits. She saw Anne Boleyn being devoured by dogs, and Henry recrucifying Christ with his adultery, and predicted that their marriage would bring disaster and lose the king his throne. More had visited the nun shortly before Cromwell had her arrested and brought before the Star Chamber accused of high treason. It was her 'damnable and diabolical instrumentality' that had turned the pope against the king, so claimed Thomas Audley, More's replacement as lord chancellor. Barton herself was then taken with her retinue of priests from the Tower to St Paul's Cross, where she stood on a scaffold and publicly confessed that her prophecies were fraudulent. An Act of

Attainder was passed by parliament confirming her treason, and naming as accomplices More and John Fisher, the hardline bishop of Rochester and Tyndale's old foe.

More assured Cromwell that, in his talks with the nun, 'we talked no worde of the Kinges Grace or anye great personage ells'. He sidestepped this issue neatly enough, but Cromwell was concocting another in parliament that he could not evade without betraying his faith. An Act of Succession was introduced, pronouncing the marriage of Henry and Catherine to be 'void and annulled'; it implicitly dismissed papal jurisdiction and authority by adding that no power had the right to uphold such a marriage. Anyone who said or wrote anything 'to the prejudice, slander or derogation of the lawful matrimony' of Henry and Anne would be guilty of high treason. The new Act required every English man and woman who was called upon to swear an oath 'that they shall truly, firmly, constantly, without fraud or guile, observe, fulfil, maintain, defend and keep the whole effect and contents of this Act'.

'After this day,' an MP's brother wrote of the Act, 'the Bishop of Rome shall have no manner of authority within the realm of England.' The heretics and 'newe men' against whom More had fought for so long now had their triumph. A cascade of further Acts – of Supremacy, Annates, Appeals, Peter's Pence and Dispensations – stripped the pope of titles, monies, privileges, visitations and powers of appointment. A new heresy law ended the system of ecclesiastical jurisdiction that More had struggled to maintain. No longer was it an offence to speak ill of the pope. The changes might seem technical and remote; headship of the church apart, liturgy and theology had hardly changed, and a contemporary visitor to a service in a parish church might think himself still to be in 1434. More knew, however, that the old faith was bruised and bleeding internally, and he feared that the time was close when 'it shall seeme that there shall bee than no chrysten countreyes left at all'. He attended Sunday mass at St Paul's on 12 April

1534; after he left, an official of the royal council handed him a summons to appear at Lambeth Palace the next morning to swear the Oath of Succession.

More returned to Chelsea and spent the night in prayer. The next morning he attended mass in Chelsea parish church. Then he bade his family goodbye and walked to the jetty at the edge of his garden, on the north bank of the Thames close to where Battersea Bridge now stands, and his boatmen rowed him downriver to the archbishop's palace at Lambeth. There he was taken in front of Cromwell, Archbishop Cranmer, Thomas Audley and William Benson, the abbot of Westminster. He read a copy of the Act of Succession and carefully compared it with the Oath. He then said that 'unto the oath that is here offered to me I cannot swear, without the jeoparding of my soul to perpetual damnation'. Audley replied that 'we are all sorry to hear you say thus'; he added that 'it will cause the King's highness to conceive great suspicion of you and great indignation toward you'. Audley showed More a printed roll with the signatures of those who had sworn from the Lords and Commons. 'I myself cannot swear,' More said, 'but I do not blame any other man that has sworn.'

For the next four days More was held in the custody of the abbot of Westminster. On 17 April he was taken by river to the Tower, landing at the Traitor's Gate, where he was met by his 'good friend and old acquaintance' Sir Edmund Walsingham, the Lieutenant of the Tower. He was lodged in one of the apartments kept for the prisoners of consequence – 'at the lest wise it was strong ynough' he remarked of its thick walls – and his servant John à Wood was permitted to attend him. Three days after his arrival, he had a terrible reminder of the reversal in fortune that he and Catholic loyalists had undergone. Elizabeth Barton, and five priests who had supported her, were taken from their cells in the Tower and tied to hurdles. They were dragged through the filth and mire of the London streets to Tyburn, where Marble Arch now stands. Here, the 'holy maid' was hanged. Each priest was hanged until he was half dead; his penis was then cut off and thrust in his mouth, before his stomach was opened up and he was eviscerated and decapitated. The heads were parboiled and set on poles on London Bridge.

More, who had wished heretics the dreadful death of 'the shorte fyre', now faced the traitor's equal agony of hanging, drawing and quartering. He feared 'duresse and harde handelinge' and 'violent forceable waies', and he discovered 'my fleshe much more shrinkinge from payne and from death, than me thought it the part of a faithfull Christen man'.

The sea change in England passed Tyndale by. His ever faulty political antenna failed to register that, as the Reformation deepened into the fracture and schism of Western Christendom, he might now be safer in London than in Antwerp.

More, the great enemy, was locked away in the Tower, dispatched there by Cromwell and Cranmer, men sympathetic to Tyndale's cause, and by Audley, the weathervane of the king's whims. By contrast, Antwerp was becoming more dangerous as Charles V, humiliated by his inability to repress Lutheranism in Germany, redoubled his efforts to strangle it in his hereditary dominions. These included the Low Countries, where penal ordinances of increasing severity were let loose on heretics of every hue. The possession of vernacular Bibles or any book proscribed by the ultra-orthodox theologians of Louvain, the attendance of any meeting of heretics, 'disputing about Holy Scripture', and 'want of due respect to the images of God and the Saints', attracted capital punishment. '*Les hommes par l'épée, les femmes par la fosse, les relaps par le feu*', the ordinance ran, 'the men beheaded by the sword, women buried alive in a ditch, the relapsed burnt'.

Informers were promised liberal rewards and a share in the confiscated goods of convicted heretics. Lax officials were warned of the severe consequences of dereliction of the duty to search for heretics. The Inquisition, established in the Low Countries but not in England, had the right to arrest, torture, confiscate property and execute heretics without right of appeal.

The citizens of Antwerp guarded their freedoms and tolerances as best they could. A printer publishing any work without a licence, a category into which all Tyndale's writings fell, in theory faced a minimum sentence of the branding of a cross so deeply that it could not be effaced, to which the judge could add the removal of an eye or a hand; in practice, they continued to print without asking the permission of the theologians of Louvain.

Within the confines of the English House, Tyndale was effectively protected by the freedom from arbitrary arrest extended to English merchants. Outside it, there was little reason for an imperial officer to take notice of a foreign heretic who was, in local terms, of no consequence. Any officer who did investigate Tyndale, moreover, would find that he had favoured the cause of the emperor's aunt in the annulment debate.

Tyndale was thus vulnerable to the imperial writ, but only if someone with influence and money activated it. No one in the Low Countries had reason to do so. The powerful officials who enjoyed office in England wished him well, not ill. As the summer and autumn of 1534 passed into winter, More remained in the Tower. His legal situation deteriorated further after parliament passed the Act of Supremacy in November. This confirmed the king to be 'the only supreme head in earth of the Church of England, called *Anglicana Ecclesia*'. At the same time, a new Treason Act made it an offence subject to the death penalty to 'maliciously wish, will, or desire, by words or by writing' to deprive the king of any of his titles or dignities, or to call him 'heretic, schismatic, tyrant, infidel'. A man could thus be executed for high treason if he refused to swear that he believed the king to be head of the English Church, on the grounds that he had denied one of the king's titles.

Like Frith, however, in whose death he had rejoiced, More enjoyed substantial privileges in the Tower. He walked in the gardens. His daughter Meg visited him. She failed to persuade him to take the Oath – they wept together and chanted the Litany – but her maid Dorothy Colley ran errands from the Tower for him. He was able to arrange for straw mats to be laid on the floor and hung on the walls. His friend Antonio Bonvisi sent him a camlet gown for warmth; he wrote to thank him for it. Bonvisi was the friend whom Vaughan and Cromwell suspected of providing money to the diehard Catholic friars Peto and Elstow in Antwerp. A frisson of suspicion might have stirred Tyndale had he known that More retained a link with Antwerp, but he did not know.

More had books and pen and paper. He exchanged letters with Fisher, his fellow prisoner in the Tower. More's old friend Cuthert Tunstall, and Stokesley, his replacment in London with whom More had worked closely in his heretic hunts, had surrendered and taken the Oath easily enough. Of all the bishops, only Fisher had refused, and in his correspondence with More the go-betweens were Fisher's servant Richard Wilson and, remarkably, George Golde, the servant of Edmund Walsingham, the Lieutenant of the Tower. Security was lax indeed. More wrote perhaps the finest of all his works, *A Dialogue of Comfort against Tribulation*, in his cell. He also started his last work *De Tristitia Christi*, On the Sadness of Christ. The authorities became suspicious of his activities. Towards the end of 1534 he was put in harsher confinement. He wrote to his daughter that he was being held in 'close keping' because of 'some newe causeless suspicion' and 'some secret sinister informacion'. He warned her that 'some new sodain searches may happe to be made in every house of ours as narrowly as is possible'. For a time, he was allowed no visitors and prevented from attending daily mass in the chapels of the Tower. He wrote a memorandum to himself about perjury, concluding that it would be wrong to betray a secret lawfully entrusted to him. What secret?

De Tristitia was smuggled out of the Tower. It was eventually taken to Spain, where it was deposited in the reliquary closet of the Chapel of Relics of the Royal College of Corpus Christi in Valencia. It was written in Latin, though More's granddaughter Mary Bassett translated it into English. At the end of the original copy of this translation, William Rastell, More's nephew and printer, wrote: 'Sir Thomas More wrote no more of this work. But when he had written this far, he was in prison kept so straight all his books and pen and ink and paper were taken from him, and soon after he was put to death.'

The work is unfinished – it breaks off with the words 'and they laid their hands on Jesus' as Judas led the soldiers to arrest him – but it tells us what More was thinking.

His writing blazes with hatred of heretics. He compares them to Judas. Like Judas, he says, who betrayed Christ with a kiss, heretics claim love for Christ while continuing their treacheries against him. Judas is like the heretic facing the fire. Even after the moment of betrayal, he can repent and God will welcome him back if he desires it, but he is too steeped in evil to abjure.

Sustaining himself in his own wretchedness in the Tower – '*tristician timorem tedium et dirae mortis horrorem*', 'sadness, fear, boredom and horror of ghastly death' – More described his feelings on the fate of the heretic: 'The air longs to blow noxious vapours against the wicked man. The sea longs to overwhelm him in its waves, the mountains to fall upon him, the valleys to rise up to him, the earth to split open beneath him, hell to swallow him up after his headlong fall, the demons to plunge him into gulfs of ever-burning flames . . .'

At the close of 1534, Thomas More was thinking of William Tyndale, and what he wished to happen to him.

On 21 May 1535, the day of his betrayal, Tyndale had sixteen months more to live. More had a little over six weeks.

That spring, a charming young Englishman arrived in Antwerp. Henry Phillips – he called himself Harry – was in his middle twenties. He came from a good family. He was the third son of Richard Phillips, a Dorset landowner who served as a Member of Parliament and who had a profitable appointment as customer of the port of Poole. Harry's nephew Edward Phillips was to become Master of the Rolls; he also built Montacute, the most exquisite Tudor mansion in England, which remained in the family until it passed to the National Trust in 1931. Harry was well schooled. He peppered his letters with Latin tags and referred often to his literary leanings. He graduated from Oxford as a Bachelor in Civil Law in February 1533. He had grace and presence, a 'comely fellow like as he had been a gentleman'. He had a servant with him in Antwerp, 'but wherefore he came, or what purpose he had been sent thither, no man could tell'.

Tyndale was relaxed enough by now to enjoy a social life among the merchants, and he was often 'desired forth to dinner and supper amongst merchants'. He met Harry Phillips and took a shine to him. He brought him back to his lodgings in the English House and invited him to dine with him on several occasions. He allowed him to see his books 'and other secrets of his study'. Thomas Poyntz, however, sensed that something was amiss with Phillips. When he asked Tyndale how he had met him, Tyndale replied that Phillips was 'an honest man, handsomely learned and very conformable'. The last was the word evangelicals used for those who conformed to their own beliefs. Poyntz became even more uneasy when Phillips asked him to walk with him to show him the layout of the town. Phillips made a point of showing Poyntz that he was well moneyed, though whence the money came he did not say. He also said that he 'bare no great favour' to Henry VIII. But Poyntz could not pin down his suspicions.

If Harry Phillips had ever been what he appeared to be – friendly, honest, scholarly and true – he ceased to be so after he left

Oxford. He robbed his father of a sum of money entrusted to him
to settle an obligation, and thereafter lived off his wits. Having
squandered the money, he wrote to his mother 'piteously begging'
her to intercede with his father on his behalf. He said that he had
'chanced to fall into play' while he was in London to deliver his
father's money to a Mr Medlee. He had lost £3 or £4 gambling
and, fearing his father's wrath, had not dared to come home. Later
he also lost his 'spending money', and 'by fortune he was driven he
whist not whither'.

In fact, he had come to Louvain, the centre of hardline Catholic
sentiment, a clue, alas, that Tyndale and Poyntz were missing. At
some stage late in 1534, Harry Phillips came into a considerable
amount of money, some of which he had used to enrol in the university of Louvain on 14 December 1534. Louvain, and its
university, were strictly and energetically Catholic. Had Tyndale
suspected that his young friend had connections with Louvain, he
would have dropped him at once.

But Tyndale, so worldly in his writing, and so artless with men,
was easy prey. It is sad that he should have treated Harry Phillips
with the same honest affection as he had John Frith; perhaps the
cause was the same, the paternal instinct of a childless man who
had written so tenderly of matrimony, a state denied to him by his
fugitive life. Two of Phillips's genuine interests – he had a great flair
for languages and a love of literature – coincided with Tyndale's
own. Their backgrounds, too, of the West Country and Oxford,
were similar, and Tyndale must have enjoyed speaking the language in which he laboured all day with somebody new. On his
side of the Narrow Sea English was very seldom heard.

After spending three or four days in Antwerp, Phillips went to
the imperial court at Brussels, where he arranged that the procurer
general, the imperial attorney and other government officers
should go to Antwerp to seize Tyndale. This, so Foxe surmised,
was 'not done with small charges or expenses, from whomsoever it

came'. A resident of the English House was a sensitive person to arrest, given the importance of English trade, and it is likely that Phillips had to grease some important palms. He also had to make sure that the victim was lured outside the House before being arrested.

A short while later, Phillips's servant came to the English House. Poyntz was sitting by the door and the man asked if Master Tyndale was there. He said his master was coming to see him. Poyntz's presence may have delayed matters, for nothing more was heard of Phillips until the merchant left for a month to attend to business at Barrow, eighteen miles from Antwerp.

Phillips returned on 21 May. He told Poyntz's wife that he wished to dine with Master Tyndale, and she confirmed that he was working in his study in the House. He asked if she had some good meat. 'Such as the market will give,' she replied. He went out, supposedly to the market, in fact to position the officers he had brought from Brussels in the lane by the House. He returned at noon. He went to Tyndale's study and asked him to lend him 40 shillings, saying that he had lost his purse in the street that morning. It was easy to get money from Tyndale, so Foxe wrote, 'for in the wily subtleties of this world he was simple and inexpert'. Perhaps Foxe is gilding the story here – Phillips's 40 shillings make too neat a match for Judas's thirty pieces of silver – but perhaps not. Phillips had stolen from his father; as we shall see, fraud and trickery continued in his future. Touching a victim for a loan was perfectly in character for Harry Phillips, that much is certain. It probably amused him.

'Master Tyndale, you shall be my guest here this day,' Phillips suggested.

'No,' said Tyndale. 'I go forth this day to dinner, and you shall go with me, and be my guest, where you shall be welcome.'

At dinnertime – they ate early in those days, well before noon – the two men left the house, which was set back from the lane by a long and narrow entry that would not take the two of them abreast. Tyndale therefore gestured for Phillips to go ahead. With a great show of courtesy, Phillips insisted that the older man lead. As they walked, Phillips, who was a head taller than Tyndale, pointed down at him to identify him to the waiting officers.

The arrest was quiet and easy. The officers told Poyntz later that they 'pitied to see his simplicity when they took him'. Tyndale was taken to the procurer general, who gave him dinner: a distinguished scholar was not a run-of-the-mill criminal. From there he was taken to the castle of Vilvoorde, an eighteen-mile trip from Antwerp. The procurer general searched Tyndale's lodgings in the English House. He took away all his possessions, 'as well his books as other things'.

22

The Paymaster

odern Vilvoorde is now a northern suburb of Brussels, off the ring road close to the city airport, a place of freight yards, shopping centres and new housing estates built on the sites of demolished factories. The only relics of the medieval town are the church and a much-patched stone tower on the Langemollerstraat.

The castle where Tyndale spent his last days was torn down at the end of the eighteenth century. It was replaced by a white-washed penitentiary that served until the late 1940s as a landmark for travellers on the road from Brussels to Antwerp. The courtyards are now used as a park for municipal fire engines and ambulances. One cell block remains, a flaking cliff of barred windows and crumbling masonry, where firefighting and first aid equipment is stored. Some of the material from the old castle was recycled for the penitentiary. It is possible that a brick or stone survives from Tyndale's time; and the spur of the River Zenne, where the prisoners slopped out their cells, also remains, green and stagnant.

Vilvoorde was separated from Brussels by six miles of open country when Tyndale was taken there. The castle was its major feature, built in 1374 by a duke of Brabant on the same lines as the recently completed Bastille in Paris. It had seven towers and a river-fed moat with three drawbridges; it was dank, its walls running with damp, and secure and well guarded, for it was the main state prison of the Low Countries, and its dungeons were designed to lodge eminent men.

Here, Adolf van Wesele, lieutenant of the castle, assigned Tyndale a cell. Van Wesele was not a sympathetic old acquaintance, as Walsingham was to More. There were no walks in the gardens for Tyndale, no correspondence or visitors, no gifts of warm camlets. The last surviving words that Tyndale wrote tell of his suffering from the cold and damp, and from the darkness. The letter is in Latin, apparently to the marquis of Bergen, an imperial official whom Cromwell was petitioning for Tyndale's release. It is not dated, but it was almost certainly written five or six months after his arrest, in the autumn of 1535.

It is a simple and patient letter, written before Tyndale knew his fate, in which his prime concern remained the scripture, and it deserves to be quoted in full. He asks 'by the Lord Jesus, that if I am to remain here through the winter, you will request the commissary to have the kindness to send me, from the goods of mine which he has, a warmer cap; for I suffer greatly from cold in the head, and am afflicted by a perpetual catarrh, which is much increased in this cell; a warmer coat also, for this which I have is very thin; a piece of cloth too to patch my leggings. My overcoat is worn out; my shirts are also worn out. He has a woollen shirt, if he will be good enough to send it. I have also with him leggings of thicker cloth to put on above; he also has warmer nightcaps. And I ask to be allowed to have a lamp in the evening; it is indeed wearisome sitting alone in the dark. But most of all I beg and beseech your clemency to be urgent with the commissary, that he will kindly permit me to have the Hebrew bible, Hebrew grammar, and Hebrew dictionary, that I may pass the time in that study. In return may you obtain what you most desire, so only that it be for the salvation of your soul. But if any other decision has been taken concerning me, to be carried out before winter, I will be patient, abiding the will of God, to the glory of the grace of my Lord Jesus Christ; whose Spirit (I pray) may ever direct your heart. Amen. W Tindalus.'

There was no rush to burn him. He had time to convert his keeper and his keeper's daughter, or so Foxe claims; others among the castle staff, impressed by his fortitude and sincerity, said to one another that if Tyndale 'were not a good Christian man, they could not tell whom they might take to be one'. Even Pierre Dufief, the ferocious prosecutor, agreed that his prisoner was *homo doctus, pius et bonus*, a learned, pious and fine man.

While Tyndale lay quietly within the Vilvoorde walls, protests burst outside. His friends in Antwerp, led by Poyntz, complained to the imperial government that the arrest violated the privileges of the English House, and appealed to the imperial court at Brussels for clemency.

Cromwell, too, was anxious to secure Tyndale's release. A direct appeal by the English government to the emperor was unlikely to bear much fruit, however. Charles V still owed Henry no favours, and Tyndale could serve as an ideal object lesson to other heretics, like Luther, who were nominally imperial subjects, but whom the emperor could not reach. Cromwell's main hope was to establish what lay behind the arrest.

The plan had been well constructed and carefully carried out. It was also expensive. Harry Phillips had been penniless before he appeared in Antwerp and he was soon penniless again. Somebody had paid him to betray Tyndale – Phillips himself spoke of a 'commission' – and, whoever that person was, he soon disappeared from Phillips's life.

This was not the start of the counter-reformation. It was not part of a series of attacks on English heretics in exile. It was a one-off. No other reformer on the Continent was touched. Someone so hated Tyndale that he commissioned his arrest by an agent, who then used 'all diligent endeavour' to ensure that Tyndale was brought to trial and executed.

Who? This person was skilled in intelligence gathering and in the recruitment and use of agents. He had some contact or influence with the imperial authorities in the Low Countries, whose cooperation was needed in taking Tyndale and in sentencing him. He had access to funds. He wished to destroy Tyndale for the latter's heresy; we know of nothing else, no love affairs, no money troubles, that could have been a motive. This person was English-based. Phillips made it clear that he had been recruited in England and not locally. The authorities in England no longer had any desire to harm Tyndale. On the contrary, Cranmer and Cromwell, respectively the senior officials of Church and State, were shocked by news of the arrest and tried hard to secure Tyndale's release. Cromwell's godson, Thomas Tebold, was setting out on a visit to Nuremberg. Cromwell often gave him intelligence assignments on his journeys, and he asked him to visit Antwerp, to make local inquiries into the arrest.

Tebold wrote to Cromwell from Antwerp on 31 July 1535 to say that he had succeeded in speaking with Phillips. 'He that did take Tyndale is abiding in Louvain, with whom I did there speak,' he reported, 'which doth not only there rejoice of that act, but goeth about to do many more Englishmen like displeasure; and did advance this, I being present, with most railing words against our King, his Highness, calling him "*Tyrannum ac expilatorem reipublicae*", tyrant and robber of the commonwealth. He is appointed to go shortly from Louvain to Paris in France, and there to tarry, because he feareth that English merchants that be in Antwerp will hire some men privily to do him some displeasure.' That Phillips should fear retaliation shows the respect and affection in which the Antwerp merchants held Tyndale.

The same day, Tebold wrote to Cranmer, whom he also knew well. He told the archbishop that he had travelled to Louvain from Antwerp. There he had met Dr Buckenham, former Blackfriars prior in Cambridge. Buckenham was a papal loyalist who refused to accept the royal supremacy, and who had 'passed the reme' – fled from the realm first to Scotland and then on to the Low Countries, 'full indiscreetly to the continuance of his mind, and aid of the abused bishop of Rome'. Tebold noted that Buckenham had another English friar with him, and that neither of them had any visible means of support in Louvain.

'All succour that I can perceive them to have is only by him which hath taken Tyndale, called Harry Phillips,' Tebold wrote, 'with whom I had a long and familiar communication, for I made him believe that I was minded to tarry and study at Louvain.'

A mysterious benefactor had supplied the two other loyalist friars, Peto and Elstow, with the funds to survive in Antwerp. Vaughan had investigated this on behalf of Cromwell. The most likely source was thought to be Thomas More, either directly or through his friend Antonio Bonvisi; this same friend had provided More with the camlet to ward off the winter chills in the Tower, and More was able to correspond with him from his cell.

Tebold said, however, that it was 'conceived both in England and in Antwerp' that George Joye had been Phillips's accomplice in the taking of Tyndale. This suspicion was based on the ill feeling between the two over Joye's unauthorised revision of Tyndale's Testament. Tebold put this to Phillips, who said that he 'had a commission out also for to have taken Doctor Barnes and George Joye with other'. He added that 'he never saw George Joye to his knowledge, much less that he should know him'. This was no doubt true. Joye had left Antwerp and on 4 June was to be found in Calais, then an English-owned city, staying in the house of Edward Foxe, the king's almoner, whom he had known at Cambridge, and through whom he was petitioning Cromwell to be allowed to return to England. Tebold said that he mentioned this because 'Joye is greatly blamed and abused among merchants, and many others that were [Tyndale's] friends, falsely and wrongfully'.

Though Phillips claimed that 'there was no man of his counsel but Gabriel Donne', a monk from Stratford abbey in London who was studying at Louvain, it was clear that the plot originated in England. Tebold reported that Phillips was so frightened of a revenge attack by the English merchants that he had sold his books in Louvain, to the value of £20, and 'doth tarry here upon nothing but of the return of his servant'. He had sent the servant to England with letters and the man was slow in returning; by 'cause of his long tarrying', Phillips 'is marvellously afraid lest he be taken' and the letters 'come into Mr Secretary's [Cromwell] handling'.

Phillips explained his wealth by claiming that he enjoyed a well-endowed position in the Church. Tebold clearly did not believe him. 'Either this Phillips hath great friends in England to maintain him here,' Tebold wrote to the archbishop, 'or else, as he showed me, he is well beneficed in the bishopric of Exeter.' No record of his holding such a benefice exists, though Phillips later sent begging letters to Dr Thomas Brerewood, the chancellor to the bishop of Exeter, seeking money to pursue his student life and university career. Tebold was right to be sceptical of Phillips's cover story; he was right, too, to add that Phillips was certain 'that Tyndale shall die', a fate which he 'procureth with all diligent endeavour, rejoicing much therein'.

No hard evidence has ever emerged to link Phillips with his paymaster. Contemporaries found nothing. As the English throne stumbled between Henry's children, from Protestant Edward to Catholic Mary and back to Protestant Elizabeth, both sides threw up fresh martyrs who concerned them more than Tyndale. It was only later – four hundred years later – that suspicion settled on John Stokesley.

Stokesley was the bishop of London who had been active with More in the persecution of Lutherans in 1531 and 1532. His servant, John Tisen, was seen by exiles in Antwerp in January 1533. This was the man whom Tyndale noted wore a beard and avoided other Englishmen, and whom he had known at Oxford. Another servant of the bishop, called Docwraye, a public notary, visited Antwerp for two weeks in July 1533. In addition, Foxe had made a sarcastic reference to 'the valiant champion Stokesley', who, while he was lying on his deathbed in 1539, rejoiced that he had sent thirty-one heretics 'unto the infernal fire'. This, so Tyndale's pre-war biographer J. F. Mozley wrote, makes it reasonable to see Stokesley as 'the chief backer if not the prime engineer' of the plot to betray Tyndale.

There the matter has rested. But the case against Stokesley is thin indeed. Antwerp was London's prime trading partner and the leading commercial city of northern Europe. The bishop of London had many servants. It would have been strange had some of them not had business in Antwerp. Docwraye was later to become the first master of the Stationers' Company. He was known to have visited Antwerp printers, not to ask after Tyndale, but to place orders for the London diocese for the devotional books that Stokesley was importing from Antwerp. As part of his campaign against heretical books, Stokesley was actively promoting orthodox texts on his own account; an example was a fiery attack on Luther by the Catholic theologican and debater Johann Eck. Vaughan mentioned Docwraye's visit in innocent terms in a letter to Cromwell on 3 August 1533. 'The bishop of London has had a servant in Antwerp this fortnight,' he said. 'If you send for Henry Pepwall, a stationer in Paul's Churchyard, who was often with him, he will tell you his business.' Vaughan was much more concerned with the threat posed by Peto. 'A friar comes from

John Stokesley, friend of Thomas More and a heretic-hunting bishop of London from 1530. He was a careerist, however, who ever sought to 'invent some colorable device' to promote himself. It is unlikely that he would have risked the wrath of Cromwell and the king by paying to have Tyndale betrayed.

(National Portrait Gallery)

England every week to Peto,' he wrote, adding that 'More has often sent books to Peto in Antwerp.' Vaughan was worried enough to arrange for a colleague, George Cole, to 'advertise you [Cromwell] in my absence whatever he learns of Peto and his accomplices'. Peto, he added, 'is much helped out of London with money'.

As for Stokesley's dying boast, not only was the figure of thirty-one burnt heretics absurd – he can be linked to five or six at most – but Foxe would most certainly have mentioned it if any rumour then current had linked the bishop to Tyndale's death. Why, too, if he was bragging, did he not crow that Tyndale was among them? Stokesley had, in fact, lamented his own 'helpless-ness' and 'cowardice' in the 'face of advancing heresy', and had declared that he wished that he had had the same 'courage' to resist heretics that Bishop Fisher had displayed. He would hardly have berated himself so if he had engineered the death of the great heretic.

Stokesley was a difficult man, loud, bad-tempered, opinion-ated and tactless, quite the reverse of whoever so smoothly and secretly spun the web that caught Tyndale. Nothing suggests that Stokesley had any singular obsession with Tyndale, or that he was capable of finding a Harry Phillips and using him to such effect.

Stokesley was fifty-five in 1535, fifteen years older than Tyndale. He had missed teaching young Tyndale at Oxford only because he had become involved in an outbreak of academic infighting. Stokesley had been elected an Oxford fellow in 1495, and two years later became an usher at Magdalen School, which the boy Tyndale was soon to attend. After a spell at Magdalen Hall, Tyndale's old college, Stokesley was appointed praelector in philosophy and vice-president of Magdalen College in 1505. His appointment was a catalyst for bitter academic politicking at the college, which split into two hostile camps. Stokesley was accused of every ill that rival scholars could imagine. Heresy, theft, perjury and adultery were deemed insufficient, and witchcraft, neglect of duties and christening a cat were added to an official complaint. The bishop of Winchester, alarmed at the state of the college, was obliged to intervene. Stokesley denied all the charges against him on oath in January 1507. No witness came forward against him and he was cleared. It was recorded that the fellows 'in sign of unity all drank of a loving-cup together', but the harmony was forced. Stokesley's Oxford career was over, and Magdalen gave him two livings, a rectory and a vicarage, on the far side of Gloucestershire. The rectory was at Slimbridge, Tyndale's possible birthplace. There is no record that Stokesley ever visited the parish, however, being content merely to draw his stipend.

Stokesley earned his rise in fortunes to currying favour with the king. He became a chaplain and almoner to Henry. Erasmus described him in 1518 as 'well-versed in the schoolmen', a back-handed compliment, and classified him with More and Tunstall as a credit to the court. In 1520, he attended Henry as his chaplain to the Field of the Cloth of Gold, the lavish Anglo-French spectacle of jousts, feasting and fruitless diplomacy held in a field near the present motorway exit to the Calais docks. He thrived on the king's 'great matter'. He travelled to France to persuade universities to come out in favour of the divorce, claiming to be the 'principal cause and instrument' of winning them over. On the same mission to Italy in 1530, he boasted that he had 'recovered' the king's cause 'when it had slipped through the ambassador's fingers and was despaired of'. He used Wolsey's 'lack of such forwardness in setting forth the King's divorce as his grace looked for', so William Roper wrote, to 'invent some colorable device' to turn Henry against the cardinal. This he then 'to his grace revealed, hoping thereby to bring the King to the better liking of himself, and the more misliking of the Cardinal; whom his highness therefore soon after of his office displaced . . .'. Stokesley was rewarded with the bishopric of London.

In September 1533 he christened the future Queen Elizabeth at Greenwich; he was a royal councillor and a leading member of Convocation. He accepted the royal supremacy and induced the London Carthusians to submit to the king. He failed to support More's stand over the supremacy and made no attempt to protect his erstwhile ally. Stokesley had, moreover, particular reason to be careful at the time that Phillips was commissioned.

Cromwell disliked him – he found him awkward on doctrinal change – and informers were watching him and listening to his sermons. Stokesley was required to send the king a copy of a sermon he had preached. He excused himself by saying that he never wrote out his sermons. 'If I were to write my sermons,' he said, 'I could not deliver them as they are written, for much would come to me without premeditation much better than what was premeditated.' Throughout 1535, Cromwell continued to subject him to 'vexatious proceedings' of this sort.

Stokesley had also run foul of Queen Anne. She secured the release of Thomas Partmore, a former member of Gonville Hall at Cambridge and the parson of Hadham in Hertfordshire. Partmore had been accused of heresy by Stokesley in 1530 and had languished without trial in the Lollards' tower. After securing his release, Anne passed Partmore's petition on to the king. Henry ordered a commission of nine men to be set up in 1535, whose members included Cromwell, Cranmer and Hugh Latimer, to investigate Partmore's charges of mistreatment against Stokesley and his vicar general, Foxford. It is fanciful to suppose that Stokesley, who had founded his career as a royal toady, should turn on his master and risk his neck by conspiring to destroy Tyndale.

But if not Stokesley – then who?

One man, of course, has all the obvious attributes. Thomas More had the motive. He despised, feared and loathed Tyndale; he, and his English Testament, were the obsessions of More's life. His hatred was not slaked by the savaging he had given Tyndale in his *Dialogue*, nor by the half a million words he had poured into the *Confutation*; this was a mere flood of ink, where More was satisfied only by blood and the flames of the 'shorte fyre'.

Any man who had sworn to uphold the royal supremacy would be guilty of treason, if he conspired to arrest a heretic without the authority of the king, as the supreme head of the English Church. Stokesley, and every bishop except Fisher, had so sworn. More had not. He argued in his *Confutation* that, whatever the position of the pope, the Church was still the Church. The Church had found Tyndale, 'and his own fellow friar Barnes, too', to be heretics; and to More, almost uniquely, heretics they remained.

At the time that Phillips came into his money, in the autumn of 1534, More was recording his thoughts in his cell in the Tower. His fury was not dulled by loss of office or by imprisonment. It was, rather, renewed by them, for they were evidence that his instincts were correct, and that Tyndale and his like were ushering the Antichrist into the seat of power. More was writing and dreaming of 'noxious vapors', of crashing waves and collapsing mountains, fissures in the earth, and of demons plunging the heretic 'into gulfs of ever-burning flames . . .'.

We know, too, that More was a skilful user of *agents provocateurs* in the Phillips mould. This was how he had obtained Frith's fateful treatise on the sacraments. One copy had come to him from the tailor Holt, who masqueraded as an evangelical, as Phillips had done to Tyndale – convincing him that he was 'conformable'. More's network was so fertile that he boasted of receiving two other copies. 'If you have three copies of a work which I especially desired to keep secret,' Frith had complained to More, 'then indeed I must have traitors around me.' More's agents also brought him copies of letters that John Frith received from Tyndale and George Joye in the first part of 1533, even though Tyndale had taken care to address his to 'Jacob'.

Stokesley took no initiatives to have Frith executed. It was More who used the treatise to ensure that Frith went to the stake. He did so when he had been out of office for many months, in the pursuit of a personal vendetta rather than State policy. His resignation as chancellor did not curtail his hunt for heretics, and his use of agents and subterfuges.

He boasted of this, as we have seen, in the letter to Erasmus after his fall, in which he said that he wished to be 'as hateful to [heretics] as anyone can possibly be'. We know that he regarded any tactic – perjured evidence, the use of informants and lowlifes, illegal arrests and detention, disregard for safe conducts – as fair in this war.

More revelled in burnings. The leather seller Tewkesbury 'burned as there was never wretche I wene better worthy'; Hitton, the 'devil's stinking martyr', was pleasingly to suffer 'ye fyre ever lastynge' after the 'shorte fyre of Maidstone'; Frith, whom all the rest of England seemed to love, was a 'proud, unlearned fool' for whom 'Cryste will kyndle a fyre of fagottes . . . & make hym therin swete the bloude out of hys body'.

In terms of local knowledge and contacts in the Low Countries, More was well placed. He had spent several months in Antwerp, if some time before, and we know that Vaughan suspected Bonvisi of financing Peto and Elstow. More corresponded with Bonvisi and he had sent books to Peto. Peto, Vaughan said, was 'much helped out of England with money'. By whom, if not by More? More had, too, political renown among Catholic statesmen. In particular, he was highly regarded by Charles V.

Whoever betrayed Tyndale clearly enjoyed the confidence of the imperial government. The empire had no great reason to bother itself with Tyndale. His heresy had been directed entirely at England. The translator had made no attempt to spread his views among the emperor's subjects. He kept to himself, and to the small English community, and he had proved a most discreet expatriate. The pope might be happy enough to see him burnt, but he was no more than a symbolic irritant to the secular powers. He had done them no damage.

After the arrest, it is true, English appeals for clemency ran into the sands. Charles V's ill feeling towards Henry remained. Imperial subjects had been burnt at Smithfield for heresy, and the English could not complain too strongly if there was a measure of reciprocity at Vilvoorde.

But the taking of Tyndale was bothersome: it involved assembling a snatch squad to make sure that the victim was taken in the street, and not within the sensitive confines of the English House; it upset relations with the English merchants, it led to petitions, and inquiries from Cromwell. Antwerp had a floating population of English heretics. Tyndale alone was seized.

To arrange it needed influence, as well, no doubt, as some palmgreasing by Phillips. More was admired by the emperor personally. Charles V had written him a letter of support and encouragement for his efforts on Queen Catherine's behalf, while he was still chancellor. More had tactfully declined to receive it from Chapuys, but the ambassador made it clear that More remained 'loyal' and 'affectionate' to the emperor. 'He begged me for the honour of God to forbear,' Chapuys reported to Charles, 'for although he had given already sufficient proof of his loyalty that he ought to incur no suspicion, whoever came to visit him, yet, considering the time, he ought to abstain from everything which might provoke suspicion; and if there were no other reason, such a visitation might deprive him of the liberty which he had always used in speaking boldly in those matters which concerned your Majesty and the Queen.' More went on to pledge his most 'affectionate service' to the Emperor.

The arrest of Tyndale would have been a fitting *quid pro quo* for a man who had fought as best he could for the emperor's aunt, and who now risked death for the emperor's religion.

*

Henry Phillips told Tebold that his mysterious benefactor had commissioned him to effect the arrest of Barnes and Joye, as well as Tyndale. Barnes, too, fits More. The ex-chancellor hated him.

In the preface to the *Confutation*, More devoted almost as much space and vitriol to Barnes as to Tyndale. Barnes, an Augustinian friar who had been the prior of his order in Cambridge, had abjured in 1526 and fled abroad two years later. He met Luther in Wittenberg and later moved to Antwerp. Barnes wrote *A supplicatyon unto kinge henrye the eyght* in 1531, a vigorous attack on 'oure spiritualtye', accusing the clergy of usurping the king's authority, and forcing a 'true preacher' such as himself into exile. His views on the pope coincide with Henry's over the annulment – 'can not the pope erre? let hym rede his awne lawe' – and a copy was sent from Antwerp to Cromwell by Stephen Vaughan.

Henry did not greatly care for its theology – the first 'comon place' of faith it listed was the Lutheran insistence that 'Alonlye faith iustefyeth before god' – but he was flattered by its praise for the royal prerogatives. Barnes offered to return to England to 'eyther proue these thygnes by godes worde agenst you al or els I wylk suffer at hys gracis plesure . . .'. The king had refused a similar offer from Tyndale but he accepted the one from Barnes. Cromwell arranged a safe conduct and Barnes arrived on a visit to London of six to eight weeks at the end of 1531.

More had him followed by spies, intercepted his letters, and interrogated those whom Barnes met. He noted that Barnes was sporting a beard and wore merchant's clothes; he wrote of meetings that Barnes had 'in the house of hys secret hostes at the sygne of the botell at Botolfes wharfe', and said that he visited friends in London who subsidised him while he was abroad. Humphrey Monmouth, Tyndale's old benefactor, may have been among them; in his will, Monmouth named Dr Barnes as one of those he would like to preach at his funeral, and he left Barnes £10 and a gown. Barnes was allowed to debate with senior clerics. Although he had licence 'wythout perell to saye what he wolde', More gloated of a debate with Stephen Gardiner, Barnes 'was therin confuted so clerely & so playnly, that all hys evangelycall bretherne of hys hundred sectes, wolde haue ben ashamed to se it'.

More would have sent him to the stake. He wrote that Barnes 'hath so demeaned hym selfe hys comynge hyther that he hath clerely broken & fofayted hys saufe conductede, and lawfully myght be burned for hys heresyes'. In fact, Barnes had shown his safe conduct to Frith, who reported that it had no conditions, and no time limit other than that Barnes must start his visit to England before Christmas 1531, which he had done; it would thus have been illegal to have burnt him. Frith said that Barnes feared for his life because of More, despite his safe conduct; he therefore kept himself as 'secreatly' as he could, and thought it best 'prively to departe the realme'.

The royal safe conduct prevented More from acting, but his comment on Barnes's safe departure is chilling. 'Lette hym go thys ones,' More wrote, 'for god shall fynde hys tyme full well.'

Barnes left England early in 1532. Only his reputation remained in England, and this More savaged in the preface to *Confutation*. 'Of all [the reformers'] bookes that came yet abroade in englysshe . . . was never none yet so bad, so folysshe, nor so false as hys,' More wrote, claiming that, on his visit to England, Barnes was 'in suche wyse fynally confounded wyth shame that he was in a mamerying [hesitation] whyther he wolde retourne agayne over the see, or tary styll here and renounce hys heresyes agayne, and tourne agayn to Crystes catholyke chyrche . . .'. More lashed him as a grotesque, a renegade and apostate, writing a mocking '*Confutation of Friar Barnes' Church*', in which he linked the 'contrarye folies' of Barnes and Tyndale.

He claimed that Barnes was a Zwinglian, who denied the real presence at the Eucharist, and who had converted Tyndale to the same belief. Barnes was stung enough to write 'a letter to me of hys own hand,' More recorded, 'wherein he wryteth that I lay that heresye wrongfully to his charge, and . . . he sayth he wyll in my reproche make a boke agaynst me . . .'. Barnes did not, in fact, devote a book to refuting More, as Tyndale had. Instead, unlike Tyndale, he turned the sea change that had overcome the fortunes of the reformers to good use. He was soon busy in Germany as a diplomatic agent on behalf of Cromwell. He also began work on a revised edition of his *Supplication*, in his new role as a propagandist for the king.

Barnes was back in England in October 1533 to prepare for a diplomatic mission to Hamburg. He returned to London in the summer of 1534 with an embassy from the Hanseatic cities of Lübeck and Hamburg, lodging with the envoys in the Steelyard. The revised edition of his *Supplication* was published in London in November 1534 bearing the colophon of the printer John Byddell. It was the first work by a foe of More to be openly printed in England and it revealed the increasing confidence of the reformers. Barnes was less strident than he had been in the first edition – 'masyter Moore . . . layeth to my charge, that I counted all the spiritualitie to be noughte . . . I confesse many good men to have shaven crownes and also long gownes' – and he showed real sympathy for the plight of his now imprisoned adversary.

Though More had used 'foule and shameless wordes' against him, Barnes said that 'truely, as God shall iudge me, I am sory for his trouble, yf I coulde helpe hym with any lawfull meanes, I wolde do my best . . .'. More was abandoned, alone in the Tower with Fisher and his conscience. 'Yea, his owne churche is agaynste hym', Barnes wrote, and it was true, for the 'Byshoppes, Universities and best learned' of the realm had submitted to the royal supremacy and showed less compassion for the disgraced lord chancellor than a heretic.

Whether More was aware of Barnes's noble sentiments towards him, we do not know; it is possible, given the lax regime at the

Tower, that a copy of *Supplication* found its way to him. But it will not have softened More's attitude to Barnes; on the contrary, it was the way in which the influence of such reformers was swelling that most frightened and enraged him.

When Phillips came calling on Tyndale in May 1535, Barnes was safe in England; he was shortly to be sent to Wittenberg as a royal chaplain on Henry's behalf to persuade Luther's fellow worker and successor, Philip Melanchthon, to pay a visit to England. Whoever wished Phillips to seize Barnes as well as Tyndale was playing with the betrayal of a royal diplomat to a foreign power, an act that was classified as treason. We know of only one man who thought that Barnes should be arrested for heresy, regardless of a royal safe conduct, but that in any event 'god shall fynde hys tyme'. That, of course, was Thomas More.

There appears to be one overriding reason why More cannot have commissioned Phillips. He was locked up in the Tower of London when the betrayal took place, and he had only a few weeks to live.

In April 1535 the priors of the Charterhouses of London, Beauvale in Nottinghamshire and the Isle of Axholme in Lincolnshire, and a Carthusian monk of Sion, who were imprisoned with More in the Tower, were tried for refusing to acknowledge the king as head of the Church. They were sentenced to be hung, drawn and quartered at Tyburn on 4 May 1535. Meanwhile, they were chained up by the leg and neck to posts in their cells and More's adopted daughter, Margaret Clement, visited them secretly and brought them food.

On 30 April, the day after the trial of the first Carthusians, More was examined in the Tower by Cromwell and several lawyers. When asked whether he would acknowledge the king as the supreme head of the Church, he refused to answer. Fisher was interrogated separately. On 3 June, a fortnight after Tyndale's betrayal, More was again examined in the Tower by Cromwell,

Cranmer, Audley, Suffolk and Wiltshire. He was told that Henry ordered him to say whether he agreed that the king was the head of the Church.

More answered that the question was a double-edged sword. If he did not believe the king to be the supreme head – and he would not say whether he thought this or not – then, by swearing he believed it, he would perjure his soul, and by refusing to swear it he would imperil his life. He did not think it right that a man should be forced to answer what he believed in under these circumstances. Cromwell replied that More, when chancellor, had forced suspected heretics to answer whether they believed that the pope was the head of the Church, knowing just as More did now that, if they answered yes, they violated their conscience, and if no they would burn. So why should More not be asked? More replied that there was a distinction. When he was examining heretics, every country in Christendom laid down that the pope was head of the Church, whereas the new doctrine that the king was head of the Church was accepted in only one country and rejected by every other in Christendom.

A few days later, the authorities found that More had written letters at the end of May to Fisher, carried by More's servant. In them, he told Fisher that he was refusing to reply when asked for his opinions on the king's position in the Church; he suggested that Fisher adopt a different line, so that it would not seem that they were colluding. On 12 June, More was deprived of writing materials, and also of his books. As chancellor, he had ordered that heretics should not be allowed books or pen and paper, so he was hard pressed to complain. He was questioned about the letters on 14 June. He said that he had written only to comfort Fisher, whom he knew to be a fellow prisoner in the Tower.

On 22 May, the pope, hearing that Fisher was in danger of the death sentence, had created him a cardinal. The papal motive was to safeguard Fisher with a public demonstration of support.

Instead, infuriated, Henry declared that he would send Fisher's head to Rome for the pope to place a cardinal's hat on it. Three more Carthusians were hung, drawn and quartered at Tyburn on 19 June. On 22 June, Fisher was beheaded on Tower Hill for high treason in denying the royal supremacy.

More was brought to trial on the same charge in Westminster Hall on 1 July before special commissioners sitting with a London jury. The judges were hardly impartial, for Cromwell, Norfolk, Suffolk, and Anne Boleyn's father and brother, Wiltshire and Rochford, were among the commissioners with the lord chancellor, Audley, presiding. Unlike Fisher and the Carthusians, More denied that he had ever said that the king was not head of the Church, and that silence could never be construed as high treason.

The law required evidence of a 'malicious' denial of one of the king's titles, making this a great legal difficulty for the prosecution. But the solicitor general, Sir Richard Rich, then gave evidence of a conversation that he had had with More on 12 June. Rich had visited More in the Tower that day in another attempt to have him take the Oath of Supremacy, and also apparently to remove More's books and writing materials. Rich said to More that the king in parliament could enact any law and that all subjects were bound to obey. He asked More whether, if parliament passed an Act requiring everyone to swear allegiance to Rich as king, More would be compelled by law to comply. More admitted that he would be forced to obey such a law, or so Rich alleged, but added that this was a 'light' case, and he would put a 'higher' case to Rich: if parliament passed an Act that God should no longer be God, would this Act take effect? More claimed that Rich was lying. If so – and he had made a long career as a lackey of the crown – Rich perjured himself enough to ensure that More was found guilty. The jury was out for only fifteen minutes.

More addressed the court before sentence was pronounced. He said that parliament had no power to abolish the papal supremacy over the Church. Audley interrupted to claim that most learned doctors took the opposite view. More said, in silent reproach to his erstwhile friends, Tunstall and Stokesley, that for every bishop supporting the royal supremacy, there were a hundred learned men throughout Christendom who supported his own position. He added that all the General Councils of the Church for the last thousand years stood firmly against the Act of parliament. 'Not only have you no authority, without the common consent of Christians all over the world, to make laws and frame statutes, acts of parliament or councils against the said union of Christendom,' he said, 'but you and the others sin capitally in doing so.'

It was the brave speech of a courageous man, whose love for the old religion was equal to Tyndale's rapture with the new. But the tide was against him. For refusing to swear the Act of Succession, legitimising the Boleyn marriage, he was sentenced to life imprisonment. For refusing the Act of Supremacy, Audley sentenced him to be hanged, cut down while still alive, castrated, his entrails cut out and burnt before his eyes, and then beheaded. The king in his graciousness commuted this to beheading.

More was to die on 6 July 1535. The night before his execution, he sent his daughter Meg his hair shirt, so that she could treasure their secret link; and he wrote her a last letter with a piece of coal. 'I would be sorry if it should be any longer than tomorrow,' he wrote. 'For it is St Thomas Even; and therefore I long to go to God; it were a day very mete and convenient for me. I never liked your manner toward me better than when you kissed me last; for I love when daughterly love, and dear charity, hath no leisure to look to worldly courtesy. Farewell, my dear child, and pray for me, and I shall for you and all your friends, that we may merrily meet in Heaven.'

Meg brought out the tenderness in this strange, tortured and cruel man. She could not bring herself to attend the execution, and it was his adopted daughter Margaret Clement who took the headless corpse to Meg at the church of St Peter ad Vincula in the Tower, where the family had permission to bury it. The head of Sir Thomas More was boiled before being exhibited, to preserve it and add terror to its demeanour, overboiled in fact, so that it turned black. It was put on the pole on London Bridge which Fisher's head had occupied for the past fortnight. After a few days, Meg Roper bribed a constable of the watch to take it down and give it to her. She hid it and eventually it was placed in the Roper family vault in St Dunstan's, Canterbury.

News of Tyndale's arrest would clearly have lightened More's steps to the block. The drama and courage of his death, and his confinement in the Tower, do not diminish the probability that More commissioned Tyndale's betrayal. In Scottish law, juries may return a verdict of 'not proven'. This is very far from 'not guilty'. The jury recognises that the prosecution has failed to prove guilt beyond reasonable doubt, but it does not find the accused to be innocent.

Henry Phillips, last seen in Vienna in 1542, disappeared from history without revealing his employer's identity. There is no hard evidence to prove the involvement of More – a 'not proven' verdict is inevitable – but the background points inexorably at More and at no other. He had an overwhelming motive: the destruction of heretics was the grand obsession of his life, and he placed Tyndale at the head of the dark galaxy of the Antichrist. He had the skills, in selecting and running double agents; he believed that the foulest methods were fair in heretic hunting, writing that safe conducts need not be honoured in such cases; he approved of the stake, the fate now awaiting Tyndale, fretting only that it was not used enough. His fall from office, and his imprisonment, encouraged rather than diminished his hatred of heresy.

And, even from the Tower, he had the opportunity. Phillips received his commission and his money during the autumn of 1534, probably in October or November. By 21 December, he had already arrived in the Low Countries and was matriculating at Louvain. More was under very loose guard in the Tower at the time the commission was made. The Tower itself was part royal palace as well as prison; Anne Boleyn had spent the night before her coronation in one of its luxurious apartments, and among the 'liberties' of the Tower that More was able to enjoy was the royal menagerie, with its exotic birds and lions. He had his own man-servant and the use of a maid. His friend Antonio Bonvisi had contacts in Antwerp and the Low Countries. He was able to write freely and to smuggle lengthy manuscripts out of the Tower.

Such treatment was not exceptional. More had himself commented with dismay that John Frith was released from the Tower at Christmas 1532 as a favour by the bishop of Winchester; claims were also made, as we have seen, that the underkeeper at the Tower – Thomas Phelips or Philips – had 'lett hym [Frith] go at liberty in the nyght' to visit John Petite and other evangelicals. When Petite was himself in the Tower, the same underkeeper had allowed him to remove a board in his cell to enable him to join Bilney for supper in the cell above. Frith had received letters, from Tyndale among others, and he was able to write his treatise on the sacraments and other works. The conditions were not ideal, but his work, *The Bulwark against Rastel*, was lucid and compelling enough to convert his critic John Rastell, the brother-in-law of Thomas More.

The kindly man at the Tower seems to be the Thomas Philips whom More had interrogated at Chelsea and committed to the Tower while he was still chancellor. In his *Chronicle* of 1548, Edward Hall said that this Philips, also called Thomas, had himself been a prisoner in the Tower before – acting as some sort of guard – he had procured an English Bible for Sir Nicholas Carew to read for solace in the Tower in the days before Carew was beheaded for treason in 1539. Hall also mentioned that Philips had been 'sore troubled' by More. It would not have been unusual for Philips being kept in the Tower for a lengthy period after More sent him there in 1529 before being formally convicted, and being given a privileged position as a staff helper, and retaining it after acquittal. The Tower was far from a paradigm of high security; it had its own working arrangements, perks and privileges.

More also had privileges. He was free to move in the Tower grounds and to receive letters and visitors. It was only at the end of 1534, after Harry Phillips had arrived in Louvain, that More wrote to his daughter that he was being held in 'close keping' because of 'some newe causeless suspicion' and 'some secret sinister informacion'. He was allowed no visitors for some time, and barred from attending mass in the chapels of the Tower.

We do not know what this 'causeless suspicion' was. The strict regimen did not last very long, however, because More was soon enough writing to Fisher. It was a serious matter indeed for the authorities to have the two most high-profile prisoners in the kingdom writing to each other, with all the opportunity it gave them for collusion. They did so, however; and it is clear that More was not only in the frame of mind to commission Tyndale's destruction, but also that the physical circumstances of his imprisonment in the Tower did not prevent him from doing so.

If God was More's stated motive for wishing Tyndale harm, Phillips's was money. More had that, too; stories that his family were reduced to burning bracken to stay warm after his fall are fable.

More had been one of the best paid men in the country for many years. In 1520, he was paid £173 6s 8d as under-treasurer, the second highest salary in the treasury. He more than doubled this with other grants and sinecures. He was granted a licence to export a thousand woollen cloths, which he was able to sell on to a merchant. He received a pension from the king of France, and he was paid a retainer by the earl of Northumberland. He was handsomely paid for commercial work. As a young lawyer, he had worked for the city livery companies, and he continued to work for the Mercers. He was also paid for arranging the protection of merchant ships sailing from the Low Countries.

As Speaker of parliament, he had received a bonus doubling his £100 a year salary, and he picked up a lucrative sinecure as collector of the parliamentary subsidy in Middlesex. He speculated in property. In 1523 he paid £150 for Crosby Place in Bishopsgate Street in London, a 'very large and beautiful' building, selling it on eight months later for £200. In 1524, he bought seven acres of land in Chelsea for £30, and seven and a half acres in Kensington. He also bought the guardianships of two rich landowning lunatics.

The bishops wished to reward him for his work in parliament on behalf of the clergy in 1532. His son-in-law, William Roper, wrote that 'they agreed together and concluded upon a sum of four or five thousand pounds at the least, to my remembrance, for his pains to recompense him'. He was able to refuse this, telling Tunstall that 'I wolde rather have caste theyre money into the Temys thenne take yt'. More said later that 'loke I for my thanke of god that is thyr better, and for whose sake I take the labour and not for theyres'. He knew that Tyndale had accused him of money-lust, and he wanted to deny it and show himself as a simple soul who 'carried the Crosse in procession in his parish Churche at Chelsey'.

His circumstances were reduced after his resignation but he was still a rich man. He retained the income of a king's counsellor until 1534, together with estates in Oxfordshire, Hertfordshire and Kent. His wife Alice complained that she would be 'utterlye undone' if his 'landes and tenementis' were confiscated. She remained a wealthy woman in her own right, however; on the death of her first husband, John Middleton, a wealthy silk merchant, she had inherited estates in Essex and Yorkshire. It seems that the family had spirited valuable 'moveable goodes' away from Chelsea before the arrest.

More thus had motive, money and – despite his imprisonment – opportunity. Phillips, feckless, wayward and shallow, was
professional when it came to his craft; he was discreet, but when he
did let a name drop from his past, when he was later poverty-
stricken and in Rome, it was More's.

23

'Though I gave my body even that I burned . . .'

Thomas Poyntz, Tyndale's host at the English House, and the man who knew Tyndale best, struggled the hardest to free him. In his writing, Tyndale was witty, bitter, wounding – he could strip the enamel from an opponent's reputation with a phrase – and seldom kind. He was not a likeable man in print. Those who knew him in everyday life, however – the Walshes, Monmouth, now Poyntz and his wife – grew fond of him.

Tyndale was as harsh on himself as he was to others. 'God made me ill-favoured in this world,' he had written to Frith, 'speechless and rude, dull and slow-witted.' But this self-deprecation had its own charm. It was part of his raw honesty and his courage; together with the joy he had in his work, it stopped him from sliding into bigotry, and it touched those he met, and made them protective of him. He was not betrayed by an acquaintance, but by a stranger, Phillips, who used his professional guile to exploit his victim's artlessness in the ways of the world.

In person, Tyndale inspired affection, not malice. Despite his own desperate circumstances in the Tower, John Frith took pains to defend his friend from the attacks on him made by Thomas

More in his *Letter* to Frith. He wrote of Tyndale's poor apostle's life,' adding that Tyndale 'hath a faithful, clear, innocent heart' that no man should reprove.

Poyntz was prepared to risk his life for him. Speed was essential. The longer Tyndale was held in Vilvoorde, without sanctions or ill effect on the English trade with Flanders, the less likely his release became. Tebold's visit produced little. On 25 August 1535, Poyntz wrote to his brother John, the lord of the manor of North Ockenden in Essex, an evangelical sympathiser and a former courtier whom Poyntz hoped would be able to lobby the English authorities on Tyndale's behalf.

He said that the king 'has never a truer hearted subject this day living' than Tyndale, who 'hath lain in my house three quarters of a year'. He explained that Tyndale had been arrested 'by procurement out of England', and that 'it is clear it must be the papists who are at the bottom of it'. These 'privy lurkers', he said, feared that the king might summon Tyndale to return to England and 'hear him charitably'. They had betrayed him to prevent him harming the papal cause. Poyntz said that Tyndale was in grave danger of execution, and told his brother that his death 'will be a great hindrance to the gospel, and to the enemies of it one of the highest pleasures'. He warned that there were two Englishmen at Louvain – he did not name them, but they were probably Phillips and Buckenham – who were 'taking great pains to translate out of English into Latin those things that may make against him, so that the clergy here may understand it'. Poyntz had a good notion of the books and papers that had been confiscated from Tyndale's rooms in the English House, and he knew that the prosecutors would find 'opinions contrary to their business, the which they call the order of the holy church'. The letter ended with an appeal to his brother to solicit 'the king's grace' to help Tyndale; 'in my conscience there be not many perfecter men living, as knows God'.

His brother duly forwarded the letter to Thomas Cromwell. By then, Cromwell had already sounded out Henry VIII. A memorandum records that he had made a visit to the palace, probably in August, 'to know the king's pleasure for Tyndale, and whether I shall write or not'. The king agreed that efforts should be made to save Tyndale. This may have been at the prompting of Queen Anne; she was again pregnant, and she retained her husband's favour for the moment. Cromwell wrote two letters to members of the privy council in Brabant in September 1535. One was addressed to the president, Carondolet, who was also the archbishop of Palermo; the other was to the marquis of Bergen-op-Zoom, the man whom Tyndale may have petitioned for books and warm clothes while in prison. The letters have not survived. They must, however, have appealed for clemency as a matter of grace rather than law. Heresy was an international crime, in the sense that the courts of any territory in which a suspect was seized were competent to try him or her, regardless of nationality. Tyndale was thus charged under the laws of the Low Countries.

The letters were handed to Stephen Vaughan to be sent on to Flanders. Vaughan acknowledged their receipt – he described them to Cromwell as 'your two letters devised for Tyndale' – but he feared they would achieve little. He said that 'it were good the king had one living in Flanders, that were a man of reputation', and, in the absence of such a heavyweight ambassador, he held out little hope of success. Vaughan sent the letters on to Robert Flegge, one of the English merchants at Antwerp. Flegge received them promptly, and replied to Cromwell on 22 September.

The marquis of Bergen-op-Zoom had left the court at Brussels two days earlier, to travel to Germany as escort to the eldest daughter of the king of Denmark. Flegge asked Poyntz to ride after him. Poyntz rode with all speed and overtook the party at Alken. After the marquis had read the letter, he told Poyntz irritably that some Flemings 'were burned in England not long before', and that the English themselves burnt Anabaptists at Smithfield. As Poyntz protested, the marquis cut him short by saying that 'the princess is ready to ride'. Poyntz followed the marquis's party for fifteen miles until it stopped again at Maastricht. By now, the marquis was in better humour, and invited Poyntz to dine with him, complaining at the treachery of the times, and saying of his escort of men-at-arms that 'we know not whether we ride among our friends or enemies'. After breakfast the next morning, he gave the Englishman a letter for the council in Brussels, and replies for Flegge and Cromwell.

Poyntz rode hard for Brussels and then went on to Flegge at Antwerp. The marquis's letters were not encouraging. He told Flegge that he was sorry to be away from court, and so 'unable to render the king's highness . . . such service as he would wish'. He had written to Archbishop Carondolet, begging him to help, and could do no more. The archbishop in turn spoke with the queen-regent and the council, and wrote to Flegge to report that they had turned down the appeal. Flegge asked Poyntz to take the correspondence to Cromwell and the privy council in London. This Poyntz did, kicking his heels in England until the end of October, waiting for Cromwell to compose a new batch of letters.

Poyntz delivered these to the imperial council in Brussels. While he was waiting for a reply, he was told by a contact in the emperor's chancery that 'Master Tyndale should have been delivered to him according to the tenor of the letters', but Phillips, who was in Brussels, had 'followed the suit against Master Tyndale'.

Worse followed. Phillips now turned on Poyntz. He told Pierre Dufief, the procurer general who had arrested Tyndale, that Poyntz was 'a dweller in the town of Antwerp, and there had been a succourer of Tyndale'. He added that Poyntz himself was a heretic – he was 'one of the same opinion' as Tyndale – and that the campaign to free Tyndale was Poyntz's 'own labour and suit and no man's else'. Poyntz was arrested on or about Hallowtide,

1 November, on Phillips's accusation. Dufief had him held in the
house of one of his sergeants of arms.

The procurer general and an official from the imperial
chancery interrogated Poyntz each day for a week. They were
interested in general intelligence on the English court as well
Poyntz's suspected heresy, for they asked him 'of the king's affairs
as of the message concerning Tyndale, of his aiders and of his religion'. After this long examination, Dufief drew up two dozen
articles or charges, and delivered them to the commissioners
appointed to hear his case. A copy was given to Poyntz, who was
allowed to have an advocate and proctor to help in his defence.
He was given eight days to reply to the articles against him; the
prosecution was to have eight days to respond to that, and so matters would drag on at eight day intervals 'till the process were
ended'. Poyntz was forbidden to send messengers or letters any-
where, except by the Brussels town post, where Dufief could
intercept and read what was sent; he was not allowed to send or
receive correspondence in any language but Flemish; and he was
to speak Flemish at all times so that his captors knew what was
being said.

One exception was made to the last rule. A Carmelite provincial
was invited to dine at the house where Poyntz was being held, and
he brought a young English novice with him. The novice had
'much pretty talk' with Poyntz about the deaths of Thomas More
and John Fisher, whom the young man held to be martyrs; he was
clearly being used as an *agent provocateur* to winkle an indiscretion
out of Poyntz. For weeks, Poyntz played cat and mouse with the
commissioners, using excuse after excuse to delay answering their
list of charges. He 'trifled them off,' Foxe recorded, 'from
Hallowtide until Christmas even, with dilatories from eighth day
to eighth day'. On the morning of 24 December, the commissioners warned him that he would be condemned whether he had
replied to them or not. He now used an advocate to help him

ensure that his replies were unsatisfactory enough to warrant further delays and questions.

He was alarmed to find that, whenever the commissioners visited him, Phillips 'accompanied them to the door, in following the process against him, as he also did against Master Tyndale'. Poyntz had now been detained for three months, and he realised that he would most likely be executed if he did not flee. At the beginning of February 1536, at night by a method that Foxe did not specify, Poyntz broke out of the house where he was being held and hid until the city gates of Brussels were opened at dawn. A hue and cry was raised for him, but he knew the countryside well and slipped through to the coast and found a boat for England. One of his captors, John Baers, was given a heavy fine of £80 by the imperial council for his negligence in allowing the escape of 'a prisoner accused of Lutheranism, named Thomas Poyntz, an Englishman'.

Poyntz was banished from the Low Countries. He lost his business, his property and his family, for his wife, Anna van Calva, was Flemish and refused to bring the children to join the impoverished merchant in England. He inherited the manor of North Ockenden on his brother's death a decade later, but he seems to have been too poor to live there. He had gladly ruined himself for his friend.

Poyntz was gone and Cromwell's entreaties had been ignored. Tyndale was helpless and imprisoned in wretched conditions. The castle at Vilvoorde was notoriously damp; dank vapours from the moat and the Zenne added to the sluicing Flemish rains. He had to pay for his own food and the other expenses of imprisonment. An account was kept by Adolf van Wesele of the money paid out by him for 'the keeping of a certain prisoner named Willem Tintalus, Lutheran . . . for a year and one hundred and thirty five days, at forty stivers the day'. A stiver was worth about one English penny, and his jailers took their cut of his daily 3s 4d before a pittance was used to buy his food. Cash was raised by selling the prisoners' assets. Tyndale's were the tools of a heretic's trade – grammars, Bibles in Hebrew, Greek and Latin, and illicit ones in English and German – and would not have been easily sold. Some of his possessions survived. Works he had written on the sacraments, and on the controversial will of William Tracey, were recovered by his friends from some hiding place in the English House, and later published.

We know from his prison letter – 'I ask to be allowed a lamp . . . the Hebrew bible, Hebrew grammar and Hebrew dictionary' – that he wished to devote his imprisonment to working on the Old Testament. If he did translate more, and the time he spent in Vilvoorde was enough for him to have completed the Bible, the work has not survived. Any writings found in his cell may have been burnt on the day of his execution, as had happened to John Huss.

The most grievous loss to the English-speaking world was with the poetical books. Tyndale's death robbed us of the beauty that he would have brought to Psalms and the Song of Solomon. Among the *Sarum Use* epistles from the Old Testament, that he translated and published in his 1534 revised New Testament, is the most exquisite rendering of the second chapter of the Song of Songs, the epistle on the visitation of our lady.

'I am the floure of the felde,' Tyndale wrote, 'and lyles of the valeyes. As the lyle amonge the thornes so is my beloved amonge the daughters . . . Beholde my beloved sayde to me: up and haste my love, my dove, my bewtifull and come away, for now is wynter gone and rayne departed and past . . . Up haste my love, my dove, in the holes of the rocke and secret places of the walles. Shew me thy face and let me hear thy voyce, for thy voyce is swete and thy fassyon bewtifull.'

King James's men did well enough, perhaps, but see what is lost; speak it aloud and hear what is lost. '*Up and haste my love, my dove, my bewtifull and come away . . .*' Tyndale continues to flow, where the King James Version stutters with less urgency and command: '*Rise up, my love, my fair one, and come away.*' Tyndale writes: '*For now is wynter gone and rayne departed and past.*' It is a sentence warm with the promise of spring. King James bumbles: '*For lo, the winter is past, the rain is over, and gone.*' That is a weather report. Tyndale has the intimacy of direct speech: '*Beholde my beloved sayde to me . . .*' King James's divines are crabbed and formal: '*My beloved spake, and said unto me . . .*' *Beholde* catches the eye and ear, and lifts what Tyndale's beloved then *sayde to me*, where King James's beloved both *spake* and *said* in dull repetition.

We know Tyndale's Isaiah only from the fragments in the same epistles. 'For heaven shall vanyshe awaye as smoke,' he writes in the epistle on the first Friday in Advent, 'and the erthe shall weare awaye as a vesture, and the in habiters therof shall peryshe awaye after the same manner, but my salvacion shall endure ever, and my ryghteousness shall not perishe.' For the King James committee, the earth did not *weare awaye* but *waxed old*. Its *in habiters* became the clumsy *they that dwell therein*; and the Lord's righteousness *shall not be abolished* rather than the more cadent *shall not perishe*.

There are moments in the epistles where Tyndale is outdone. 'He is despised and rejected of men,' reads the King James in Isaiah 53, '*a man of sorrows . . .*'. For that echoing phrase, Tyndale has the duller '*one who has suffered sorrow*'. He has '*as a sheep led to be slain*' where the King James excels with '*brought as a lamb to the slaughter*'. But in other places – 'with his stripes we are healed', 'sins as red as scarlet', 'the Lord shall rise as the sun over thee' – the epistles show the brilliance that we would now enjoy in the final Old Testament books but for Harry Phillips.

The investigation of a suspect heretic, particularly one as distinguished as Tyndale, was a lengthy business. He was first examined by the procurer general, Pierre Dufief, and a notary. They questioned him under oath on his career, his writing and his beliefs. This preliminary set of interrogations lasted, in Poyntz's case, for a week; the process with Tyndale was more complex, and will have lasted at least a fortnight. It established that the prisoner had a case to answer. The queen-regent, the emperor's aunt Margaret of Austria, then appointed a set of commissioners to try the case. One or more of them was present at each subsequent interrogation.

Dufief was the main member of the commission, and the archives show that he was paid the handsome sum of £128 for his services. He had a reputation for venality as well as cruelty; he benefited from the sale of goods confiscated from his prisoners, and extortion and embezzlement seem to lie behind his eventual removal from office. He was joined by three theologians, Ruard Tapper, Jacobus Latomus and Jan Doye. Each was a doctor of divinity, and a canon at Louvain, the stamping ground of Catholic diehards and Phillips's base camp. It was their task to prove that Tyndale's beliefs amounted to heresy. The theologians shared a payment of £149 with Willem van Caverschoen, the secretary to Jacques de Lattre, the inquisitor general of the Low Countries. Four privy councillors made up the rest of the commission; one of them, Godfrey de Mayers, was well rewarded with £54, probably for doing much of the legal work.

These were experienced and inflexible men. Tapper was almost fifty, a veteran professor, recently appointed as chancellor of the university of Louvain, and dean of St Peter's, the most fashionable church in the town. He had been active against heretics since 1523, when he was the theological assessor at the trial of Augustinian monks of Antwerp. After the Tyndale case, the pope gratefully appointed him inquisitor general of the Low Countries. His colleague Jacques Masson, who had adopted the Latin name of Jacobus Latomus, was a professor of fifty-nine, a brilliant scholar and a future rector of Louvain who disliked Erasmus and the liberal humanists as heartily as he did Luther.

The three canons shared More's enthusiasm for the fire. The theological faculty at Louvain, of which each was a member, had sent a letter to the archbishop of St Andrews in 1528. It congratulated him on the burning of the Scottish protomartyr Patrick Hamilton as a 'worthy deed' that had 'given us great courage'. A certain horror attaches to this letter, because Hamilton had visited Louvain as a nineteen-year-old while studying on the Continent, and the theologians who revelled in his death will have known him as a teenager.[1]

Henry Phillips was active, 'following the suit against Master Tyndale', moving between Louvain, Vilvoorde and Brussels, at hand if needed, sometimes accompanying the commissioners to the door of Tyndale's cell. It seems that he was one of the two Englishmen whom Poyntz recorded as translating passages of Tyndale's writing from English into Latin, to aid the commissioners, who had no English. The other may have been Dr Buckenham, the former prior whom Phillips had identified to Tebold as his friend at Louvain.

Translation took time. Cromwell's intervention in September 1535 had also to be attended to. It was unlikely that the articles of accusation were drawn up until the end of 1535; Mozley thought that January 1536 was possible. Tyndale's writings were thick with self-incriminating evidence. He wrote that faith alone justifies, and that salvation flows from grace and forgiveness of sins offered in the gospel, and not from good works; he denied the freedom of the will, the existence of purgatory, and the papal supremacy; he held that Church rulings based on human traditions cannot bind the conscience; he proclaimed the inefficacy of prayers to the saints, pilgrimage, and confession to priests.

Each of these was proof of heresy. It is doubtful whether a full confession and abjuration would have saved him. More had been at pains to claim that Tyndale had already abjured in his Little Sodbury days, in 1523, in front of John Bell, the chancellor of the

Gloucester diocese. More wrote in his *Dialogue Concerning Heresies* that Tyndale had escaped Bell only because he 'glossed his words with a better sense, and said and swore that he meant no harm'. The assertion that Tyndale 'swore' was fabricated by More to ensure that, if Tyndale faced a later trial, he would be treated as a relapsed heretic, for whom the death sentence was automatic. Tyndale was aware of More's intention, and he stressed in his *Answer to More* that he was never asked to make an oath. 'He sware not,' he wrote of himself, 'neither was there any man that required an oath from him.'

In the event, the question of a previous abjuration was not raised because it was irrelevant. Tyndale – like More himself – refused to try to buy his life with his conscience and remained steadfast in his beliefs. He refused the offer of an advocate and a proctor, and undertook his own defence. Foxe reported that 'much writing' and 'great disputation' passed to and from between Tyndale and the Louvain theologians.

The process was conducted in private, but Latomus sent an account of his dealings with Tyndale to a friend. From his cell, Tyndale wrote a long paper – Latomus calls it 'a book' – on his central belief, *sola fides justificat apud Deum*, faith alone justifies before God. The theologians responded with their own book, in which Latomus claimed that 'we took away his key, and put another in its place'. Tyndale had 'no reasonable answer to make', Latomus recalled with self-satisfaction, 'yet preferred to make a show of replying rather than to acknowledge his error'. Tyndale's reply obliged the divines to write again at length. 'We plainly overturned his foundations and demonstrated the absurdity of his opinion', Latomus wrote. Nonetheless, because Tyndale asked for elaboration, and 'we were unwilling to decline any request of his', a third book of arguments against Tyndale was prepared.

The exchanges, or at least Latomus's account of them, were better tempered than those between Tyndale and More. A scholarly civility was kept, for each side hoped, however forlornly, to convert the other. No whiff of torture entered the debate. In such trials it became common to rack the prisoner between each question put to him, while the inquisitor kept up an endless chant – 'Tell the truth, for the love of God' – through bloodless lips. The duke of Alva imposed this fate on scores of evangelicals in the struggle to maintain Catholicism and Spanish rule in the Low Countries; but the duke, and his *Bloedraad,* or Bloody Council, were still some years off. Latomus and his colleagues put their questions to Tyndale with the courtesy due to a fellow scholar, and they replied meticulously to the points he raised in return. If they had a patronising air – 'reflect upon all this,' they advised Tyndale, 'and you will clearly see the absurdity in which you are landed' – it reflected their strength as divines admired by society and by the emperor himself, and the weakness of the wretched prisoner who opposed them.

Much of the skirmishing was on the old battleground of faith and works. Tyndale claimed that good works simply declared a man's goodness; they did not make him good, 'just as the fruit of the tree shows, and does not create, the healthiness of the stock'. Latomus admonishes him: 'The simile is a bad one; for the bearing of the fruit weakens the tree, but good acts strengthen the mind; a fountain and its water would suit your purpose better.' Tyndale returns to the attack. Good works, he says, are not needed by God, and they benefit him no more 'than the bitter draught, drunk by a patient, benefits the physician who prescribes it'. Latomus admits that: 'I agree with you here.' But he adds that God 'rewards us as if he needed our works . . . [I]f good men merit no reward of God, what are we to say of sinners?' Tyndale held that 'In work we ever sin, and our thoughts are impure', or so Latomus paraphrased him. 'Therefore we live by faith as long as we are in the flesh; and by faith we overcome the world.' To Tyndale, citing I John 5, this is the 'victory which overcometh the world, even our faith, our faith in God through Christ'; for through it 'the love of him who overcame all the temptations of the devil shall be imputed to us'. To Latomus, this position collapses when it is examined; 'it cannot stand, it is riddled with difficulties.'

Other subjects were raised. Latomus worked his way through the sacraments, prayers to saints, fasting, images, papal authority. More had defended these great Church traditions with emotion and at the cost of his life. Latomus made much use of quotations from the ancient Fathers – 'that you may see,' he told Tyndale, 'how great and of what nature are the men, whom you have deserted for Luther' – but his arguments were dry and donnish.

The nub of the case, and its passion, lay in Tyndale's attachment to the Christ he had rediscovered in the gospel, and in his certainty that salvation lay in faith and in the love that God manifests through the Son. Latomus rightly identified this conviction as Bible-based. 'If, as you write, you desire to be instructed,' he remarked to Tyndale, 'be careful not to regard the sacred text as a storehouse of arguments for your part.' But that, of course, was precisely what Tyndale did believe; for him, the Bible was the sole storehouse of divine truth. Latomus urged him to think again. 'Consider, I beg of you, Tyndale,' he wrote, 'to what absurdity you are come to by leaving the well trodden paths and the teachings of the fathers.' There is sympathy in that remark, and pity; and acceptance that things had run their course. He knew that Tyndale would not abjure, and it may be that he admired him for it.

In his third book – the exchange of writings went on for several months – Latomus said that he had accepted the conclusion of Tyndale's last treatise, where the latter said that he had laid out his opinions 'with a good conscience'. If Tyndale's beliefs were true, Latomus replied, then 'you are rightly displeased with those that imprison you in the name of the pope and emperor, and treat you as a malefactor'. But there was another side to the matter, of 'what we believe, what we hold', with equally good conscience; and it was upon this – 'what we have learned in the catholic, orthodox, and, if you will permit the word, also Roman church' – that the prisoner would be judged.

Any hopes of help from England slowly slid away in the early months of 1536. Catherine of Aragon died on 8 January. She wrote Henry an affectionate last letter, addressed to 'My dear lord, king and husband', forgiving him the hurts he had done her, praying him to protect their daughter Mary, and concluding: 'Mine eyes desire you above all things.'

Her letter pricked Henry's conscience. A few days later, Queen Anne miscarried a stillborn son; the male heir who would have guaranteed her survival eluded her. Henry turned against her and her evangelical sympathies ceased to carry weight. The king was said to have fallen in love with Jane Seymour, whose 'disposition was tempered between the gravity of Catherine and the gaiety of Anne'. In April, Chapuys informed the emperor of a plot to destroy Anne, which he welcomed for the damage it would do to the reformers' cause. 'Whoever could help in its execution would do a meritorious work,' the ambassador wrote, 'since it would prove . . . a remedy for the heretical doctrines and practices of the concubine – the principle cause of the spread of Lutheranism in this country.'

The same month, on 13 April, the ever-optimistic Stephen Vaughan thought of Vilvoorde in a letter he wrote to Cromwell. 'If now yow sende me but your lettre to the privye counsail, I could delyver Tyndall from the fyre,' he said, 'so it come by tyme, for elles it will be to late.' Cromwell could recognise a lost cause. We know of no reply, nor of any further English petitions to the imperial council at Brussels.

On May Day 1536, the king rode off abruptly from a tournament at Greenwich, leaving the queen behind. She was arrested the next day and brought up the Thames to the Tower. A secret commission investigated charges of adultery with her own brother, Lord Rochford, whose wife had turned on him and who 'prejudiced the king with her own extravagant apprehensions and filled his head with many false reports'. Four commoners, Norris, Weston and Brereton, all royal servants, and Smeton, a musician, were also said to have enjoyed the queen's favours. All denied it except Smeton, who confessed in a misguided attempt to curry favour.

Anne's uncle, Thomas Howard, the duke of Norfolk, presided over the judges and announced the verdicts. All were found guilty of high treason. The day before her execution, Anne sent a message to the king, asserting her innocence, recommending their daughter Elizabeth to his care, and thanking him for 'advancing her first to be a marchioness, then to be a queen, and now, when he could raise her no higher upon the earth, for sending her to be saint in heaven'. An executioner was sent specially from France, where a sword rather than the brutal English axe was used for beheading. On being told of his skill, she laughed and said it was as well, for she had a short neck.

She was brought out to Tower Green a little before noon on 19 May 1536. On the scaffold, she is said to have given a book of devotions to one of her maids of honour. Two books owned by the Wyatt family vie for the honour. One, now in the British Library, has metrical versions of thirteen psalms translated into English by John Croke, the same metrical psalms later chanted by puritan troopers in the English civil war. The other has twelve evangelical prayers and thanksgivings. 'Grant us most merciful father,' one runs, 'the knowledge of thy holy will and glad tidings of our salvation, this great while oppressed with the tyranny of thy adversary of Rome and his faulters and kept close under his Latin letters . . .' Tyndale, in his distant cell, would have approved of that.

She prayed on the scaffold, and said simply: 'To Christ I commend my soul.' After execution, Anne's body was thrown into an elmwood crate, made for shipping arrows to English soldiers in Ireland, and buried in the chapel of the Tower. Eleven days later Henry married Jane Seymour.

Anne's death was seen as a grave blow to the English Bible and Cranmer tried to gloss over her support for it. The archbishop admitted to Henry that: 'I loved her not a little, for the love which I judged her to bear towards God and his gospel.' But, he hastened to add, 'if she be proved culpable, there is no one that loveth God and his gospel that ever will favour her . . . for then was never creature in our time that hath so much slandered the gospel'. Cranmer begged the king not to allow his rightful anger to colour his views of the Bible. 'I trust that your grace will bear no less entire favour unto the truth of the gospel, than you did before,' he pleaded, 'forsomuch as your grace's favour to the gospel was not led by affection unto her, but by zeal unto the truth.'

Nicholas Shaxton was more forceful. He was the evangelical whom Anne Boleyn had helped make bishop of Salisbury, and whom Bishop Nix of Norwich wished he had burnt in place of Bilney. He wrote to Cromwell begging him '*in visceribus Jesu Christi*' – 'in the very guts of Christ' – to continue to uphold the gospel as Anne had exhorted him to do. He may have asked him, too, to intercede for Tyndale. Cromwell could do nothing for the prisoner, and the king would not.

Phillips was another matter. Tebold had supplied Cromwell with evidence that Phillips was slandering the king, as a 'tyrant' and 'despoiler'. This was treasonable talk, and Cromwell used it to try to have Phillips seized.

Orders were issued in the king's name on 23 March 1536 to the consul in Nuremberg to 'intercept and send to England' two English criminals believed to be at large in the city. These were James Griffith, described as 'of low birth, guilty of treason, robbery, manslaughter and sacrilege', and 'a rebel named Henry Philipp' who was thought to be 'on his way from Flanders to Italy'. The following day, Henry wrote to Charles V to say that the 'rebels' Phillips and Griffith, who had committed 'grievous crimes', had taken refuge in the emperor's dominions, where they 'stir up causes of dissension'. The king asked for them to be delivered up for punishment.

The intelligence was correct. Phillips had left Flanders, his money now gone, and believing Tyndale to be safely incarcerated, and was making his way to Italy. On 3 May, the English agent in Rome, Sir Gregory de Casalis, wrote to Cromwell to inform him that Phillips had surfaced in the city, where he was seeking out a powerful cardinal and the pope. As Tyndale's betrayer, Phillips could expect to be rewarded in Rome; he was also claiming to be a relation of Thomas More, who was a martyr in Roman eyes.

De Casalis was Henry's man in Italy. He began in royal service by buying high-grade war horses in Naples for the king's personal use, and distributed royal gifts of falcons to influential Italians and Frenchmen. Henry and the pope had used him as a trusted go-between. His easy access to the curia had been shown in a letter to Wolsey. 'Hearing that a post was to be dispatched today,' he wrote, 'I have been with the pope.' Henry had knighted him, and used him over the annulment. De Casalis made little progress there, of course, and the king showed his displeasure by cutting back on payments to him. 'If greater regard is not had to my expenses,' de Casalis complained, 'no Englishman coming to Rome will find me at my home, but that I have moved to the nearest hospital.' He had ingratiated himself with Cromwell, and with Queen Anne, hoping that 'she will not wrongfully condemn such an old and faithful servant'. He made the transition smoothly and remained the king's agent until 1537.

In his report on 3 May, de Casalis said that Phillips 'aspires to the pope's friendship'. He said that Phillips was introduced to the papal court by Cardinal Caracciolo, who 'commends him as learned and noble, and as a kinsman of Thomas More'. The cardinal had added that Rome was indebted to More, 'persecuted by the king for asserting the authority of the Holy See'.

Caracciolo was a senior member of the curia and he was closely allied with Charles V. He owed the emperor his career; Charles had used him on diplomatic missions to Venice, and had appointed him imperial chancellor of Milan. 'Being pressed by the imperialists,' Gregory de Casalis had reported to Cromwell on 1 June 1535, 'the pope has promoted to the cardinalate the protonotary Caracciolo . . .' The cardinal was described as 'a good servant of the emperor'.

Why did Phillips make straight for Caracciolo when he came to Rome? Perhaps because More had described him as a potential friend at the Roman court; certainly because he was likely to prove sympathetic. Caracciolo was the emperor's man, and Charles V had every reason to be grateful to More's memory, and to his surviving friends and relatives. Had he not written to More to thank him personally for the support he had given to his aunt over the annulment? Caracciolo's own interest in More was such that another cardinal, Nicholas of Capua, had sent him a letter on 12 August 1535 which included 'an account of the death of Sir Thomas More just received from England'.

Why, too, did the cardinal describe Phillips to the pope as 'a kinsman of Thomas More', as well as 'learned and noble'? It is most unlikely that Caracciolo simply accepted the word of a stray Englishman that he was an aristocrat and a relation of More. De Casalis was not taken in for a moment, and Caracciolo was no fool. He had at least ten years' experience of survival in the dangerous swill of Italian politics; he had been chancellor of Milan, one of the liveliest places in Europe, and he was currently negotiating a peace settlement between Charles V and Francis I of France. He promoted Phillips, it seems, because he was satisfied that there was a link between the young man and the martyred lord chancellor of England. To support Phillips was a way of recognising More, as well as rewarding Tyndale's betrayer, and Caracciolo was confident enough that this would please both emperor and pope to commend Phillips to the pope.

The new pope had equal grounds to be generous to Phillips. Clement VII, indecisive to the last, had died in 1534. His successor, Paul III, had the usual vices of Renaissance pontiffs. He was the brother of a papal concubine, a stylish nepotist, a promoter of bullfights and horse races, a lecher known as 'Cardinal Petticoat', and the father of three sons and a daughter, whom he shamelessly entertained with his daughters-in-law at Vatican banquets. But he had virtues as well. He was a patron of art and scholarship, who enriched the Vatican Library and appointed Michelangelo architect-in-chief of St Peter's; he encouraged Church reform and favoured new orders, issuing the papal bull that founded the Jesuits. He was firm in his defence of Catholicism and the pursuit of heretics like Tyndale; he revived the Inquisition and condemned Henry VIII for the execution of Bishop Fisher and More. He had created Fisher a cardinal in May 1535, as a warning to the king not to treat him as a traitor; but Fisher was dead before the traditional red hat arrived – 'the hat came as far as Calais, but the head was off before the hat was on' – and More followed shortly after.

But for de Casalis, Phillips might well have received the payment or pension he sought from the pope. De Casalis told the papal secretary that Phillips was 'of humble birth and a great scoundrel', adding that if such a man was allowed to have his way with the curia, 'all the thieves in England will come too, and say they were driven out for the sake of the Holy See'. The secretary was 'obliged for the hint', so de Casalis reported to Cromwell, and Phillips was frustrated.

The last to be heard of him, while Tyndale was still alive, was that he had made his way from Rome to Paris. Here he was discovered, 'all ragged and torn', by an Oxford friend who found him clothes and lodging. True to form, Phillips rewarded this generosity by stealing from his benefactor.

At the last in Vilvoorde, so Foxe wrote, Tyndale 'prayed that he might have some English divines come unto him: for the manners and ceremonies in religion in Dutchland (said he) did much differ from manners and ceremonies used in England'. It added that 'divers divines from Louvain, whereof some were Englishmen' were sent to him; other Catholic refugees had fled from England to join Phillips and Buckenham in Louvain. The note closes abruptly: 'and after many examinations at the last they condemned him'.

Tyndale was found guilty of heresy in the first days of August 1536. He was told that he was to be degraded from the priesthood and relaxed to the secular power for sentence. John Hutton, the government agent in the Low Countries, wrote to Cromwell from Antwerp on 12 August to say that he had dined with the procurer general in the English House two days before. The official 'certified to me that William Tyndale is degraded, and condemned into the hands of the secular power, so that he is very likely to suffer death this next week'. Hutton said that he had been unable to learn the articles on which Tyndale had been condemned; he promised that when he had the details, they 'shall be sent to your lordship by the first'.

The degradation – or unhallowing, in which the disgraced man was ceremoniously stripped of his priestly dignity – almost certainly took place after 5 August and before Hutton's dinner engagement on 10 August. A deed was signed in The Falcon Inn at Vilvoorde on 5 August in which the inquisitor general for the Low Countries, Jacques de Lattre, delegated his powers to Ruard Tapper. The deed was witnessed by Latomus and by the other theologian in the case, Jan Doye. The way was now clear for Tapper to authorise the ceremony with Pierre Dufief, the procurer general.

Dufief submitted the expenses he ran up in staging the 'unhallowing of Guillem Tindal, an Englishman'. They came to some £19 – the authorities paid them promptly at the end of the month – and covered the cost of hiring carriages for visiting dignitaries, and for fees for 'the serjeants and servants of the town'. The interrogations and trial had been carried out in secret, but the degradation was a public spectacle, staged to strike fear into heretical hearts. It was carried out, so Dufief's expenses record, by 'the bishop suffragan and the two prelates assisting him . . . while other ecclesiastics and laymen were present'.

The ceremony may have been held in the main church of Vilvoorde, or on the large square in front of it, little more than 200 yards across the stagnant moat from the castle where Tyndale had his cell. Protocol demanded that the inquisitor general and his secretary, Willem van Caverschoen, be present together with the Louvain canons and the other commissioners from the case. An event of this drama will have attracted spectators from across the region, encouraged by their parish priests, anxious that their flock witness the humbling of the new religion. The inquisition had a fine sense of theatre; it transformed burnings and humiliations into *autos-da-fé*, acts of faith, in which ritual and entertainment blended into a living morality play in which a mass audience watched heretics pay the price for their evil.

The process was unchanged from the days of John Huss. The three bishops – the suffragan was from Cambrai – were seated on a high wooden platform. Tyndale was led to it, in the vestments of a priest about to celebrate mass, and made to kneel in front of the bishops. His hands were scraped with the blade of a knife, symbolically removing the oil with which he had been anointed at his consecration. The sacraments were placed in his hands and taken away. As the cup was removed from him, the bishops intoned a solemn curse: 'O cursed Judas, because you have abandoned the counsel of peace and have counselled with the Jews, we take away from you this cup of redemption.' Other curses were pronounced as his stole and chasuble were stripped from him, one by one, and he was reclothed as a layman.

At the end, the bishops intoned the final curse: 'We commit your soul to the devil.' Having deprived him of all ecclesiastical rights, the bishops then ensured that the Church would not be stained with Tyndale's blood by proclaiming: 'We turn him over to the secular court.' Ritual demanded that Dufief acknowledge this by saying: 'I am the one who wields the temporal sword.' Tyndale was now doubly condemned. The *poena sensus* was to be achieved by his strangulation and burning; this was to be followed by the *poena damni*, confirming his absolute separation from God in the eternity of hell.

Hutton expected that Tyndale would die within the week. Instead, he lived for two more months. We do not know the reason for the delay, but the Dominicans and priests assigned to the prisoner will have used the time to try to persuade him to recant. A condemned man who reconciled himself to the Church saved his immortal soul, if not his life and body; and a coterie of monks accompanied him to the stake in the hope of a last-minute change of heart. When a prisoner accepted the faith at Logrono in Spain, as the torch was waved before his eyes, the Dominicans attending him, in the moments before his pyre was lit, 'began to embrace him with tenderness and gave infinite thanks to God for having opened to them a door for his conversion . . .'. Tyndale denied his interrogators the famous victory they sought. He

The executioner strangles Tyndale moments before burning him at the stake in Vilvoorde. His last words – 'Lord ope the King of Englands eyes" – became part of Protestant mythology. Contemporaries noted no such words, however, only that the strangling was bungled and that he suffered terribly.

(Hulton Getty)

reminded himself no doubt of the advice that he had given to Frith in the same circumstances; to 'cleave fast to the rock of the help of God, and commit the end of all things to him', and, when the friars tempted him to abjure, to 'be not overcome of men's persuasions'.

He was executed early in October 1536, probably before noon on 6 October. A stout stake or beam was set up in a public place, perhaps in the main town square between the church and the castle, now, prosaically, a parking area and pedestrian zone leading to a supermarket and shopping arcade. Iron chains were fastened to the top of the stake, and a noose of rope passed through it at neck height. Kindling and faggots were piled up in a pyramid around the stake. Dufief and the commissioners were present to witness the event. Tyndale was brought from the castle, with a small retinue of guards and friars. After refusing a final opportunity to recant, he was securely bound to the stake, by his feet, and by the iron chains around his calves and chest. The noose was placed round his neck. He had then a brief period in which to pray. Foxe says that he cried, with fervent zeal and loud voice: 'Lord, open the king of England's eyes.' The executioner, standing immediately behind the stake, tightened the noose at Dufief's signal. It had not been shown that Tyndale was a relapsed heretic, and he qualified for the mercy of being strangled in the moments before the fire was lit.

It appears that the executioner bungled his work, however, and that Tyndale was still alive as the flames engulfed him. 'They speak much of the patient sufferance of Master Tyndale at the time of his execution,' Hutton later wrote to Cromwell.

The executioner added fuel to the fire until the body was utterly consumed. The ashes were then disposed of, probably by throwing them into the sullen waters of the River Zenne, so that no trace of the heretic remained to defile the earth.

But Tyndale's traces are everywhere, of course. 'That old tongue, with its clang and its flavour,' as the critic Edmund Wilson wrote of the Bible, 'that we have been living with all our lives', is Tyndale's tongue. Its cadence, its rolling and happy phrases, its consolations and the elegance of its solace, are his.

Eight years before, he had anticipated his death. 'There is none other way into the kingdom of life than through persecution and suffering of pain,' he wrote, 'and of very death after the ensample of Christ.' In this belief, at least, and in the firmness of their faith, he and More are at one.

He did not write his own epitaph. A passage he left from I Corinthians serves as well: 'And though I gave my body even that

I burned, and yet had no love, it profiteth me nothing.' That he used *love* and not *charity* was technical evidence of his heresy, of course, and a prime reason why More wanted him burnt. But Tyndale did not die for charity; he died for love, for the love of God's words and of their readers, and the most familiar work in the English language is thereby given the added grace of being a labour of love.

24

Aftermath

Back among the living, we catch several later glimpses of Harry Phillips. He fled from Paris to escape further English accusations. He was back in Louvain in 1537, where he tried to charm his way into the entourage of Reginald Pole. Pole was a former favourite of Henry VIII, who became passionately opposed to the divorce and the royal supremacy. He left England for Italy in 1532. The pope created him a cardinal and sent him as papal legate to the Low Countries. Henry declared Pole a traitor, and set a price on his head. In England, Pole's brother and mother were beheaded.

Phillips had long since squandered his Tyndale pieces of silver. He may have intended to betray Pole for the reward money. Certainly, this is what Pole and his entourage feared.

John Hutton, the English agent in Brussels, was instructed by Cromwell to have Pole seized as a traitor in Liège in May 1537. Hutton wrote to Cromwell on 26 May to explain that the Regent, Margaret, had refused to arrest Pole on the grounds that 'in all treaties the Pope's legate was exempt'. Hutton added, however, that a renegade named Vaughan – not Stephen, but another of the same name who had 'fled from England for manslaughter' – had revealed to him that he had 'applied to Henry Phillippis, an Englishman in Louvayn, who offered to get him in to service with Card. Pole, knowing one of his gentlemen named Thrognorton.' Vaughan told Hutton that Phillips was soon to sail for Cornwall with Throckmorton, carrying letters to Cardinal Pole's friends as well as to Phillips's father, 'baked within a loaf of bread'. 'I advised him to encourage the enterprise,' Hutton wrote to Cromwell, 'and gave him forty shillings.'

It was, of course, the last that Hutton saw of his money. Phillips was not found landing in Cornwall. But he did write a series of begging letters to his family that have survived. God knows the anxiety and poverty he had suffered, he said, and what 'jeopardy' he was now in. Unless he was helped, he said, he 'must go to the wars or be a serving man'. He pleaded with his father for cash and reconciliation. 'I call upon you for succour your miserable child Henry Phyllypps,' he wrote. 'I desire your blessing and help *contra calumniam*, which has followed me through Flanders, Allmaygne, Italy, and France. I have offended you, but never my country as my adversaries *falso asserunt*. I desire that the error of my youth may not destroy the hope of your goodness.'

Another screed was sent to Dr Brerewood, the chancellor of Exeter, who had taught him and whom he flattered as 'my Maecenas'. He asked for help in his 'extreme necessity'. He has been falsely vilified, he wrote, and 'cannot bear to be deprived of both country and literature at the same time'. He asked if he might become a servant of anyone whom Brerewood had educated in the arts. He wrote to his brother Thomas, saying that he acknowledged that he had 'dyvasted' his claim on the family fortune, but that 'I desire to purchase grace for other three years' study'. He said that he was now but ten days' journey from Thomas. 'Only they who gave the bearer these letters know where I am,' he ended. 'Whoever is sent must be instructed by this bearer, where he got these.'

When this failed, he wrote to his brother William, this time giving an address: 'it is in your hand to save or spill me . . . you may be here within 10 days . . . it is in Brabant, at Lovayn, in the house of Lambert Croolys, who knows always where I am'.

He realised that he was vulnerable himself – Hutton was looking for him – and fled from Louvain. He was back in the town in January 1538, sending further begging letters to Chancellor Brerewood in Exeter.

On 1 October 1538, Cromwell had further news of Phillips and 'Michael Frognorton' from his godson Thomas Tebold at Padua in Italy. It appeared that Throckmorton had indeed been in England. Tebold reported that Throckmorton was 'merrily disposed and boasted how he had deceived Cromwell' when he had taken Cardinal Pole's messages to England, saying that 'but for his crafty and subtle conveyance, Cromwell could have beheaded him'.

It was soon clear that Throckmorton was far from being a friend of Phillips, as Hutton had suggested. The next time he met Tebold, Throckmorton was 'clothed in a coat of wolf skins and a cap of mail, as pale as ashes, blowing and puffing like unto a raging lion'. He said he had not slept all night. The reason was that 'one Harry Philleps, sometime student in Lovayn, where he betrayed good Tyndall, had come out of Flanders, either driven by poverty to ask help of Pole, or because of evil behaviour.' Phillips had been serving with the imperial army to keep body and soul together. He was 'arrayed like a Svycer', a Schweizer, a Swiss mercenary; he was 'a ruffling man of war, with a pair of Almain boots'. He had arrived on foot, but Pole's entourage, 'thinking they perceived he had worn spurs, and for other suspicions, concluded he had been sent by Cromwell to destroy Pole or be a spy on him'.

Throckmorton feared that when Pole 'rode out as usual with five or six horses unarmed', Phillips could destroy him 'with the help of three or four hardy fellows' and escape to the mountains –

'this is the Italians' practice, or poison'. Pole and Throckmorton persuaded the Venetians to force Phillips to quit their territory; Tebold reported that they were so thoroughly afraid of Phillips that 'every wagging of a straw maketh them now afraid'.

Phillips himself approached Tebold for help, 'pretending great repentance'. He claimed to be 'so troubled and dismayed that half his life was gone'. Tebold refused to give him money. Desperately short of cash, Phillips sold his doublet of velvet and damask, and his cloak of English cloth. Tebold advised him to sue for pardon and grace in England, and he said he would return and submit himself.

Phillips was back in Flanders early in 1539, and seemingly contrite. The new English ambassador in Brussels, Sir Thomas Wriothesley, wrote in high excitement to Cromwell on 5 February 1539. 'I trust by tomorrow night to have Henry Phillips yield himself to me as the King's prisoner, or else lay him fast,' he wrote. 'If he come I shall send him to England, and for my word's sake, be a suitor for his pardon.' Wriothesley said that a repentant Phillips would be an ideal agent for the crown, 'as his language in many tongues is excellent and his experience great'.

All appeared to go well. On 7 February, Wriothesley reported to Cromwell that Phillips 'hath submitted himself to me as the King's minister'. The ambassador did not interrogate him – 'I forebore to examine him here, fearing that delay and curiousness in examination might frighten him' – but was confident that Phillips would 'perform what he has promised me'. He said that he had at first refused to shake Phillips's hand, at which Phillips had knelt before him. 'Sir,' Phillips said, 'I come to submit myself wholly to the King's Majesty's mercy. I have so offended that I am unworthy to live, yet perhaps report has made my doings seem worse than they were . . .' Wriothesley warned him that a liar would deserve no mercy, but the king was a most merciful prince, and Phillips might be pardoned by 'telling the whole truth of thy life since thou hast been of this naughty sort'. Phillips 'promised to follow my advice', and the ambassador bid him stand and, trustingly, shook him by the hand. He was charmed by Phillips. 'The fellow hath great wit,' he wrote to Cromwell. 'He is excellent in languages . . . he hath freely yielded himself, thinking it better to be hanged than to live like a traitor.'

The two men bid each other goodnight. It was agreed that Phillips would leave for England the next morning. He was given a chamber in Wriothesley's house for the night, with two men to 'keep him in sight until he was on horseback in the morning'.

Between 6 and 7 a.m. the next morning, 8 February, Phillips disappeared. So did 'more or less to 2000 crowns of the sun', and some rings and jewellery belonging to the ambassador, to a total value of 2400 crowns. 'I sent out my horse every way, sent men to the seven gates here to watch for him,' Wriothesley wrote on 9 February. 'There was such running and riding and stirring about the town as has not been seen these hundred years.' The ambassador offered a reward of 1000 gold guilders to any who brought Phillips back to him, and 100 crowns for information that led to his capture. Wriothesley railed and fumed – 'Mr W takes his escape so heavily,' an acquaintance wrote, 'that I fear a return of his ague' – to no effect. Phillips was gone.

In April 1539, he was reported to be in the service of the duke of Cleves. His name was included in a Bill of Attainder of 28 April 1539, as 'having traitrously maintained the pope's headship of the church of England'. He was later sighted in Italy.

Sir Thomas Seymour, writing to Henry VIII from the camp of the king of Hungary outside Buda, on 8 August 1542, reported that Phillips was in danger of having his eyes put out. Phillips had been in Vienna, where he had confessed to an Englishman 'that he hath been ambassador for the Turk divers time by the space of V [five] years'. This made him a traitor to the Hungarian king, and in peril of losing his eyes or his life. He appears to have escaped again, but the trail goes cold on the Hungarian plain. No more is heard of him, other than Foxe's final comment that, or 'the saying so goeth', having lived from the blood of others, Phillips was finally 'consumed at last with lice'.

Thomas Poyntz from the English House suffered poverty and the break-up of his family for his loyalty to Tyndale. He petitioned the king in 1536, having been 'banished the Emperor's countries for matters of religion, and repaired to England', for the restoration of his son Fardinando Poyntz to him. Poyntz had placed the boy in a school in Burton upon Trent, but the lad had been taken away 'by the petitioner's wife, who remains apart from him in Antwerp'. He died in 1562 and is fondly remembered by a Latin epitaph near his tomb. It praises his 'ardent profession of evangelical truth' for which he 'suffered bonds and imprisonment beyond the sea, and would plainly have been destined to death, had he not, trusting in divine providence, saved himself in a wonderful manner by breaking his prison. In this chapel he now sleeps peacefully in the Lord, 1562.'

Stokesley, the bishop of London, remained hostile to the English Bible. Archbishop Cranmer divided Tyndale's New Testament into 'portions' which he distributed to the 'best learned bishops' so that they could correct any errors. Stokesley was assigned Acts. He refused even to read it. 'I marvaile what my lorde of Canterbury meaneth,' he wrote, 'that thus abuseth the people in gyvyng them libertie to reade the scriptures, which doith nothing else but infecte them with herysies. I have bestowed never an hower upon my portion, nor never will.' He also continued to oppose clerical marriage; he told a married priest that he 'had better have a hundred whores than be married to his own wife'.

But he fell in with Cromwell's regime happily enough. When colleagues of the martyred monks of the Charterhouse continued to mutter against the royal supremacy, Cromwell's agent Sir John

Whalley suggested that reliable and amenable bishops such as Stokesley should preach to them. Stokesley duly won the monks over, and in January 1536, under his supervision, they wrote that they had been persuaded to submit to the crown not by 'fear of bodily pain, penury or death' but by 'duty informed and ordered . . .'. Stokesley and Cranmer administered the Oath of Supremacy to them a few days later. Stokesley was no rebel or risk-taker. He died in 1539 and was buried before the altar of the Lady Chapel in St Paul's, the cathedral having been draped in black cloth from the west door to the high altar.

Stephen Vaughan survived the dangers of his times and calling. After missions to France and Germany, in 1536 he was employed to spy on Queen Catherine in her retirement from court to Kimbolton Castle in Huntingdonshire. Vaughan was rewarded with a permanent post at the Mint from 1537, and with a grant of Church lands in 1544. He died as the well-respected Member of Parliament for Lancaster in 1549.

George Constantine remained a betrayer. He returned to England at a date before 1536 and became vicar of Llawhaden in Pembrokeshire, and was later registrar of St David's diocese. In 1554, after the Catholic Queen Mary came to the throne, Constantine was one of those who accused the bishop of St David's, Robert Ferrar, of heresy. Ferrar was burnt the following year 'for the example and terror of such as he seduced and mis-taught'. Constantine took a wife – his daughter married a future archbishop of York – before his own death in 1559.

Nicholas Udall, survivor of the Oxford fish cellar, versifier and headmaster, was dismissed from Eton in 1541 for complicity in the theft of valuable silver images and college plate, and conduct unbecoming, and was imprisoned in the Marshalsea.

Thomas Cromwell went on to issue injunctions in 1536 and 1538 that every church should be provided with a Bible. He arranged the dissolution of the monasteries between 1536 and

1540, benefiting personally from confiscated estates. Conservative intrigues, and his arrangement of the marriage between Henry VIII and Anne of Cleves, whom the startled monarch described as 'a Flemish mare', cost him his head in 1540. Henry himself survived until 1547.

As to Sir Thomas More, posterity has treated him well. His general revelry in the stake and the fire, and his individual and obsessive hatred of William Tyndale, are largely forgotten. He progressed smoothly from beatification in 1886 to canonisation in 1935, sharing a feast day, 22 June, with the fiery bishop of Rochester, Saint John Fisher. He is plentifully honoured, in the names of schools, colleges, housing estates, and streets, by statues and monuments, and by the film, *A Man for All Seasons*.

John Paul II did him the ultimate honour on 31 October 2000, proclaiming him to be the patron saint of politicians. The pope's motive, so Cardinal Roger Etchegaray explained, was to remind politicians 'of the absolute priority of God in the heart of public affairs'. But is it wise – is it Christian? – to remind politicians of a man who held his incinerated opponents to be 'well and worthily burned'?

Tyndale's honours are less obvious. He is unsainted, of course, and few Anglican churches keep his feast day, October 6; his statues and memorials – on a slope of the Cotswolds, by the Victoria Embankment in London, in a car park in Vilvoorde – are obscure compared to those of his great enemy. But his life's work triumphed. His ploughboy soon had his English Bible.

In 1535, Miles Coverdale had published the first complete English Bible, dedicated to Henry VIII, and probably printed at Zurich. Coverdale based this on Tyndale and the Vulgate, translating the outstanding Old Testament books from Luther and Zwingli, and with reference to the Vulgate.

'Matthew's Bible', so called because its title page claimed it to be 'truly and purely translated by Thomas Matthew', the alias of John Rogers, was printed at Antwerp in 1537. It was dedicated to the king, who licensed 1500 copies. These were for legal sale in England and for general reading for the first time. Rogers, martyred at Smithfield under Queen Mary, was the chaplain to the English merchants at Antwerp and Tyndale's friend. He used Tyndale's New Testament, and Pentateuch, and other Old Testament books, from Joshua to 2 Chronicles, with the remaining OT books from Coverdale. The initials 'W. T.' between the two testaments recognise it as being predominantly Tyndale's work.

Other Bibles followed. Copies of the 'Great Bible', printed under Thomas Cromwell's patronage at Paris in 1539, were placed in all the churches of England. A definitive Tyndale Testament – 'after the last copye corrected by his lyfe' – was 'imprynted at London by Richard Iugge, dwellynge in Paules churchyarde, at the signe of the Bible An. M.D.xlviii'. It seems fitting of Tyndale's ultimate triumph that the first English printer to put his name to a Tyndale testament, in 1548, should have lived where so many Tyndale bibles had been burnt.

The 'Geneva Bible' of 1560 was also known as the 'Breeches' Bible', for translating a phrase in Genesis as 'they made themselves breeches' instead of 'aprons'. It had the full elaboration of the printer's art: maps, tables, concordances, prefaces, illustrations, and marginal notes and glosses. The 'Douai-Reims Bible' of 1582 and 1610 were, ironically, Roman Catholic translations.

Tyndale's genius was ultimately enshrined in the great 'Authorised Version' or 'King James' Bible. A body of fifty-four translators – all but one of them ordained – was appointed by James I to produce a new version. They were divided into six companies, two meeting at Westminster under the dean, and two apiece at Oxford and Cambridge under the direction of their

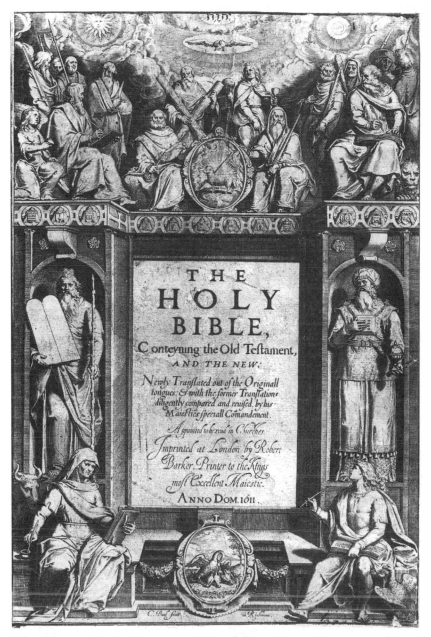

The title page of the King James Bible of 1611. Little of it was, as claimed, 'Newly Translated out of the Originall Tongues'. It serves rather as Tyndale's undying memorial. More than four-fifths of the New Testament is directly his, and three-quarters of the Old Testament books that he translated.

(Hulton Getty)

professors of Hebrew. They completed their work in 1611. Within a generation, it had displaced all its competitors. With its revisions, the Revised Version of 1881–5 and the American Standard Version of 1901, it has remained the most familiar – to many, the only – English Bible.

It is, as we have seen, overwhelmingly Tyndale's Bible. Almost any passage in the New, and most in the Old Testament, can serve as his memorial. Let us take the opening of John's gospel as our example:

In the begynnynge was the worde, [writes Tyndale], and the worde was with God: and the word was God. The same was in the begynnynge wyth God. All thinges were made by it and with out it was made nothinge that was made. In it was lyfe and the lyfe was the lyght of men. And the light shyneth in the darknes but the darknes comprehended it not.

In the beginning was the word, [echo King James's fifty-four divines], and the word was with God, and the word was God. The same was in the beginning with God. All things were made by him, and without him was not any thing made that was made. In him was life and the life was the light of men. And the light shineth in darknesse, and the darknesse comprehended it not.

SOURCES

Tyndale's original writings include the prefaces and prologues to his translations, the *Exposicion of the fyrst Epistle of Seynt Jhon* and *An exposicion upon the v, vi, vii chapters of Mathew,* and the *Parable of the Wicked Mammon, The Obedience of a Christen Man, The Practyse of prelates* and *An Answere unto Sir Thomas Mores dialoge.* Three volumes of the original works were edited for the Parker Society by the divine and antiquary Henry Walter; *Doctrinal Treatises and Introductions* (Cambridge, 1848); *Expositions and Notes* with *The Practice of Prelates* (Cambridge, 1849); and *An Answer to Sir Thomas More's Dialogue* (Cambridge, 1850).

The first brief narrative of Tyndale's life appeared in 1548 in Edward Hall's *The Vnion of the Noble and Illustre Famelies of Lancastre and Yorke.* John Bale included a short note in Latin on 'Guilhelmus Tyndale' in his *Illustrium Maioris Britanniae Scriptorum* of 1548. John Foxe published detailed accounts of Tyndale in different versions in his *Actes and Monuments.* Commonly known as *Foxe's Book of Martyrs,* four editions (1563, 1570, 1576 and 1583) appeared during Foxe's lifetime. The work became a Protestant classic and many abridged and edited versions were published over the following three centuries. *The Life and*

Story of the true Servant and Martyr of God, William Tyndale is from pp. 114–34 of *Acts and Monuments*, edited by S. Cattley, vol. 5 (London, 1837). This includes detail of Phillips's behaviour in Antwerp and his betrayal of Tyndale. Reference is also made to the eight-volume edition of 1877, edited and revised by J. Pratt and introduced by the ecclesiastical historian John Stoughton.

The major Victorian biography, *William Tindale* by Robert Demaus, was published in 1871 by The Religious Tract Society of St Paul's Churchyard in London, a few yards from the site of the fires on which many of Tyndale's Testaments were burnt. Demaus was himself senior curate of St Luke's, Chelsea, close to the site of Thomas More's house. J. F. Mozley's *William Tyndale* (London, 1937) is the painstaking between-wars work, which had the field largely to itself until David Daniell's *William Tyndale* (New Haven and London, 1994).

Professor Daniell is a brilliant if solitary champion for Tyndale. He edited and introduced modern spelling versions of *Tyndale's Old Testament, being the Pentateuch of 1530, Joshua to 2 Chronicles of 1537, and Jonah* (New Haven and London, 1992), the 1534 *New Testament* (New Haven and London, 1989) and Tyndale's *The Obedience of A Christian Man* (London, 2000). Professor Daniell also wrote the preface to the 1526 *New Testament*, in its original spelling, which was edited by W. R. Cooper (London, 2000). A reprint of Tyndale's 1534 *New Testament* in the original spelling was introduced by Isaac Foot and edited by N. Hardy Willis (Cambridge, 1938). A facsimile of the Cologne fragment, *The Beginning of the New Testament Translated by William Tyndale 1525*, edited by A. W. Pollard, was published at Oxford in 1926.

The Oxford University *Register of Congregation 1505–17* refers to 'Willelmus Hychyns' and to his receipt of his BA and MA degrees. See also *The History of the University of Oxford*, vol. II, *Late Medieval Oxford* (Oxford, 1992), edited by J. I. Catto and R. Evans. In a brief study, *William Tyndale* (London, 1996),

Andrew J. Brown suggests that Tyndale was born rather earlier than supposed, by April 1491, and that he grew up in the part of Gloucestershire that lies to the west of the Severn, and not in a village – like Nibley or Slimbridge – that is to the east of the river.

The *Calendar of Letters and Papers, Foreign and Domestic, of the Reign of Henry VIII*, twenty-one volumes, edited by J. S. Brewer, J. Gairdner, R. H. Brodie et al. (London, 1862–1932), more simply known as *L&P*, is a consummate source of detail for the period. In particular, it details the attempts made to track down and then to win over Tyndale, and gives flesh to the strange figure of Henry Phillips. References (year/letter or paper number) include: the 'articles ministered against Humfrey Munmouthe of the parish of All Saints Barking' in vol. IV, pt. ii 1528/4260, and Monmouth's Petition to Wolsey in ibid. 1528/4282; and John Hackett to Wolsey: 1528/4511 The agent and friar John West to Hackett is ibid. 1528/4693, while Hackett complains to Wolsey that the burgesses of Antwerp demand Harman's release in ibid. 1528/4714. Herman Rinck to Wolsey is ibid. 1528/4810; Hackett to West ibid. 1528/5078; and West to Wolsey asking for funds to go to the Frankfurt Fair vol. IV, pt. iii 1529/5402. Stephen Vaughan wrote to Henry VIII in vol. V 1531/65/153/201/246, and to Cromwell ibid. 1531/247/248/303. Charles V wrote to Henry VIII refusing the latter's request to extradite Tyndale in 1531/354. Vaughan wrote further to Cromwell, fearing that More had terrified Constantine into giving evidence against him in ibid. 1531/532/533/574.

The interrogation of Bainham is ibid. 1531/583. Sir Thomas Elyot wrote to the Duke of Norfolk on the difficulty of catching Tyndale in ibid. 1532/869 and to Cromwell ibid. 1532/1554. Tyndale's letter to Frith, a copy of which More obtained, is vol. VI 1533/403/458. Vaughan wrote to Cromwell of More's relations with Peto in Antwerp, mentioning that Peto had money out from

England, in ibid. 1533/934. Thomas Poyntz to John Poyntz, his brother, is vol. IX 1535/182, to Cromwell ibid. 1535/405, and Poyntz's petition to the king vol. X 1536/222. Vaughan's last despairing letter of 13 April 1536 – 'if now you sende but your lettre . . . elles it wilbe to late' – is ibid. 1536/663. The begging letters of Henry Phillips to his mother, father, brothers and Dr Brerewood, the chancellor of Exeter, are in vol. IX 1535/1138–1144. The letter from Sir G. de Casalis to Cromwell on 'an Englishman named Philip' at Rome claiming to be 'a kinsman of Thos. More' is vol. X 1536/796. Ambassador Hutton to Cromwell on Phillips's supposed trip to Cornwall is vol. XII 1537/1293; Henry Phillips to Thyomas Bryerwod (Brerewood) vol. XIII, pt. ii 1538/99; Thomas Theabold (Tebold) to Cromwell ibid. 1538/507 and to Cranmer ibid. 1538/509; Ambassador Wriothesley to Cromwell on his going to Louvain to search for Phillips vol. XIV, pt. i 1539/233; Wriothesley on Phillips pleading for forgiveness ibid. 1539/247; Edward Carne to Cromwell on the Phillips escape ibid. 1539/248; Wriothesley to Cromwell on the escape, adding that he has been robbed ibid. 1539/264.

The *Biographical Register of the University of Oxford 1501–1540*, edited by A. B. Emden (Oxford, 1974), also contains the *L&P* references to Phillips – variously as Pfelepes, Philippes, Phylleppes and Phyllyps – on a volume basis.

The *Calendar of Letters, Despatches and State Papers relating to negotiations between England and Spain*, seventeen volumes, edited by G. A. Bergenroth et al. (London, 1862–1965) includes ambassadors' dispatches, the correspondence of Catherine of Aragon and references to the divorce, as does the *Calendar of State Papers and Manuscripts relating to English Affairs preserved in the Archives of Venice and in the other Libraries of Northern Italy*, seven volumes, edited by L. Rawdon-Brown et al. (London, 1864–1947).

*

As to Tyndale's great enemy, *The Yale Edition of the Complete Works of St. Thomas More* (New Haven and London, 1963–) contains the attacks More made on him and his fellow evangelicals. The relevant volumes are:

Vol. 4, *Utopia*, ed. Edward Surtz S. J. and J. H. Hexter (1965)

Vol. 5, pts 1 and 2, *Responsio ad Lutherum*, ed. John M. Headley, trans. Sister Scholastica Manderville (1969)

Vol. 6, pts 1 and 2, *A Dialogue Concerning Heresies*, ed. Thomas M. C. Lawler, Germain Marc'hadour and Richard C. Marius (1981)

Vol. 7, *Letter to Bugenhagen, Supplication of Souls, Letter Against Frith*, ed. Frank Manley, Germain Marc'hadour, Richard C. Marius and Clarence H. Miller (1990)

Vol. 8, pts 1, 2 and 3. *The Confutation of Tyndale's Answer*, ed. Louis A. Schuster, Richard C. Marius, James P. Lusardi and Richard J. Schoeck (1973)

Vol. 9, *The Apology*, ed. J. B. Trapp (1979)

Vol. 12, *A Dialogue of Comfort Against Tribulation*, ed. Louis L. Martz and Frank Manley (1976)

Vol. 14, pts 1 and 2, *De Tristitia Christi*, ed. and trans. Clarence H. Miller (1976).

More's account of Thomas Hitton and his description of him as 'the devil's stinking martyr' is vol. 8, pp. 16–17: More writes in p. 16, l. 32 to p. 17, l. 2, that Hitton was 'delyuered in concluson for his obstinacye to the seculare handes, and burned uppe in his false fayth and heresyes, wherof he lerned the great parte of Tyndales holy bokes and nowe the spirit of errour and lyenge, hath taken his wretched soule with hym strayte from the shorte fyre to ye fyre euer lastyng. And this is lo syr Thomas Hytton the dyuyls stynkyng martyr of whose burnynge Tyndale maketh boste.' More celebrates the death of John Tewkesbury in vol. 8, p. 21, ll. 32–5: 'For which thynges and dyuers other horryble heresyes, he was delyuered at laste vnto the secular handes and burned, as there was neuer wretche I wene better worthy.' He mocks Tyndale for praising Tewkesbury's courage, p. 20, l. 37 to p. 21, l. 5: 'I here also that Tyndale hyghly reioyceth in the burnyng of Tewkesbery but I can se no very grete cause why but yf he reken it for a grete glory that the man dyd abyde styll by the stake when he was faste bounden to it. For as for the heresyes he wolde haue abiured thyem agayne wyth all hys harte, and haue accursed Tyndale to, yf all yt myghte haue saued hys lyfe.'

Richard Bayfield is also mentioned in the preface to the *Confutation of Tyndale's Answer*, again with an accusation of cowardice and also of bigamy, in p. 17, l. 17 to p. 18, l. 3: 'Then haue ye hadde here burned synnys at London of late Rycharde Bayfelde, late a monke and a preste, whyche fell to heresye and was aiured and after that lyke a dogge returnynge to his vomyte, and being fled ouer the sea, and sendynge from thense Tyndales heresyes hyther wyth many myscheuouse sortes of bokes . . . [H]e went about two wyues, one in Brabande [Brabant], a nother in Englande . . . Of Bayfeldes burnynge hath Tyndale no great cause to glory. For though Tyndales bokes brought hym to burnynge yet he was not so constante in his euangelycall doctryne, but that after he was taken, all the whyle that he was not in vtter dyspayre of perdon he was well contente to haue forsworen yt agayne . . .' He expresses his satisfaction at the burnings, for which he blames Tyndale, in a passage in which he also rehearses the legal fig leaf by which the clergy did not condemn the heretics to death but instead tried them and then handed them to the civil power to impose the death sentence, in p. 589, l. 39 to p. 590, l. 7: 'of whiche sorte there hathe of late some be burned in Smythfelde, as Bayfelde, Baynom and Teuxbery [Bayfield, Bainham and Tewkesbury]: the clergy maketh them nat hereytkes nor burneth them neyther. But Tyndales bokes and theyr owne malyce maketh them heretykes. And for heretikes as they be the clergy dothe denounce them. And as they be well worthy, the temporaltie dothe burne them. And after the fyre of Smythfelde, hell doth receyue them where the wretches burne for euer.' More rejoices in the prospect of Tyndale burning in hell with Thomas Bilney on p. 22, ll. 34–7: 'For whych the pore wreche lyeth now in hell and cryeth out on hym,' he writes of Bilney, and Tyndale 'yf he do not amende in tyme, he is lyke to fynde hym when they come togyther, an hote fyrebronde burnynge at hys bakke, that all the water in the worlde wyll neuer be able to quenche.' He claimed that Bilney was finally 'conuerted vnto Cryste and hys trew catholyke fayth' in a passage on p. 23, ll. 8–26 in which he wrote that God 'of hys endles mercy brought [Bilney's] hys body to deth, & gaue him yet ye grace to turne and saue hys soule'. A further section on 'Bilnes returne to the catholik faith' is on p. 518. More deals with his interrogation of George Constantine, and the way in which the prisoner confessed his knowledge of how Tyndale's 'deuelysshe bokes' were smuggled, with 'the shypmannes name that had them, and the markes of the ferdellys [packing crates]', on pp. 19–20. More's condemnation of women preachers is on p. 27. He thinks it right on p. 179, ll. 3–8, 'to prohybyte the scrypture of god to be suffered in englyshe tonge amonge the peoples handes, lest euyll folke by false drawyng of euery good thynge they rede in to thye colour and mayntenauns of theyr own fone fantasyes, and turnynge all hony in to posyn, myght both dedly do hurte vnto theym selfe, and sprede also that infeccyone farther a brode'. More expresses his desire, on p. 338, ll. 25–6, that Tyndale and his like should 'haue an hot iren thruste thorow thyr blasphemouse tonges'.

More denied harming any of the heretics he held in his Chelsea house in his *Apology*, vol. 9, p. 118, ll. 33–7: 'And of all that euer came in my hande for heresy, as helpe me god, sauynge as I sayd the sure keeping of them and yet not so sure neyther but that George constantyne coulde stele awaye: ellys had neuer any of them any strype or stroke syuen them, so mych as a fylyppe on the forhead.' However, he goes on to confirm that Constantine was being held in the stocks with which More had equipped his Chelsea home when he broke free. Constantine, More says on p. 119, ll. 4–9, was 'neyther so feble for lacke of meate but that he was stronge inough to breke the stockes, nor waxen so lame of hys leggys wyth lyenge but yet he was lyghte inough to lepe the wallys nor by any myssehandelyng of his hed so dulled or dased in hys brayn, but that he had wytte inough whan he was onys out, wysely to walke hys waye'. More went on to deny ill treatment of Segar Nicholson on p. 119, ll. 118–26: 'But now tell the brethren many meruaylouse lyes, of myche cruell tormentynge that heretykes hadde in my house, so farforth that one Segar a boke seller of Cambrydge whyche was in myne house about foure or fyue days, and neuer hadde eyther bodely harme done hym, or fowle worde spoken hym . . . hath reported syns . . . that he was bounden to a tree in my gardeyn, and thereto pytuousely beten and yet besyde that bounden about the hed wyth a corde & wrongen, that hye fell downe dede in a swowne.'

More makes his chilling prediction of John Frith's future in vol. 9, p. 122, ll. 18–21: 'I fere me sore that Cryst wyll kyndle a fyre of fagottes for hym, & make hym therin swete the bloude out of hys body here, and strayte frome hense send hys soule for euer into the fyre of hell.' He confided his own fear of the defeat of Catholicism in a world with 'no chrysten countreyes left' in vol. 13, p. 173.

For Thomas Philips, the inmate of the Tower who helped Frith, see vol. 9, p. 166 – 'Thomas Philippis of London letherseller, mowe prysoner in ye towre' – and the note to 126/12 on pp. 372–4.

The Correspondence of Sir Thomas More, edited by E. F. Rogers, was published at Princeton in 1947.

Contemporary accounts of *The Life and Death of Cardinal Wolsey*, by George Cavendish, and *The Life of Sir Thomas More*, by

William Roper, have been edited in one volume by Richard S. Sylvester and Davis P. Harding (New Haven and London, 1962). The two men have also been compared in *The Statesman and the Fanatic* by Jasper Ridley (London, 1982). *The Life of Thomas More* by Peter Ackroyd (London, 1998) and *Thomas More* by Richard Marius (New York, 1984) are excellent modern biographies.

For Tyndale's predecessors, see F. D. Matthew's *The English Works of John Wycliffe* (London, 1880), J. A. Robson's *Wycliffe and the Oxford Schools* (Cambridge, Mass., 1961), J. Stacey's *John Wycliffe and Reform* (Philadelphia, 1964) and J. Bale's *Brief Chronicle of Sir John Oldcastle* (Parker Society, vol. 36, London, 1902).

Tyndale's meddlesome colleague Joye is the subject of *George Joye* by C. Butterworth and A. Chester (Philadelphia, 1962). F. L. Clark writes on *William Warham: Archbishop of Canterbury 1504–1532* (Oxford, 1993). His successor is the subject of *Thomas Cranmer* by Diarmaid MacCulloch (New Haven and London, 1996), and of J. Strype's two-volume *Memorials of Archbishop Cranmer* (London, 1812). The question of the sacraments is in *The Mass and the English Reformers* by C. W. Dugmore (London, 1958). *The Letters of Erasmus* were translated and edited by F. M. Nichols in three volumes (London, 1901–18).

Humanism, Reform and Reformation: The Career of Bishop John Fisher, edited by B. Bradshaw and E. Duffy (Cambridge, 1989), portrays the fiery bishop of Rochester. *The English Works of John Fisher*, edited by J. E. B. Mayor, was published in London in 1876. See, too, *The Works and Days of John Fisher: An Introduction to the Position of St John Fisher* by E. Surtz (Cambridge, Mass., 1967). *Henry VII's Conservative Scholar* by Andrew A. Chibi (Berne, 1997) deals with Bishop John Stokesley and the divorce, royal supremacy and doctrinal reform. The work of John Frith is introduced and edited by N. T. Wright (London, 1978). *The Life*

and Letters of Thomas Cromwell are the subject of two volumes
edited by R. B. Merriman (Oxford, 1902); see also D. Burton's
Thomas Cromwell (London, 1982), A. G. Dickens's *Thomas
Cromwell and the English Reformation* (London, 1959). Foxe deals
with Monmouth in *Acts and Monuments* in vol. iv, p. 617, with
Bilney at length in pp. 619–56 of vol. iv (London, 1837 edn), as
well as with Frith, Barnes, et al. Bilney is also covered in *The Life
and Acts of Matthew Parker* by the indefatigable J. Strype (Oxford,
1821, vol. I, pt I).

The *Reformation Parliament*, dealing with political and consti-
tutional change, is by S. E. Lembert (Cambridge, 1970). *The
Reformation and the English People* is by J. J. Scarisbrick (Oxford,
1984). E. Duffy's *The Stripping of the Altars* (New Haven and
London, 1992) powerfully portrays *Traditional Religion in
England 1400–1580*, as does R. Finucane's *Miracles and Pilgrims:
Popular Beliefs in Medieval England* (London, 1977). G. R. Elton's
body of work includes *England under the Tudors* (1955), *Policy and
Police* (1972), *Reform and Renewal* (1973) and *Reform and
Reformation* (1977).

For further views, see J. J. Scarisbrick's *Henry VIII* (London,
1970), Q. Skinner's *The Foundations of Modern Political Thought*,
vol. 2, *The Age of Reformation* (Cambridge, 1978); *The English
Reformation* by A. G. Dickens (1964).

For Anne Boleyn and her sympathy for reform, see *Anne Boleyn
and Reform* by Maurice Dowling in the *Journal of Ecclesiastical
History*, vol. 35, no. 1, January 1984. The *Ecclesiastical Memorials
of John Strype*, vol. I, pt I (Oxford, 1822), includes further detail
on Anne Boleyn, and much else besides. *The Rise and Fall of Anne
Boleyn* is by R. M. Warnicke (Cambridge, 1898); *The Six Wives of
Henry VIII* are the subject of books by Alison Weir (London,
1991) and Antonia Fraser (London, 1992); *Anne Boleyn* is by E.
W. Ives (Oxford, 1986).

On Thomas Cromwell, see *The Life and Letters of Thomas Cromwell* by Roger B. Merriman (Oxford, 1902); *Thomas Cromwell* by B. W. Beckingrale (London, 1978); *Treason in Tudor England* by Lacey Baldwin Smith (London, 1986).

For biblical translation and history, see: *English Biblical Translation* by A. C Partridge (London, 1973); *The English Bible*, two vols, by J. Edie (London, 1876): *The Literary Lineage of the King James Bible* by C. C. Butterworth (Philadelphia, 1941); *A History of the Bible as Literature*, vol. 1, *From Antiquity to 1700*, by David Norton (Cambridge, 1993); R. A. Knox's *On Englishing the Bible* (London, 1949); W. Schwarz's *Principles and Problems of Biblical Translation* (Cambridge, 1955); F. F. Bruce's *The English Bible, A History of Translations* (London, 1961); *The Semantics of Biblical Language* by J. Barr (New York, 1960); H. W. Robinson's *The Bible in its Ancient and English Versions* (1940). *The West from the Reformation to the Present Day* (Cambridge, 1963); and *Wide as the Waters* by Benson Bobrick (New York, 2001). For a comparison between ancient and modern translations, see the *Eight Translation New Testament* (Wheaton, Ill., 1974). This gives, on the same page, The King James Version, The Living Bible, Phillips Modern English, Revised Standard Version, Today's English Version, New International Version, Jerusalem and the New English Bible.

The early history of printing, as well as being essential to this book, is remarkable in its own right for the speed of progress. Within a generation, italic, Roman and bold typefaces had appeared in upper and lower case and in a variety of fonts; books were illustrated by woodcuts and engravings; colour printing was in use, together with bindings both plain and elaborate; and books of greatly differing size were being sold at the great (and surviving) Frankfurt and Leipzig Fairs. *The Reformation and the Book 1517–1570* edited by Jean-Françoise Gilmont (Aldershot, 1998); *The Printing Revolution in Early Modern Europe* by Elizabeth L. Eisenstein (Cambridge, 1983); *The Coming of the Book* by Lucien

Febvre and Henri-Jean Martin (London, 1976) provide overviews. *The Printed Bible* by Michael H. Black in vol. 3 of the *Cambridge History of the Bible* (Cambridge, 1963) covers early printed Bibles. *Worldly Goods* by Lisa Jardine (London, 1996) is set in a Renaissance context. The subject of F. C. Avis's *England's Use of Antwerp Printers 1500–1540* in *Gutenberg-Jahrbuch* (1973) is self-explanatory, as is H. S. Bennett's *English Books and Readers 1475–1557* (Cambridge, 1952). E. G. Duff's *The Printers, Stationers and Bookbinders of Westminster and London from 1476 to 1535* was published in London (1906) and reprinted in New York (1977). *Antwerp, Dissident Typographical Centre: The Role of Antwerp Printers in the Religious Conflicts in England* published by the Plantin-Moretus Museum at Antwerp (1994) shows how the Antwerp printers, having benefited from printing illegal Protestant books in English, switched to Catholic books after these were banned in turn under Elizabeth I.

On smuggling and shipping, see *The Maritime Trade of the East Anglian Ports* by N. J. Williams (Oxford, 1988); *The Ship in the Medieval Economy* by Richard W. Unger (London, 1980); and *English Merchant Shipping 1460–1540,* by Dorothy Burwash (Newton Abbot, 1969).

The Tyndale Society's excellent Journal includes articles on the *Stuttgart Tyndale Bible,* no. 7, July 1997; *Cuthbert Tunstall, Tyndale's 'Still Saturn',* by Margaret Clark, vol. 3, 1998; *William Tyndale and the Making of the English Churches,* by David Daniell, no 9, April 1998; and much else of interest.

Of particular note is *How Much of the King James Bible is William Tyndale's?* by John Nielson and Royal Skousen, no. 3, 1998. This shows an average of 83.7 per cent of the King James New Testament to be found in Tyndale, 2.4 per cent in Coverdale, 2.2 per cent in the Great Bible, 4.7 per cent in the Geneva Bible, 2.2 per cent in the Bishops' Bible, 1.9 per cent in the Rheims Bible, and 2.8 per cent to be original to the King James. Of the

Old Testament books that Tyndale translated, 75.7 per cent of the King James is found in Tyndale, 6.1 per cent in Coverdale, 9.6 per cent in the Geneva Bible, and 8.7 per cent is original to the King James.

As well as the debt owed to the Society, and to Professor Daniell, I am again grateful for the skilful research supplied by former students of Clive Holmes at Lady Margaret Hall, Oxford, in this case my niece, Victoria Stiles.

NOTES

Preface   On the Burning of Heretics

1   A spring halfway down the hill at Lutterworth is said to have
begun flowing after one of Wycliffe's fingers fell on the spot as
his bones were carried down the slope. This local legend is one
of which Wycliffe himself, hostile to superstition and loose
talk of miracles, would heartily disapprove.

1   Youth

1   Cardinal's College was renamed Christ Church after Wolsey's
fall, and remains the grandest of the Oxford colleges.

2   Decision

1   And to Continental ones, of course. Erasmus not only wrote
but spoke in Latin during the several years he spent in England.
In the Latin-speaking academic and government circles in
which he moved there was no need for him to learn English.

2   Hooper was appointed bishop of Gloucester in 1550. Five
years later, when Catholicism was (temporarily) restored in
England, Hooper went to the stake in the city as a heretic.

3 Unnamed by Foxe, but probably William Latimer, a friend of
   Erasmus – and of More – who had taught at Oxford while
   Tyndale was an undergraduate, and who held two
   Gloucestershire livings in his retirement.

13 The Flight to Hamburg
1 The Turks did not leave Belgrade until 1867.
2 In fact, the work extended over a very long period and was not
   all done at Alexandria.
3 Tyndale certainly thought them to be the work of Moses. In
   the nineteenth century, however, it became widely accepted
   that the Pentateuch was compiled from previously written documents dating from the ninth to the fifth centuries BC.

17 The Confutation
1 The chancellor, Thomas Parker, failed to have the sentence of
   exhumation and burning imposed by the secular arm, and the
   very large fine of £300 was imposed on him for his negligence.

20 'A fellow Englishman, who is everywhere and nowhere'
1 The Apocrypha, or 'hidden things', are the biblical books
   accepted by the early Church as part of the Greek Septuagint,
   but not included in the Hebrew Bible. Luther included the
   Apocrypha (1 and 2 Esdras apart) as an appendix to his 1534
   Bible as 'useful and good to be read', and it is likely that
   Tyndale would have done the same had he completed his work.
   Later Protestant leaders, wishing to return to strict biblical
   authority stripped of later additions, did not recognise it as true
   scripture.

23 'Though I gave my body even that I burned . . .'
1 James Beaton, the archbishop of St Andrews, escaped the
   reformers' revenge. His successor and nephew, the cardinal

archbishop David Beaton, was hunted down and murdered in his castle of St Andrews in 1546 by Protestant conspirators dressed as building workers. He locked himself in his apartments but they smoked him out by crying 'fire!' and burning coals at the door. 'I am a priest,' he cried as he opened the door. 'Ye will not slay me!' But they did, John Knox, the great Scottish reformer, among them.

INDEX

Page numbers in *italics* denotes illustration/caption